FIELD BOOK OF
AMERICAN WILD FLOWERS

With 30 colored plates and over 300 black-and-white illustrations drawn from nature by F. Schuyler Mathews and Eduardo Salgado

F. Schuyler Mathews'

FIELD BOOK OF

AMERICAN

WILD

FLOWERS

Completely revised and enlarged by

NORMAN TAYLOR

G. P. Putnam's Sons   New York

Library of Congress Catalog Card
Number: 55-5778

MANUFACTURED IN THE UNITED STATES OF AMERICA
·
VAN REES PRESS • NEW YORK

PREFACE

This revision of the oldest and most widely used guide to our wild flowers is long overdue. The late F. Schuyler Mathews originally published the book in 1902; it was an immediate success, as it has been ever since. No real revision could be undertaken before the completion of major works on the flora of our range. Two such technical works have recently been published. First came the eighth edition of *Gray's Manual of Botany,* after forty years of work by the late M. L. Fernald of Harvard. Early in 1953 the New York Botanical Garden published the completely new edition of Britton and Brown's *Illustrated Flora* by Dr. H. A. Gleason, a huge undertaking in three volumes, with an illustration for every species.

No revision of Mathews' *Field Book of American Wild Flowers* could have been made without constant reference to both these technical works. Although they differ in details, they reflect the current knowledge of our flora that has accumulated since the first edition of Mathews' *Field Book,* which was issued before motor travel made available for study many regions and plants that were all but inaccessible in the horse-and-buggy days. They also embody all the research that has been done on the interpretation of specific identities, their ranges, Latin nomenclature, and many other features. Such books make rather hard reading for the amateur.

That two such outstanding authorities as Gleason and Fernald should always agree is unthinkable. Where they differ this revision of Mathews' book has, in general, followed the *Illustrated Flora,* because of my conviction that for the next fifty years this will be the standard, and by far the most practical, reference work in its field. In the new *Gray's Manual,* for instance, there are thousands of somewhat controversial forms, varieties and reputed hybrids, the identification of which is very confusing to the average seeker.

To sift out these complexities and make this new edition of Schuyler Mathews' book as simple as can be has been the guiding principle in its revision.

NORMAN TAYLOR

Elmwood
Princess Anne, Maryland

CONTENTS

HOW TO USE THIS BOOK

The total flora of our area contains many thousands of species—4,660 according to the *Illustrated Flora,* but 5,523 according to *Gray's Manual.* To the latter must be added 2,817 named forms, varieties, and hybrids recognized by Dr. Fernald, making a grand total of 8,340 different plants, if all these are in fact actual entities. Dr. Gleason does not think so, nor does he give most of them nomenclatorial rank.

We are here concerned only with those likely to be of interest to the amateur. Leaving out practically all shrubs and trees, all the ferns and grasses, all sedges and rushes, greatly reduces this number. But the remainder is still over 3,000 species—an unwieldy mass for all except the expert.

In order to keep the book within reasonable size—a pocket guide in fact—a drastic selection from these 3,000 species has to be made. To include them all would be impossible. The basic species chosen by Mathews half a century ago are all included, and to them have been added as many as the size of the book warrants, having in mind the increase in new plants and the fact that the patience of the reader is likely to wear thin if too many technicalities are included.

The technical jargon of the manuals inspires terror in the amateur, if not something like rage. Such terms are avoided here, although their precise significance is often without as precise an English equivalent. Plants, after all, like ourselves, have organs to which simple terms are applied—leaf, stem, flower, inflorescence, corolla, calyx, stamen, pistil, etc. Some of these are used here because to avoid them is like talking about pneumonia without mentioning the lungs. The few that are used have been listed and defined in the Glossary which closes this introductory part of the book.

OUR RANGE

The area covered by the book is an unfortunate one, but there seems no escape from using it. Plants are not held back by political boundaries, but one must stop somewhere or the book would include too much. The area selected, therefore, is essentially that of the two reference books already cited. It includes all of northeastern North America with the following boundaries:

NORTH: Up to and including Ontario, Quebec, Newfoundland, Labrador and Greenland

SOUTH: The line comprising the southern boundaries of Virginia, Kentucky and Missouri

EAST: The Atlantic Ocean

WEST: The 96th meridian. This takes in nearly all of the states of Minnesota, Iowa and Missouri. To have stretched it to the 100th meridian would have made it necessary to include scores of Far Western species that are really not part of our Eastern flora.

This is a huge area—well defined, the most populous—about which more is known floristically than perhaps any such area in the world, with the possible exception of the British Isles.

It would have been desirable to define the area by ecological rather than political boundaries, but that is impossible here. Any student, however, will profit by understanding how our flora is distributed and why.

At the time of the last glaciation—some estimates give forty thousand years ago, others more—nearly all the existing flora was pushed down from the arctic regions of North America. As the ice retreated poleward, which it is still apparently doing, this predominantly northern element tended to become restricted to the cooler, moister sites in the area. These include, of course, the regions in the north today, but also the mountains comprising the Allegheny chain, stretching, with some breaks, from New England to the Great Smoky National Park in North Carolina. Some especially arctic or alpine types never get farther south than the Adirondacks; others stop in the White Mountains; still others are now confined to regions of maritime Canada, where icy sea water replaces elevation in creating a cool environment.

Another large element of our flora is southern in its affinities. These species push up the coastal plain and piedmont (the hilly region east of the mountains), some to Maryland, some to New Jersey. A few stop on Long Island, and still fewer go farther north. They live in a region of greater heat and generally poorer soils than the inhabitants of better sites.

A third and perhaps the largest element of our flora is scattered more or less indifferently along the coast, in the mountains, and often west of them to the limits of our range. That brings us to a distinctly Western element that creeps eastward from the prairies into Illinois, Indiana, Ohio, and western Pennsylvania, but rarely or almost never east of the Alleghenies.

It is the interpenetration of these floral elements from the north, south, and west that makes our present flora so varied and so beautiful. To the student who stumbles upon a tiny arctic-alpine rhododendron on the summit of Mt. Washington its beauty and certainly its interest will be enhanced if he knows that it is a relict from ancient times of glaciation. And to find a meadow-beauty (*Rhexia*) in a New Jersey bog will bring up visions of an overwhelmingly tropical family with this northern outpost far from the center of the *Melastomaceæ*. Hundreds of such examples could be cited if this book were not wholly devoted to the identity of plants. The plant geography of our area is another fascinating aspect of its flora.

In citing the range of individual species these facts have been kept in mind. Some are given as *Me. to Fla. and La.*, for example. This indicates a predominantly coastal species. Others are given as *Que. to N. C.* Most of these follow the mountains, or at least the highlands, and may be rare or wanting on the coastal plain.

If any species included in the book extend beyond our range, their limits are always stated, so that readers who live beyond our area will know that many of their plants have come from our region to theirs.

CLASSIFICATION

There is no perfect system for the classification of plants. But without some system vegetation is not much more than a bundle of hay. Seventy years ago Engler and Prantl in Germany devised a scheme which attempted to show, in the arrangement of plant families, the evolutionary history of the plant kingdom. Starting with the so-called flowerless plants (fungi, algae, mosses and ferns), they progressed to the cone-bearing trees, through the lilies, grasses, and their allies to the orchids. Then came those plants without petals, then those with separate petals, those with a united corolla, and finally the *Compositæ* or Daisy Family, where scores of tiny flowers are crowded into a head—like the chrysanthemum, aster and goldenrod.

The scheme has been nibbled at ever since, but not one of its proposed modifications has concurrence by all the experts. For this reason the authors of both the *Illustrated Flora* and *Gray's Manual* follow the system of Engler and Prantl, well knowing that it is not perfect but not quite knowing what to do otherwise. It has also been followed here, for the same reason.

For many people the quickest way to find the description of an unknown plant is to thumb through the pictures, or else to consult the Color Guide that follows. These may be short cuts, but they tell little or nothing about why plants are sorted into families, genera, and species or why these are arranged in a definite order in a book like this.

Such terms as *family, genus* and *species* are best defined before we can understand how they are sorted.

FAMILY: *A usually large group of plants related by similarity of structure, often containing many genera.*

An example is the Pea Family (*Fabaceæ*). It comprises many genera, such as pea, bean, clover, locust, lupine, peanut and scores of others. Each separate family has a brief description.

GENUS (plural *genera*): *A usually smaller group of plants, within a family, more closely related by structure.*

An example is the genus *Lilium,* containing all the lilies, but no other plants of the *Liliaceæ* or Lily Family, such as smilax, asparagus, lily of the valley, Solomon's-seal, trillium, etc.

SPECIES: *An individual plant, within a genus, like no other except its own kind.*

An example would be *Lilium canadense,* the Canada or yellow meadow lily. It has two names: *Lilium* to tell us it belongs to the genus that contains only the lilies; and *canadense,* that it is only the Canada lily. This final or specific name sets it off from the wood lily, the Turk's-cap lily, or any other lily.

All the plants in this book, therefore, have first a generic name like *Lilium,* and a specific one like *canadense.* Such designations are precise, but many amateurs will ignore them and rely only upon common or vernacular names which are always included if the plant has one.

The order or sequence in which the families are arranged follows the system of Engler and Prantl, which, in spite of its imperfections, gives us a reasonable method of arranging the material in a book like this. Reduced to its simplest terms, this system characterizes plants by definite and rather diagnostic features which apply to whole groups of families. For those who would like to have some inkling of the significance of this the following scheme is presented:

I. Plants with the veins of the leaf parallel (not net-veined or reticulated), and parts of the flower—petals, sepals, etc.—generally in threes or multiples of three. Here come all the lilylike plants, iris, orchids, etc., comprising the families on pages 2 to 106.

II. Plants with the veins of the leaf netted or reticulated, and parts of the flower—petals, sepals, etc.—generally in fours or fives or multiples of these, never in threes. This group includes all the plants from page 108 to the end of the book. Such a large group must be divided for purposes of identification. It falls quite readily into three main divisions.

1. Flowers with no petals or with no sepals, sometimes without either; individually mostly inconspicuous, but often crowded into fairly conspicuous clusters. Here come all the families contained on pages 108 to 124, including many weedy plants such as goosefoot, lamb's-quarter, dock, etc. None of these have true petals, and the individual flower is often chaffy or membranous. Note carefully the difference between an individual flower and a *cluster* of them. The latter is often, but incorrectly, called a flower.

2. Flowers with true petals, or with sepals colored like petals (as in the hepatica); the petals *always separate,* not united into some sort of bell-shaped or tubular corolla. This large group contains so many families that for convenience it can be divided into two categories.

    a. Flowers regular; *i.e.,* not lopsided or one-sided, not pealike or violetlike; always symmetrical. Here belong all the families on pages 124 to 334 (except a few noted below).

    b. Flowers never regular, always irregular; *i.e.,* with a spur, or violetlike or pealike; the petals not in a symmetrical pattern (as they are in the common buttercup, for instance). Three subdivisions are:

        (1) Flowers pealike: the Pea Family, pages 220 to 242.

        (2) Flowers violetlike: the Violet Family, pages 288 to 296.

        (3) Flowers spurred, as in the columbine, etc., pages 158 to 162.

3. Flowers with a *united corolla,* which may be bell-shaped, funnel-shaped, or tubular; never of separate, divided petals (except in a few instances noted where they occur). This group includes all

the rest of the flowers in the book, beginning at page 336. For convenience they may be subdivided thus:

a. Flowers in some sort of compact head, the individual flowers minute, but the head usually conspicuous. This includes the Daisy or Composite Family (*Compositæ*), made up of such plants as aster, goldenrod, chrysanthemum, sunflower, etc., pages 492 to 578.

b. Flowers not so arranged.

    (1) Flowers regular; *i.e.,* not lopsided, one-sided, or spurred; generally symmetrical. Here come the families on pages 336 to 394. (See also pages 464 to 488.)

    (2) Flowers not regular, always irregular and unsymmetrical. Here belong many plants with an irregular corolla, such as the mints, borage, snapdragon, lobelia, etc., pages 394 to 462.

Such a simple segregation of plant families is all that one needs to understand the basic scheme of classification used here. But there are readers for whom the color of a flower is its most noticeable feature, and most of the plants in the book are arranged by color in the list that follows. Such a list has many advantages for quick and easy identification. But it should never be forgotten that Nature can play tricks with any such list. Plants vary in color from time to time, and some species can be pink in one place and white in another. In the Color Guide only the usual color can be stated.

COLOR GUIDE

AN INDEX TO ASSIST IN THE IDENTIFICATION
OF A FLOWER OR ITS FRUIT BY MEANS
OF THE COLOR

FLOWERS ONE-QUARTER INCH IN SIZE AND LARGER

WHITE

Arrowhead, 10-12.
Water Arum, Wh. Arrow Arum, 16, 18.
Mud Plantain, 30.
Clintonia umbellulata, 36.
Trilliums, 48-52.
Wh. Adder's Tongue, 62.
Star-of-Bethlehem, 64.
Atamasco Lily, 68.
Showy Orchis, 92.
Habenaria nivea, 96.
Wh. and Rag. Fr. Orchises, 98, 100.
Wh. and Sh. Lady's Slippers, 104, 106.
Spring Beauty, 124.
Starry and Blad. Campions, 128.
Catchfly. Eve. Lychnis, 130.
Sandworts, 134.
Chickweeds. Stitchworts, 136-138.
Water Lily, 138.
Lar. Wh.-flowered Anemone, 144.
Anemones, 142-146.
Rue Anemone, 148.
Goldthread, 158.
Twinleaf, May Apple, 166, 168.
Bloodroot, 168.
Fumitory. Dutch. Breeches, 172, 174.
Squirrel Corn, 174.
Toothworts. Cresses, 178-182, 184.
Whitlow-grass, 182.

Horseradish, 184.
W. Stonecrop, 194.
Saxifrages, Mitrewort, 196, 198.
Grass-of-Parnassus, 200.
Cloudberry, 208.
Dalibarda, Avens, 208, 210.
Strawberries, 212.
Potentilla tridentata, 214.
Indian physic, 218.
Lespedeza capitata, 236.
Wood Sorrel, 252.
Snow-on-the-Mountain, 266.
Round-l., and Musk Mallows, 274, 276.
Rose-mallow, 276.
Sweet Wh. and Lance-leaved Violets, 292.
Pale Violet, 296.
One-flowered Wintergreen, 338.
Shinleaf, Round-l. Pyrola, 340.
Indian Pipe. Pine-sap, 340-342.
Cr. Snowberry. Bearberry, 344-346.
Tr. Arbutus. Checkerberry, 344.
Mountain Laurel, 348.
Sheep, and Pale Laurels, 348-350.
Wh. Swamp Honeysuckle, 350.
Star Flower, 360.
Pimpernel, 364.
Lance-leaved Sabatia, 368.
Sp. Dogbane, 378.

WHITE

Bindweeds, 386-388.
Forget-me-not. C. Gromwell, 396-398.
Black Nightshade, 436.
Thorn Apple, 438.
Moth Mullein, 440.
Turtle-head, 444.
Houstonia, 464.
Hobble-bush, 472.

Marsh Bellflower, 486.
Bonesets. Thoroughworts, 494-496.
White Snakeroot, 496.
Wh. Asters, 514-532.
Daisy Fleabane, 532.
Pearly Everlasting, 538.
Mayweed, 552.
Oxeye Daisy, Feverfew, 554.
English Daisy, 560.

FLOWERS EXTREMELY SMALL, OR COMMONLY GROUPED OR MASSED

WHITE

Water Plantain, 8.
False Spikenard, 40.
False Solomon's Seal, 40.
Lily-of-the-V., 44.
Tall Meadow Rue, 148.
Black Snakeroot, 162.
Wh. and Red Baneberries, 164.
Bitter Cress, 180.
Whitlow-grass, 182.
Shep. Purse. Peppergrass, 188.
Sundews, 192.
Mitreworts, *Mitella,* 198.
Burnet, 218.
False Spirea, 220.
False Mermaid, 252.
Seneca Snakeroot, 260.
Enchanter's Nightshade, 314.
Br. Sarsaparilla, 316.
Dw. Ginseng, 318.
W. Carrot. Hemlock Parsley, 320.
Cowbane. Cow Parsnip, 322.
Water Parsnip, 324.
Caraway. W. and P. Hemlocks, 326.
Sweet Cicely, 330.
Water Pennywort, 332.
Pyxie. Featherfoil, 356.
Glaux maritima, 364.
Virginia Stickseed, 394.
Corn Gromwell, 396.
Eu. and White Vervains, 402.
Perilla frutescens, 410.
Balm, 414.

Wild Mint, Bugleweed, 414.
Cut-1. Water Horehound, 414.
Mountain Mint, 418.
Horehound, 430.
Culver's Root, 448.
Thyme-leaved Speedwell, 450.
Eyebright, 456.
Plantains, 462-464.
Cleavers, *Galiums,* 466-468.
Elders, 470.
Coral-berry. Snowberry, 474.
Swamp, and Gar. Valerians, 480.
Corn Salad, 480.
Eupatoriums, 494-496.
Wild chamomile, 552.

CREAM or YELLOWISH WHITE

Clintonia, 36.
Wild Oats, 46.
Bunch Flower, 54.
Ladies' Tresses, 82.
Rattlesnake Plantains, 84.
Goat's Beard, 204.
Rough Avens, 210.
White Clover, 226.
Lespedeza hirta, 236.
Pale Violet, 296.
Pipsissewa, 336.
Poke Milkweed, 384.
Lithospermum officinale, 398.
False Gromwell, 398.
Castilleja, 454.

CREAM or YELLOWISH WHITE
Partridge-berry, 466.
Elder, 470.
Galinsoga, 498.
White Golden-rod, 504.
Sweet and C. Everlastings, 540.
Rattlesnake-root, 572.
Lion's foot. Tall W. Lettuce, 574.

LILAC WHITE
Hepatica, 146.
Many Asters, 514-532.

GREENISH WHITE
Twisted Stalk, 36.
Stenanthium, 56.
Wild Leek, 64.
Rattlesnake Plantains, 84.
Green Wood Orchis, 94.
Habenaria leucophæa, 100.
Ragged Fringed Orchis, 100.
Buckwheat, and Cl. False B., 118, 120.
Virgin's Bower, 140.
Long-fruited anemone, 142.
Thimble-weed, 144.
Orangeroot, 164.
Hairy Rock Cress, Arabis 1., 182.
Saxifrage. Mitrewort, 196, 198.
Strophostyles helvola, 240.
Whorled Milkwort, 262.
Seaside Spurge, 264.
Cl. Bittersweet, 270.
Spikenard. Sarsaparilla, 316-318.
Bunchberry. Fl. Dogwood, 334.
Pyrolas. Shinleaf, 338-340.
Gentiana villosa, 376.
Indian Hemp, 380.
Asclepias verticillata, 386.
Cow Wheat, 458.
Wild Liquorice, 468.
Cl. Wild Cucumber, 482.

One-seeded Bur-cucumber, 482.
Galinsoga, 498.
Antennarias, 534.

WHITISH or YELLOWISH BROWN
Cat-tails, 2.
Bur Reeds. *Sparganiums,* 4-6.
Beech-drops, 460.

GREEN
Jack-in-the-pulpit, 14.
Green Dragon, 16.
Arrow Arum, 16.
Calamus, 20.
Cat Brier, 34.
Solomon's Seal, 44.
Indian Cucumber, 52.
Indian Poke, 54.
Gr. Adder's Mouth, 78.
Green Orchises, 94, 96.
Hexastylis arifolia, 108.
V. Snakeroot. Dutchm. Pipe, 110.
Docks, 112-114.
Sheep Sorrel, 114.
Smartweed, 116.
Tearthumb, 118.
Lamb's-quarters. Jeru'm Oak, 120.
Pigweeds. Tumbleweed, 120, 124.
Early Meadow Rue, 148.
Alumroot. Gold. Saxifrage, 198, 200.
Spurges, 264.
Pinweed, 288.
Ludwigia polycarpa, 304.
Asclepias amplexicaulis, 384.
Horseweed, 532.
Gt. Ragweed. Roman Worm-wood, 542.
Beggar-ticks, 550.
Wormwood, 556.

YELLOW-GREEN or GREEN-YELLOW
Carrion Flower, 32.
Asparagus, 40.

YELLOW-GREEN or GREEN-YELLOW

Broad-lipped Twayblade, 80.
Isotria verticillata, 90.
Knotgrass. Er. Knotweed, 116.
Blue Cohosh, 166.
Ditch Stonecrop, 194.
Milk Vetch, 230.
Cypress Spurge, 266.
Ginseng, 318.
Sanicle, 332.
Bartonia, 376.
Clammy Ground Cherry, 436.
Physalis, 436.
Painted Cup, 454.
Beefsteak Plant, 458.
Tall Wormwood. Mugwort, 556.

YELLOW

Yellow-eyed Grass, 22-24.
Bellwort, 46.
Meadow Lily, 58.
Day Lily, 66.
Star Grass, 70.
Pussley, 124.
W. Plantain Spearwort, Sm. Fl. Crowfoot, 150.
Hooked Crowfoot, 152.
Ear. and Swamp Buttercups, 154.
Bristly Crowfoot, 154.
Creep. and Bu. Buttercups, 154.
Tall Buttercup. M. Marigold, 154, 156.
Celandine. Prickly Poppy, 170, 172.
Yellow Rocket. Mustards, 184, 186.
Golden Saxifrage, 200.
Peck's Geum, 210.
Cinquefoils, 212-216.
Potentillas, 212-216.
Silverweed. Five-finger, 216.
Agrimony, 218.
Wild Indigo. Rattlebox, 220.
Black Medick, 230.
Partridge Pea. *Cassias*, 242.
Sorrels, 252-254.

Yellow Flax, 258.
Pale Jewel-weed, 272.
Flower-of-an-hour, 278.
Great St. John's-wort, 280.
St. Peter's-wort. St. A's Cross, 280.
Frostweed. *Hudsonia*, 286.
R-1. and Downy Y. Violets, 290, 294.
Prickly pear, 298.
Seedbox, 304.
Evening Primrose, 312.
Sundrops, 312.
Loosestrifes, 360-362.
Horse Balm, 406.
Virginia Ground Cherry, 436.
Mullein, 438.
Butter-and-eggs, 440.
False Foxgloves, 450.
Eyebright. Yellow Rattle, 456.
Pedicularis lanceolata, 458.
Squawroot, 460.
Yel. Bedstraw, 466.
Fly-honeysuckle, 474.
Bush Honeysuckle, 478.
Cup-plant, 498.
Goldenrods, 502-514.
Coltsfoot, 538.
Elecampane, 540.
Cone-flower, 542.
Oxeye, 544.
Sunflowers. B. Marigolds, 546-550.
Sneezeweed, 552.
Arnica, 560.
Yellow Thistle, 564.
Canada Hawkweed, 570.
Dandelion, Wild Lettuce, 574-578.
Sow Thistles, 578.

GOLDEN or ORANGE YELLOW

Golden Club, 20.
Turk's Cap Lily, 60.
Carolina Lily, 60.
Dogtooth Violet, 62.
Habenaria integra, 96.
Yel. Cr. and Fr. Orchises, 98.

GOLDEN or ORANGE YELLOW
Yel. Lady's Slipper, 104.
Yel. Pond Lily, 140.
Celandine Poppy, 170.
Golden Corydalis, 176.
Geum aleppicum strictum, 210.
Yel. Hop Clover. Melilot, 228.
Wild Senna, 242.
Spotted Touch-me-not, 272.
St. John's-wort, 280-284.
Wild Parsnip, 322.
Flame Azalea, 352.
Loosestrife. Moneywort, 360-364.
Lithospermum canescens, 398.
Golden Aster, 500.
Gray Goldenrod, 512.
Cone-flower, 544.
Chrysogonum, 554.
Tansy. Golden Ragwort, 556, 560.
Dwarf and Fall Dandelions, 566, 568.
Rattlesnake-weed, 570.

ORANGE
Day Lily, 66.
Blackberry Lily, 74.
Flame Azalea, 352.
Butterfly Weed, 382.
Butter-and-eggs, 440.
Tawny Hawkweed, 570.

SCARLET
Wood Lily, 56.
Tiger Lily, 60.
Columbine, 158.
Hibiscus coccineus, 278.
Pimpernel, 364.
Oswego Tea, 420.
Painted Cup, 454.
Trumpet Honeysuckle, 478.

RED
Water Purslane, 306.
Monarda, 418.
Cardinal Flower, 488.

MAROON
Wakerobin, 48.
Ground Nut, 238.

PINK
Water Plantain, 8.
Tradescantia rosea, 26.
Large-fl. Trillium, 50.
Erythronium, 64.
Atamasco Lily, 68.
Tearthumbs, 118.
Spring Beauty, 124.
Sleepy Catchfly, 130.
Ragged Robin, 134.
Sand Spurry, 138.
Pale Corydalis, 176.
Meadowsweet. Hardhack, 202.
Queen-of-the-Prairie, 204.
Rabbit-foot Clover, 222.
Alsike Clover, 226.
Rose-Mallows, 276.
Trailing Arbutus, 344.
Mountain Laurel, 348.
Pinxter Flower, 350.
Pyxie, 356.
Rose and Sea Pinks, 368-370.
Sabatia stellaris, 370.
Large Marsh Pink, 370.
Spreading Dogbane, 378.
Four-leaved Milkweed, 386.
Ground Pink, 390.
Partridge-berry, 466.
Coral-berry, 474.
Snowberry, 474.
Climbing Hempweed, 494.
Common Fleabane, 534.
Tickseed, 542.
English daisy, 560.

CRIMSON
Ragged Robin, 134.
Live-forever, 194.
Long-plumed Avens, 210.
Red Clover, 226.
Milkwort, 260.
Swamp Milkweed, 382.

CRIMSON PINK
Snake Mouth, 88.
Moccasin Flower, 106.

CRIMSON PINK
Lady's Thumb, 116.
Deptford and Maiden Pinks, 126.
Wild Pink, 128.
Fumitory, 178.
P. Flowering Raspberry, 204.
Alsike Clover, 226.
Marsh Mallow, 274.
Sheep, and Pale Laurel, 348-350.
Large Marsh Pink, 370.
Swamp Milkweed, 382.
Lopseed, 402.
Monarda, 420-422.
Twin-flower, 472.

MAGENTA or RED PURPLE
Stemless Trillium, 48.
Arethusa, 86.
Nodding Pogonia, 90.
Showy Orchis, 92.
Corn Cockle, 134.
Fumitory, 178.
Pitcher Plant, 188.
Sundew, 192.
Marsh Five-finger, 216.
Tick Trefoils, 230-234.
Bush Clover, 234.
Beach Pea, Wild Bean, 238, 240.
Herb Robert, 248.
Wild Geraniums, 250.
V. Wood Sorrel, 254.
Flowering Wintergreen, 258.
Milkworts. Polygalas, 260.
Crowberry, 268.
Broom Crowberry, 268.
Pur. Poppy Mallow, 276.
Loosestrifes, 298-300.
Meadow-beauty, 302.
Fireweed. H. Willow Herb, 306-310.
Rhodora, 352.
Shooting Star, 358.
Lesser Centaury, 366.
Purple Milkweed, 382.
Hound's Tongue, 394.
Lopseed, 402.
Am. Germander, 406.

Hedge Nettle, 434.
Figwort, 444.
Gerardias, 452.
Beefsteak Plant, 458.
Garden Valerian, 480.
Joe-Pye-Weed, 494.
New Eng. Aster, 518.
Robin's Plantain. Fleabane, 532-534.
Purp. Cone Flowers, 542.
Burdocks. Thistles, 562-564.

MAGENTA PINK
Twisted Stalk, S. roseus, 36.
Grass Pink, 88.
Purple Fringed Orchis, 102.
Bouncing Bet, 128.
Squirrel Corn. P. Corydalis, 174, 176.
Cut-leaved Toothwort, 178.
Canadian Tick Trefoil, 239.
Bush Clover, 234.
Wild Geranium, 250.
Cr-l. and Sh-l. Milkworts, 260.
High and Musk Mallows, 276.
Pinweed, 288.
Clammy Cuphea, 302.
Pyrola asarifolia, 340.
Dw. Canadian Primrose, 358.
Centauries, 366-368.
Four-leaved Milkweed, 386.
Blue Curls, 404.
Wild marjoram, 410.
Swamp Valerian, 482.

PURPLE
Indian Turnip, 14.
Isotria verticillata, 90.
Purple Orchis, 102.
Leather Fl. P. Virgin's Bower, 140, 142.
Purple Avens, 210.
Alfalfa, 230.
Lespedezas, 234-236.
Common Vetch, 236.
Common Violet, 292.
Canada and Dog Violets, 296.
Thaspium, 324.

PURPLE
Rhododendrons, 350-354.
Pimpernel, 364.
Downy Phlox, 390.
Viper's Bugloss, Vervain, 400-402.
American Germander, 406.
Mints, 412-414.
Savory, 418.
Wild Bergamot, 422.
Downy Blephilia, 422.
Ground Ivy, M. D. Skullcap, 422-424.
Self-heal, 428.
Wild thyme, 430.
Dittany, 430.
Nightshade, 434.
Small Snapdragon, 444.
Monkey-flower, 446.
Naked Broomrape, 462.
Venus's Looking-glass, 484.
Bellflower, 484.
Tall Blazing Star, 498.
Asters, 514-532.
Marsh Fleabane, 538.
Tall Blue Lettuce, 578.

MADDER PURPLE
Twayblades. Coral Roots, 78-80.
Wild Ginger, 108.
Feverwort, 472.
Ironweeds, 494.

LILAC
Field Larkspur, 162.
Wild or Hog Peanut, 240.
Bird-f. and Marsh Violets, 288.
Epilobiums, 306-310.
Pale Laurel, 350.
Rhododendron, 350-354.
Ague-weed, 372.
Com. Milkweed, 384.
W. Blue Phlox, 390.
Catnip. *Monarda,* 420-422.
False Dragon Head, 428.
Motherwort, 430.
False Pimpernel, 448.

Houstonias, 464.
Heart-leaved Aster, 518.
Calico, and N. Y. Asters, 524-526.
Daisy Fleabane, 532.
Robin's Plantain, 532.
Canada Thistle, 566.
White Lettuce, 572.
Lactuca hirsuta, 576.

VIOLET
Crested Dwarf Iris, 72.
Ragged Robin, 134.
Tall Larkspur, 158.
B. False Indigo. B. Lupine, 222.
Cow Vetch, American Vicia, 238.
Flax, 258.
Violets, 288.
Downy Gentian, 374.
W. Bl. Phlox. Gk. Valerian, 390-392.
Jacob's Ladder, 392.
W. Comfrey. Eu. Stickseed, 394.
Small, and Viper's Bugloss, 400.
Narrow-1. Vervain, 402.
Blue Curls, 404.
False Pennyroyal, 406.
Hyssop. Am. Pennyroyal, 418.
Lyre-leaved Sage, 420.
Blephilia, 422.
Scutellarias, 424-428.
Nightshade, 434.
Blue Toad-flax, 440.
Valerianella olitoria, 480.
Harebell. T. Bellflower, 486-488.
Great, and Downy Lobelias, 490-492.
Liatris spicata, 498.
Asters, 514-532.
Robin's Plantain, 532.

VIOLET BLUE or ULTRAMARINE
Day Flowers. Spiderwort, 24-28.

**VIOLET BLUE or
   ULTRAMARINE**
Pickerel Weed, 30.
Blue Flags. Iris, 70-74.
Blue-eyed Grasses, 74-76.
F. Larkspur. Monkshood,
   162.
Gentians, Ague-weed, 372-
   376.
Virginia Cowslip, 394.
Bugle, 410.
Balm, 414.
Cornflower, 562.
Chicory, 568.

LAVENDER
Pale Violet, 296.
Sea Lavender, 366.
Am. Pennyroyal, 420.
Purple Thorn Apple, 438.
Blue Toad-flax, 440.
Culver's Root, 448.
Am. Brooklime, 448.
Speedwells, 448-450.
Marsh Bellflower, 486.
Heart-leaved Aster, 518.

BLUE
Forget-me-nots, 396.
Cornflower, 562.

COLORS OF BERRIES

WHITE
White Baneberry, 164.
Creeping Snowberry, 344.
Snowberry, 474.

ORANGE SCARLET
Bunchberry, 334.
Feverwort, 472.

RED
Twisted Stalk, 36.
Lily-of-the-valley, 44.
Trilliums, 48-52.
Red Baneberry, 164.
Checkerberry, Wintergreen,
   344.
Bittersweet or Nightshade,
   434.
Partridgeberry, 466.

Fly Honeysuckle, 474.
Red-berried Elder, 470.
Hobble-bush, 472.
Coral-berry, 474.

LT. PRUSSIAN BLUE
Clintonia borealis, 34.

**BLACK or BLACK
   with bloom**
Carrion Flower, 32.
Cat Brier, 34.
Clintonia umbellulata, 36.
Solomon's Seal, 44.
Indian Cucumber-root, 52.
Bl. Snakeroot, 162.
Sarsaparilla, 318.
Elder, 470.

GLOSSARY OF TERMS

Achene. A small, dry, one-seeded fruit that does not split.

Adventive. A foreign plant not completely established.

Annual. A plant that lives one year and dies, depending for perpetuation on seeds.

Anther. *See* **Stamen.**

Biennial. A plant that lives two years, blooms the second year, and depends for perpetuation only on seeds. *See* **Perennial.**

Bract. A small, leaflike structure often found on flower-stalks or among the inflorescence.

Calyx. The outer envelope of a flower, usually green, but sometimes colored like petals; its individual segments called *sepals.*

Cleistogamous. Said of a flower that never opens and is self-fertilized; as in the basal cleistogamous flowers of some violets and other plants.

Compound. Said of a leaf that has two or more leaflets, as in the strawberry, lupine, and most plants of the Parsley Family. Some leaves are twice or thrice compound, as in poison hemlock.

Corolla. The usually showy inner envelope of a flower, its individual segments called *petals.* Some corollas have united segments and are hence cup-shaped, funnel-shaped, or otherwise united.

Dioecious. Having male and female flowers on separate plants.

Disc or **Disk.** The inner, central portion of the flower-head in the *Compositæ,* composed of only tubular flowers. *See* illustration at Sneezewood, page 552.

Filament. *See* **Stamen.**

Glaucous. Gray or grayish-green or bluish-green.

Herb. A usually fleshy plant, whether annual, biennial or perennial, that dies down to the ground each winter. Most plants in this book are herbs; distinguished from shrubs and trees which are woody, not fleshy.

Inflorescence. A flower-cluster.

Irregular Flower. *See* **Regular Flower.**

Monoecious. Having male and female flowers separate, but on the same plant.

Monopetalous. Having the petals united. *See* **Corolla.**

Naturalized. A foreign plant completely established.

Ovary:Ovule. *See* **Pistil.**

Perennial. An herb that dies down to the ground (but some are evergreen) each winter, and persists, often for years, from new shoots produced by its roots or rootstock, annually. *See* **Annual** and **Biennial.**

Perfect Flower. One that contains calyx, corolla, stamens and pistil.

Perianth. Collective term for petals and sepals.

Petal. *See* **Corolla.**

Pistil. The female organ of a flower, composed of a swollen base, the *ovary,* in which are the *ovules* (future seeds), a shanklike stalk, the *style,* and a usually sticky, club-shaped or divided tip, the *stigma,* upon which pollen is deposited for the fertilization of the ovules, which then ultimately become seeds.

Pistillate. Said of a flower that bears only pistils.

Pollen. *See* **Stamen.**

Polygamous. A plant that bears some pistillate, some staminate and some perfect flowers.

Polypetalous. Having separate petals. *See* **Corolla.**

Pubescent. Hairy.

Rays. The outer, petal-like structures found in many flower-heads of the daisy family. *See* pages 498 to 578. Often mistakenly called petals, as the "petals" of the common white daisy.

Regular Flower. One that is symmetrical, uniform in the number of its parts, never lopsided, one-sided or 2-lipped or otherwise unsymmetrical, which would then make it an *irregular* flower.

Rostellum. *See* Orchid Family, page 76.

Sepal. *See* **Calyx.**

Spadix. A club-shaped or thickened stalk upon which are crowded many minute flowers, often surrounded by a hooded, leaflike *spathe. See* Jack-in-the-Pulpit, page 14.

Spathe. *See* **Spadix.**

Staminate. A flower that bears only stamens.

Stamen. The male organ of a flower; composed of a slender, threadlike stalk, the *filament,* which is topped by a small knoblike tip, the *anther.* This produces the usually yellow dustlike *pollen* which is the male fertilizing element. Pollen is carried to the stigma of other flowers by the wind, insects, hummingbirds, or by the water, to ensure cross-fertilization.

Stigma. *See* **Pistil.**

Stipules. Small leaflike structures found at the base of some leaf stalks.

Style. *See* **Pistil.**

Unisexual. A flower bearing stamens or pistils, but not both.

FIELD BOOK OF
AMERICAN WILD FLOWERS

CAT-TAIL FAMILY. *Typhaceæ.*

Perennial marsh herbs with stemless, ribbonlike leaves and with flowers of two kinds, male and female on the same plant, lacking petals or sepals, and wind-pollinated. Both species are gregarious, often forming immense cat-tail marshes.

Cat-tail
Typha latifolia   Yellow-brown, June-July

The light olive-green, flat leaves usually exceed the flower-stem in height. The upper half of the cylindrical flower-spike consists of the stamens, and the lower half of the pistils; the abundant, yellow, powdery pollen of the staminate flowers scattering itself over the pistillate flowers below, fertilizes them.

It is the compact down of the pistillate flowers tipped with red-brown that forms the familiar cat-tail of August and September. At that time only a few lingering remnants of the staminate flowers remain on the withering tip of the stem above. The completely developed cat-tail measures fully 1 inch in diameter. In June it is important to note that the two kinds of flowers are not appreciably separated by a gap as in the next species. The color of the staminate flowers is a variable olive yellow-brown, or brownish yellow, according to age.

Typha is the old Greek name of these plants. The plant is 4-8 feet high, and is common in swamps everywhere, but mostly inland.

Narrow-leaved Cat-tail
Typha angustifolia   Yellow-brown, June-July

The slenderer species known specifically as *angustifolia,* that is, narrow-leaved, is remarkable for the distinct and considerable separation, on the stem, of the two groups of flowers; this is usual, but not without exception. This cat-tail is narrow, rarely measuring over ¾ inch in diameter. The leaves are slightly ridged on the back. The plant is 4-9 feet high, and grows mostly near the coast from Que. to Fla., rarely inland. Closely related is *Typha domingensis,* with flat leaves, but found only from southeastern Va. southward.

2

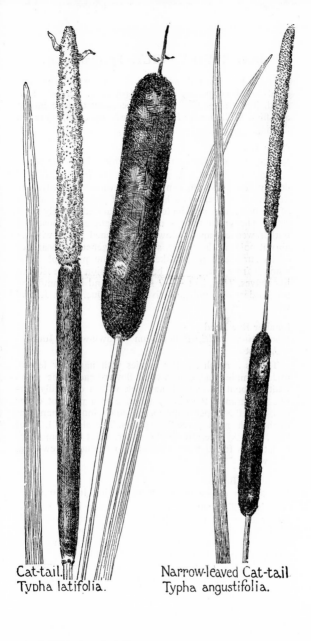

Cat-tail.
Typha latifolia.

Narrow-leaved Cat-tail.
Typha angustifolia.

BUR REED FAMILY. *Sparganiaceæ.*

Marsh herbs with flowers arranged in separate spherical heads, without petals, the heads bristly. Largely self-fertilizing, but assisted in the process by aquatic insects and flies. While most of the bur reeds are erect, some are floating.

Great Bur Reed
Sparganium eurycarpum　Brown-white, May-August

The deep green leaves are about ⅝ inch wide. The downy flowers are in dense round heads scattered along the top of the stem, and like those of the cat-tails consist of the two kinds, staminate and pistillate, absolutely separated. The green fruit is a burlike sphere composed of nutlets wedge-shaped below, and flattened above with an abrupt point in the center, so that the general appearance of its surface is not unlike that of the pineapple. The name is from σπάργανον, a band, in allusion to the ribbon-like leaves. The plant is 3-7 feet high, and is common on the borders of ponds and rivers from Que. to N. J., and west.

Smaller Bur Reed
Sparganium multipedunculatum　Brown-white, June-August

This is a much smaller species with narrower leaves, and a simple stem and row of flower-heads. The green fruit is about ¾ inch in diameter, with a decidedly bur-like appearance, the nutlets tapering to a point at either end, and the upper point being *much* longer than that of the fruit in the preceding species. The plant is 1-2 feet high, and is generally in the water, erect or sometimes afloat; it is found from Labrador to northern New Eng. and west.

Branching Bur Reed
Sparganium androcladum　Brown-white, June-August

This familiar variety, which is common in all bogs, is larger than the foregoing in many respects, and it is distinguished for its somewhat angular flower-stem; the latter grows out at the point where the leaf is joined with the plant-stem. The plant is 1-2 feet high, and is distributed from Que. to Va.; also in Ohio and west to Minn. and Mo. It is the same plant listed as *S. lucidum* in our last edition.

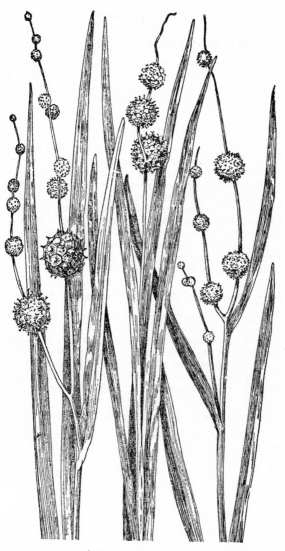

Great Bur Reed. Sparganium Branching Bur Reed.
Sparganium multipeduncu- Sparganium
eurycarpum. latum. americanum.

Sparganium americanum   **Brown-white, June-August**

The same height as *S. androcladum,* but the flower-stalk always branched. Leaves thin and pliant, barely ½ inch wide. Fruit-heads stemless or nearly so. Bogs or shallow water. Que. to Fla. and westward.

Sparganium chlorocarpum   **Greenish-brown, June-August**

A northern species with a stout stem and thin, narrow leaves ¼ inch more or less wide, with a thin, dry, color-less margin toward the base. Flower-heads stemless or nearly so, the lower ones growing from a point slightly above the junction of plant and leaf stem. Fruit-head 1 inch or less in diameter. 1-2 feet high. Borders of ponds and sluggish streams. Que. to southern N. Y., W. Va., Ind. and Iowa. A dwarf form 4-12 inches high, with fruit-heads ½ to ¾ inches in diameter is sometimes dis-tinguished as the variety *acuale,* and is found with the typical form, but also west to S. D.

Sparganium angustifolium   **Dull brown, July-August**

A slender and very narrow-leaved species floating in deep water. Leaves long, ⅛ inch or less wide, and opaque. Flower-stalk simple, the heads a trifle above the leaf junction, ¼-⅔ inch in diameter, and with or with-out a very short stem. 1-4 feet high. In ponds and slug-gish streams, or mountain tarns, Newf. to N. J., Pa. and Mich. It is closely related to *S. multipedunculatum.*

Sparganium fluctuans   **Dull brown, July-August**

A long and slender-stemmed species with thin leaves ¼-½ inch wide. Flower-stalk branched, the 2-3 branches bearing 3-5 heads ¾ inch in diameter. 2-3 feet high. Margins of cold ponds, often in 3 feet of water. Newf. to Conn. and Pa., west to Minn.

Sparganium minimum   **Greenish-brown, July-August**

A small and slender species common in cold, shallow ponds and streams of the north. Leaves thin, limp, and grasslike. Flower-stalk simple; the fruit-heads less than ½ inch in diameter, stemless. 4-16 inches high. Labrador to northern N. J. and Pa., west to Mich.

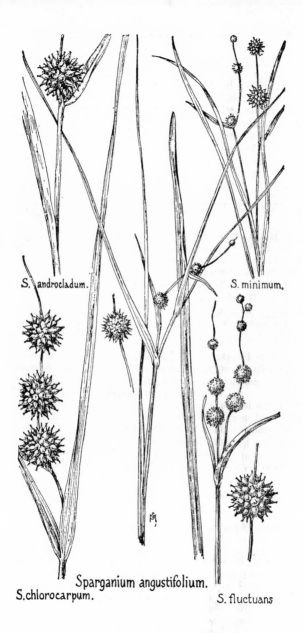

S. androcladum.

S. minimum.

S. chlorocarpum.

Sparganium angustifolium.

S. fluctuans

Midway between the bur reed family and the water plantain family is a large group of floating or submerged aquatic plants, the pond weeds, belonging to the genus *Potamogeton*. They have tiny flowers, without petals, followed by small nutlike fruits much beloved by aquatic birds. The differences between the 20-30 species are so troublesome that the reader is referred to the technical manuals for their identification.

WATER PLANTAIN FAMILY. *Alismaceæ.*

Marsh or aquatic herbs with long-stalked leaves, and flowers with 3 green sepals and 3 white or pinkish petals.

There are two genera below, the familiar arrowhead, often with arrowhead-shaped leaves, and the water plantain with small flowers in much-branched clusters.

Water Plantain
Alisma Plantago-aquatica White or pale pink, July-September

The leaves, all from the root, are olive-green, strongly veined, and elliptical but very variable in shape, broader or longer, and sometimes heart-shaped at the base, 2-6 inches long. The flower-stem is tall and symmetrically branched, displaying the three-petaled, very small white flowers to great advantage. The flowers are perfect, with six stamens and a pistil. The plant is 1-3 feet high, and is found in the shallow water of ponds and sluggish streams from Que. to southern N. Y., west to Mich. and Wisc. Forms in deep water have narrower leaves.

Alisma subcordatum Magenta-pink, July-September

Closely similar to *A. Plantago-aquatica* but the leaves narrower and flowering stems less spreading. There are 2-4 flower-stalks all taller than the long-stemmed, linear lance-shaped or elliptical leaves. The delicately pale often pink flowers with a yellow base are about ³⁄₁₆ inch broad, and are borne in 1-2 whorls or circles about the tall stalk on rather thick stems. 1-3 feet high. Local in shallow water from Vt. to Fla., west to Minn.

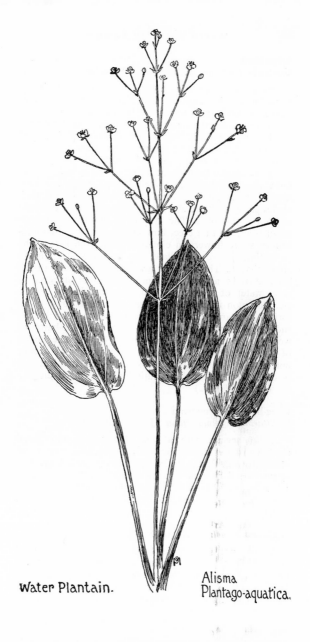

Water Plantain.

Alisma
Plantago-aquatica.

Arrowhead
Sagittaria latifolia   White, July-September

The genus *Sagittaria,* always white-flowered, is remarkable for its manifold leaf phases. The most common is *S. latifolia* in which the leaves are deep lustrous green and distinctly arrow-shaped; hence the name derived from the Latin *sagitta,* an arrow. The forms of *S. latifolia* are extremely diverse. Some have very broad obtuse leaves. In others the leaf-blades and their lateral bases are oblong lance-shaped, and acute. In still another form the leaf-blades and their lateral bases are narrowly linear. Finally, a form is also found with the leaf-blades partly sagittate and partly lance-shaped or elliptical without basal lobes. The typical *S. latifolia* is smooth throughout, with an erect flower-stalk carrying the three-petaled white flowers in circles of three, the lowest one (sometimes more) pistillate; the leaves nearly always arrow-shaped. The seed, or achene, is obovate with the beak at right angles. 4-40 inches high. In sluggish or quiet water of streams, and on the margins of ponds, etc. Common nearly everywhere, at least in some of its forms. Its starchy rootstocks were used as food by the Indians. The var. *pubescens* is a distinct fine-hairy or woolly form with very broad, blunt leaves. The pollen of the arrowhead is distributed by a variety of agents, not least of which are the insects which frequent wet places, among them the beautiful glassy-winged dragonfly. (*Color Plate 1.*)

Long-beaked Arrowhead
Sagittaria Engelmanniana   July-September

A tall species with a stout flower-stalk and broad sagittate, obtuse leaves. Flowers with the 2-4 lower circles pistillate, with flower-stalks less than ½ inch long. The obovate seed or achene with a long, nearly erect beak. 1-2½ feet high. In swamps, and on the margins of ponds and cold springs. Mass. to Del., and Pa. south to Ala. and Fla.

Sagittaria cuneata   August-September

A small northern species 8-20 inches high, with broad acute sagittate leaves having spreading lobes, or the blade reduced to a narrow segment. The plant grows both in and out of the water, and in the latter case develops very long-stemmed leaves, and also a number of

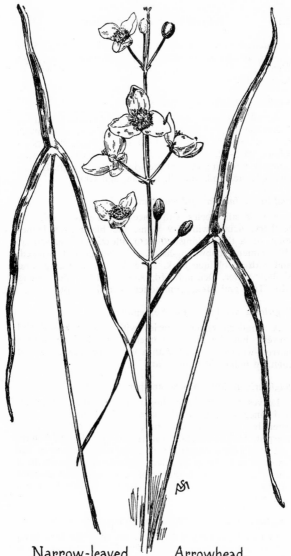

Narrow-leaved   Arrowhead.
A narrow-leaved form of Sagittaria latifolia. The
typical broad-leaved form has foliage more like
illustration of Sagittaria brevirostra.

broadened stems without leaves called phyllodia. Seed winged all about and with a tiny erect beak. 8-18 inches high. Que. to central Me., south to N. J., and west to Kan. and Cal.

Sagittaria brevirostra   July-September

A tall and stout western species, with acute, sagittate leaves the lobes of which are as long as the blade. Flower-stalk simple or branched 8-20 inches long, flowers in whorls of 5-12. Achenes with a tiny, nearly erect beak scarcely extending beyond the wing. 2-4 feet high. Rivers, swamps, etc., Ind. and Ill. to Kan. and Okla.

Sagittaria falcata   July-September

A very tall species with lance-shaped leaves, thick or leathery, acute, with 5-9 veins, the blade 5-18 inches long, on a thick elongated stem. Flowers white, showy, the filaments cobwebby-hairy. Achenes curved, winged, and with an oblique beak. 2½-5 feet high. Swamps and shallow water. Del. and Md., south to Fla., and west to Mo., Tex. and Mex. Commoner near the coast.

Sagittaria ambigua   July-September

A smaller, western species with similar leaves and flowers, but the anther filaments smooth. The achene narrow-winged, slender, with a very short beak. 1-2 feet high. In ponds, Mo. and Kan.

Sagittaria rigida   July-September

Leaves very variable, linear, lance-shaped, elliptical, and lance-ovate with two narrow, short basal lobes, or often but one. The plant may be erect or lax or sub-merged. The flower-stalk, shorter than the leaves, is limp and finally prostrate. Flowers white, the pistillate of the lowest circle almost stemless. Achenes obovate, with a long erect beak. 8-30 inches high. Swamps and margins of ponds. Que. to Del., Pa., Ohio, and west to Minn. and Neb.

Sagittaria graminea   White or pinkish, July-September

Leaves lance-shaped to linear on long slender stems, 3-5 veined, or sometimes reduced to mere phyllodia (leafless stems), acute-pointed. Flowers staminate or the lower circle pistillate, the petals often pale magenta-pink, filaments dilated and fine-hairy. Achenes tiny and almost

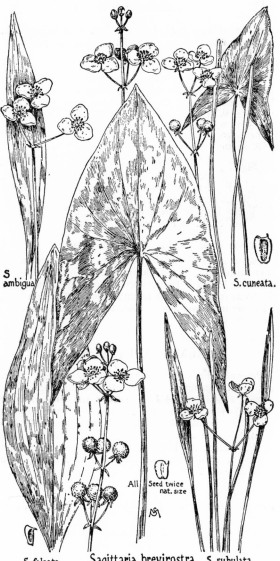

S ambigua

S. cuneata.

S. falcata.   Sagittaria brevirostra.   S. subulata.

All Seed twice nat. size

beakless, slightly winged, and ribbed. 4-20 inches high. Newf. to Fla. and westward. Early leaves purplish.

Sagittaria teres   August-September

Generally with cylindrical, pointed phyllodia, rarely bearing a linear blade. Flowers minute, in 1-3 circles, ½ inch broad, with 12 dilated fine-hairy filaments. Achene obovate, with tiny erect beak, the sides ridged. 4-16 inches high. Ponds, Cape Cod, Mass., L. I., N. Y., possibly southward; an erect aquatic.

Sagittaria subulata   July-September

A dwarf species with linear or lance-shaped leaves, or all reduced to phyllodia. Flowers small, and with 6-8 smooth filaments. Achene tiny, short beaked and ridged. 2-7 inches high. In tide-water mud, or shallow water on the coast. N. Y. to Fla. and Ala.

Sagittaria montevidensis   July-September

Leaves elliptic-lance-shaped, acute at each end in the submerged form in the illustration, but often erect and arrowhead-shaped. Flowers with about 15 stamens, the filaments roughened with minute scales. 8-30 inches high. River swamps and ponds, Del. to Fla., west to S. D., Tex. and Cal.

ARUM FAMILY. *Araceæ.*

Perennial herbs possessing a sharp, peppery juice, somewhat uncommon in the north but numerous in the tropics, containing the *Philodendron* and *Anthurium* of the florists as well as the famous breadfruit. Flowers sometimes perfect, but generally with staminate and pistillate on the same plant, or the staminate and pistillate on different plants. The flowers very minute, crowded on a club or spadix enclosed within or surrounded by a hood or spathe.

Indian Turnip or Jack-in-the-pulpit
Arisæma triphyllum   Purple-brown and green, April-July

Generally with two long-stemmed, tri-parted dull green leaves without a gloss, which overshadow the hooded flower below at the junction of the leaf-stems. The flowers, on the clublike spadix within the hood, are grouped

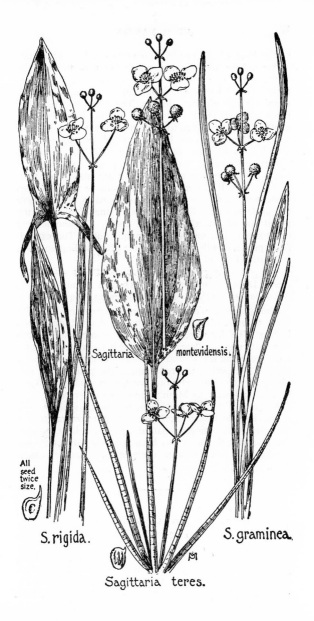

S. rigida.

Sagittaria montevidensis.

All
seed
twice
size.

S. graminea.

Sagittaria teres.

at the base of the spadix and are sometimes staminate and pistillate on separate plants, that is to say, the stamens are abortive on one plant and the pistils are abortive on another; but often one plant develops both staminate and pistillate flowers. The novel and beautiful green and purple-brown striped spathe is variable in depth of color; exposed to sunlight it is usually quite pale, while in the dark woods it is exceedingly purple; as a rule the plant prefers the shaded, wet woods. The handsome clustering berrylike fruit is at first green and finally, in late August, brilliant scarlet. The plant attains a height of 1-2½ feet. It is common in the woods in wet situations from Nova Scotia to Fla. and westward to Minn. There are at least three distinct forms of the plant: (1) the pulpit striped green and brown inside, (2) another red or brown inside, and (3) the pulpit fluted. The exceedingly peppery bulb becomes edible after boiling and was a favorite food of the Indians.

Green Dragon, Dragon-root, or Dragon Arum
Arisæma Dracontium   Dull white-green, May-June

The species generally has a single compound leaf with seven or more obovate-lanced-shaped, pointed, dull green leaflets. The long spadix is usually composed of both staminate and pistillate flowers, and it tapers to a slender point, reaching far beyond the rolled-up, greenish, pointed spathe. The berries are red-orange. The plant is 1-3 feet high, and grows in wet woods or low grounds from Que. to Fla. and west to Minn.; comparatively rare.

Suggesting the green dragon, but much smaller, is a recent introduction from Japan, *Pinellia ternata*. It is a low plant with a single 3-parted leaf, and a long, pointed green spathe. So far it has been seen only under rhododendrons and in lawns in southern N. Y. and northern N. J.

Arrow Arum
Peltandra virginica   Green, May-June

The rich green leaves are arrow-shaped with one prominent vein or nerve. The flowers are staminate and pistillate on the same plant, covering the long, tapering spadix; the pointed green spathe, rolling and wavy on the margin, is 4-7 inches long. The cluster of berries is green, and is at first enclosed in a green sheath, the fleshy

Dragon Arum.
Arisæma Dracontium.

Jack-in-the-pulpit.
Arisæma triphyllum.

base of the spathe. The plant grows 1-1½ feet high, in shallow water, from Me. south, and west to Mich. It derives its name from πέλτη, a target or shield, and ὑνήρ, man, from the targetlike form of the stamen.

Yellow Arrow Arum
Peltandra luteospadix   White-green, May-July

A southern species with wider leaves than those of *P. virginica,* the basal lobes divergent, the stems 8-20 inches long, as long or longer than the flowering stalk. The spathe with a green-white expanded margin, and acute apex; the yellow tapering spadix about one half the length of the spathe. The matured berries red. In swamps and springy ground from southern Va. to Fla.

Water Arum
Calla palustris   White, June

A little swamp flower resembling the calla-lily; the latter is, of course, not a lily, and, curiously enough, not a true calla, it is a *Zantedeschia.* The deep green leaves of the water arum are long-heart-shaped with long stems. The open and rolling edged spathe is white above and greenish beneath. The yellow spadix is entirely covered with flowers, the lower ones perfect, i.e., with all the parts complete, and the upper ones *often* staminate. Fertilization is assisted by insects and pond-snails. The berries, red and distinct, in a head like those of the Jack-in-the-pulpit, are ripe in August. The plant grows 5-10 inches high and is at home in cold bogs, from Me., south to Va., and west to Minn. The name *Calla* is ancient and obscure, *palustris* is the Latin name for swamp.

Skunk Cabbage
Symplocarpus fœtidus   Dark purple-red and green, Feb.-April

A single species, of the earliest appearance in spring, having a fetid odor, which attracts numerous insects, and a closely coiled purple-red streaked and blotched, green, leathery spathe which entraps them to their death. The stout spadix is compactly set with perfect lavender flesh-colored flowers, i.e., flowers with stamens and pistil. The conspicuous anthers are a grayish-straw color. The fruit

Arrow Arum.
Peltandra virginica.

Water Arum.
Calla palustris.

is the enlarged and fleshy spadix enclosing round bullet-like seeds immediately beneath its surface which ripen in September. The name is from συμπλοκή, connection, and καρπός, fruit, alluding to the connection of the ovaries forming compound fruit. The color of the shell-like spathe is not without æsthetic interest; the madder purple, green, and yellow-green are blended and streaked with a peculiar charm; inside, the red is darkest. The leaves will at first be found in a compactly coiled, pointed spike close beside the ruddy spathe. Later when the coarse 1-2 feet long, cabbagelike leaves are unfolded the origin of the common name becomes evident. The odor of the flower is *imitative* of decaying flesh, but it is not wholly bad; it reminds one of the smell of a mustard plaster, and raw onions—the cut stem *decidedly* suggests the latter. The plant is found in swamps, beside brooks, and in wet glades. Common from Que. to N. C., west to Iowa and Minn.

———

Golden Club
Orontium aquaticum   Golden-yellow, April-May

A single species, perennial and aquatic, whose prominent golden-yellow spadix (the club), scarcely larger around than its long, snaky stem, is thickly clustered with the completely developed flowers of generally six sepals, as many golden stamens, and a pistil. The spathe is undeveloped and removed from the spadix, appearing like a mere leaflet on the flower-stem. Fruit green and bladderlike. The long-stemmed, oblong, dark green leaves float upon the water. It is a beautiful aquatic plant whose flowers deserve close examination under the glass. 1-2 feet high, common in the shallows of ponds, from Mass., south, and generally found near the coast. Name from the Syrian river Orontes.

———

Calamus or Sweet Flag
Acorus Calamus   Yellow-green, June-July

The stiff, swordlike, light green leaves give the plant a rigid character. It has inconspicuous flowers compactly covering a tapering cylindrical spadix which grows angularly from the side of a two-edged stem resembling the flat ribbonlike leaves. The individual flower has a pistil,

Skunk Cabbage.   Symplocarpus fœtidus.

six stamens, and as many sepals of a dull yellow-green color. The fruit is a small berry, at first gelatinous and finally dry, but the plant is mostly propagated by its stocky roots. Name, *Ἄκορας*, for some plant with an aromatic root. The horizontal, pungent, and pleasantly aromatic rootstock is a familiar commodity of the apothecary. There is a striped-leaved variety. The plant grows 1-4 feet high, or more, and is found beside small streams and in wet ground, from Que. to Fla. and west to Minn., Tex. and Colo.

YELLOW-EYED GRASS FAMILY.
Xyridaceæ.

Perennial herbs with narrow, grasslike leaves, and perfect, regular, yellow flowers with three spreading lobes and a slender tube borne from between tightly pressed scales of a conelike cluster.

Yellow-eyed Grass
Xyris flexuosa   Yellow, July-August

A little swamp plant with grasslike, or rather slender rushlike, light green leaves which twist as they grow old, and flowers about ⅓ inch across, of three yellow petal-like divisions, three stamens, and as many sepals, the flowers proceeding from a conelike head composed of brownish-green leafy scales. The fruit is an oblong many-seeded capsule. The name is from *Ξυρίς*, an unknown Greek plant with two-edged leaves. The plant grows 6-16 inches high, in sandy bogs or morasses, from N. J. to Fla., Tex. and Ark.

Northern Yellow-eyed Grass
Xyris montana   July-August

A dwarf and slender species found in mountain regions, with a straight or slightly twisted stem, not bulbous at the base. Leaves narrow and linear about 2 inches long, not twisted. The small ovoid flower-heads about ¼ inch thick. 3-12 inches (rarely 12) high. Generally in peat bogs. Newf. and the White Mts., south to Pocono Mts., Pa., west to Wisc.

Golden Club.
Orontium aquaticum.

Sweet Flag.
Acorus Calamus

Xyris caroliniana   June-August

A tall but variable species; the stem not bulbous at the base. Leaves grasslike, 3-8 inches long and about ¼ inch wide. The ovoid head about ⅓ inch in diameter. 10-16 inches high, rarely taller. In bogs and wet sandy lake shores, Nova Scotia to Fla. near the coast, and west to Mich. and Tex. The plant is so variable that names for some of its forms have been proposed, such as *X. difformis* and *X. elata,* but it is doubtful if they are valid.

Xyris Smalliana   July-September

A very tall species 15-36 inches high, with broad linear or sword-shaped leaves often ¾ inch wide, rather rigid and not twisted. Flower-stem slender and flattened near the top. Heads long-ovoid, ½ inch in diameter, the green scales with an ochre-yellow edge. In rich soil of boggy shores, and often in water. East Mass. to Fla.

Xyris fimbriata   July-September

Another tall, stout species, with broad straight, linear leaves, and a straight flower-stem flattened and roughened on the edges toward the top. Heads ellipsoidal, ½ inch in diameter, the long fringed sepals extending conspicuously beyond the bracts. 2-3 feet high. Wet pine barrens of N. J., to Fla. and Miss.

SPIDERWORT FAMILY. *Commelinaceæ.*

Herbs with jointed and often leafy branching stems, the leaves sheathed at the base, and generally perfect flowers, i.e., flowers with stamens and pistil. The family contains many tropical genera, among them the Wandering Jew of the florists.

Virginia Day Flower
Commelina virginica   Light violet-blue, June-September

The grass-green leaves are lance-shaped, and brown-sheathed at their junction with the plant-stem; the sheath is hairy-edged. The flowers are three-parted and irregular, that is, unequal in size, form, and structural parts; two of the light violet-blue petals are larger than the third. The leaf immediately below the flowers is heart-shaped and clasping, forming a hollow from which the flower-stem proceeds. The flowers expand only in the morning.

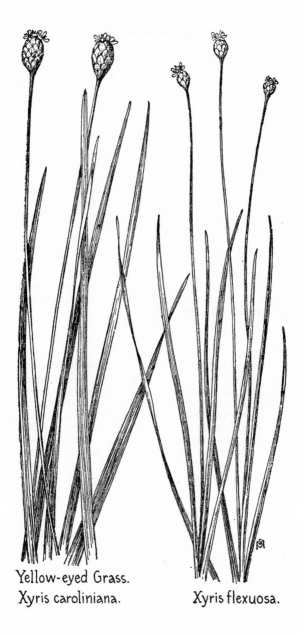

Yellow-eyed Grass.
Xyris caroliniana.

Xyris flexuosa.

The plant is erect, stout-stemmed, and grows 2-3 feet
high and is the most common of the wild species. It is
named for the early Dutch botanists, Kasper and Jan Com-
meljin. Fond of damp and shady, but warm places, from
southern N. Y. south and west to Mo.

Asiatic Day Flower
Commelina communis   Light violet, July-October

A tall and slender species naturalized from Asia, with
lance-shaped leaves, and a heart-shaped acute spathe, the
margins of which are not united. Flowers light violet
½ inch or so broad. Stems 1-3 feet long. A common
annual weed of dooryards and gardens in the northerly
part of its range. On moist alluvial banks, eastern Mass.
and Del. to Ala., west to Neb. and Tex.

Commelina erecta   August-October

A slender southern species with linear lance-shaped
leaves. Cells of the ripened fruit one-ovuled and one-
seeded. The spathe hood-shaped. 1-2 feet high. Moist
ground, N. Y. to Fla., Tex. and Ariz. (*Illus. for this and*
C. communis *are opposite page 32.*)

Spiderwort
Tradescantia virginiana   Light violet-blue, May-August

This species has mucilaginous sap and upright stems,
with light green, narrow, and linear leaves. The flowers
are regular with three purplish ultramarine-blue petals
which richly relieve the golden anthers within; the latter
are widely removed from the prominent stigma. It is also
a familiar, old-fashioned garden flower, common beside
the farmhouses of the north. It is named for John
Tradescant, gardener to Charles I. of England. It grows
1-1½ feet high, usually in rich or moist ground, from
Me. south, and west to Minn. and Mo. There are variable
forms of this species, as well as another slenderer
southern species with smaller *pink* flowers, 6-12 inches
high, named *Tradescantia rosea,* var. *graminea.* It is distributed from Va., south along the coastal plain to Fla.

Tradescantia longipes   Purple-violet, magenta-pink, May

This is a local species with large purple-violet or magenta-pink flowers. It is often stemless or nearly so, and
extremely soft-hairy. Leaves linear lance-shaped, the

Virginia Day Flower.   Spiderwort.
Commelina virginica.   Tradescantia virginiana.

flower-stems long, slender, and fine-hairy. Stem (if present) only 1-4 inches high. In dry or moist sandy soil in Mo.

Tradescantia subaspera   Blue-violet, June-August

Tall and stout with a zigzag stem and broad deep green leaves; the whole plant more or less fine-hairy. Leaves lance-shaped and acute-pointed. ½-1½ inches broad. The profuse flowers are light blue-violet. 1-3 feet high. Shrubby and shady banks of streams, W. Va. and Tenn. to Ill. and Mo.

Tradescantia subaspera, var. *montana*

A southern species similar to *Tradescantia virginiana*, but the flowers smaller and the calyx smooth. The leaves are broader and a deeper green than those of *T. ohiensis*. From Va. and Ky., south. The typical *T. subaspera*, with a more twisting stem, is found west of the Alleghenies.

Tradescantia ohiensis   Blue-violet, May-June

A slender and smooth species with long linear leaves and many light blue-violet flowers in a cluster. The narrow bracts and smooth flower-stems finally turned downward. In wet places and on prairies, Mass. to Fla., west to Minn. and Tex. It may be only naturalized in Mass.; common on midwestern prairies.

Tradescantia bracteata   Blue-violet

A western species, the upper part of the plant glandular, fine-hairy, of a dull color. The bracts beneath the flowers relatively large, folded together, and curved backward, their bases sometimes an inch broad. Flowers blue-violet, 1-1¼ inches in diameter. Prairies, Ind. to N. D. and Kan.

Tradescantia occidentalis   Light violet, magenta-pink

Another slender western species with narrow linear incurved leaves with an enlarged dry, thin base. Bracts narrow. The large flowers light violet or sometimes magenta-pink. Wisc. and Minn., west to Mont. and south to Tex. and Ariz.

———

A recently introduced plant, *Aneilema Keisak,* closely related to the day flowers and spiderworts, has been found in brackish marshes in southeastern Va. It is a low, creeping plant with solitary, stalked flowers with pink petals. Native of eastern Asia.

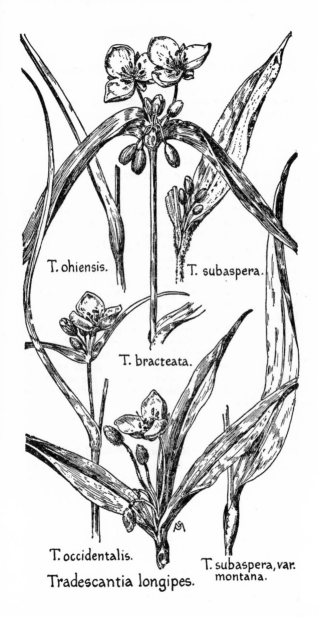

T. ohiensis.

T. subaspera.

T. bracteata.

T. occidentalis.

T. subaspera, var. montana.

Tradescantia longipes.

PICKEREL-WEED FAMILY. *Pontederiaceæ.*

Aquatic herbs with perfect (i.e. having stamens and pistil), more or less irregular flowers issuing from a spathe or leaflike envelope, which are mostly fertilized by insects.

Pickerel-weed
Pontederia cordata   Light violet-blue, June-September

A tall plant with one blunt arrowhead-shaped, dark green, thick leaf, varying to a very elongated triangle shape, and a showy flower-spike about 4 inches long crowded with ephemeral, violet-blue flowers which are marked with a distinct yellow-green spot. Immediately below the spike is the small spathe. Sometimes the flowers are white. The flower-cup is funnel-formed and six-divided, the upper three divisions united, and the three lower ones spread apart. The six stamens are three of them long and protruding, and three short which are often abortive; the blue anthers are so placed that it is impossible for an insect to enter the flower-cup without brushing against them and detaching the pollen. The fruit is a bladderlike receptacle containing one seed. The plant is named for Giulio Pontedera, a professor of botany at Padua. Pickerel-weed grows 1-3 feet high, and is commonly found in the shallows of ponds and sluggish streams, sometimes associated with the arrowhead. It is closely related to the still more showy water hyacinth of Fla.

———

Mud Plantain
Heteranthera reniformis   White or bluish, July-August

A small water plant with deep green, floating, round, kidney-shaped leaves on long stems, and 2-5 white or pale blue perfectly developed flowers, which, like those of the preceding species, are exceedingly short-lived. The tiny flowers proceed from a spathe or leafy enclosure projecting from the sheathed side of a leaf-stem. The flower with six nearly equal divisions spread above its slender tube. The plant is named for its unlike anthers, ἑτέρα different, and ανθηρά anther; the specific *reniformis* means kidney-formed, in allusion to the shape of the leaf. It grows about 12 inches high, in mud or shallow water, from Conn. to N. J., south to Fla., west to Tex. and Neb.

Pickerel Weed. Mud Plantain.
Pontederia cordata. Heteranthera reniformis

Smaller Mud Plantain
Heteranthera limosa   **Blue or white, July-August**

A similar low herb common in the southwestern states, generally found in shallow water. The stems with many branches at the base. The leaves ovate, oblong or lance-oblong, blunt at the tip, rounded at the base or else slightly heart-shaped, 1 inch long or less, the stems 2-5 inches long. The spathe or leafy bract encloses but one flower which is usually larger than that of *H. reniformis,* generally blue and with a white spot near the base, or all white. 6-15 inches high. Ky. and Ill., southwestward to Tex. and Tropical Am.

Water Stargrass
Heteranthera dubia   **Light yellow, July-October**

This species is a submerged grasslike plant with a slender stem and translucent deep green leaves; the flow-ers only reach the surface of the water. Leaves linear, flat, sharp-pointed, and finely parallel-veined. The spathe one-flowered, the flower light yellow with six narrow divisions and a very long, slender tube, the stamens longer than the style, with arrow-shaped anthers. 2-3 feet high. In shallow, quiet water, from Que. south, and west to Ore. and Mex. Also known as *Zosterella dubia.*

There is still another mud plantain known only from Mo. and Kan., *Heteranthera peduncularis,* which re-sembles *H. reniformis,* and is considered by some as a mere form of it. *H. peduncularis* is a stouter plant with larger leaves.

LILY FAMILY. *Liliaceæ.*

An enormous group of often very showy perennial herbs in temperate regions, but treelike in the tropics. Familiar examples include, besides the true lilies, the tulip, onion, lily of the valley and asparagus. Flower parts usually in sixes, often cuplike, but with separate petals in some. Over 3,000 species are known, of which those below in-clude only the native kinds.

Carrion Flower
Smilax herbacea   **Green-yellow, May-June**

The light green veiny-corrugated leaves are mostly round-ovate and heart-shaped at the base, pointed at the

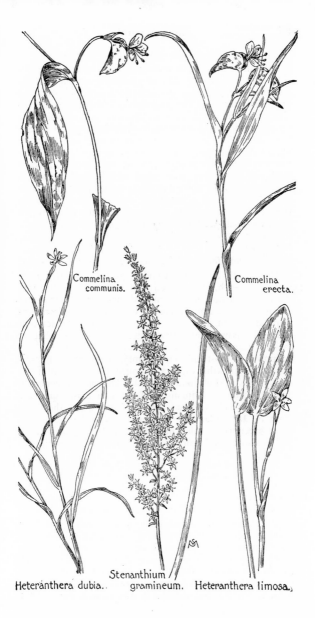

Commelina
communis.

Commelina
erecta.

Heteránthera dubia.   Stenanthium   Heteranthera limosa.
                        gramineum.

tip, and devoid of gloss, their stalks greatly varying in length, measuring 1/3-3 inches; with a tendril at either side. The long flower-stalk proceeding from between the tendrils is topped by a hemispherical flower-cluster with spokelike stemlets. The greenish-yellow flowers are insignificant and putrid-odored; the staminate and pistillate on separate plants, show their dependence upon insects for fertilization, particularly upon those flies which are attracted by carrion. The cluster of berries is first green and finally blue-black with a bloom. It is, indeed, a beautiful and decorative vine, most unfortunate in the repellent odor of its flowers at the time of bloom. It is very variable, grows to a length of 4-15 feet, and frequents river banks and thickets. Common in some of its forms from the coast west to Neb. and Wyo.

Cat Brier
Smilax rotundifolia   Light green, May-June

The slightly zigzag stem and branches, the latter more or less squarish, are covered with scattered prickles, and the broadly ovate, short-stemmed, light green leaves are 2-3 inches long and pointed. The leaf-stalk is bent upward at a right angle; in the angle are the slender tendrils. The flower-stalk bears fewer flowers than that of the preceding species. The berries are blue-black. It is common in most thickets, forming dense, prickly, impenetrable growths; often a nuisance. Common from the coast west to Mich. and Tex. Also known as greenbrier, and not always distinguished from two close relatives: *Smilax Walteri,* with red berries, found along the coast from N. J. to Fla. and Tex., and *Smilax laurifolia,* another greenbrier, which has longer and evergreen leaves and is also coastal from N. J. to Fla. and Tex., and also in Ark.

Clintonia
Clintonia borealis   Yellowish-green, June-early July

A handsome woodland plant with from two to four (usually three) shiny, light green, large oval-oblong leaves; a slender flower-stalk, about 7 inches high, bears from three to six yellowish-green, drooping flowers greenish on the outside. The flower is formed of six distinct sepals, and is perfect, having six stamens and a pistil; its form is lilylike and dainty. It was named for DeWitt

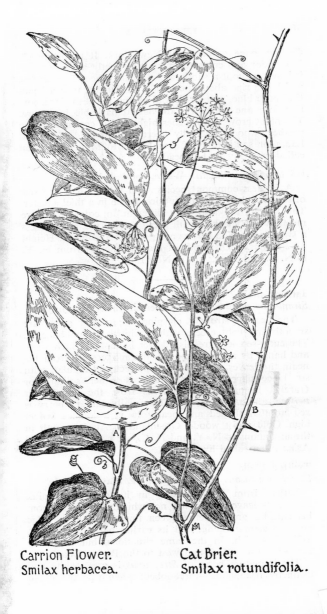

Carrion Flower.
Smilax herbacea.

Cat Brier.
Smilax rotundifolia.

Clinton, once governor of New York. It unfortunately lacks odor and color to make it perfectly attractive, but it is not without a subtle and delicate grace. The berries, which are ripe about the middle of August, turn a beautiful pure blue, a color devoid of any purplish tinge, and therefore one which is rare and remarkable in nature. The plant grows 6-16 inches high, and is common in the northern woods, especially where they are cold and moist. Labrador south to N. C., and west to Manitoba; often called corn lily or bluebead.

Clintonia umbellulata   White, spotted, May-June

A far less common species, with flowers half the size of those of the foregoing species, borne in a thick cluster. The flowers are also very different in color; they are mostly white speckled with green and purple, and possess a sweet odor. The berries are globular and black. Height 8-22 inches. Rich woods of the Alleghenies from N. Y. to N. C. and Tenn.; not in New Eng.

Twisted Stalk
Streptopus amplexifolius   Greenish-white, May-July

The leaves, strongly clasping the zigzag stem, are smooth and light green, with a whitish bloom beneath. The curly-sepaled, greenish flower is about ½ inch wide, and hangs by a long, crooked, threadlike stalk from beneath the leaves. The flower is perfect and regular, with six lance-shaped segments, and is either solitary or (rarely) in pairs. The name is from the Greek, for *twisted,* and *stalk* or *foot.* The usually solitary berry is red, football-shaped and nearly ½ inch long. 2-3 feet high. Cold moist woods. Greenland to Alaska, south in the mountains to N. Y. and N. C., west to N. Mex. and Ariz.; often called liverberry.

Twisted Stalk
Streptopus roseus   Dull purple-pink, May-early July

Differs from the preceding in its dull purple-pink flower, its leaves which are not whitened with a bloom beneath, but are altogether green, finely hairy at the edge and not stem-clasping; and its earlier period of bloom. 1-2½ feet high. In the same situations, but extending farther south to Ga., and west to the Pacific Coast.

The immature berry of *Streptopus* is green-white and distinctly triangulate—three-lobed; when ripe the ovoid

Clintonia
umbellulata.

Clintonia borealis.

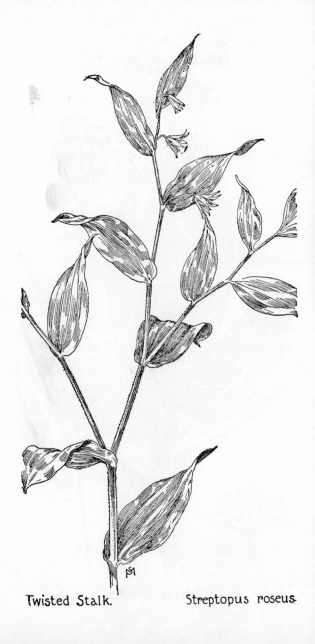

Twisted Stalk.   Streptopus roseus

False Spikenard.   Smilacina racemosa.

berry is a translucent cherry-red; the slender stems are abruptly bent near the middle. A form of *Streptopus roseus*, known from Ont. to Pa. west to Mich. and Wisc., was included in our last edition as *Streptopus longipes*. It is here considered as a mere form of *S. roseus*, differing in having elongated instead of matted rootstocks.

Asparagus
Asparagus officinalis Green-yellow, June

This beautiful perennial, so well known as a vegetable, is not quite as familiar to us in its æsthetic dress. Its leaves (or properly, its branchlets) are threadlike; and it assumes a bushy, almost larklike figure as it grows older, and becomes decorated with round, scarlet berries. The tiny green-yellow flowers are six-parted, and rather inconspicuous. The name is ancient. Adventive from the old country, and a frequent escape from kitchen gardens everywhere. It is a favorite among the farmers' wives who use it decoratively in their homes; certainly it is not less decorative than the florist's famous *Asparagus plumosus*.

False Spikenard
Smilacina racemosa White, May

A really beautiful woodland plant slightly resembling Solomon's Seal, but bearing its Spiræalike cluster of fine white flowers at the tip of the stem. The light blue-green leaves are oblong and ovate-lance-shaped, taper-pointed, and with very short stalks—hardly any, in fact. The tiny flower has six distinct white sepals, and is perfect, with six stamens and a pistil. The flower cluster is pyramidal, and the zigzag plant-stem gracefully inclines. The berries, smaller than peas, are at first greenish then yellowish-white speckled with madder brown, and finally, in late September, a dull ruby-red of translucent character. They possess an aromatic taste. The name is a diminutive of Smilax, without appropriate application. Common in moist copses and besides woodland roads. 1-3 feet high. Nova Scotia, south to Ga. and Miss., west to Ariz.

False Solomon's Seal
Smilacina stellata White, May-early June

A much smaller species than the foregoing, with a very small but pretty starry cluster of white flowers at

False Solomon's Seal.
Smilacina stellata.

Smilacina trifolia

the tip of the stem. The leaves, light blue-green and very firm, clasp the zigzag stem. The flower is ¼ inch wide. The berries, which are few, are at first spotted and finally dull reddish-black, striped black. 8-16 inches high. Moist banks and meadows. Newf. to Va., west to B. C. and Cal.

Three-leaved False Solomon's Seal
Smilacina trifolia White, May-early June

A still smaller species, with generally three leaves, but sometimes two or even four, tapering to a sheathing base; flowers smaller than those of the preceding species, and the berries red like those of the next species. 2-6 inches high. In bogs or wet woods. Newf. to B. C., south to Pa., west to Minn.

Although the resemblance of *Smilacina trifolia* to *Maianthemum canadense* (the next species described) is close, the differences are easily detected by a careful observer. The (usually) three leaves of *Smilacina trifolia* clasp the stem but are in no way heart-shaped at the base. This species also has *six* flower segments and as many stamens, and the whole plant is invariably smooth, not fine-hairy as is *sometimes* the case with the next species. The berries of *Smilacina* and *Maianthemum* are closely similar, but those of *Smilacina stellata* are in a measure harder, more opaque than any of the others, and reddish-black, while those of *Maianthemum* are pale red.

Wild Lily of the Valley
Maianthemum canadense White, May-June

A tiny woodland plant resembling *Smilacina trifolia*, with small white flowers which differ from those of the genus *Smilacina* in having only four segments and as many stamens. It has two to three light green, shiny leaves which are ovate-lance-shaped or broader, with a somewhat heart-shaped base. The berries are yellow-white, spotted with madder brown until early fall, when they turn a dull translucent pale red.

A familiar plant in nearly all woods, generally in moist places. 3-6 inches high. The name is from *Maius*, May, and ἄνθεμον, flower. Labrador west to Minn. and Iowa, south to N. C.

Wild Lily of the Valley.
Maianthemum canadense.

Lily of the Valley.
Convallaria majalis.

Lily of the Valley
Convallaria majalis   White, May-early June

There is only one true species, familiar in cultivation. It has two oblong leaves, shiny and smooth, and a
slender stalk bearing a one-sided row of tiny white
flowers, extremely sweet-scented and dainty. Flower-cup
bell-shaped, with six lobes recurved, and six stamens.
Berry red, but rarely seen. The name is from the Latin
convallis, valley, and the Greek for lily. Identical with
the European flower of the gardens which rather uncom-
monly escapes to the wilds. It also grows on the higher
Alleghenies, from Va. to Tenn., and is thought to be
native there.

————

The pendulous position of the flowers in Solomon's
Seal is in a great measure protective; the wind and
weather can not injure or uselessly scatter the pollen. The
flowers, moreover, have short styles and long anthers,
and are unquestionably cross-fertilized by bumblebees
which are common visitors, together with innumerable
small insects.

Solomon's Seal
Polygonatum pubescens   Pale green, April-June

The oblong-ovate, light green leaves finely hairy and
paler beneath, arranged alternately either side of the
slender, smooth stem; the cylindrical and tassel-like perfect flowers (each having six stamens) depend in clusters
of two, rarely three, below them. An extremely pretty
and graceful plant when under cultivation. The fruit, at
first a green berry with a whitish bloom, at last becomes
blue-black and resembles a small Concord grape; it im-
parts an additionally decorative appearance to the plant.
1-3 feet high. Common in thickets beside woodlands, and
on hillsides. Nova Scotia, south to Ga. and west to
E. Kan., Neb., and Tex. In our last edition listed as *Polygonatum biflorum.* A related plant, *P. canaliculatum* with
smooth leaves is found from Mass. to Ga. and west to
Okla. and Tex.

Great Solomon's Seal
Polygonatum biflorum   Pale green, May-early July

The plant is taller and smooth, *without* the fine hairiness. Leaves ovate, pointed, and partly clasping the plant-
stem, 3-8 inches long, and many-ribbed. Flowers in

Solomon's Seal.   Polygonatum pubescens.

clusters of from two to eight. Stem stout and round. 2-8 feet high. Meadows and river banks, New Eng. south to Fla., and west to Ind. and Miss. The interpretation of these two species has long been confused. The easiest way to identify the two is by stature. The first species is rarely over 3 ft. high, while the great Solomon's Seal is generally over 4 ft. high. The plants take their name of Solomon's Seal from seal-like scales on the rootstock.

———

Bellwort
Uvularia perfoliata   Pale yellow, May-June

A graceful woodland plant, smooth throughout, with a forking stem (one to three leaves below the fork), the deep green ovate-lance-shaped leaves appearing as if perforated by it. The delicately fragrant flower-cup, granular-rough inside, is attenuated but lilylike, with six distinct pale yellow segments. Flowers perfect, with six short stamens and a pistil. Flower segments with a deep honey-bearing groove within, ridged on either edge.

Seed pod a three-parted capsule, appearing as if chopped off at the end. Name from *uvula,* palate, referring to the way the flower hangs. It grows 6-18 inches high, in rich woods, from Que. to Ohio, and south to Fla. and Tenn.

Large-flowered Bellwort
Uvularia grandiflora   Pale yellow, April-June

This is the commoner bellwort from western New Eng., west and south, mostly in the mountains. The deep-green leaves are fine-white-hairy beneath; the large pale yellow flower, inclining to green at the summit, is fully 1½ inches long, and *smooth* inside. Stem with a single leaf or none below the fork. Que. to Conn. and W. Va., west to Minn. and Okla.

Wild Oats
Uvularia sessilifolia   Cream-yellow, May-June

Similar in some respects to the foregoing but with marked differences. Stem angled. The deep green leaves, fine-hairy beneath, conspicuously three-grooved, sharp-pointed, and stemless, or slightly clasping. The six divisions of the flower less pointed, no ridges within the flower-cup, the latter more buffish cream-colored, but still yellowish. The seed capsule three-sided, resembling a

Uvularia
perfoliata.

Large-flowered Bellwort.   Wild Oats.
Uvularia grandiflora.   Uvularia sessilifolia.

beech nut. The one or two flowers on slender stalks, at first terminating the plant stem, but finally appearing opposite the leaves by reason of the growth of the branches.

Stem 6-13 inches high. It is very common in the north woods. Que. south to Ala., and west to Minn. and Ark

Mountain Bellwort
Uvularia pudica   Yellow, May-June

A southern plant of the mountain woods found at an altitude of 5000 feet in Virginia. The rather stocky angular stem slightly fine-hairy. Leaves ovate, pointed, rough-edged, and a bright shining green on both sides. Flowers pale yellow, bell-shaped, with six perianth divisions, the styles separated nearly to the base and not longer than the anthers. 8-15 inches high. N. J.; but mostly in the mountains of Va. and W. Va., also in Ga.

Toadshade
Trillium sessile   Dull magenta-red, April-May

The trilliums or wakerobins are handsome woodland plants with stout stems, ruddy purple at the base; their perfect flowers have three green sepals which remain until the plant withers, three petals much larger, and six stamens. *T. sessile* has stemless, slightly fragrant erect flowers with narrow petals and sepals, the former rather erect and spreading, dull magenta-red, varying to a greenish tone. Leaves stalkless, somewhat four-sided but ovate, and often blotched with lighter and darker green. Red berry spherical or nearly so, ½ inch deep. The name is from *triplum,* triple, a characteristic of all parts of the plant. 5-10 inches high. Moist woods. Pa., south, and west to Minn. and Ark. A closely related species is *Trillium recurvatum,* which differs from the preceding in the following particulars. The leaves are narrowed at the base into a stalk, and the flower has reflexed sepals, and pointed petals narrowed at the base. 6-16 inches high. Rich woods. Mich. to Ohio, west to Wisc. and Neb.

Wakerobin, or Birthroot
Trillium erectum   Maroon, or white, etc., April-June

A very common eastern species, with four-sided ovate leaves scarcely stemmed, and abruptly pointed, and flowers, with a reclining stem, varying in color from white to pink, brownish purple-red or maroon, with flat, ovate, spreading petals nearly 1½ inches long, the sepals

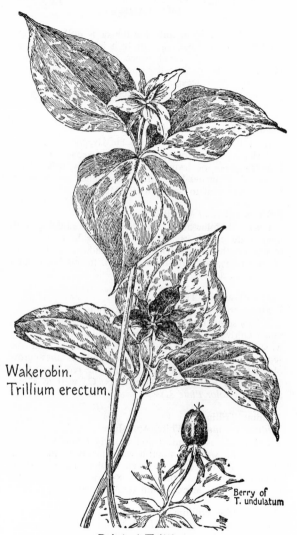

Wakerobin.
Trillium erectum.

Berry of
T. undulatum

Painted Trillium.
Trillium undulatum.

a trifle shorter. Sometimes the flower is dull pink, of a
brownish purple tone, and rarely it is greenish. It is ill-
scented, and as a consequence attracts carrion-loving
insects, such as the flesh-fly, who find the raw-meat color
of the flower as acceptable as the odor. Berry dark red,
round-ovate. 7-15 inches high. Rich woods. Que. to N. C.,
Ga. and Tenn. (*Color Plate 2.*)

Trillium viride   **Greenish, April-May**

A similar species to *T. sessile* but larger. Leaves ovate
and sharp-pointed, often mottled, the sepals spreading.
Flowers green or brown-purple, or yellow, with linear
petals. 12-15 inches high. Moist woodlands and hillsides.
Ky. to Ga., west to southern Ill., Mo. and Ark.

Trillium Gleasoni   **White, May**

Leaves rhombic-ovate. The white flower nodding, with
long ovate petals; its stalk 1½-2 inches long. The filaments less than half as long as the anthers. Woodlands,
Mich. to Ky., west to Minn. and Mo. In our last edition
listed as *T. declinatum*.

Large Flowering Trillium
Trillium grandiflorum   **White, May-June**

A handsome, large-flowered species flowering later, and
much cultivated by the florists and wild gardeners. The
waxy-white petals 1½-2 inches long, larger than the
sepals, curve gracefully backward, and, as they grow
older, turn pink. 10-18 inches high. The red berry fully
1 inch long. Rich woods. Que. to N. C., west to Minn.
and Ind. (*Color Plate 3.*)

Nodding Trillium
Trillium cernuum   **White, April-June**

Leaves almost stemless and broadly four-sided ovate.
Flower with white or pinkish wavy petals ¾ inch long,
and with a short stem recurved so that the blossom is
often hidden beneath the leaves. 8-14 inches high. Moist
woods. Que. to Minn., south to Ala. and Mo.

Dwarf White Trillium
Trillium nivale   **White, March-May**

A very small species with ovate leaves, 1-2 inches long,
and flowers whose white petals, less than 1 inch long, are
scarcely wavy. Berry red, about ⅓ inch in diameter, flattened and spherical, with three rounded divisions. A

Erect *flower of*
Trillium recurvatum.

Nodding Trillium.
Trillium cernuum.

Dwarf White Trillium.
Trillium nivale.

dwarf plant 2-5 inches high. Rich woods. Pa. and Ky.
to Minn. and Neb.

Painted Trillium
Trillium undulatum   White, crimson-striped, May-June

One of the most beautiful of the genus, and very common in the rich woodlands of the north. Leaves ovate
and tapering to a sharp point. Green sepals quite narrow, and the gracefully recurved, wavy-edged white petals
strongly marked with deep or pale red or even purple
streaks. The dark scarlet ovate berry ¾ inch long, ripe
in September and falling at a touch. 8-16 inches high.
Cold damp woods and beside woodland brooks, Que. to
Ga., in the mountains, west to Mich. and Wisc.

———

Indian Cucumber-root
Medeola virginiana   Greenish-yellow, May-June

The only species, the thin, circling, long ovate, light
green leaves of which are arranged around the middle,
and the three ovate ones around the top of the thin stem.
The inconspicuous nodding, but perfect, flower is ⅔
inch wide, greenish-yellow, accented by the reddish terra-
cotta color of the six stamens, and the three long, recurved terra-cotta-brown stigmas, i.e., the three divisions
of the tip of the pistil; the three petals and three sepals
are also recurved. In September about two or three
purple-black berries replace the flowers at the apex of
the plant. Named for the sorceress Medea on account of
its supposed medicinal virtue. The common name alludes
to the succulent, horizontal, white tuberous root which
tastes like cucumber, and was in all probability relished
by the Indians. 1-3 feet high. Rich damp woods, Que. to
Ga. and west to Minn.

Medeola virginiana is a characteristic woodland plant,
common in the White Mountain woods. It is adapted to
subdued sunlight, and is interesting in both flower and
fruit. The blossoms, often beneath the three upper leaves,
are thus protected from the dripping of the trees in wet
weather; their colors are æsthetic. Crawling insects can-
not easily mount the (at first) woolly stem and rob the
flower of its pollen, flying insects readily find the blossom, and in September the three crowning leaflets beneath
the berries are stained with dull crimson, the color
attracting birds to the fruit. It is therefore evident that
the plant depends in some measure upon visitors.

Indian Cucumber-root.   Medeola virginiana.

Blazing Star, or Devil's Bit
Chamælirium luteum   White, June-July

The stem bearing light green, flat, lance-shaped (blunt) leaves at the base with several shorter, narrower ones farther up, and terminated by a feathery spike 4-10 inches long of small, fragrant flowers, white with a tinting of the yellow stamens characterizing the male, and inconspicuous white the female ones. It is quite dependent upon insects for cross-fertilization, the male flowers growing on one plant and female on another; the flower-cup has six narrow, spreading white segments. The female plant is more leafy. Fruit an oblong capsule. The name, which was first applied to a half-grown, low specimen, is from χαμαί, on the ground, and λείριον, lily. The wand-like stem 1-4 feet high. Low grounds and bogs, from Mass. to Fla., west to Neb. and Ark.

———

Bunch Flower
Melanthium virginicum   Cream-yellow, turning brown,
June-August

The lowest leaves nearly 1 inch wide, the few upper ones small, and linear or grass-shaped. Flowers polygamous, i.e., male and female, and perfect on the same plant. It does not, therefore, rely fully upon insects for fertilization. Flower-cup of six separate, greenish cream-yellow segments turning brown with age. Fruit, an ovoid-conical capsule, three-lobed. The name is from μέλας, black, and ἄνθος, flower, in allusion to the dark color which the flower assumes upon withering. The leafy, slender stem is 3-5 feet high. It grows in wet woods and meadows, from N. Y. south to Fla., west to Minn. and Tex. *Melanthium hybridum,* which has broader leaves and blunter flower segments, is found from Conn. to Ga. and W. Va., but is not so common as *M. virginicum.*

———

Indian Poke or American White Hellebore
Veratrum viride   Dull yellow-green, May-June

A leafy perennial herb with very poisonous coarse roots, remarkable in the early stage of its development for its beautiful pure yellow-green color, which becomes darker and dull within four weeks, and finally withers to an unsightly brown before the summer is in its prime.

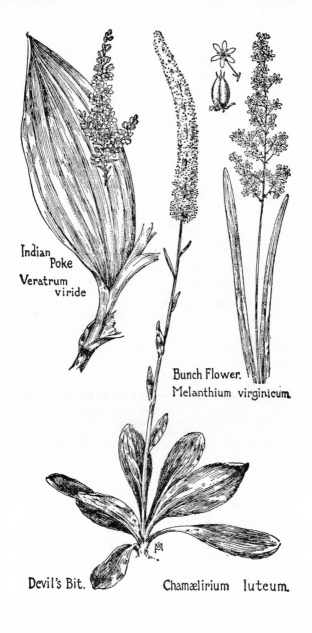

Indian Poke
Veratrum viride

Bunch Flower.
Melanthium virginicum

Devil's Bit.   Chamælirium luteum.

The broad ovate, clasping leaves are scored with numerous ribs, and crinkled in parallel lines. The large flower-
spike is dull yellow-green turning brownish with age;
the flowers, like those of the preceding genus, are polygamous, but small, with six green sepals. Capsule also like
that of *Melanthium*. Name from *vere,* truly, and *ater,*
dead black, in allusion to the blackening (really turning
brown) of the plant upon withering. The plant is poisonous in all parts, but has recently been widely cultivated
as an American source of *veratrine,* a drug found to be
useful in high blood pressure, and for certain heart af-
fections. It grows 2-7 feet high, in wet meadows and low
grounds nearly everywhere.

Stout Stenanthium
Stenanthium gramineum   White or green, July-August

Stem leafy, stout and erect, with grasslike leaves.
Flower-spike sometimes 2 feet long; the flowers are also
polygamous. Flower-cup whitish-green or white with six
narrow spreading lance-shaped sepals, ⅓ inch long.
Leaves grasslike. Fruit capsule pointed long-ovate. The
name is from στενός, narrow, and ἄνθος, flower, alluding
to the slender sepals and flower-cluster. 3-5 feet high.
Pa. to S. C., west to Ohio and Tenn. (*Illus. opp. page
32.*)

The lily group is distinguished for its handsome bell
shaped flowers, of six distinct spreading segments with a
honey-bearing groove at the base of each. Flowers perfect with six prominent stamens, and a long pistil the tip
of which is a three-lobed stigma. Fruit an oblong capsule
containing many flat seeds. The bulb scaly. The name
Latinized from the Greek λείριον.

Wood Lily or Wild Orange-Red Lily
Lilium philadelphicum   Orange-scarlet, July

The most beautifully colored wild lily of all, with bright
green leafy stems, flower-cup opening *upward,* and the
six flower segments narrowing to a stemlike slenderness
toward the base. The color varying from orange-scarlet
to scarlet-orange or paler, and spotted with purple-brown
on the inner part of the cup. The segments do not re-
curve. From one to three flowers are borne at the branch-

Wood Lily.   Lilium philadelphicum.

ing summit of the plant-stem. 1-3 feet high. Dry and sandy soil, common in the borders of thin woods, Me. to N. C., west to Minn. and Mo. The var. *andinum,* a western form, has linear leaves alternately or irregularly distributed on the stem, and generally deeper red flowers. The pod narrowed at the base. Rich and dry soil of prairies, and in bogs, Ohio to Colo., N. Mex., and northwest.

Pine Lily
Lilium Catesbæi var. *Longii*   Orange-scarlet, July-August

Similar to *L. philadelphicum,* but the linear leaves alternately or irregularly distributed. The orange-scarlet flower solitary, with widespread wavy-margined divisions, long-clawed at the tip, and madder-purple-spotted at the yellow base. 1-2 feet high. Moist pine-barrens, Va. to Fla., Ala. and Mo.

Yellow Meadow Lily or Canada Lily
Lilium canadense   Buff yellow spotted purple-brown, June-July

The common lily of the north, found most often upon low meadows. The stem is slender or stout, very light green and smooth, and bears the light green lance-shaped leaves in circles. The stem divides into several branches (really flower-stalks) each of which bears a pendulous flower, buff yellow on the outside and a deeper orange buff spotted purple-brown on the inside. The nectar is protected from the rain by the pendulous position of the flower-cup; it is gathered mostly by the wild honey-bee, and the leaf-cutter bee, which visit the flower to gather the brown pollen as well. These insects are therefore the most potent means of fertilizing this lily. It grows 2-5 feet high, and frequents moist meadows and copses, from Que., south to Ala. and west to Ohio, Ind. and Minn.

Lilium canadense is probably the most popular wild lily of our range. However, it certainly does not possess the beauty of color that characterizes the wood lily, nor the subtle delicacy of the Turk's Cap; but the graceful curves of its pendulous bells are unsurpassed in any wild or cultivated flower, and it must always command the greatest admiration for that matchless quality. Of the three wild lilies this one is also the most prodigal of its charms.

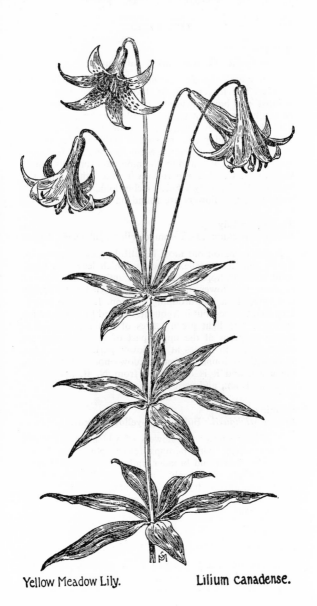

Yellow Meadow Lily.   Lilium canadense.

Bell Lily
Lilium Grayi   Orange-scarlet, July-August

A mountain species confined to the southern Alleghenies. The leaves smooth, broad lance-shaped, acute-pointed, and borne in whorls or circles of 4-8, the lowest generally irregularly scattered. Flowers spreading horizontally or slightly drooping, deep orange-scarlet, yellow at the base and profusely spotted with madder purple; the divisions without claws. Stem slender, 2-3 feet high. Peaks of Otter, Va., and on the mountain summits, southwest to N. C. In comparison with the other lilies this flower is small—only 1½-2¼ inches long, and very rarely more than two flowers are found on a single plant.

Turk's Cap Lily
Lilium superbum   Buff orange-yellow, July-early August

A less common but most beautiful species remarkable for its completely reflexed petals, which leave the handsome stamens, tipped by the brown anthers, fully exposed to view; the flower-cup is thickly freckled with brown, and hangs in a half-drooping position. It is also largely fertilized by bees, but is frequently visited by the monarch butterfly. The light green leaves of this lily hold alternating positions at the upper part of the stem, but are more or less in circles at the lower part. 3-7 feet high. It is oftenest found in wet meadows not very far from the coast, and it is distributed from N. B. and Mass., south to Tenn., and west to Ohio.

Carolina Lily
Lilium Michauxii   Buff orange-yellow, August

A similar species the flowers of which have far less reflexed sepals, with perhaps fewer spots. The leaves are darker green and broader, rather blunt-lance-shaped. 2-3 feet high. Commonly found along the coast from Va. to La., also in dry woods and among the mountains. Va., south to Fla. In our last edition listed as *Lilium carolinianum*.

Tiger Lily
Lilium tigrinum   Orange-scarlet, July-August

An Asiatic species escaped from gardens, and commonly found beside old farmhouses. Its leaves are lance-shaped and scattered along a stiff, straight, cottony,

Turk's Cap Lily.   Lilium superbum.

dark-colored stem, with black bulblets at the point where they join the plant-stem. The flower segments are strongly spotted and reflexed. Me. to N. Y.

————

Dogtooth Violet or Yellow Adder's Tongue
Erythronium americanum　Dull gold-yellow, April-May

A small, lilylike flower distinguished for its brown-purple-tinged (outside) gold-yellow color; sometimes the purple tinge is wanting in the flower, but the two leaves are almost always strongly mottled with it; these are elliptical, pointed, nearly stemless, and proceed from the root. The flower is perfect, with six stamens and a pistil, and it is especially adapted to long-tongued insects. Other occasional visitors are the small yellow and white butter-flies. It is probable, too, that many species of flies are attracted to this plant on account of its mottled color; but the majority of flies are poor pollen disseminators. The name, Greek, for *red,* in allusion to the European species which is purple-red. The little plant, 5-10 inches high, is common in moist woods and beside brooks in swampy places, from Nova Scotia south to Fla. and west to Minn.

White Adder's Tongue
Erythronium albidum　White or violet-white, March-May

A very similar species with narrower leaves mottled less distinctly or not at all, smooth, thick, and whitish-green. The flowers are white, or dull, pale violet-tinged outside, and yellow-tinged at the heart; the six divisions of the flower-cup strongly recurved. As the white stigma in *Erythronium* matures in advance of the golden anthers, it is, generally speaking, cross-fertilized; its most frequent visitor is the bumblebee. 5-8 inches high. Ont. south to Ky., but rare eastward. Also in Ark. and Okla. In our last edition *Erythronium mesochoreum* was listed as a species. It is now considered as merely a variety of *E. albidum,* differing, if at all, in having no lateral offshoots to the corm. It is found only in Mo., Neb. and south to Tex.

Yellow Adder's Tongue.
Erythronium americanum.

Erythronium albidum.

Erythronium propullans   Rose-pink, May

A western species with a peculiar fleshy offshoot proceeding from a slit near the middle of the stem. Leaves small and generally slightly mottled. Flowers bright crimson or rose-pink, yellow at the base, half an inch long. Stigmas united. 6-8 inches high. Rich woods of Minn., and very rare.

———

Star-of-Bethlehem
Ornithogalum umbellatum   White, May-June

A slender ornamental plant of Europe, escaped from gardens. The dark green leaves are narrow and linear, and the flowers are borne in a branched cluster; they are white inside, green-lined outside, and they open only in the sunshine. Name from the Greek, meaning *bird's milk,* supposed to allude to the egg-white color of the flower. 4-12 inches high. Found most often in fields and meadows near farmhouses, Newf. to N. C., west to Miss., Kan. and Mo.

———

Wild Leek
Allium tricoccum   Greenish-white, June-July

In spring the wild leek develops two or three light green, flat, oblong-lance-shaped leaves 8-10 inches long, and about 1 inch wide or more, and by summertime when these are withered, the white or greenish-white flowers begin to bloom, in a spokelike cluster from a spathe or leaflets at the top of a naked stem. The perfect flowers, with stamens and pistil, are six-parted, with six green-white segments. It is an onion-scented herb whose name is the Latin for garlic, and it is not remarkable for its beauty. It grows 4-15 inches high, in rich woodlands from Que., west to Minn. and Iowa, and south among the Alleghenies to N. C. and Tenn.

Wild Garlic
Allium canadense   Pale pink or white, May-June

A more commonly distributed, extremely narrow-leaved species frequenting wet meadows, the flower-cluster of which is sparse in bloom or else is replaced by a thick cluster of bulblets—a frequent occurrence with *Allium.* The flower's segments are narrow and obtuse, and quite as long as the stamens. 8-24 inches high. Me. to Minn.,

Star-of-Bethlehem.   Ornithogalum umbellatum.

and south to the Gulf. Commonly cultivated alliums are
the true onion, chives, garlic and the wild onion, all of
them natives of the Old World and likely to become
escapes from gardens. Among native species, other than
the wild garlic and wild leek, are several onion or leek-
like plants. These are the wild onion (*Allium cernuum*),
with pinkish flowers; and a related plant, *Allium stel-
latum*. Both are more common westward than along the
coast. Other native species occur on the prairies, but
their identification is possible only by reference to technical manuals.

Day Lily
Hemerocallis fulva   Tawny orange, July-August

A native of Europe and Asia, escaped from gardens.
Leaves angled in section, tapering to a sharp point, narrow and light green. The flower-stalk tall, bearing usually eight or nine blossoms which open one or two at a
time. The flower divisions six, three narrow, and three
wide and blunt, very fragile, and rusty or tawny light
orange, with a veined texture. The name is from the
Greek, and means *beautiful for only a day*. 2-5 feet high.
Found usually on meadows and upon the borders of
streams, but often a pest in gardens, from its propensity
to spread by rootstocks. Mass. and N. Y., south to Va.
and Tenn. (*Color Plate 4.*)

Lemon Lily
Hemerocallis flava   Yellow, June-July

A beautiful but far less common species, occasionally
escaped from country gardens, with narrow leaves and
pure bright yellow flowers more delicate and slender in
form, having a delightfully fragrant odor. 2-3 feet high.
The leaves of both these plants grow thickly, and are
characterized by graceful, drooping curves.

Hemerocallis fulva is rapidly becoming established as
a wild flower in many parts of the country. Its tenacity
of life under apparently adverse conditions is remarkable.
It propagates rapidly by its spreading roots, and sometimes takes complete possession of by-ways and spare
corners where the environment is favorable. In various
parts of New York State the plant is abundant. Less
attractive in figure than the delicate yellow *Hemerocallis*

Wild Garlic.
Allium canadense.

Wild Leek.
Allium tricoccum.

flava, and odorless besides, it makes up for such discrepancies by a magnificent tawny orange matched by few if any members of the Lily Family. The flowers bloom for one day only.

The foregoing do not comprise all the plants of the lily family likely to be found within our range. Many showy cultivated plants are frequent or infrequent escapes from gardens, all of them being natives of Eurasia. Among those reported as escapes are the autumn crocus (*Colchicum*), the toad lily (*Tricyrtis*), the tulip (*Tulipa*), the grape hyacinth (*Muscari*), the plantain lily (*Hosta*) and the squills (*Scilla*). Descriptions of these will be found in *Taylor's Encyclopedia of Gardening.*

Among *native* plants in the lily family any of the following are likely to be found, but they are usually less common than the plants already noted. These are: *Disporum,* which is related to the bellworts; *Nothoscordium,* an onionlike plant, but without the onion odor; the star grass (*Aletris*); the swamp pink (*Helonias*); the Spanish bayonet (*Yucca*); bog asphodel (*Narthecium*); wild hyacinth (*Camassia*); *Zygadenus,* which contains the white camass and other species; the fly-poison (*Amianthium*); and the turkeybeard (*Xerophyllum*). Descriptions of these and their range must be sought in the technical manuals.

The true yams (not the sweet potato), comprising the genus *Dioscorea,* are twining vines with small white or greenish flowers and immense underground tubers. They are only occasional within our area, being mostly tropical.

AMARYLLIS FAMILY. *Amaryllidaceæ.*

Perennial herbs, with generally showy, perfect lilylike flowers—with stamens and pistil—having six generally equal divisions of the flower-cup. It contains very few native species, but many cultivated ones like narcissus, snowdrop, tuberose, and the century plants.

Atamasco Lily
Zephyranthes atamasco　　**Pink or white, May**

Leaves somewhat thick, blunt, and shining deep green, long and straight. The flower perfect with six stamens and a pistil, the former very much shorter than the flower-

Atamasco Lily.
Zephyranthes Atamasco.

Star Grass.
Hypoxis hirsuta.

cup. The flower-cup is symmetrical and divided into six
distinct lobes, crimson pink, white with a magenta tinge,
or white; it is rarely eight-lobed. The name is from the
Latin and Greek, *Zephyrus,* the west wind, and ἄνθος,
a flower. The fruit is a depressed capsule. 6-15 inches
high. In moist localities, Va. to Fla. and Ala.

Star Grass
Hypoxis hirsuta   Yellow, April-July

The leaves are deep green, linear, grasslike, and covered with hairs. The perfect flower is six-parted, with six
stamens of unequal lengths; it is deep yellow inside, and
hairy and greenish outside. There are perhaps three
flowers at the top of the hairy stalk, which, by a plentiful
supply of pollen, attract both smaller bees and butterflies.
The star grass is commonly found in meadow grass, in
dry situations. The name is of Greek origin, alluding to
some unknown plant with sour leaves. 3-6 inches high.
Me. south to Ga., Miss. and Tex., west to Minn. Three
other species are known within our area, but they are
distinguished only by technical characters.

A spider-lily (*Hymenocallis occidentalis*), with a terminal cluster of large, showy white flowers, is found from
southern Ind. and Mo. to the Gulf of Mexico.

IRIS FAMILY. *Iridaceæ.*

Perennial herbs mostly found in damp or moist situations, having straight straplike leaves and showy, perfect
flowers of three and six parts. Besides the few native
species, it contains garden favorites like the crocus and
gladiolus, as well as the garden montbretia.

Larger Blue Flag or Fleur-de-lis
Iris versicolor   Violet-blue, May-July

A handsome, and decorative plant, with light green,
straight, flat leaves, and three-parted perfect flowers
blooming one by one from a green bract or leaflet at the
tip of a somewhat irregular stalk. The stamens are hidden and inserted at the base of the three larger and more
showy divisions of the flower, which are beautifully
veined with deep violet over a whitish ground tinted at
the base with yellow. The stamens are under each of the

Blue Flag.   Iris versicolor

three straplike divisions of the style (the middle portion of the pistil) which directly overlie the showy purple-veined petals or divisions. Thus the insect, generally a bee, in order to reach the honey must alight upon the showy petal, crawl beneath the overhanging style-division, and brush past the anther hidden below it, dislodging the yellow pollen in its passage. At the tip of each style-division is the stigma, and upon this some of the pollen is deposited as the bee passes; but it is really the pollen from some previously visited flower which possesses the greater fertilizing power. Fruit a long three-lobed capsule. The name is from 'Ιρις, the rainbow, in allusion to the prismatic colors of the species. 16-30 inches high. On the wet margins of ponds, and in swamps, from Newf. south to Va. and west to Minn. and Manitoba.

The very showy water flag (*Iris pseudacorus*) of Europe, with handsome yellow flowers, is common in swamps and wet ditches nearly throughout our range.

Slender Blue Flag
Iris prismatica   Violet-blue, May-June

A slender-stemmed species with very narrow grasslike leaves, and a smaller flower with generally narrower proportions and an extremely short tube, but a long slender stem proceeding from smaller bracts or leaflets. The fruit capsule narrowly three-lobed and angular. This species is mainly found near the coast in brackish swamps, or wet grounds. 1-3 feet high. Nova Scotia to Ga., but also in the *var. austrina* in the mountains of N. C. and Tenn.

Dwarf Iris
Iris verna   Violet-blue and yellow, April-May

A usually one-flowered, small, slender-stemmed species with grasslike leaves scarcely over seven inches long, the flower with the three principal divisions narrowed toward the base, slightly woolly, and deep gold-yellow at the narrowing part. Sometimes the flowers are white. The fruit capsule is obtusely triangular and short. 4-8 inches high. On wooded hillsides, from southern Pa. to Ga., Miss. and Ky.

Crested Dwarf Iris
Iris cristata   Light violet, April-May

A lance-shaped leaf tapering at both ends distinguishes this species from all others; the leaf is bright green, 4-9 inches long, and about ½ inch wide. The flowers are

Crested Dwarf Iris. Blackberry Lily.
Iris cristata. Belamcanda chinensis.

very light violet with the broad outer divisions *crested;*
i.e., they are marked with three raised parallel flutings
along the center, the middle one of which is orange-
yellow. The flower is exceedingly delicate in color and
dainty in form. The fruit capsule is sharply triangular and
ovate in outline, hardly twice as long as it is wide. 3-6
inches high. It is a very dwarf plant common on the
hillside and along streams, from Md. south to Ga., and
west to southern Ind. and Okla.

The tall-bearded or German iris (*Iris germanica*) of
Europe is commonly cultivated and sometimes escapes
from gardens.

Blackberry Lily
Belamcanda chinensis   **Golden-orange, magenta-spotted,
August-September**

An Asiatic plant escaped from cultivation, similar to
the iris but much more branched. The leaves flat and
light green, like those of the iris, the perfect flowers with
six even divisions of a light golden-orange color mottled
with dull magenta spots. Three prominent stamens. Several flowers in bloom at once. The fruit capsule is fig-
shaped, 1 inch long, and when the scales or divisions
of the shell fall in August, the blackberrylike, fleshy-
coated black seeds are exposed to view. The name is
East Indian. 2-4 feet high. The plant has escaped from
gardens to roadsides and low hills, from Conn. and Pa.,
south to Ga., and west to Kan.

Blue-eyed Grass
Sisyrinchium angustifolium   **Deep violet-blue, May-July**

A stiff grasslike little plant with linear, pale blue-green
leaves less than the somewhat twisted and flat flower-stem
in height. The flowers are perfect, with a prominent pistil, and three stamens; the six divisions are blunt and
tipped with a thornlike point; they are violet-blue, or
sometimes white; the center of the flower is beautifully
marked with a six-pointed white star accented with bright
golden-yellow, each one of the star-points penetrating the
deeper violet-blue of the petal-like division. The flowers
of this and other species are very fleeting. Seed capsule
globular. The name is Greek in origin, and was applied
by Theophrastus to some other plant. 6-13 inches high.
In fields and moist meadows, common from Newf. south
to Va., and west. Stem $\frac{1}{16}$-$\frac{1}{8}$ inch wide.

Blue-eyed Grass.

Sisyrinchium angustifolium. Sisyrinchium graminoides.

Stout Blue-eyed Grass
Sisyrinchium graminoides Deep violet-blue, May-June

A similar species which has usually two unequal branches springing from a conspicuous grasslike leaf; the leaves a trifle bloomy and very light green; less stiff than those of the preceding species, and ³⁄₁₆-¼ inch wide. The flower petals are also sparsely woolly on the outer surface. 8-16 inches high. In grassy places, and sometimes on the borders of woods, from Newf. to Minn., south to Fla. and Tex.

Eastern Blue-eyed Grass
Sisyrinchium atlanticum Violet-blue, May-June

A tall, bending species, similar to the preceding but lighter green and somewhat woolly; a slenderer and weaker stem, sometimes nearly 2 feet long, and reclining, terminating in two or three almost equal branches. Leaves very narrow, bracts somewhat purplish and dry papery; the flower a trifle smaller, the outside somewhat woolly. The seeds but slightly pitted or nearly smooth. In wet meadows or brackish marshes or sandy soil, Me. to Fla., near the coast; west to Miss. and Mo.

ORCHID FAMILY. *Orchidaceæ.*

An enormous family of chiefly tropical plants, familiar enough from the display in florists' windows, but with many native kinds. Ours are perennial herbs having perfect flowers, the various parts of which are irregular in structure but symmetrical in arrangement. There are three similar sepals colored like petals, two lateral petals, and below these a third unique petal called the *lip,* conspicuously colored, often spurred, and containing nectar which attracts insects. The latter in the effort to reach the nectar invariably dislodge the peculiarly adhesive pollen-clusters and eventually carry them to the next blossom. The ingenious mechanical device of the flower to insure cross-fertilization is simple but effective. The orchids, except *Cypripedium,* have but one stamen which is united with the style into one common column placed at the axil of the flower facing the lip. The stigma, the usual termination of the style, is a gummy surface located directly below the so-called rostellum, the receptacle of the anther, and the *actual* termination of the style. In

Green Adder's Mouth.   Malaxis unifolia.

the two anther-cells above the rostellum there are two
pollinia, or stemmed pear-shaped pollen-clusters, each
composed of several packets of pollen tied together by
elastic threads; these threads running together form the
stem terminated by a sticky disc. It is these discs which
attach to the tongues or heads of insects and insure the
transportation of the pollen-masses to the gummy stigma
of another flower. The orchids as a general rule are in-
capable of self-fertilization, and are wholly dependent
upon long-tongued insects for the transportation of their
pollen. In *Cypripedium,* the stigma is not a gummy surface but is in a cavity between the anther-cells.

Green Adder's Mouth
Malaxis unifolia   Whitish-green, July
A small species with tiny white-green flowers in a
small cluster about the size of mignonette. A single oval,
pointed leaf clasps the slender stem about halfway up.
The sepals are oblong, and the lip three-pointed. Fruit
capsule oval. The name from the Greek, meaning soft,
perhaps because the plant tissue is soft. 4-9 inches high.
In cold woods or bogs, from Newf. to Fla. and west to
Manitoba and La.

Large Twayblade
Liparis liliifolia   Madder purple, June-July
A small but showy species with rather large shiny
leaves 2-4 inches long, light green. The flowers showy,
brownish or madder purple, with reflexed sepals and
petals, the latter exceedingly narrow, the lip ½ inch long
and broad. Flowers numerous, the cluster sometimes 5
inches tall. The Greek name in allusion to the shining
leaves. 4-9 inches high. Me., south to Ga., west to Minn.
and Mo.

Early Coral Root
Corallorhiza trifida   Dull madder purple, May-June
A small species commonly found in evergreen woods,
with a ruddy, irregular root resembling coral, and a
straight yellowish-brown leafless but scaly stem bearing
small, uninteresting madder purple flowers with tiny
sepals and petals and a whitish lip; the seed capsule
nearly ½ inch long. The name, Greek, meaning *coral*
and *root.* Rather rare, in swamps and damp woods, from
Newf. south to N. J., in the mountains to Ga., and west
to Ore.

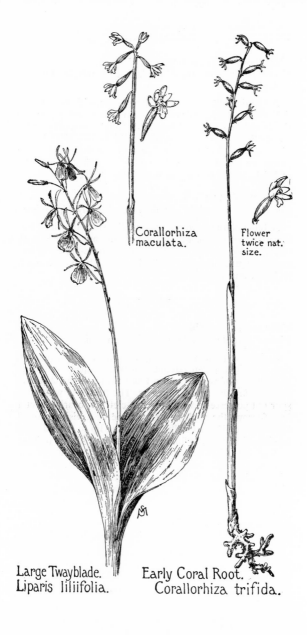

Corallorhiza
maculata.

Flower
twice nat.
size.

Large Twayblade.
Liparis liliifolia.

Early Coral Root.
Corallorhiza trifida.

Small-flowered Coral Root
Corallorhiza odontorhiza   Dull madder purple, July-
September

A slender but generally taller species with very small,
dull purple-brown flowers drooping on a stiff stem; the
lip whitish, spotted, and the sepals and petals marked with
purple lines. The flower-stem purplish-brown. 6-12 inches
high, leafless, but with one or two sheathing scales. In
evergreen woods, especially under arborvitæ. From Me.
to Mich., south to Fla., and southwest to Tex.

Large Coral Root
Corallorhiza maculata   Madder purple, July-September

A taller, large-flowered species, the stem of which has
several close scales. Many slightly fragrant flowers, with
the white lip spotted and lined with purple-brown. Common in spruce woods. 10-18 inches high. Newf. south
to N. J., and west to Cal.

Heart-leaved Twayblade
Listera cordata   Madder purple, June-July

A delicate plant with a very slender stem bearing two
opposite light green, stemless leaves shaped somewhat
like the *ace of spades,* and a loose cluster about 2 inches
long of *tiny* dull purple flowers. The flower is without a
spur but possesses a very long two-cleft lip, bearing nectar
in a furrow; the slightest disturbance of a visiting insect
causes the delicate rostellum above the lip to explode and
forcibly eject a sticky fluid which is sure to hit the pointed
tops of the pollen-masses lying just over the crest of the
rostellum. Thus, the insect coming in contact with the
sticky fluid withdraws fluid and pollen-masses. 3-10 inches
high. Named for Martin Lister, an early English botanist.
Moist woods, Greenland to N. Y., and west to Cal.

Broad-lipped Twayblade
Listera convallarioides   Greenish-yellow, June-July

A similar species with leaves less heart-shaped and
flowers with a wedge-oblong lip, much longer than the
narrow sepals and petals. Sepals purplish. In damp woods.
Newf., south to N. Y., in the mountains, and west to
Alaska.

Heart-leaved Twayblade.   Listera cordata.

Ladies' Tresses
Spiranthes cernua   Yellowish-white, August-September

A marsh orchid, with a peculiarly twisted or spiral flower-spike and very light green linear leaves not nearly as tall as the flower-stem. The flowers translucent yellowish-white, or variably cream-white, odorless or fragrant, the whiter ones generally most fragrant, the lower sepals not upturned or joining with the upper, the latter arching and joined to the petals; all these parts with the curly-edged broader lip forming the bugle-horn-shaped tiny flower. It is fertilized by some of the smaller bees, moths, and butterflies. In *Spiranthes* the rostellum holds in its center a narrow boat-shaped disc containing a sticky fluid; it is covered by a membrane easily ruptured by an insect. After the rupture the exposed sticky fluid glues itself to the tongue of the insect and the boatlike disc is withdrawn together with the pollinia which are already attached to it at the back. When the flower first opens, the tube or passage between the rostellum and the lip is exceedingly narrow; hence, the former is easily ruptured by visitors. Later the space widens as the column topped by the rostellum moves upward in the maturer development of the flower. As a consequence, only those flowers which are mature are sufficiently open for the insect to reach the stigma and thereon leave the pollen of a younger flower. The name is from the Greek, for *coil* and *flower,* alluding to the spiral arrangement of the flowers. 6-24 inches high. In wet meadows and grassy swamps. Newf., south to Fla. and west to Minn. and S. D.

Slender Ladies' Tresses
Spiranthes gracilis   Cream-white, August-October

An exceedingly slender and tall species, smooth or rarely woolly above, bearing small withering bracts or leaflets along the flower-stem which is terminated by a very much twisted cluster of many slender flowers, translucent cream-white, and very fragrant. The odor of *Spiranthes* is peculiarly aromatic, reminiscent of the horse-chestnut but remarkably sweet. The sepals of the flower are a little longer than the lip, which is greenish above with white margins. The ovate leaves at the root wither before the flowers bloom. Visited by the bumble-bee and the small bee. 10-22 inches high. Common in dry situations, in pastures, fields, and half-wooded hillsides. Nova Scotia south to Fla. and west to Minn. and Tex.

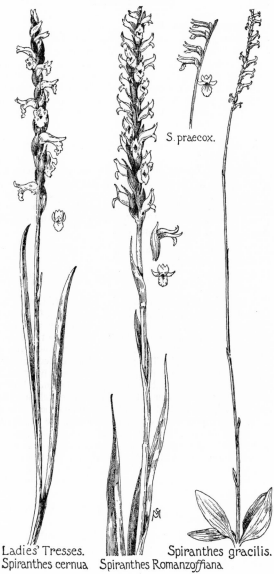

S. praecox.

Ladies' Tresses.   Spiranthes gracilis.
Spiranthes cernua   Spiranthes Romanzoffiana

Grass-leaved Ladies' Tresses
Spiranthes præcox Yellowish-white, July-August

A slender and tall species with grasslike light green leaves, and a leafy stem bearing a much twisted flower-spike of yellow-white spreading blossoms. The lateral sepals free, the upper one closely connected with the two petals, the lip often dark-striped. 10-30 inches high. In moist grassy places. A southern species confined to the Atlantic seaboard from N. J. to Tex.

Spiranthes Romanzoffiana White, creamy or greenish, July-August

Spiranthes Romanzoffiana is a plant of northern regions, and is not common there. It has a thick and short flower-spike, with very fragrant greenish cream-white flowers somewhat hooded by the combined sepals and petals. Leaves linear. 6-12 inches high. Labrador to N. Y. and Pa., west to Minn. and Cal.

————

Rattlesnake Plantain
Goodyera repens White, creamy or greenish, July-early August

A remarkably odd and attractive little orchid, with the very dark blue-olive green leaves marked with darker cross-veins. It has a scaly, slender, slightly woolly one-sided flower-stalk with translucent greenish or creamy-white small flowers; the saclike lip of the flower has a recurved wavy margin. The pollen-masses, called pollinia, are made up of numerous packets connected by threads which run together and form a single flattened brown ribbon the end of which is fastened to the rostellum. The rostellum when rubbed is removed and carries with it a bit of membrane to which the pollinia are attached; this clings to the tongue of the bee, and all is properly withdrawn, and carried to another probably more mature flower, whose stigma is easily accessible, as in the case of *Spiranthes*. Named for John Goodyear, an early English botanist. 5-8 inches high, rarely higher. Under hemlocks and spruces, in the northern woods. Newf. to N. H. (frequent in the White Mts.), south to the Great Smoky Mts. of N. C., west to Mich. and Minn.

Goodyera tessellata White, creamy or greenish, August

The commonest species in northern New England, with a stouter stem than that of the preceding species,

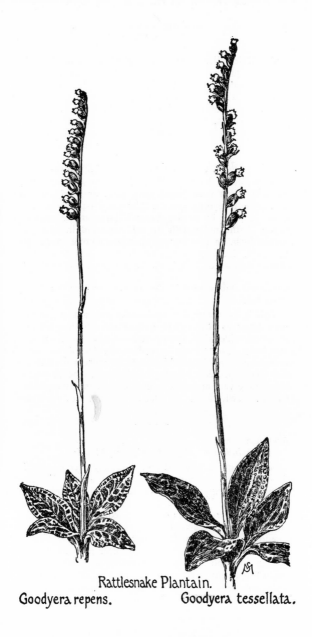

Rattlesnake Plantain.

Goodyera repens.   Goodyera tessellata.

and a little taller. Leaves 5-9 ribbed, the veins bordered by pale green pencilings, the whole leaf irregularly mottled with light and dark green, rarely without the markings. The lip of the flower is less sac-shaped, with a less recurved margin. In hillside woods. Newf. to northern N. Y., south to the Catskills and Conn., west to Mich. and Ohio. In our last edition the rattlesnake plantains were listed as *Epipactis,* a name no longer valid.

Goodyera decipiens   White, creamy or greenish, August

Stem stout, leaves stiff, plain green or indistinctly marked, often with broad white ribs, or *rarely* mottled as in the foregoing species. The flower-spike thick and one-sided; the lip of the flower is large at the base and tapers to the point with the edges curved inward. 8-20 inches high. In dry woods, generally among evergreens. Que., N. B., and along the Great Lakes from Lake Huron westward. This is the largest of all the species.

Goodyera pubescens   White, creamy or greenish, July-August

This is the commoner rattlesnake plantain of southern New Eng.; its flower-spike is thick, blooms upward, and is *not* one-sided. The flower-stem is stout, densely woolly, and bears several lance-shaped scales. The flower has a pronounced sac-shaped blunt lip the margin of which is not recurved. Leaves dark blue-olive green, white-veined, the middle vein broad. 6-18 inches high. In dry evergreen woods, Newf. to N. C., Ala. and Tenn., west to Minn.

Arethusa
Arethusa bulbosa   Magenta-crimson, May-June

A large single-flowered and delicately scented orchid, the light magenta-crimson petals and sepals of which point upward like the fingers of a half-open hand viewed in profile. The lip of the flower is recurved and spreading, with the broad apex often fringed, magenta blotched, and crested in three white hairy ridges; this forms a conspicuously colored landing platform for the visiting insect, usually a bumblebee, which, after pressing beneath the column and sipping the nectar, backs out brushing against the edge or lid of the anther, opening it and emptying the enclosed pollen upon his head, as is also the case with *Pogonia ophioglossoides.* The column is

Rattlesnake Plantain.
Goodyera pubescens.

Arethusa bulbosa.

topped by the lidlike anther instead of the usual rostellum, and the pollen-masses are not pearlike and stemmed. The solitary leaf is linear, and hidden in the sheathed scape; it appears after the flowering season. Rarely a plant produces two flowers; these vary from 1-2 inches in length. Fruit capsule elliptical, about 1 inch long. 5-10 inches high. Common in bogs, from Newf., south to S. C., west to Minn. and Ind. Named for the fountain nymph Arethusa.

Grass Pink
Calopogon pulchellus Magenta-pink, June-July

A smaller flowered, but very beautiful orchid, slender-stemmed, and with one linear bright green leaf. Flower-stalk bearing 3-9 magenta-pink sweet-scented flowers with a long spreading lip crested with yellow, orange, and magenta hairs; the anther and pollen are as in *Arethusa*. Name from the Greek, *beautiful* and *beard*, referring to the handsome bearded lip. 10-16 inches high. In bogs, from Newf., south to Fla. and Tex., and west to Minn. and Mo. Often found in company with the next.

Snake Mouth
Pogonia ophioglossoides Crimson-pink, June-July

A most delicate little orchid bearing generally solitary, raspberry-scented crimson-pink flowers with a small light green lance-shaped leaf halfway up the stem, and a tiny one just below the blossom; sometimes a long-stemmed leaf proceeds from the root. The flower has sepals and petals of equal length overhanging a beautifully crested and fringed lip, curved like the hollow of one's hand, which furnishes an alighting platform for the visiting insect, which pushes forward in the narrow space between the stigma and the lip, scraping pollen off its back in its progress. The pollen attaches to the gummy stigma. In retreating, the lid of the anther catches on the back of the visitor, swings open, and fresh pollen is deposited for the benefit of the next flower. This orchid has no rostellum and its pollen is not in stemmed pearlike masses. The name, Greek, *bearded*, from the bearded lip of some of the species. 8-13 inches high. In wet meadows and bogs, Newf., south to Fla. and west to Minn. Frequently found in company with *Calopogon*.

Grass Pink.
Calopogon pulchellus.

Snake Mouth.
Pogonia ophioglossoides

Nodding Pogonia
Triphora trianthophora   Light magenta, August-
   September

A local species less showy than the foregoing but remarkable for its dainty pendulous flowers, which are
considerably smaller. With 2-8 tiny leaves, alternating,
and clasping the stem. There are 1-6 long-stalked flowers
which proceed from between the stem and leaf. 3-8 inches
high. In rich woods, Me. to Fla., west to Wisc. and Ark.
(*Color Plate 5.*)

———

Five-leaves
Isotria verticillata   Purple and green-yellow, May-June

Distinguished by its circle of five light green leaves at
the summit of the stem. Flower dull purple with long
stem and long narrow greenish sepals, erect or inclining
above the circle of leaves. 8-12 inches high. Moist
woods. Me., south to Fla., west to Ind. and Wisc. Rare in
the east. In our last edition listed as *Pogonia verticillata*.

There are no points of resemblance between five-leaves
and *Triphora trianthophora;* the former has a circle of
leaves, the latter scattered leaves. In *I. verticillata* the
sepals are extremely long, narrow and madder purple-
stained; in *T. trianthophora* they are short and faintly
magenta-tinged. Both species grow in either moist or
dry woods, yet both will surely be found near water.

Isotria medeoloides   Yellow-green, May-June

A small plant, with yellow-green flowers the lip of
which is crested over its whole face; the sepals but a
trifle longer than the petals. The five smaller, narrower
leaves circled as in *I. verticillata* immediately below the
one or two flowers. 8-9 inches high. Moist woodlands,
Me. to Va., and probably our rarest orchid. Listed in
our last edition as *Pogonia affinis*.

———

Cleistes divaricata   Magenta-pink, May-June

A dainty and beautiful species with pale magenta-pink
or nearly white flowers; the long, narrow sepals a dull
greenish-brown. There is one oblong lance-shaped leaf,
3-7 inches long, borne just above the middle of the stem,
and another bractlike one below the flower. 12-20 inches

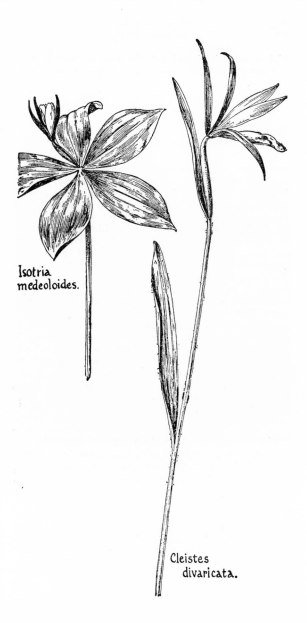

Isotria
medeoloides.

Cleistes
divaricata.

high. Marshy land, and wet pine barrens from N. J. to
Fla. and Miss. In our last edition listed as *Pogonia divaricata.*

————

Showy Orchis
Orchis spectabilis Magenta and white, May-June

This, with another more northern species, is our only
true *Orchis*. There are two light shiny leaves proceeding
from the base of the stem; the latter is thick and angular
in section, bearing at its summit a few showy flowers
with magenta sepals and petals united in a hood, and
beneath them the conspicuous, almost white lip; behind
the lip is the rather long spur, in which is secreted an
abundant supply of nectar for the thirsty visiting insect;
the latter, generally a queen bumblebee, is a common
visitor and thrusts its head into the spur, brushing care-
lessly past the rostellum at the top of the column and,
rupturing its thin membrane, exposes the two sticky
round discs attached to the pear-shaped pollen-clusters.
These discs immediately fasten upon the bee's face or
forehead, and when the creature retires it carries with it
discs and pollen-clusters. Finally when the next flower is
visited the pollen is scraped off upon its sticky stigma.
Orchis spectabilis is 5-10 inches high, and frequents rich
moist woods, especially hemlock groves, from N. B.
south to Ga., and west to Minn. and Neb. It is found
in the valley of the Connecticut west of the White Mts.
Orchis is the old Greek name for a European species.

Orchis rotundifolia Magenta and white, June-July

Orchis rotundifolia is a less common species with but
one leaf, oval or nearly round, and smaller flowers about
the same color but deeper than those of *O. spectabilis.*
From Greenland, south to northern N. Y., Mich. and
B. C. westward. Flower lip white magenta-spotted.

It is a much slenderer species than *O. spectabilis,* and
the small flowers are not more than ⅔ inch long. Each
blossom springs from the junction of a small bract with
the plant stem, and its slender spur is not longer than the
three-lobed, spotted lip, the middle lobe of which is
notched sufficiently to simulate all four lobes.

Showy Orchis.
Orchis spectabilis.   Isotria verticillata.

Green Wood Orchis
Habenaria clavellata Greenish-white, June-July

A slender species with a single obtuse lanceolate leaf less than ⅓ of the way up the stem, and two or three tiny scalelike ones above it. The 5-12 insignificant very small greenish-white flowers with tiny sepals and petals, a wedge-shaped lip, and a characteristic long slender spur curved upward, and around to one side. The pollen-clusters of the *Habenarias* are short-stemmed and terminated with a sticky gland which is so arranged that it easily fastens upon the heads or faces of visiting insects. The plant is 6-18 inches high. Name from the Latin *habena*, a bridle or rein, alluding to the narrow lip of some species. In bogs and wet places, Newf. west to Minn., and south to Fla. and La.

Tubercled Orchis
Habenaria flava Yellow-green, June-July

A very common yellow-green-flowered species, with a stout stem, several lance-shaped leaves, and small flowers with yellow-green sepals and petals, the blunt lip toothed on either side and slightly protuberant in the center at the base, the slender spur twice its length. 10-24 inches high. Common in all wet places, from Que. to Fla. and west to Minn. and Tex.

Habenaria hyperborea Green, yellow-green, June-July

A tall and leafy northern species, with green, or yellow-green flowers, erect lance-shaped leaves, and a dense narrow flower-spike sometimes 12 inches long, or longer. Flower-spur short and incurved, petals, sepals, and lip much shorter than the ovary. 8-30 inches high. Cold, wet woods. Greenland to Pa., westward to Ind., Neb. and N. Mex.

Habenaria dilatata Greenish-white, June-July

A very similar species with much narrower leaves and greenish-white flowers with small obtuse sepals. The white lip lance-shaped from a lozenge-shaped base. Cold, wet bogs. Greenland to Mass., N. J., and west to Colo. and Cal.

Hooker's Orchis
Habenaria Hookeri Whitish yellow-green, June-August

The two large, shining, nearly round, or broadly oval light green leaves usually lie upon the ground, but are

Green Wood Orchis.
Habenaria clavellata.

Tubercled Orchis:
Habenaria flava.

sometimes raised above it. The somewhat twisted and *bare* stem bears 10-20 upright flowers, with green lateral sepals curving backward, narrow yellow-green petals, and the throat accented by two lateral spots of yellow-ochre. The lip is lance-shaped, incurved, and pointed; the slender white-green spur nearly 1 inch deep is especially adapted to the long tongues of the moths. 8-15 inches high. Woods and borders of wooded swamps from Que. south to W. Va., west to northern Mich. and Minn. (*Color Plate 6.*)

Green Round-leaved Orchis
Habenaria orbiculata   Whitish yellow-green, July-August

A larger species, the two nearly round leaves of which are sometimes 7 inches across, and lie flat upon the ground; they are light green and shining above, and silvery-white beneath. The stem is *not* bare, but bracted; the whitish yellow-green flowers in a loose cluster, with the upper sepal nearly round, the lateral ones ovate, and the narrow lip obtuse and drooping, almost three times the length of the small lance-shaped petals; the slender, curved, whitish spur nearly 2 inches long thickened toward the blunt point is peculiarly adapted to the long tongue of one of the lesser sphinx-moths. "A larger individual might sip the nectar it is true, but its longer tongue would reach the base of the tube without effecting the slightest contact with the pollen" (Wm. Hamilton Gibson). The pollen is usually withdrawn fastened upon the moth's eyes. 1-2 feet high. Rich evergreen woods. Me., south to N. C. in the mountains, west to Minn.

Yellow Orchis
Habenaria integra   Orange-yellow, July

This southern species has one or two foliage leaves and several smaller ones upon its slender stem, and a dense flower-cluster, orange-yellow. 10-20 inches high. Wet pine-barrens. N. J., south to Fla. and Tex.

Snowy Orchis
Habenaria nivea   White, July-August

Another southern species, with several very narrow leaves low on the stem, and a loose many-flowered spike of small, fragrant, slightly greenish-white flowers, each with an exceedingly slender curving spur. Wet pine-barrens. N. J. to Fla. and Tex.

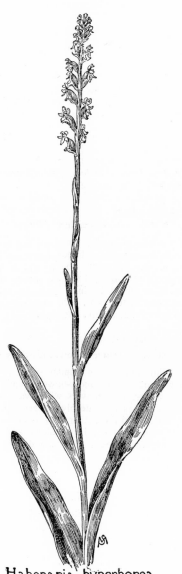

Habenaria hyperborea.

Bracted Orchis
Habenaria viridis, var. *bracteata*   Light green, June-August

Characterized by the numerous bracts or leaflets from the bases of which the tiny flowers spring. The lower leaves broadly ovate, the upper ones mere long bracts scarcely three times the length of the pale green flowers. The lip of the flower toothed at the tip and oblong, twice as long as the white spur. 6-20 inches high. Damp woods and meadows, from Newf. south in the mountains to N. C., west to Colo. and B. C. In our last edition listed as *Habenaria bracteata,* a Eurasian species which is doubtfully in our area.

Yellow Crested Orchis
Habenaria cristata   Orange-yellow, July-early August

This is a southern species among a group of fringed orchids, with narrow lance-shaped leaves below, diminishing to the size of bracts above, and orange-yellow flowers with narrow fringed petals and a very deeply fringed lip. Spur about ¼ inch long. The anther cells widely separated at the base. 8-20 inches high. In bogs, Mass. and from N. J. to Fla. and Ark.

Yellow Fringed Orchis
Habenaria ciliaris   Orange-yellow, July-early August

An exceedingly handsome slender species, with lance-shaped leaves and a large many-flowered spike of showy golden or orange-yellow flowers with ovate sepals, narrow fringed petals, and a deeply fringed lip. The spur long and slender, and the anther cells as in the preceding species. 12-24 inches high. In meadows and wet sandy barrens, from Mass., south to Fla. and west to Mich., Wisc. and Mo.

White Fringed Orchis
Habenaria blephariglottis   White, July-early August

A similar species. The white fringed flowers a trifle smaller, with a less deeply fringed lip; the latter ⅓ the length of the spur. 12-21 inches high. In swamps and bogs from Newf. to Va., Fla. and Miss., west to Mich. Blooms a few days earlier than *H. ciliaris* where the two grow together.

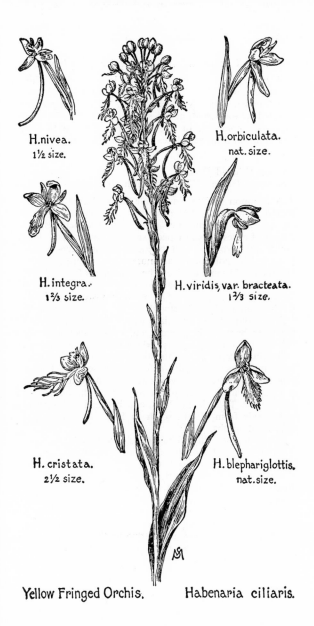

H. nivea.
1½ size.

H. orbiculata.
nat. size.

H. integra.
1⅔ size.

H. viridis, var. bracteata.
1⅔ size.

H. cristata.
2½ size.

H. blephariglottis.
nat. size.

Yellow Fringed Orchis.   Habenaria ciliaris.

Habenaria leucophæa   White, greenish, June-July

A western species with fragrant large greenish-white or white flowers, the fan-shaped lip three-parted, broad, and fringed. Spur 1½ inches long, so it is especially adapted to the long-tongued sphinx-moths. 18-30 inches high. Not common. In bogs from Nova Scotia to Ont. and Ohio; also in wet places in Minn. and Neb.

Ragged Fringed Orchis
Habenaria lacera   White, greenish, June-July

A common species remarkable for its lacerated three-parted flower-lip, and unsubstantial translucent white flower which is sometimes greenish and sometimes yellowish. Leaves lance-shaped, smaller above. The long flower-spike crowded with the inconspicuous deep-spurred flowers. The pollen-cells are not widely separated. Wm. Hamilton Gibson describes the structure of the flower thus, after remarking that no botanist has mentioned its distinct peculiarity. "The nectary instead of being freely open is abruptly closed at the central portion by a firm protuberance or palate which projects downward from the base of the stigma, and closely meets the lip below." The opening is thus divided into two lateral ones, each lying directly beneath a sticky elongated pollen-disc. Thus the insect, generally a butterfly, inserts its tongue exactly where the latter will touch the disc which is sure to clasp it and be withdrawn together with the pollen. *H. lacera* is 10-22 inches high, and is found in bogs and wet woods from Newf., south to S. C. and Ark., and west to Manitoba.

In appearance this white orchis is distinctly different from all others. Although its similarity to the next species is marked, it is *structural* and therefore not so evident to a casual observer. The flower is well named; its lacerated flower-lip is literally torn to divisions of threadlike fineness, and the general effect is accordingly unique. No other orchis is like it; the flower of *H. psycodes* has a compact settled figure; that of *H. clavellata* is distinct and has a swirling appearance due to the curving spur; while that of *H. blephariglottis* is a characteristically fringed affair of orderly appearance. But *this* orchis is a thing of "shreds and tatters."

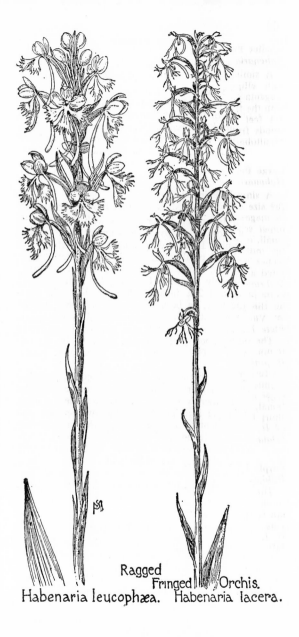

Ragged
Fringed Orchis.
Habenaria leucophæa.   Habenaria lacera.

Smaller Purple Fringed Orchis
Habenaria psycodes   Magenta-pink, July-early August

A similar species but of more imposing proportions, with elliptical and lance-shaped leaves, and fragrant magenta-pink or lilac-pink flowers variably pale or deep, with the fringed lip three-parted, and a spur ⅔ inch long. 1-3 feet high. Commonly found in swamps and wet woods from Newf. south to N. C. and Tenn., west to Manitoba.

Large Purple Fringed Orchis
Habenaria fimbriata   Magenta-pink, June–early August

A similar but much larger species with flowers twice the size of those of *H. psycodes,* fragrant, and variable in magenta-pink from a deep tone even to white. The upper sepal and petals close together, the lateral sepals small, ovate and acute. The three divisions of the broad lip more deeply fringed. Flower-spike sometimes 12 inches long and 2½ inches across. Anther cells separated at the base. In both flowers, *H. psycodes* and *H. fimbriata,* fertilization is generally effected by moths and butterflies whose heads and eyes are often decorated by the pear-shaped pollen-masses. Que. to N. C. and W. Va., west to Ohio, mostly in the mountains. (*Color Plate 7.*)

The difference between *H. psycodes* and *H. fimbriata* is not very well marked, and some authorities consider *H. fimbriata* a mere variety of *H. psycodes;* there is often confusion in the identification of the two species, and it must be evident to a close observer that intergrading types are not infrequent. *H. psycodes* has more conventional, compact flowers with an even (not ragged) very short fringe, and they are about half the size of those of *H. fimbriata.* Where the two grow together *H. fimbriata* blooms about a fortnight earlier than *H. psycodes.*

Purple Orchis
Habenaria peramœna   Purple, July-August

This is a truly *purple flowered* species found in the south and southwest. The fan-shaped lip is toothed but not fringed, and the leaves are somewhat narrower. The long spur curved. 12-30 inches high. Wet meadows, N. J. south to N. C., Tenn. and Ala., west to Ohio and Mo.

Smaller Purple Fringed Orchis.   Habenaria psycodes

White Lady's Slipper
Cypripedium candidum   White, May-early July

A handsome but rather small-flowered orchis, with
3-4 light green narrow elliptical leaves; the flower with
two wavy and twisted narrow green petals, three broader,
green, purple-blotched sepals, and a pouch or lip open
at the top by a fissure, white outside, purple-streaked
inside, containing nectar at its base. Two of the sepals
are joined together under the lip. The column of *Cypripedium* is flanked on either side by a fertile stamen
bearing a two-celled anther, opening lidlike, the pollen
loose and sticky-powdery within—in this respect the genus
is distinctly different from those already described. The
stigma is hidden beneath the third sterile stamen crowning
the column, exactly between the anthers; it is moist and
roughish. In the process of fertilization by the insect,
generally a bee, the latter enters the pouch by the fissure,
sucks the nectar from its base, and escapes by crowding
through the small opening immediately beneath one of
the anthers, receiving upon its back the sticky pollen in
the exit. In the next flower the insect brushes *first* against
the stigma, leaving some of the pollen as it takes its
departure in the manner described. The rather rare *C.
candidum* is 6-10 inches high, and is found in bogs and
wet meadows from N. Y. and N. J., west to S. D. and
Mo. The name is from Κύπρις, Venus, and πόδιον, shoe—
Venus's shoe.

Yellow Lady's Slipper
Cypripedium calceolus   Yellow, May-July

This is a taller species, with a slender leafy stem, and
showy fragrant yellow flowers the petals and sepals of
which are madder-purple-streaked; the narrow petals are
usually twisted, and the bright golden-yellow lip as well
as the summit of the column is more or less blotched
and striped with madder purple. 12-24 inches high.
Woods and woodland bogs. Newf. south among the
mountains to Ala., and west to La. and N. Mex. *C.
calceolus,* the parent species, is found in our area in two
varieties. One of them, var. *parviflorum* has smaller flowers, while the var. *pubescens* is a large form of this
species, characterized by its greater height and larger
flowers.

Yellow Lady's Slipper.   Cypripedium calceolus var. parviflorum.

Showy Lady's Slipper
Cypripedium reginæ   White, crimson-magenta, June-
   July

This is perhaps the most beautiful plant of the whole
genus. The stem is stout and leafy to the top, the flower
fragrant; its pouch is white, more or less blotched
or stained with velvety light crimson-magenta, the sepals
and petals white, broad and not longer than the rotund
pouch. The sterile stamen long-heart-shaped, stained yellow at the tip and spotted crimson, crowns the column
(see *C. acaule*). 1-2 feet high. Swamps and wet woods,
Newf. south to Ga., west to N. D. (*Color Plate 8.*)

Moccasin Flower or Stemless Lady's Slipper
Cypripedium acaule   Crimson-pink, May-early July

The commoner and more familiar lady's slipper, with
two large leaves from the root, without a plant-stem,
the slightly fragrant flower terminating a long slender
stalk with a green leaflet or bract at the point of junction;
the pouch crimson-pink (rarely white) veined with a
deeper pink, sepals and petals greenish and brown, more
or less curved and wavy. The third, or sterile, stamen
of *Cypripedium* crowning the column and overhanging
the stigma is variable according to the species: in *C.
acaule* it is angularly six-sided, in *C. candidum* lance-
shaped, *C. calceolus* var. *pubescens* long triangular, and
in *C. reginæ* heart-shaped; beneath these is the hidden
stigma which receives pollen from the backs of visiting
bumblebees or honeybees, or most frequently from the
smaller bees. In *My Studio Neighbors,* Wm. Hamilton
Gibson describes at length the fertilization of *C. acaule*
by the bumblebee. 8-12 inches high. Newf. to S. C. and
Ala., west to Alberta.

*   *   *

From here to the end of this book the wild flowers
have a fundamentally different structure from those here-
tofore noted. For this basic difference in plant structure,
and hence in the sequence of families, see "How To Use
This Book" in the Introduction.

The most primitive types of the plants that begin here
are those that have catkinlike flower clusters, usually
without petals, sometimes without sepals, and often without either. If trees were included in this book, here would

Moccasin Flower.   Cypripedium acaule.

come the willow, poplar, oak, beech, birch, walnut and hickory, and the alder.

A few herbs also have primitive flower structure, but they are too inconspicuous to merit much attention. Those interested in identifying these wild flowers should refer to the technical manuals for the following: lizard's-tail (*Saururus*), nettles (*Urtica, Laportea, Bœhemeria*), and bastard toad-flax (*Comandra*).

BIRTHWORT FAMILY. *Aristolochiaceæ.*

A small family of twining or low herbs, having perfect flowers—with six or more stamens and a pistil. The leaves stemmed, and either alternate or proceeding from the root. The flower-cup comprises a petal-like calyx, but the plant is without petals. The cup is united with the ovary or fruit receptacle, and lobed or irregular. Assisted in the process of fertilization by various smaller insects.

Wild Ginger
Asarum canadense Brown-purple, April-May

The two long-stemmed deep green veiny leaves soft woolly, and heart-shaped, their stems hairy; the flower with three distinct pointed brownish or madder purple divisions to the calyx which is closely united to the solid seed receptacle or ovary, green outside; the cup white below marked by a hexagon in purple-brown. A curious woodland plant whose odd flower is half concealed by its low position and its sober color, which not infrequently resembles the leaf-mold just beneath it. Its proximity to the ground and the frequent visits of the fungus gnats and the early flesh-flies suggest that these have most to do with the fertilization of the plant. 6-12 inches high. Common in rich woods from Que. south to N. C. and Ala., west to Minn. and Ark.

Heart-leaf
Hexastylis arifolia Green-purple, April-June

A southern species with evergreen leaves arrow-heart-shaped, and urn-shaped flowers dull green outside, dull purple-brown inside, with three short blunt lobes. One leaf only put forth each year. In woods from Va., south to Tenn., Ala. and Fla.

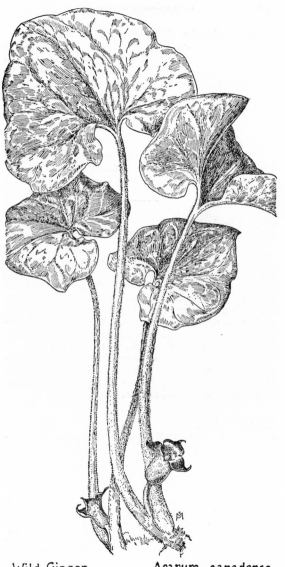

Wild Ginger.   Asarum canadense.

Hexastylis virginica **Brown-purple, May-June**

A southern species confined to mountain woods, with 1-3 leaves, round-heart-shaped, smooth and leathery in texture, and about 2 inches broad, the surface generally mottled white-green. The brown-purple flower about ¾ inch long with 3 blunt lobes, net-veined inside. Filaments shorter than the anthers. Va. and W. Va. to Ga. and Ala.

Hexastylis Shuttleworthii **Greenish-purple, April-May**

Similar in character, but with very large bell-shaped flowers 1¼-2 inches long. Mountains, Va. and W. Va. to Ga. and Ala.

———

Virginia Snakeroot
Aristolochia Serpentaria **Dull green, June-July**

A woolly-stemmed and familiar medicinal herb, the long heart-shaped leaves thin and green on both sides, and the dull greenish flowers with curving crooked long stems, near the root, as in *Asarum* the calyx curved like the letter S. Sometimes the flowers are fertilized in the bud without opening, but often they trap many of the smaller insects—notably gnats which possibly assist fertilization. Fruit an ovoid-ribbed capsule. 8-20 inches high. Conn. and N. Y., south to Fla., west to Ill. and Mo.

There is also a southern form of *Aristolochia Serpentaria* called var. *hastata,* with very narrow lance-shaped or linear-oblong leaves, arrowhead in outline, which is found from Va. to Fla., and La.

Dutchman's Pipe
Aristolochia durior **Dull green, purple-brown, May-June**

A familiar tall vine in cultivation from N. Y. south, trailing most frequently over arbors, porches, and piazzas. Smooth heart-shaped light green leaves, and hook-shaped flowers, the yellow-green veiny tube with a flat, three-lobed purple-brown throat, resembling a Dutch pipe; it entraps early small insects—gnats and flies. 10-25 feet high. In rich woods southern Pa., south to Ga.

The Dutchman's pipe is one of those vigorous, stolid, and satisfactory vines, big leaved and curiously flowered, which commends itself to the horticulturist. It responds readily to cultivation far north of its natural range.

Flower of
A. durior.

Virginia Snakeroot.　　　　Aristolochia serpentaria.

Pipe-Vine
Aristolochia tomentosa   Dull green, purple-brown, May-June

A similar vine, but characterized by an extreme woolliness; leaves round-heart-shaped, veiny, and smaller than those of *A. durior*. The flowers are a yellower green, with calyx exceedingly woolly, the deep purple-brown throat nearly closed and oblique. Kan. to Ind., and south to Ark. and Fla.

BUCKWHEAT FAMILY. *Polygonaceæ.*

Herbs with alternate toothless leaves and swollen-jointed stems, usually a stipule or leaflet above each joint, and small, generally perfect flowers (or sometimes diœcious, monœcious, or polygamous ones) without petals, the calyx 2-6 parted. Over 900 species are known, many of them noxious weeds, but it also contains the garden rhubarb.

Patience Dock
Rumex patientia   Green, May-June

The docks are mostly uninteresting northern weeds that cumber fertile ground, and decorate waste places; many of them, like the patience dock, come from the old country. This species has smooth broad lance-shaped leaves, broadest just above the base, and the flowers are green, tiny, inconspicuous and drooping, replaced by seed-wings or heart-shaped discs resembling miniature palm-leaf fans. 2-5 feet high. Nearly everywhere in cultivated or waste land.

Great Water Dock
Rumex orbiculatus   Green, July-August

Dark green smooth leaves, the lowest very long, a branching, stout stem, and densely flowering, circling clusters; the tiny flowers nodding, replaced by seed-wings similar to those of the preceding species. 3-6 feet high. In wet situations, Newf. to N. J., west to N. D. and Neb.

Swamp Dock
Rumex verticillatus   Green, May-July

A smooth deep green species, similar to the above, with a grooved stem and long-stemmed lance-shaped

Winged seed R.crispus.

Winged seed R.Patientia.

Curled Dock.　　　　　　　Rumex crispus.

leaves. Flowers in dense circles, the outline of the seed-wing top-shaped. 2-5 feet high. Swamps. Common from Que. south to Fla. and west to Wisc. and Tex.

Curled Dock
Rumex crispus   Green, June-August

This is the very common curled leaf dock throughout the U. S., a troublesome weed from the old country. Leaves wavy on the margin, flowers replaced by heart-shaped pointed seed-wings. 1-4 feet high. A form known in our last edition as *Rumex elongatus* does not differ from *R. crispus*.

Bitter Dock
Rumex obtusifolius   Green, June-August

Another weed from the old country, common in fields and waste places. A loose and thinly flowered spike; the stem rough and stout and the somewhat wavy leaves oblong and wider than those of the other species. The seed-wings with a few spines on either side. 2-4 feet high. Que., south to Fla., and west to Ore. and B. C.

Golden Dock
Rumex maritimus   Green, July-October

A sea-shore species, an annual; with light green, narrow, lance-shaped leaves, the plant more or less woolly, and greatly branched, the circles of the flowers crowded together into a compact spike, the seed-wings narrow and pointed, golden yellow in autumn, bearing 2-3 long spines on either side. In the sand along the shores. Que., south to Va., and from Kan. and Minn., west and north. It has been confused with *R. persicarioides* of the old country, but the latter is confined only to Que. and eastern Mass.

Field or Sheep Sorrel
Rumex Acetosella   Green, brown-red, June-September

A most troublesome small weed from the old world, with long arrowhead-shaped leaves acid to the taste, and inconspicuous flowers in branching spikes, green, or later brown-red; the whole plant sometimes turning ruddy in dry, sterile fields. It will generally flourish in one place for two or three years and then die out. The flowers are diœcious, that is, the staminate and pistillate ones are found upon separate plants, and are therefore fertilized

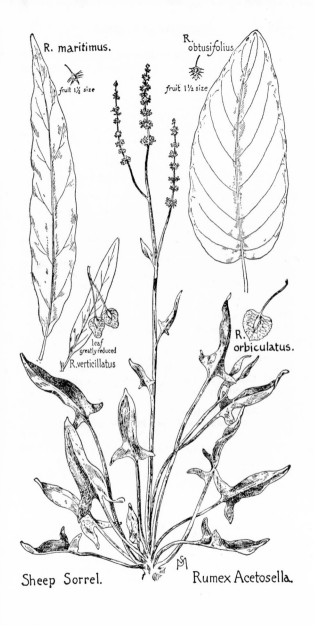

R. maritimus.

fruit 1¼ size

R. obtusifolius.

fruit 1½ size

R. verticillatus

leaf greatly reduced

R. orbiculatus.

Sheep Sorrel.

Rumex Acetosella.

by insects: bumblebees, honeybees, and the smaller butterflies are the commonest visitors. 6-12 inches high.
Growing everywhere.

———

The genus *Polygonum,* the name from πολύς, *many,*
and γονυ, *knee,* alluding to the many joints of the plants,
comprises about 150 distinct species, nearly all of which
may be characterized by the term *weed!* They are æs-
thetically uninteresting and many are extremely troublesome in the farmer's vegetable garden. They mostly bear
pink perfect flowers grouped in a slender spike.

Knotgrass
Polygonum aviculare Greenish-yellow, June-September

A slender species with a weak stem, bluish-green, small
lance-shaped leaves, scaly joints, and greenish pink-tipped
flowers. Common everywhere in cultivated and waste
ground. The blue-green leaves, alternate, or are in appearance clustered and issue from tiny brown sheaths. A
mostly prostrate weed of roadsides and found in many
confusing forms.

Erect Knotweed
Polygonum erectum Greenish-yellow, July-September

A stouter and a yellowish-green stem, leafy; the leaves
nearly oval, and the flowers greenish-yellow. A common
wayside annual weed from Que. to Ga. and west to the
Pacific Coast. The stem of this species is noticeably erect
with no tendency to sprawl.

Pennsylvania Smartweed
Polygonum pennsylvanicum Pink or white-green, July-
September

A somewhat red-jointed species, at home in wet waste
places, with shiny lance-shaped leaves, and pink or white-
green flower-clusters; the upper branching stems and
flower-stems beset with tiny hairlike glands. Common
everywhere. It has a branching, sprawling habit.

Lady's Thumb
Polygonum Persicaria Crimson-pink, June-September

A smooth-stemmed annual species from the old world,
with similar leaves and crimson-pink or deep magenta
flowers, the leaves rough and generally marked with a
darker green triangle in the middle. Very common in
waste damp places.

Smartweed.
Polygonum
Hydropiper.

Lady's Thumb.
Polygonum Persicaria.

Smartweed Water Pepper
Polygonum hydropiper   Green, July-September

A common weed in all wet waste places, naturalized from Europe and often a pest. Leaves narrow lance-shaped, very acrid and pungent, and fringed with tiny bristles. Flowers mostly green in a slim long cluster, nodding. An annual, 1-2 feet high. The indigenous species *P. hydropiperoides* with an equally wide distribution has pink or flesh-colored or greenish flowers, branching stems, and very narrow leaves, not acrid. Common nearly everywhere.

Polygonum virginianum has a smooth stem, ovate to elliptical leaves, fringed sheaths, and tiny flowers in color like the next, borne on erect slender spikes often 10 inches long. 1-4 feet high. Woodland margins, N. H. to Minn., south to Fla. and Tex.

Halberd-leaved Tearthumb
Polygonum arifolium   Pink, greenish, July-September

A perennial species with broad arrowhead-shaped leaves, and a ridged reclining stem beset with fine teeth curved backward. Leaves long-stemmed, and prickle-nerved. Insignificant pink or greenish flower-clusters. In pulling up the weed the thumb and fingers are apt to be torn with the saw-edged stems, hence the common name. 2-6 feet high and often sprawling over other plants. Common from N. B. to Ga., west to Minn. and Mo.

Arrow-leaved Tearthumb
Polygonum sagittatum   Pink, July-September

An annual species climbing over other plants, with a weak four-angled reclining stem beset with prickles only at the angles; the narrow arrowhead-shaped leaves, far apart, sometimes blunt-pointed, short-stemmed, or the smaller leaves without stems. Flowers five-parted, pink, in small dense clusters. Common in low, wet ground everywhere.

Climbing False Buckwheat
Polygonum scandens   Green-white, pale magenta-pink, July-September

A minutely roughish species, with slender climbing, reddish stem, arrowhead-shaped leaves, and leafy flower-spikes, the tiny flowers green-white or pink, the calyx five-parted. Climbing over rocks and bushes 6-12 feet

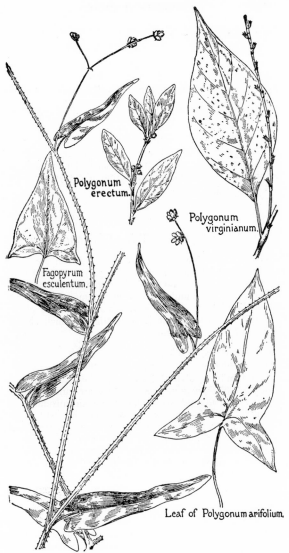

Polygonum
erectum.

Polygonum
virginianum.

Fagopyrum
esculentum.

Leaf of Polygonum arifolium.

Arrow-leaved Tearthumb.   Polygonum sagittatum.

high. In moist places, common everywhere. A rather decorative vine but often troublesome in the vegetable garden.

Buckwheat
Fagopyrum esculentum   Greenish-white, June-September

The familiar buckwheat in cultivation escaped to way-sides. From the old world; with arrowhead-shaped leaves, and greenish-white flowers sometimes pinkish, the calyx five-divided, and with eight honey-glands alternating with the stamens; the flowers fertilized mostly by honeybees; the honey of a peculiarly fragrant character but dark in color. Seed beechnut-shaped. Common everywhere, but not usually persisting.

GOOSEFOOT FAMILY. *Chenopodiaceæ.*

Uninteresting herbs—weeds, many of which are from the old country; with minute green, perfect flowers with a persisting calyx but no petals. The spinach and beet are members of this family as well as summer cypress and Good-King-Henry. Among native plants of waste places and salt marshes are species of *Atriplex,* which should be sought in technical manuals.

Lamb's-quarters, or Pigweed
Chenopodium album   Green, June-September

The family is divided into nine tribes, chief among which is *Chenopodium.* Some of these are quite western, others are of the old world and have been introduced in the east. Lamb's-quarters is common east and west. Leaves mealy-white beneath, varying from rhombic-oval to lance-shaped or narrower, the lower ones coarse-toothed. The green flower-clusters dense, and dull green. 1-4 feet high. Waste places. The name from the Greek meaning *goose* and *foot,* in allusion to the shape of the leaves of some species.

Jerusalem Oak, or Feather Geranium
Chenopodium Botrys   Green, July-September

An annual species from the old country, not mealy but with an aromatic odor. Leaves smaller, slender-stemmed, and deeply subdivided. The flowers green in dense heads, the spike leafless, the calyx three-parted. 1-2 feet high.

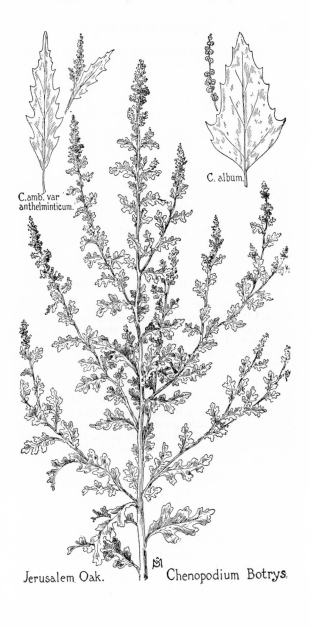

C.amb. var
anthelminticum.

C. album.

Jerusalem Oak.   Chenopodium Botrys.

In autumn the leaves fall off and leave the stem and seed-spike naked. *C. ambrosioides,* or Mexican Tea, is a similar introduced species, with a densely flowered *leafy* spike; the leaves lanceolate. Both are common in waste places. *Chenopodium ambrosioides* var. *anthelminticum,* or Wormseed, differs from the typical *C. ambrosioides* in its leaves which are more aromatic, and its flower-spike which is more elongated and nearly leafless. In the south the var. *anthelminticum* is perennial; otherwise both type and variety are annuals. 2-3 feet high. Naturalized from Tropical Am.

Often in waste places, or following a fire, the strawberry-blite, *Chenopodium rubrum,* will be found quite common. It is an erect plant 10-20 inches high, the flower cluster as if infested by red strawberries. It is almost cosmopolitan in N. Am. and Europe.

AMARANTH FAMILY. *Amaranthaceæ.*

Weeds; some of those of a ruddy color, mostly foreign, are widely cultivated. The perfect flowers without petals, have scales or leaflets (generally three) which retain their color when dry; hence the name 'Αμάραντος, meaning unfading: the cock's-comb is a familiar garden example.

Pigweed
Amaranthus retroflexus   Green, August-October

An annoying weed, common in cultivated ground and in gardens, with light green roughish leaves and stem; leaves long-stemmed and angularly ovate. The dull green flowers in a stiff bristly spike. 1-8 feet high. Common east and west, introduced from the old world.

Amaranthus hybridus   Green, August-October

A similar species, but smoother and a darker green, with slenderer linear-cylindrical, bending spikes, branching. The flowers also similar, but with more acute sepals. 2-6 feet high. Apparently indigenous in the southwest, but introduced eastward. *Amaranthus hybridus* var. *hypochondriacus* is called Prince's Feather and is a deep red form of the species in common cultivation and a frequent escape. It is a perfectly smooth annual with thick flower-spikes. Introduced from Tropical Am.

Pigweed.   Tumbleweed.
Amaranthus retroflexus.   Amaranthus græcizans.

Tumbleweed
Amaranthus græcizans   Green, July-September

A low, smooth, greenish white-stemmed species with light green, small obovate leaves, obtuse at the point, and with many branches. The flowers green, and crowded in close small clusters at the stem of each leaf. 6-20 inches high. In the west, late in autumn, the withered plant is uprooted and tumbles about in the wind, hence the popular name. Common in waste places.

PURSLANE FAMILY. *Portulacaceæ.*

A small group of low herbs with thick juicy leaves and perfect but unbalanced flowers—that is, with two sepals and five petals and as many stamens as petals, or more sepals, or an indefinite number of stamens, or sometimes the petals altogether lacking. Cross-fertilization is largely effected by bees and butterflies. Fruit a capsule filled with several or many shell-shaped or kidney-shaped seeds.

Purslane or Pussley
Portulaca oleracea   Yellow, June-September

An annual; a fleshy-leaved prostrate weed naturalized from the old world, and commonly found in gardens and dooryards. Stems thick and often a terra-cotta-pink, leaves dark green, thick, and round-end wedge-shaped. The tiny, solitary yellow flowers with five petals open only in the morning sunshine, 7-12 stamens. The branches hug the ground and spread or radiate in an ornamental circle; they are 3-10 inches long. In early days the plant was used as a pot herb. It is indigenous in the southwest, but is firmly established in the north where it flourishes under any and all conditions, and has become a very troublesome weed.

———

Spring Beauty
Claytonia virginica   Pale pink or white, March-May

A charmingly delicate flower (rarely quite white) of early spring, distinguished for its flush of pale crimson-pink, and its veins of deeper pink starting from a yellow base. The deep green leaves are linear or broader, the two upper ones located at about the middle of the

Purslane.
Portulaca oleracea.

Spring Beauty.
Claytonia virginica.

plant-stem. The flower has five petals and but two sepals.
Its golden stamens develop before the stigma is mature,
making cross-fertilization a certainty. Its visitors in
search of pollen and nectar are mostly the bumblebees,
the beelike flies and the butterflies. Stem 6-12 inches
high. In open moist woods, from Nova Scotia south
to Ga., and southwest to Tex.

Claytonia caroliniana

A species similar in all respects except that the leaves
are broader, lance-shaped, and the basal ones are quite
obtuse; the flowers are also fewer and smaller. Nova
Scotia south to N. C. among the mountains, and west
to Tenn. Named for John Clayton, an early American
botanist.

PINK FAMILY. *Caryophyllaceæ.*

Annual or perennial herbs generally characterized by
smooth stems and *swollen joints,* opposite-growing leaves
without teeth, and regular, perfect flowers, with five
(rarely four) sepals, the same number of petals, and
twice as many stamens. An immense family of plants
comprising nearly 2000 species, familiar examples of
which are the carnation, the Sweet-William and the
baby's-breath.

Deptford Pink
Dianthus Armeria   Crimson-pink, June-September

An annual escaped from gardens, naturalized from
Europe, with light green narrow, erect leaves, hairy and
small, and clustered crimson-pink, white-dotted flowers
whose five petals are toothed or jagged-edged, resembling
Sweet-William. 6-18 inches high. Fields and waysides
Que. to Ga., west to B. C. Common eastward.

Maiden Pink
Dianthus deltoides   Crimson-pink, June-August

A perennial (growing from a matlike base) smooth
or somewhat hoary, escaped from gardens, naturalized
from Europe. Leaves small and narrow lance-shaped,
erect. The little crimson-pink or white-pink flowers bloom
singly, and have broader petals which are pinked at the

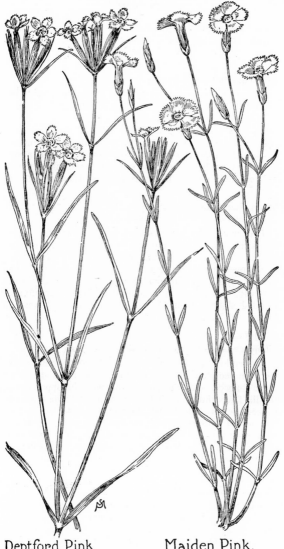

Deptford Pink.
Dianthus Armeria.

Maiden Pink.
Dianthus deltoides.

edge. 6-12 inches high. The face of the flower more nearly resembling Sweet-William. In fields and waste places. N. H. to N. J., west to Mich.

Bouncing Bet or Soapwort
Saponaria officinalis   Pale magenta-pink, June-September

A very common perennial species, naturalized from Europe, the flowers of which have an old-fashioned spicy odor; they are delicate magenta-pink and white, scallop-tipped, and grow in clusters, the single blossom remotely resembling a pink; often double-flowered in the north. Leaves ovate, 3-5 ribbed, and smooth. Stem, thick-jointed, 1-2 feet high. Common in waste places. (*Color Plate 9.*)

Starry Campion
Silene stellata   White, June-August

The lance-shaped leaves and the stem are fine-hairy; the former in distinct clusters of four. The flowers are white, arranged in a loose terminal spike, star-shaped and fringed-edged, the stamens very long. A beautiful and delicate wild flower frequently visited by the small yellow butterfly, and many moths. 2-3 feet high. Common in wooded slopes, from Mass. south to Ga. and west to Minn. and Tex.

Wild Pink
Silene caroliniana   Crimson-pink, May-June

A very low species with a somewhat sticky-hairy character immediately beneath the flowers, most of the blunt lance-shaped leaves clustered at the base, the upper leaves small. The crimson-pink flowers with somewhat wedge-shaped petals. The calyx tubular and adapted to the tongues of butterflies and moths, by which the flower is cross-fertilized. 4-9 inches high. Me., south to Tenn., west to Ohio and Mo. A form with smooth leaves is known as var. *pennsylvanica*.

Bladder Campion
Silene cucubalus   White, June-August

A delicately beautiful, foreign, perennial species which has become naturalized in this country. The deep green leaves are smooth and ovate-lance-shaped. The flowers are white with the five petals deeply two-lobed; the pale green flower-cup is greatly inflated, almost globular in shape, and beautifully veined with green markings not

Bladder Campion.
Silene cucubalus.

Starry Campion.
Silene stellata.

unlike those of a citron melon. The ten anthers (on long
stamens) are sepia brown when mature. 8-18 inches high.
In meadows and moist hollows beside the road throughout.

Sleepy Catchfly
Silene antirrhina   Pink, June-September

A homely but curious annual species whose small
flowers open only for a short time in sunshine. The joints
of the stem are glutinous and evidently prevent any
stealing of the nectar by creeping insects (such as ants)
which are useless as pollen carriers. The flower-calyx is
ovoid with the pink petals often half hidden. 10-25
inches high. Common in waste places everywhere.

Night-flowering Catchfly
Silene noctiflora   White, July-September

Like the bladder campion but smaller; a foreign species
with a beautifully marked calyx resembling spun glass,
the petals similar. The plant is hairy-sticky, the leaves
blunt lance-shaped. The white flowers are delicately fragrant, and open only at dusk, closing on the following
morning. Probably it is exclusively fertilized by moths,
as many such visitors may be seen sipping at the newly
opened blossoms in the early evening. 1-3 feet high.
Common in waste places everywhere.

Evening Lychnis or White Campion
Lychnis alba   White, July-October

A charming plant naturalized from the old country,
with densely fine-hairy, ovate-lance-shaped leaves and
stem, both dark green; the leaves opposite. The sweet-
scented flowers are white, closely resembling those of
Silene noctiflora; in *Lychnis,* however, the flower has
five styles, in *Silene,* three. Both species open their blossoms toward evening and close them during the following
morning. The white petals are deeply cleft and crowned
at the base with miniature petal-like divisions. The calyx
is inflated, and often stained maroon-crimson along the
ribs, which are sticky-hairy; after becoming still more
inflated it withers and leaves exposed the vase-shaped
light brown seed-vessel. 1-2 feet high. In waste places
and borders of fields, Nova Scotia to Ga. and west to
the Pacific Coast. (*Color Plate 10.*) A red-flowered

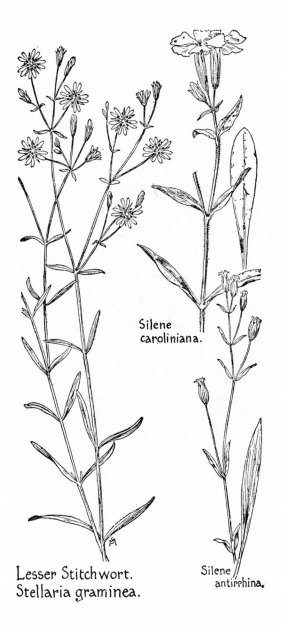

Silene
caroliniana.

Silene
antirrhina.

Lesser Stitchwort.
Stellaria graminea.

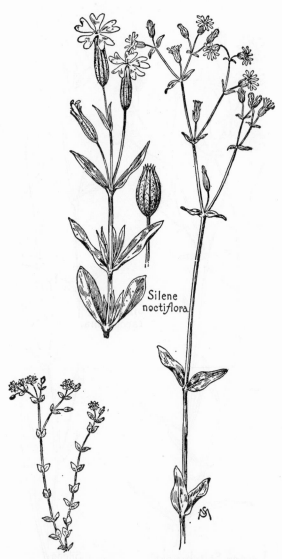

Silene
noctiflora

Arenaria serpyllifolia.   Cerastium vulgatum.

Corn Cockle   Agrostemma Githago

relative, the red campion, *Lychnis dioica,* also European, is found as a weed in eastern N. Am.

Ragged Robin or Cuckoo Flower
Lychnis Flos-cuculi **Pink or crimson, June-September**

A slender perennial, also adventive from Europe, found in old gardens. The plant is downy below, and slightly sticky above; the leaves slender lance-shaped above, and few, but blunt lance-shaped below. The pink, or crimson, or light violet petals of the ragged-looking flowers are deeply cut into four lobes each, the two lateral lobes very small. Fertilized in great measure by bees and butterflies, the bumblebee, perhaps, the most frequent visitor. 1-2 feet high. Common in wet and waste ground, from N. B. south to N. J., and southwest to Pa.

Corn Cockle
Agrostemma Githago **Magenta, July-September**

A densely hairy straight-branched annual, adventive from Europe, and found mostly in grain fields. The magenta flowers not brilliant, but broad and showy, with very long *linear* sepals much exceeding the petals in length. Fertilized by butterflies and moths. 1-3 feet high. Common or occasional throughout the country.

Thyme-leaved Sandwort
Arenaria serpyllifolia **White, May-August**

A tiny annual widely branched and rough-downy, naturalized from Europe; with small ovate leaves and miniature white flowers, the sepals of which are rather long, and rough. 2-8 inches high. Common in dry sandy places everywhere.

Mountain Sandwort or Mountain Daisy
Arenaria grœnlandica **White, June-August**

Another similar tiny, dainty plant, but with arctic proclivities, having much larger flowers with translucent white petals notched at the tip. The crowding leaves are linear and threadlike, the plant grows in a dense tuft from the root, in crevices of rocks. 2-5 inches high. Greenland and the higher peaks of N. Y., Pa., Va., and N. C. On Mt. Washington, where it is called the "Mountain Daisy," it snuggles close to the rocks in sheltered situations, holding its own—almost, if not quite, alone—on the highest points of the bleak Presidential

Field Chickweed.
Cerastium arvense.

Ragged Robin.
Lychnis Flos-cuculi.

range, from 5000 to 6290 feet above tide-water, where
snow lasts during eight months of the year.

Pine-barren Sandwort
Arenaria caroliniana   White, May-July

A *seaboard* species growing in dry sand. Branches
nearly bare, and with a few dainty white flowers about
½ inch broad. The tiny awl-shaped lower leaves densely
overlapping. 4-9 inches high. N. Y., N. J., south.

———

Chickweed
Stellaria media   White, April-October

The commonest weed of Europe, most widely distributed through N. Am. but possibly indigenous in the
farther north. A weak-stemmed low-lying annual, with
small ovate pointed light green leaves, slightly woolly
stems, and minute white flowers with five petals almost
cleft in twain, and five larger green sepals much longer
than the petals. 2-4 inches high. On damp ground everywhere. An especial favorite of birds and chickens.

Long-leaved Stitchwort
Stellaria longifolia   White, May-July

A tall very slender species with many branches, the
stem with rough angles, and the light green leaves small
and lance-shaped. The tiny flowers like white stars, with
five white petals so deeply cleft that they appear as ten,
sepals nearly equaling the petals in length. 10-20 inches
high. In wet grassy places everywhere.

Lesser Stitchwort
Stellaria graminea   White, May-July

A similar species with smaller lance-shaped leaves
widest just above their base, a four-angled stem, and
white flowers with deeply cleft petals. 12-18 inches high.
In fields and grassy waysides from Newf. to western
N. Y. and N. C., west to Minn. Introduced from Europe.
(*Illus. on page 131.*)

———

Larger Mouse-ear Chickweed
Cerastium vulgatum   White, May-September

A bothersome weed common in cultivated fields,
naturalized from Europe but probably indigenous in the
farther north. Stem hairy and clammy, leaves oblong.

Chickweed.
Stellaria media.

Mountain Sandwort.
Arenaria grœnlandica.

Long-leaved
Stitchwort.
Stellaria
longifolia.

The somewhat loosely clustered white flowers with two-cleft petals, but with *short* sepals. 6-15 inches high. (*Illus. on page 132.*)

Field Chickweed
Cerastium arvense   White, April-July

A low, rather large-flowered, handsome species, the broad petals also deeply cleft, the sepals very short, the stems downy or smooth, and the leaves rather broad linear. 4-10 inches high. In dry or rocky situations. Greenland, south to Ga. and west to Neb. and Cal. (*Illus. opp. page 134.*)

Sand Spurry
Spergularia rubra   Pink, June-August

A common little European plant in sandy waste places sometimes near the coast but not on the shore. Leaves linear and flat, in clusters about the frail stem. Tiny flowers, crimson-pink, sepals glandular-hairy. The plants grow in dense company. 2-6 inches high. Roadsides and waste places, Newf. to Ala., west to Cal.

WATER-LILY FAMILY. *Nymphæaceæ.*

Aquatic perennial herbs, with usually floating leaves, and solitary flowers with 3-5 sepals, numerous petals, and distinct stigmas or these united in a radiate disc. Fertilized by bees, beetles, and aquatic insects.

Water-Lily
Nymphæa odorata   White, June-September

The common and beautiful white pond-lily found in still waters everywhere. Leaves dark green, pinkish beneath, ovate-round, cleft at the base up to the long stem, always floating. The white, very fragrant flowers, often 5 inches in diameter when fully developed, open in the morning and close at noon or later; the golden stamens and anthers are concentric, mature after the stigma does, and cross-fertilization occurs by the agency of bees and beetles in general. A pink variety is found in southeastern Mass., and Nantucket. A variety with flowers less than three inches broad is often found along the coast from N. J. to La.

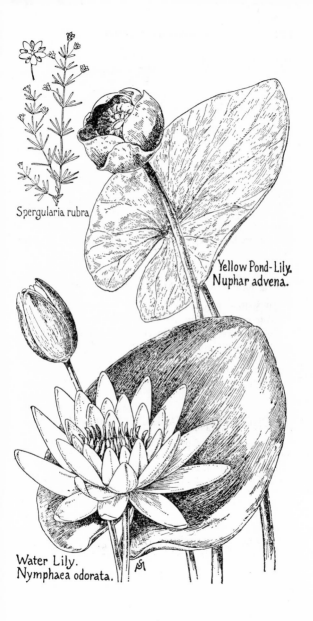

Spergularia rubra

Yellow Pond-Lily.
Nuphar advena.

Water Lily.
Nymphaea odorata.

Yellow Pond-Lily or Spatter-dock
Nuphar advena   Golden-yellow, May-September

A common odorless yellow pond-lily found often in the same water with the preceding species. With *ovate*, usually erect leaves and small green and yellow cup-shaped flowers, with 6 green sepals, sometimes purple-tinged, yellowish inside; the petals yield nectar; they are small, narrow, thick, and yellow—stamenlike. The stigma is a pale ruddy or deep golden-yellow-rayed disc, beneath which the undeveloped anthers are crowded. On the first opening of the flower there is a triangular orifice over the stigma so small that an entering insect must touch the stigma. On the following day the flower expands fully and the anthers beneath the stigma unfold, spread outward, and expose their pollen. Cross-fertilization is thus insured. A very common and familiar plant in stagnant water, with stouter stem and coarser leaves than those of the preceding species. *N. rubrodiscum* is a slenderer form the smaller flower of which has a crimson stigma. Northern Vt. to Mich. and Pa.

Small Yellow Pond-Lily
Nuphar microphyllum   Golden-yellow, June-September

This is a very slender species, with both floating and erect leaves and with flowers scarcely 1 inch wide. Sepals only three. The stigma disc dark red. In ponds and sluggish streams, N. B., south to N. J., Pa., and west to Minn.

CROWFOOT FAMILY. *Ranunculaceæ.*

A large family of perennial or annual herbs, with generally regular but sometimes irregular flowers; with stamens and pistil, or with staminate and pistillate flowers on different plants; 3-15 petals, or none at all; in the last case the sepals petal-like and colored. Generally fertilized by the smaller bees, butterflies, and the beelike flies. Common garden examples are the larkspur, peony and Christmas rose.

Virgin's Bower
Clematis virginiana   Greenish-white, July-August

A most beautiful trailing vine commonly found draped over the bushes in copses and by moist roadsides. The leaves dark green, veiny, with three coarsely toothed

Virgin's Bower.
Clematis virginiana.

Purple Virgin's Bower.
Clematis verticillaris.

leaflets; the flat clusters of small flowers with four green-ish-white sepals and no petals, the staminate and pistillate on different plants. In October the flowers are succeeded by the gray plumy clusters of the withered styles (still adherent to the seed-vessels), which appear under the glass like many tiny silky tails. The plants presenting this hoary appearance gave rise to the popular name, Old Man's Beard. The vine supports itself by a twist in the leaf-stem, the latter revolving a number of times in the course of growth. Stem about 12 feet long. Waysides and river-banks. Nova Scotia south to Ga. and La., west to Minn. and Manitoba.

Leather Flower
Clematis viorna   Dull purple, May-July

A southern species with solitary, thick, leathery, bell-shaped, dull purple flowers without petals, the purple sepals about 1 inch long. The three or more leaflets with unbroken edges or lobed. In early autumn the hoary plume is brownish. Southern Pa., south to Ga. and Miss., and west to Mo.

Purple Virgin's Bower
Clematis verticillaris   Light purple, May-June

A rather *rare* species found in rocky places among the northern hills, with leaves similar to those of *C. vir-giniana,* and showy light purple flowers, downy inside and outside, sometimes over 3 inches broad; the four purple, finely veined sepals expanding only to a cup-shape. The plumes brown-gray. Que., south to Va., and west to Manitoba.

Long-fruited Anemone
Anemone cylindrica   Greenish-white, June-August

A slender tall species the leaves and stem of which are silky-haired, leaves dark green and veiny, ornamen-tally cut (or lobed) into 3-5 parts. The solitary flowers without petals, but with 5-6 greenish-white sepals, are set on a tall stalk. The fruit a narrow, cylindrical, burr-like head 1 inch or more in length. 2-6 flowers are borne on each plant. 18-24 inches high. Common in dry woods and by wooded roadsides, from Me. to northern N. J., west to B. C. and Ariz. The name is Greek, for a flower of this group.

Thimble-weed.   Large White-flowered Anemone.
Anemone virginiana.   Anemone riparia.

Thimble-weed or Tall Anemone
Anemone virginiana   Greenish-white, July-August

This is the common tall anemone of wooded roadsides and banks. The leaves and stem are more or less hairy and deep olive-green, the leaves conspicuously veined. The flowers generally have five inconspicuous sepals white or greenish-white inside and greener outside; the flower-head usually 1 inch or less across, is succeeded by the enlarged fruit-head similar in shape to, and about as large as, a good-sized thimble. Fertilized by the bumblebees, the smaller bees and brilliant little flies. 2-3 feet high. Que., south to Ga. and Ala., west to N. D. Found in Campton, N. H.

Large White-flowered Anemone
Anemone riparia   White, June-July

A slender, tall, and handsome plant intermediate between the two preceding species, with large white flowers maturing earlier than those of the foregoing, and with smoother stem and leaves; the latter thin, and unequally cleft into coarsely and sharply toothed segments. The five thin sepals generally obtuse and a strong white. The short cylindrical fruit-head slenderer than that of *A. virginiana*. 12-35 inches high. Banks of rivers and streams, and on rocky banks, Que. to Md., west to Mich. and Minn. It may be doubtfully distinct from *A. virginiana*.

Canada Anemone
Anemone canadensis   White, May-August

A northern, rather coarse-stemmed species, very much branched, with broad, sharply toothed, three-cleft leaves; their under surfaces rather hairy. The five white sepals quite blunt, and the flower 1-1½ inches broad. The fruit-head globular. 1-2 feet high. Low moist grounds, from Que. to Md. and W. Va., west to B. C. and N. Mex.

Pasque Flower
Anemone patens   Pale violet, March-April

A silky-hairy plant of the west, bearing a single erect pale violet or lavender-white flower of 5-6 sepals (not petals) an inch more or less long. The leaves divided into many narrow linear lobes, the one below the flower stemless, the basal ones slender-stemmed. Fruiting head like *Clematis*, the silky achenes (seeds) with long feathery tails. 6-14 inches high. Prairies, Wisc., Ill., and Tex. northwestward.

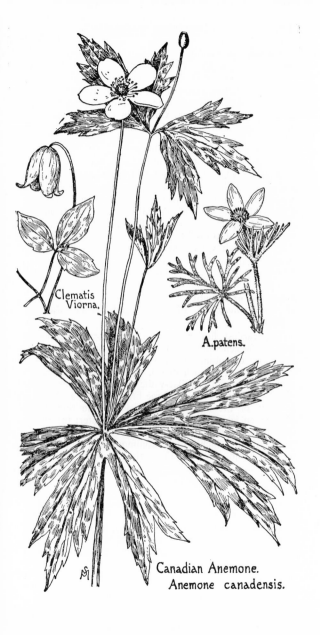

Clematis
Viorna.

A. patens.

Canadian Anemone.
Anemone canadensis.

Mountain Anemone
Anemone lancifolia White, May

A species very similar to the next but with stouter stem and three leaflets, rarely the basal ones, five-divided. The petal-like sepals ovate-oblong, the flower about 1¼ inch broad. 6-15 inches high. Chiefly in mountain woods of the south, Pa. to Ga., west to W. Va. and Ky.

Wood Anemone or Wind Flower
Anemone quinquefolia White, April-June

A beautiful, delicate, and low little plant, the most common of all the wind flowers in the early spring in woodlands. Leaves deep green, of five divisions, and frail white, or magenta-tinged blossoms of from 4-9 petal-like sepals; the solitary flower frequently 1 inch across. Cross-fertilized by the early bees and beelike flies. 4-8 inches high. Que. to Ga., and west to the Rocky Mts.

Liverwort or Hepatica
Hepatica americana Lilac-white, pale purple, March-May

The earliest flower of spring, appearing before its leaves, and generally found half hidden among the decaying leaves of autumn that cover the woodland floor. The blossom about ⅞ inch broad, with 6-12 lustrous sepals varying in color from lilac-white to pale purple and light violet, beneath which are three bracts closely resembling a calyx, or the outer floral envelope. The three-lobed olive-green leaves last throughout the winter; the newer ones together with stems and flower-stems are extremely hairy. About 3 inches high. Common from the seaboard west to Minn. and Mo. Formerly and often still called *H. triloba*.

Hepatica acutiloba

This is a species close to the preceding one and often passing into it. The leaves are three- or sometimes five-lobed, with acute tips, and the three little bracts beneath the flower are also pointed. Range the same as *H. americana*—in fact, both species are often found together in the same woods.

Wood Anemone.
Anemone quinquefolia.

Rue
Anemone.
Anemonella
thalictroides.

Liverwort.
Hepatica triloba.

Rue Anemone
Anemonella thalictroides   White, or pink-tinged, March-May

A frail and delicate spring flower, usually white but rarely magenta-pink-tinged, which often blooms in company with *Anemone quinquifolia,* but readily distinguished from it by the 2-3 flowers in a cluster, the other bearing a solitary blossom. The deep olive-green leaves in groups of three closely resemble those of the meadow rue; they are long-stemmed. The flower with usually six delicate white petal-like sepals, but there are variations of from 5-10 and sometimes they are red, or bluish-green; occasionally double. The flowers are perfect (with orange-yellow anthers). 5-9 inches high. From N. H. to Fla., and west to Miss. and Ark., usually in thin woodlands.

Early Meadow Rue
Thalictrum dioicum   Green, terra-cotta, April-May

A beautiful but not showy, slender meadow rue with the staminate and pistillate flowers on separate plants. The bluish-olive-green leaves lusterless, compound, and thinly spreading; the drooping staminate flowers with generally four small green sepals, and long stamens tipped with terra-cotta, and finally madder purple. The pistillate flowers inconspicuously pale green. An airy and graceful species, common in thin woodlands. 1-2 feet high. Que. to Ala., and west to Mo.

Tall Meadow Rue
Thalictrum polygamum   White, July-September

The commonest species, remarkable for its starry plumy clusters of white flowers, lacking petals but with many conspicuous threadlike stamens. The plants are polygamous, that is, with staminate, pistillate, and perfect ones on the same or different plants. The leaves are compound, with lusterless blue-olive-green leaflets; the stout stem light green or magenta-tinged at the branches. The decorative, misty white flower-clusters are often a foot long; the delicate-scented staminate flowers are a decided tone of green-white. This species is an especial favorite of many bees, moths, and smaller butterflies, by which it is cross-fertilized. 3-10 feet high. Common in wet meadows from Labrador to Que., west to Ohio, and south to N. C.

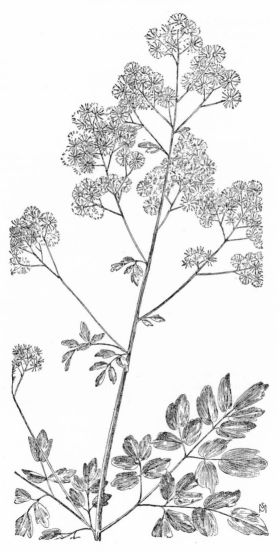

Tall Meadow Rue.   Thalictrum polygamum.

Skunk Meadow Rue
Thalictrum revolutum   White-purple, June-July

A species similar in most respects to the next, but the leaves thicker, and under a glass covered with a glandular fine-hairiness, the wavy particles (glands) easily discerned on the under side of the leaf. Rocky woods, Me., E. Mass., to N. J., and Fla., west to Mo. and Ark.

Purplish Meadow Rue
Thalictrum dasycarpum   White-purple, June-August

The stem of this species is generally stained with madder purple, but sometimes it is green with only a slight magenta tinge in parts. The leaves are three-toothed, bluish-green and similar in shape to those of the preceding species. The flowers are white with a brown-purple tinge, and are also polygamous. 3-6 feet high. On the borders of meadows and wet places, Ont. to Ohio, Ind., and southwestward.

————

Water Plantain Spearwort
Ranunculus laxicaulis   Yellow, June-August

An insignificant marsh species closely allied to the buttercup, with yellow flowers ⅔ inch broad, the 5-7 petals rather narrow. The lance-shaped leaves almost if not quite toothless, and clasping the jointed stem, which often sends out roots from the joints; the lower leaves contracted into a broad stem-clasping base. 1-2½ feet high. Common in wet places, from Del., south to Ga., and west to Tex. and Mo. Name from the classic *Rana,* a frog, referring to the marshy home of the genus.

Small-flowered Crowfoot
Ranunculus abortivus   Yellow, April-June

Rather an attractive species, commonly found beside the woodland brook, the lower leaves of which are somewhat kidney-shaped, and the upper ones slashed like those of the buttercup, but very moderately so; the leaves bright green and smooth. The small flowers with globular heads, and reflexed or drooping yellow petals; the head about ¼ inch broad. 6-24 inches high. In shady and moist ground, everywhere. The plant has many, rather confusing forms, mostly varying in the lobing of the leaves. Our illustration has somewhat more rounded leaves than the typical form.

Water Plantain Spearwort. Small-flowered Crowfoot.
Ranunculus laxicaulis. Ranunculus abortivus.

Hooked Crowfoot
Ranunculus recurvatus   Light yellow, April-June

A woodland crowfoot distinguished by its remarkably hooked seed-vessels which are gathered in a cluster about ½ inch broad. The light yellow flowers with the calyx (flower-envelope) curved backward, and with usually five small petals, are rather inconspicuous. The stem and olive-green leaves are hairy, the latter generally three-lobed, veiny, and toothed, but the root leaves are seldom divided. 10-20 inches high. Common in woods, Que. to Ga., west to Minn. and Okla.

Early Buttercup
Ranunculus fascicularis   Deep yellow, April-May

Another woodland or hillside species, with deep yellow flowers almost an inch broad. The plant rather low, with fine silky hairs on stem and leaf, the latter dark green, and deeply lobed, with 3-5 divisions. The flower with often more than five petals which are rather narrow; the fruit-head about ⅓ inch in diameter, with a slender curved spine to each seed-vessel. 6-12 inches high. Common on the borders of wooded hills, in the spring, from Ont., south to La. and Tex., and west to Minn. The first buttercup of the year; all are fertilized mostly by early bees, flies, and the smaller butterflies.

Swamp Buttercup
Ranunculus septentrionalis   Deep yellow, Late April-July

This is the next buttercup of the spring, and one confined to swamps and low wet grounds. The flowers are deep yellow and fully 1 inch broad. The hollow stem is generally smooth, but sometimes fine-hairy; the deep green leaves are divided into three leaflets, each distinctly stemmed, and three-lobed, or only the terminal one stemmed; the uppermost leaves are long, narrow, and toothless. This buttercup is very variable in both size and foliage, its branches are upright or reclining, and its leaves coarsely cleft and divided. 1-2 feet high, or more. Common in moist rich ground everywhere. Like most of the other buttercups, this one depends mainly upon the beelike flies and the little bees for fertilization.

Leaf of
Ranunculus fascicularis.

Swamp Buttercup.   Ranunculus septentrionalis.

Creeping Buttercup
Ranunculus repens   Deep yellow, May-July

A variable species of a similar character, the leaves frequently white-spotted or blotched; the deep yellow flowers nearly 1 inch broad, blooming a little later. The seed-vessel tipped with a short stout spine, thus differing from the rather deciduous long straight spine of *R. septentrionalis.* This buttercup creeps or spreads over the ground by runners. Roadsides and waste places or low grounds, generally throughout N. Am., and introduced from Europe.

Bristly Crowfoot
Ranunculus pennsylvanicus   Yellow, June-August

Often, and improperly, called a buttercup; the flower has a thimble-shaped green head formed of the pistils, and insignificant, round yellow petals surround it. It is small, scarcely ⅓ inch across, and does not in the remotest degree suggest the cup-shape of the buttercup. The stem is remarkably stiff-hairy, and irritating to the touch; it is hollow, coarse, light green, and leafy to the top. Leaves light green, three-divided, with each division three-lobed, cut and slashed like *R. acris,* and hairy above and beneath. 1-2 feet high. Common in wet situations, from Newf. to N. J. and Pa., west to Ill. and Minn.

Bulbous Buttercup
Ranunculus bulbosus   Golden or deep yellow, May-July

A small erect plant proceeding from a bulbous base or root, with hairy stem and leaf, and large bright, 1-inch-wide, deep or golden-yellow flowers, the green sepals of which are strongly reflexed. The leaves are deep green, decoratively cut and slashed, three-divided, each division three-lobed, with only the terminal one stemmed, the lateral ones nearly if not absolutely stalkless. 8-16 inches high. Roadsides and fields; abundant and naturalized from Europe. Müller records the fact that over 60 different species of insects visit these Old World buttercups, i.e., *R. repens, R. bulbosus,* and *R. acris.*

Tall Buttercup
Ranunculus acris   Golden or deep yellow, May-August

This is the common buttercup of fields and meadows, which has become naturalized from the old country. The stem is hairy, branched and less hairy above, and deep

Leaf and flower showing reflexed
sepals of Ranunculus bulbosus.

Bristly Crowfoot.   Ranunculus pennsylvanicus.

green. The leaves deep green with 3-7 stemless divisions, and these are again correspondingly divided into linear segments; they are cut and slashed in a most decorative and complicated fashion, only the upper ones showing the simple three-parted figure. The flowers, nearly 1 inch broad, are lustrous light golden-yellow within, and light yellow without, the 5 broad petals overlapping. The flowers are set on long slender stems, and sometimes continue to bloom until frost. 2-3 feet high. Common everywhere, especially upon moist meadows. The variety named *R. acris,* var. *latisectus,* is similar except in the shape of its leaf, which has *very broad* instead of linear segments, imparting to the plant a thicker and heavier appearance in the field. This variety is the common form in northern New Eng.

There are at least 33 species of *Ranunculus* in our area, so that the nine described above are to be considered as only the most common forms. For all others, the differences of which are often puzzling, the technical manuals must be sought.

————

Marsh Marigold
Caltha palustris   Golden-yellow, April-May

A thick and hollow-stemmed stocky plant common in marshes in spring, with round or kidney-shaped deep green leaves obscurely blunt-toothed, and brilliant golden-yellow flowers resembling buttercups. Often wrongly called cowslips. The flowers are perfect with 5-9 petal-like sepals, and numerous stamens; they are honey-bearing, and although the anthers and stigmas mature simultaneously, cross-fertilization is favored by the anthers opening outwardly, and the outermost ones farthest from the stigmas opening first. The flowers are chiefly fertilized by the beautiful yellow flies. The classical name *Caltha* means cup, and *palustris* a marsh—marsh-cup. 8-24 inches high. Common in wet meadows, from Me., south to S. C., and west. (*Color Plate 11.*)

Caltha natans

A species found only in northern Wisc., Minn., and the northwest, has white or palest magenta-pink flowers about ½ inch broad. Summer. Generally afloat in ponds and streams, or growing on the muddy margins.

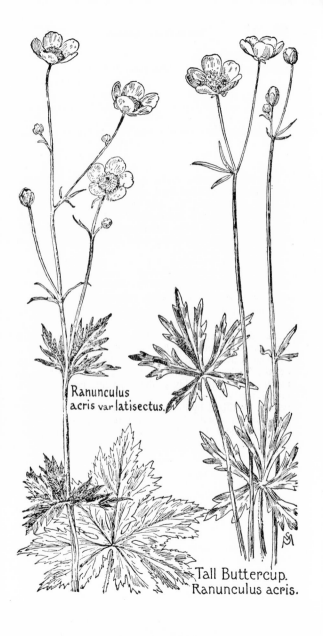

Ranunculus
acris var latisectus.

Tall Buttercup.
Ranunculus acris.

Goldthread
Coptis trifolia   White, May-July

A tiny woodland plant whose bitter golden-yellow threadlike roots contribute to the medicinal stock of the old-fashioned country housewife. The evergreen leaves are lustrous dark green, three-lobed, scalloped, finely toothed, and long-stemmed. The solitary flower terminating a long slender stem has 5-7 white sepals, and has many obscure little club-shaped petals, which are really nectaries, 15-25 white stamens with golden anthers, and 3-7 pistils on slender stalks. According to C. M. Weed, the flower is cross-fertilized mostly by a fungus gnat— a little two-winged fly, and occasionally by a small elongated beetle. 3-6 inches high. In bogs of woodlands or shady pastures, from Greenland, south to N. C., and west to Alaska. The name from the Greek *to cut,* in reference to the cut-leaf.

———

Columbine
Aquilegia canadensis   Scarlet, yellow, April-early July

A most delicate but hardy plant common on rocky hillsides and the borders of wooded glens. The long-stemmed compound leaves are light olive-green, with three-lobed leaflets. The flowers are graded from yellow through scarlet to red at the tip of the spurs. The petals are the 5 tubes culminating in the spurs, and the 5 sepals are the spreading ruddy yellow segments grading into a greenish-yellow, situated between the tubes. Stamens yellow. Fertilized by moths and butterflies. 1-2 feet high. Common in woods, Nova Scotia to Fla., west to Saskatchewan and Tex. Rarely the flowers are altogether golden yellow.

———

Tall Larkspur
Delphinium exaltatum   Light violet, July-August

A slender and smooth species of larkspur found in the woods from Pa. southward to N. C. and Tenn., and in Ohio. The deep green leaves have generally five divergent, lance-shaped or wedge-shaped lobes, and the light purple or blue-violet flowers are borne in a slim spike sometimes 10 inches long. 2-6 feet high. The *Delphiniums* are mostly fertilized by the beelike flies, honeybees, and bumblebees.

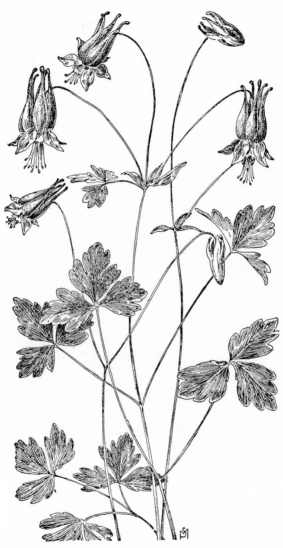

Columbine.   Aquilegia canadensis.

Floerkea
proserpinacoides
Pg. 233

Tall Larkspur.   Delphinium exaltatum.

Goldthread.
Coptis trifolia.

Monkshood.
Aconitum uncinatum.

Field Larkspur
Delphinium consolida   Lilac to ultramarine-blue, July-
    August

A European species, in cultivation and escaped to
roadsides and fields, with dissected deep green leaves
having very narrow linear lobes, and a scattered flower-
spike of showy flowers 1 inch broad, long-spurred, and
varying in color from pale magenta, lilac, and purple
to ultramarine-blue. The commoner species in cultivation
is *D. Ajacis,* an annual, with larger flower-clusters and
with woolly pods; this has also escaped over much of
our range.

———

Monkshood
Aconitum uncinatum   Violet-ultramarine, June-
    September

A handsome wild flower, slender-stemmed, weak, and
disposed to seek support. The delicate character of the
plant is not unlike that of the columbine. The deep green
leaves are toothed, have 3-5 lobes, and are rather thick.
The purple or violet-ultramarine flowers are composed
of 5 sepals, the upper one enlarged, forming the hood,
and 2 petals (three more are stamenlike, abortive, and
inconspicuous) concealed beneath the hood; the stamens
are numerous. 2-4 feet high. In woods, southern Pa., and
south along the Alleghenies to Ga., west to Ind. and Ky.

A southern relative, *Aconitum reclinatum,* with longer
stems and a hairy flower cluster, is found in Va., W. Va.,
and south to Ga.

———

Black Snakeroot
Cimicifuga racemosa   White, June-July

A tall, spreading, slender-stemmed woodland plant,
with fuzzy, feathery white flowers borne in a 6- to 20-
inch-long, wandlike cluster, having a disagreeable fœtid
odor, and compound, sharply toothed, light green leaves.
The 4-8 petals are stamenlike, and the stamens are
numerous. The flower is assisted in fertilization by the
green flesh-flies. Fruit berrylike and purplish. 3-8 feet
high. Woods, Mass., south to Ga., and west to Tenn., Ind.
and Mo. The related *C. americana,* which is scarcely different, is found only from Pa. to N. C. and Tenn.

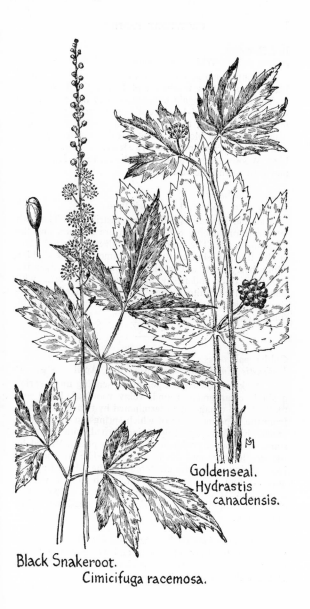

Goldenseal.
Hydrastis
canadensis.

Black Snakeroot.
Cimicifuga racemosa.

Red Baneberry
Actæa rubra   White, April-June

A bushy woodland plant with compound 3-5 parted leaves, the leaflets toothed and lobed, the lower end-leaflets sometimes again compound. The tiny white, perfect flowers with 4-10 exceedingly narrow petals and numerous stamens; the 4-5 sepals petal-like and falling when the flower blooms. Fruit a thick cluster of coral red, oval berries (poisonous); slender stems. 1-2 feet high. Woods, from Labrador southwest to N. J. and Pa., and west to Ind., Iowa and Ariz.

White Baneberry
Actæa alba   White, Late April-June

A similar species with the same distribution. The leaflets are more deeply cut, the teeth are sharper, and the lobes are acute. The narrow, stamenlike petals are blunt at the tip, and shorter than the stamens. Fruit a china white berry with a conspicuous purple-black eye; the stems are thick and fleshy, and usually red. Forms with slender-stalked white berries, and fleshy-stalked red berries occasionally occur. White baneberry is called by some *Actæa pachypoda*.

———

Goldenseal
Hydrastis canadensis   Greenish-white, April

A stocky yellow-rooted perennial, sending up in spring a single clear green, round, veiny root-leaf, lobed and toothed, and a hairy stem terminated by two small leaves, from the uppermost one of which springs an insignificant green-white flower scarcely ½ inch broad, with numerous stamens, about a dozen pistils, and no petals. Visited by the smaller bees and the beelike flies. The fruit a small head of tiny red berries clustered like the lobes of a raspberry. 1 foot high. In woods, Vt. south to Va., west to Minn. and Ark. Now very rare because of its wholesale collection for the drug *hydrastine;* sometimes called orangeroot.

Of the crowfoot or buttercup family there has been room here for only 14 genera and 37 species. For the other 9 genera and over 60 species the reader is referred to the technical manuals.

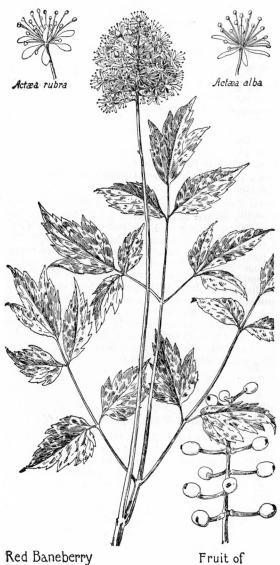

Actæa rubra

Actæa alba

Red Baneberry
Actæa rubra.

Fruit of
Actæa alba.

BARBERRY FAMILY. *Berberidaceæ.*

A family of shrubs and herbs with perfect flowers having one pistil, and as many stamens as petals (except *Podophyllum*) arranged opposite each other. The flowers of the barberry are especially adapted to cross-fertilization; but other members of the family are self-fertilized, or cross-fertilized by the agency of insects, chiefly bees.

Blue Cohosh or Papoose Root
Caulophyllum thalictroides Greenish, or yellowish, April-May

An early flowering plant common in the west, with generally but one compound leaf (at the top of the long stem) three times parted, the leaflets having 2-3 lobes; a smaller similar leaf accompanies the flower-stalk. The whole plant is covered with a white bloom when young. The simple stem is terminated by a small cluster of yellow-green, or yellowish flowers ½ inch broad, with 6 petal-like sepals, and 6 insignificant hood-shaped petals grouped closely about the central pistil. The stigma is receptive before the anthers are ripe, thus assuring cross-fertilization. Frequently visited by the early bumblebees and bees. The seeds berrylike and blue, in a loose cluster. 1-3 feet high. Rich woodlands from N. B. south to Ala., west to Manitoba and Mo.

Twinleaf
Jeffersonia diphylla White, April-May

A little plant when in flower, scarcely 8 inches tall, but attaining double that height later in the season when in fruit. The single white flower, about an inch broad, with 8 oblong flat petals, and half as many early-falling sepals, is a trifle like the bloodroot blossom, but lacks the latter's delicacy and purity of color. The long-stemmed leaf is parted almost completely into two angularly ovate lobes, whitish beneath. Finally (when fruiting) 15-18 inches high. Woods, western N. Y. and Ont., south to Ala., and west to Wisc. and Iowa.

166

The fleshy-covered cadet blue seeds
showing groups in pairs
after bursting of the
ovary.

Twinleaf.   Blue Cohosh.

Jeffersonia diphylla. Caulophyllum thalictroides.

May Apple, or Mandrake
Podophyllum peltatum White, Late April-May

A common, handsome woodland plant remarkable for its large leaves which frequently measure a foot in diameter; the *flowerless* stem of the plant bears a leaf with 7-9 lobes, peltate in character; i.e., supported by the stem in the center, as an umbrella.

The May Apple has also been called Umbrella Leaf, and, in allusion to its peculiar lemonlike fruit, Wild Lemon. The *flowering* stalks bear two less symmetrical leaves, from between the stems of which droops the ill-smelling but handsome white flower nearly 2 inches broad; it usually has 6 petals and twice as many stamens; it is without nectar, but is nevertheless cross-fertilized by the early bees and the bumblebees; these collect the pollen. Prof. Robertson believes that the plant may be occasionally self-fertilized; although the anthers do not reach out as far as the stigmas, they sometimes do touch the tip edge of the stigma. Fruit a large, fleshy, edible, lemon-shaped berry. Leaves, root and seeds poisonous, and medicinal. The plant is 12-18 inches high, and is common in damp rich woods, from Que. to Fla., west to Minn. and Tex. Rare in northern New Eng.

A plant of the woodlands so common in spring about the neighborhood of Greater New York, seems conspicuously and strangely absent in the vicinity of Boston. Our native mandrake has nothing to do with the fabulous mandrake of the Mediterranean region, which contains a narcotic poison used by Roman surgeons to deaden pain 1,800 years before the discovery of ether.

POPPY FAMILY. *Papaveraceæ.*

Herbs with a milky or yellow juice, and regular perfect flowers with 4-12 petals, generally two early-falling sepals, and many stamens. Fertilized mostly by bees. Fruit a dry capsule usually one-celled. Garden plants include the true poppy, the California poppy and cream cups.

Bloodroot
Sanguinaria canadensis White, April-May

A most beautiful but fragile flower of early spring, 1½ inches broad, with generally 8 (rarely 12) brilliant white petals four of which alternating with the others

May Apple.   Podophyllum peltatum.

are a trifle narrow, and impart a four-sided aspect to the full-blown blossom. The petals expand flatly in the morning, and become erect toward late afternoon, and close by evening. The two sepals fall when the flower opens. The golden-orange anthers mature after the two-lobed stigma, which is shriveled when the pollen is ripe; the outer stamens are somewhat shorter than the inner ones in the advanced flower, and the stigma is prominent in the new flower, so cross-fertilization is practically assured. The blossom attracts insects which gather pollen but find no honey, and its chief visitors are honeybees, bumblebees, the smaller bees and the beelike flies. As the plant breaks through the ground in early April the leaf is curled into a cylinder which encloses the budding flower; afterward the blossom pushes upward beyond the leaf. Eventually the light blue-olive-green leaf, generally with seven irregular shallow lobes, is 6-10 inches broad. The dull orange-colored juice is acrid, astringent, and medicinal in quality. Fruit-capsule elliptical-oblong with many light yellow-brown seeds. Plant finally about 10 inches high. Common everywhere on the borders of rich woods-shaded roadsides, and copses.

Celandine Poppy
Stylophorum diphyllum   Golden-yellow, April-May

A western woodland species with yellow juice, deeply lobed light green leaves slender-stemmed and smooth, and with small four-petaled poppylike golden-yellow flowers 1 inch broad, solitary, or 2-3 in a terminal cluster. Fertilized mainly by the smaller bees. The ovoid seed-pod hairy. The two sepals falling early. 12-16 inches high. In low damp woods, from western Pa., west to Tenn., Ark. and Wisc.

Celandine
Chelidonium majus   Deep yellow, May-August

A common weed naturalized from Europe and found usually in or about the eastern towns. The leaves are somewhat similar to those of the preceding species, light lusterless green, smooth, and ornamentally small-lobed. The small deep yellow flower (with four petals), ¾ inch broad or less, has a prominent green style, and many yellow stamens. The plant has a strong yellow juice. 1-2 feet high. Common in waste places nearly everywhere.

Bloodroot.
Sanguinaria canadensis.

Celandine Poppy.
Stylophorum diphyllum.

Prickly Poppy
Argemone mexicana Yellow, June-September

A yellow poppy with prickly thistlelike leaves, very light green and smooth with a slight whitish bloom, commonly cultivated, and escaped to roadsides and waste places; a native of Tropical Am. Flowers usually two inches broad or more, with four bright yellow petals, and numerous golden stamens. This poppy like all others is sought by the honeybee for its pollen; it does not yield honey. The broad surface of the stigmas of poppies in general being a convenient alighting platform for insects, the flowers are surely adapted to cross-fertilization; although the anthers ripen in the bud, and are directly over the stigma. The fruit-capsule nearly an inch long, and armed with prickles. Rarely the flowers are white. Stem stout, bristly, and 1-2 feet high. Usually found near dwellings and on the neglected borders of old highways, from New Eng. south, and west to Ill.

FUMITORY FAMILY. *Fumariaceæ.*

Near *Papaveraceæ* but the flowers irregular, sack-shaped or spurred, with 4 united petals, 6 stamens; leaves compound and finely dissected; the juice watery. They are generally weak-stemmed, quickly wilting, smooth herbs, mostly of woodlands.

Climbing Fumitory, or Mountain Fringe
Adlumia fungosa White, tinted magenta-pink, June-October

A beautiful and delicate vine climbing and trailing over thickets or shrubbery, with an attenuate, sack-shaped white flower tinted greenish and magenta-pink, or very pale pink, in drooping clusters. The leaves are compound, smooth, prettily subdivided, mostly three-lobed, and the vine climbs by means of their slender stems. The weak and slender stem 8-12 feet long. In moist situations, woods and thickets, from Que. west to Wisc., and south to N. C., among the mountains. Named for John Adlum, of Washington, a horticulturist who published in 1823 the first book on the cultivation of grapes in this country.

Celandine.
Chelidonium majus.

Prickly Poppy.
Argemone
mexicana.

Dutchman's Breeches
Dicentra Cucullaria   White, yellow-tipped, April-May

This is one of the daintiest wild flowers of the spring, common in southern N. Y., but rare in northeastern New Eng. The plant is characterized by a feathery compound leaf, long-stemmed and proceeding from the root, thin, grayish (almost sage) green in tint, blue and paler beneath; the leaflets are finely dissected. The flowering stalk also proceeds from the root, and bears 4-8, rarely more, nodding white flowers, of four petals joined in pairs and forming, two of them, a double, two-spurred, somewhat heart-shaped sack, the other two, within the sack, very small, narrow, and protectingly adjusted over the slightly protruding stamens. The spurs are stained with light yellow. The flower is cross-fertilized mostly by the agency of the early bumblebees. Honeybees collect only pollen; their tongues are too short to reach the nectar which is secreted in two long processes of the middle stamens; the proboscis of the bumblebee, 8 mm. long, reaches it, that of the honeybee, 6 mm., can not. The honeybee alights on the flower, forces its head between the inner petals, and gathers only the pollen with its front feet. Such a pendulous position as the flower compels is extremely difficult for insects other than bees to maintain. Butterflies therefore visit the flower with less success than bumblebees. Flowering stem 5-9 inches high. In thin woodlands and on rocky slopes from New Eng. south to N. C., and west to Neb., S. D., and Mo. The name from the Greek, meaning twice-spurred.

Squirrel Corn
Dicentra canadensis   White, magenta-pink, May-June

A similar species with more attenuate flowers, white or greenish-white tinted with magenta-pink, 4-8 on the stalk, all very short-stemmed, and narrow at the base, slightly fragrant. 6-12 inches high, the roots bearing many little tubers resembling yellow peas, hence the common name. Rich woodlands, from Que., south to N. C. and Ala., and west to Minn., Neb., and Mo.

Dicentra exima, the wild bleeding-heart, is a tall rare species with less finely cut leaves, large and smooth, and with narrow magenta-pink flowers. It is often cultivated. 1-2 feet high. Rocky slopes. Western N. Y. and Pa., south to Ga. and Tenn., along the mountains.

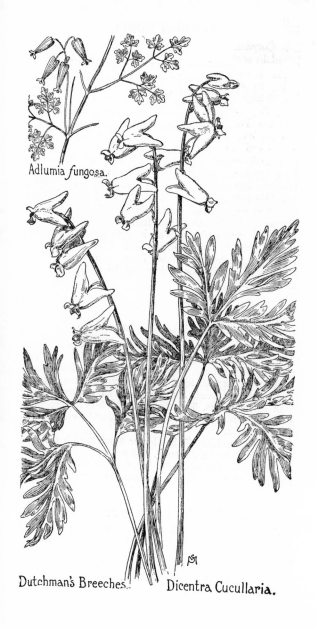

Adlumia fungosa.

Dutchman's Breeches. Dicentra Cucullaria.

Pale Corydalis
Corydalis sempervirens Pale pink, May-August

This is another conspicuously delicate wild flower of spring. Its relationship with *Dicentra* is manifested by the pale foliage and the attenuated sacklike blossom; in New Eng. it seems almost to supplant Dutchman's Breeches. The pale or whitish-green leaves are compound, and cut into ornamental segments which are generally three-lobed. The pale crimson-pink, or sometimes magenta-pink, slightly curved corolla is half an inch or more long, somewhat round at the top (which is really the bottom), and two-flanged at the bottom or mouth, which is golden-yellow. The leaves are scattered alternately on the plant-stem at the branching summit of which are groups of rarely more than four flowers. The slender and erect stem whitened with a slight bloom and often stained pinkish, is 8-22 inches high. The seed-pods are erect and slender, 1½ inches long. In rocky situations, from Newf., south along the mountains to Ga., and west to Minn. and Mont.

Golden Corydalis
Corydalis aurea Golden-yellow, March-May

A golden-yellow flowered species common in the west. The compound pale green leaves are beautifully cut into three-lobed segments, and the bright deep yellow corolla is about ½ an inch long. The seed-pod is beady in outline, slightly curved, and stands at an angle relatively with its neighbors. The slender stem 6-14 inches high. In woodlands from Que. south to Pa., and west to Wisc. and Manitoba.

The var. *occidentalis* has larger flowers, with the spur a trifle shorter than the body. The pod less lumpy or contracted about the seed, the latter acute-edged. Barrens and prairies, Ill. to Mont., southwest to Okla. and Tex.

Corydalis flavula Light yellow, May-June

A slender and smooth species, the flower-stems particularly delicate, and the tiny flower a pale golden-yellow, the spur only 1/12 inch long, outer petals sharp-pointed and slightly longer than the inner ones. Pods drooping. 6-12 inches high. N. Y. and Ont. to N. C., west to Ark. and Kan.

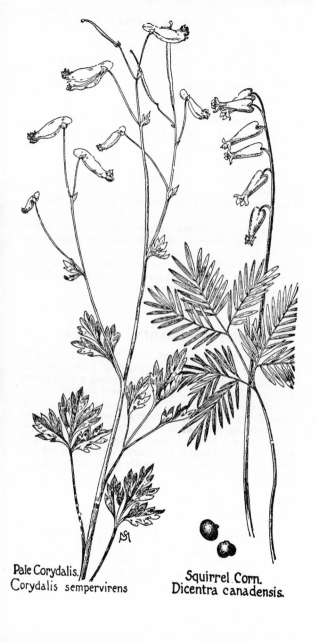

Pale Corydalis.
Corydalis sempervirens

Squirrel Corn.
Dicentra canadensis.

Corydalis micrantha   Yellow, March-April

Like the preceding but the flower scarcely spurred, and the slight crest *not* toothed, or often quite absent. Pods nearly upright. Central U. S. from Ill. and Iowa to western Fla. and Tex.

Corydalis crystallina   Deep yellow, April-June

Flowers much larger, ⅔ inch long, a deep bright yellow, spur as long as the body, stem short. 8-18 inches high. Iowa and Kan., south to Ark. and Tex.

Fumitory
Fumaria officinalis   Crimson-pink or magenta, June-September

A small delicate weed, adventive from Europe, found mostly within the seaboard states. The light green leaves are finely cut, and the small crimson-pink or magenta-pink flowers with crimson tips are borne in a dense, long, narrow spike. The reclining stem 6-20 inches long. Waste places and near old gardens, rather rare.

MUSTARD FAMILY. *Cruciferæ.*

An enormous family of often weedy plants, with watery but never poisonous juice, only a small number of which can be considered here. Among garden plants are the cabbage and its relatives, sweet alyssum, stocks, *Aubrietia* and candytuft. The Latin name of this family, from *Crux,* a cross, arose from the resemblance of the four opposing petals of its flowers to the form of a cross. There are also four deciduous sepals, one pistil, and six stamens, two of which are short; rarely there are less than six. The flowers are generally small and not showy, but they produce honey.

Toothwort or Crinkleroot
Dentaria diphylla   White, May

A low woodland plant with inconspicuous flowers ⅔ inch wide, having four petals and many yellow stamens. The basal leaves long-stemmed, three-lobed, and toothed, the two upper stem-leaves similar and opposite; all smooth. The flowers borne in a small terminal cluster. The slender seed-pods one inch long. The long root is

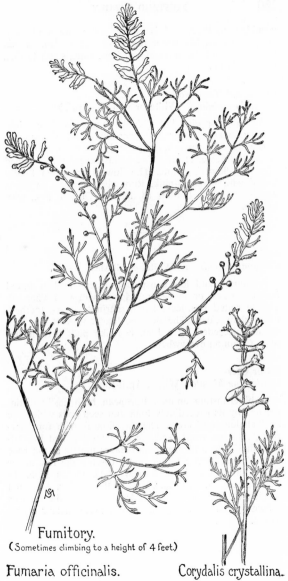

Fumitory.

(Sometimes climbing to a height of 4 feet)

Fumaria officinalis.   Corydalis crystallina.

wrinkled, toothed, and is edible, possessing a pleasant
pungent flavor, like watercress. 8-13 inches high. In rich
woodlands and damp meadows, from Que., south to Ga.,
west to Minn.

Cut-leaved Toothwort
Dentaria laciniata   White or pinkish, April-May

A similar species, but with the leaves deeply cut into
narrow lobes, sharply and coarsely toothed; three are
borne upon the smooth, or sparingly woolly, stem not far
below the flower-cluster. The basal leaves are developed
after the flowering time. The flowers are often faintly
tinged with magenta-pink. Root also peppery. In moist
woods or on the borders of thickets, Que. to Fla., west
to Kan. and Ark.

Spring Cress
Cardamine bulbosa   White, April-May

A smooth and less conspicuous, slender plant found
beside springs, or in wet meadows, with somewhat angularly round root-leaves, and sparingly coarse-toothed,
ovate stem-leaves. The flowers, like toothwort, ½ inch
broad, succeeded by a long beanlike pod. 6-16 inches
high. Common everywhere.

Bitter Cress
Cardamine hirsuta   White, April-June

A bitter-tasting annual, European herb easily distinguished by its exceedingly long thin seed-pods which are
an inch long and erect. The tiny flowers with four narrow petals are white, and are frequently visited by brilliant flies. The little compound leaves mostly at the base
of the plant form a rather pretty rosette; the few upper
leaflets are exceedingly narrow. 3-12 inches high. In
waste places, N. Y. to Ga., west to Ill. and Ky. A related
species, *C. pennsylvanica,* has leaves also on the stem as
shown by the illus. It grows in wet places nearly everywhere.

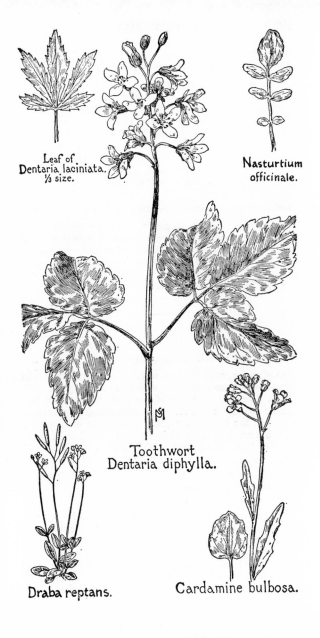

Leaf of
Dentaria laciniata.
⅓ size.

Nasturtium
officinale.

Toothwort
Dentaria diphylla.

Draba reptans.

Cardamine bulbosa.

Hairy Rock Cress
Arabis hirsuta   Greenish-white, May-July

This is a generally hairy little plant (sometimes it is nearly smooth) with a tall slim stem, terminated by a small cluster of tiny white or greenish-white flowers, beneath which in the later season of its bloom appears a succession of slim seed-pods. The clustered basal leaves are hairy, toothed, and lance-shaped, but blunt at the tip; the stem-leaves clasp the stem, and are widely toothed and small. 12-20 inches high. Found, in some of its forms, from the Atlantic to the Pacific coast.

Arabis lævigata   Greenish-white, April-May

A perfectly smooth species with a slight bloom, taller than the preceding, and with stem-leaves which clasp the stem and are almost pointed either side of it—what is sometimes called a sagittate (arrow-shaped) base. Resembling in other respects the species above described. 1-3 feet high. Que. to Ga. west to S. D. and Okla.

Whitlow-grass
Draba reptans   White, March-May

Our native whitlow-grass distinguished at once by its slender or linear seed-pods, which are longer than their stalks. The tiny flowers and the pods below them terminate a long smooth stem; the little obtuse-ovate leaves nearly at the base of the plant. An annual of miniature proportions. 1-5 inches high. In sandy and barren fields from eastern Mass., south to Ga., and west to Tex. and Cal.

Common Whitlow-grass
Draba verna   White, March-May

A species naturalized from Europe, and common throughout our range in barren fields and beside the road. The four white petals are deeply notched; the small hairy lance-shaped and toothed leaves are clustered at the base of the flowering-stems. The pods are shorter than their stems, and elliptical. Flower-stems leafless, and smooth above but a trifle hairy below. 1-5 inches high.

Hairy Rock Cress.
Arabis hirsuta.

Bitter Cress.
Cardamine pennsylvanica.

Watercress
Nasturtium officinale   White, April-August

A common aquatic plant, much prized for its pungent-tasting young leaves, which are smooth, dark green, or brownish-green in spring, and lighter green in summer. The insignificant white flowers terminate the branching stems. Leaves compound with 3-9 roundish leaflets. The scientific name is from an old Latin name for many cresslike plants. Naturalized from Eurasia. 4-10 inches high. In brooks and small streams everywhere.

Yellow Cress
Rorippa islandica   Yellow, May-August

A yellow-flowered species common everywhere, but naturalized from Europe. The leaves ornamentally cut, of usually seven segments. Pods oblong, about equaling the length of the stems. 1-3 feet high. In wet situations.

Lake Cress
Armoracia aquatica   White, July-August

An aquatic species, the finely dissected leaves under water, the upper, oblong, slightly toothed leaves above it. The white flowers on slender stems, smaller than those of the Horseradish, and in loose clusters. 1-2 feet. Que. to Fla., west to Minn. and Tex.

Horseradish
Armoracia rusticana   White, June-August

A coarse species well known for the immensely strong peppery quality of its large white roots which furnish a favorite table relish. The oblong leaves toothed and roughly veined, the basal ones large. The small white flowers rather conspicuous. Pods nearly round. Escaped from cultivation, into moist ground everywhere; naturalized from Eurasia. 20-30 inches high.

Yellow Rocket or Winter Cress
Barbarea vulgaris   Yellow, April-May

A bright yellow-flowered species with a simple stem terminated by one or more showy spikes of flowers beneath which the long curved seed-pods later appear in a loose cluster. Upper leaves stalkless, lower ones cut in

Whitlow-grass.
Draba verna.

Hedge Mustard.
Sisymbrium officinale.

usually five divisions, the terminal one very large; all deep shining green. The pretty four-petaled flowers with six stamens, four of which are quite prominent, are frequently visited by the early bees and handsome flies. They yield honey and pollen. 1-2 feet high. In moist places along the road, and in meadows nearly everywhere. Naturalized from Europe.

Hedge Mustard
Sisymbrium officinale   Light yellow, May-September

A homely straggling weed with tiny light yellow flowers, and light green, smooth leaves, with 3-6 lobes, irregularly blunt-toothed. The generally smooth stem with tall, widely spreading, wiry branches, tipped with a few flowers and curiously set with the *close-pressing pods.* 1-3 feet high. In waste places throughout our range. Naturalized from Europe.

Charlock or Field Mustard
Brassica kaber   Yellow, May-September

A coarse and vexatious weed in cultivated fields and waste places, adventive from the old country, and widely distributed throughout our range in some of its forms. The light yellow flowers over ½ inch broad, in small terminal clusters. The leaves ovate with few if any lobes, indistinctly or sparsely toothed, with short stems or none at all. The seed-pods ⅔ inch long, contracted between the seeds, and lumpy in contour. 1-2 feet high.

Black Mustard
Brassica nigra   Yellow, June-September

Another common weed in grain fields, and beside the road. A more widely branched plant than the preceding, and with far more deeply lobed leaves; one terminal large division, and generally four lateral ones, all finely toothed. The small *pure* light yellow flowers less than ½ inch broad are frequently visited by the smaller bees; the pistil, much exceeding the stamens in length, adapts the flower to cross-fertilization. The pod is ½ inch long, four-sided, and lies close to the stem; the seeds are black-brown. 2-5 feet high. Naturalized from Europe, and extending throughout our range.

Barbarea
vulgaris.

Leaf of
Field
Mustard. B. kaber.

Black Mustard
Brassica nigra.

White Mustard
Brassica hirta   Yellow, June-August

A similar but rarer species, more or less hairy, with bristly pods, contracted between the seeds; these are light yellow-brown. The flowers are a little larger. 1-2 feet high. In fields and on roadsides, escaped from gardens; naturalized from Europe.

Shepherd's Purse
Capsella Bursa-pastoris   White, April-September

A very common weed, on roadsides near dwellings and on waste ground, with tiny white flowers. The Latin name is literally a *shepherd's little purse,* in allusion to the shape of the tiny seed-pods. The root-leaves are deeply cut, and form a rosette, the stem-leaves are small, lance-shaped, and indistinctly toothed. 8-18 inches high. Naturalized from Europe, and distributed throughout our range.

Wild Peppergrass
Lepidium virginicum   White, May-September

A somewhat similar species, but more branched, remarkable for its peppery-tasting seed-pods which cluster thickly about the flowering stems in a cylindrical curving column beneath the few terminating white flowers. Basal leaves obovate (tapering to a stemlike base) with a few small lateral divisions, stem-leaves small and lance-shaped; all toothed. 6-15 inches high. Common in fields and along roadsides everywhere.

PITCHER PLANT FAMILY. *Sarraceniaceæ.*

Bog plants with pitcherlike leaves, and nodding flowers with 4-5 sepals, five petals, numerous stamens, and one pistil; represented by only one species in the northern United States.

Pitcher Plant
Sarracenia purpurea   Dull dark red, May-June

A curious and interesting plant found in peat-bogs throughout the north. The strange hollow leaves, keeled on the inner side toward the flower-stalk, are usually

Peppergrass.
Lepidium virginicum.

Shepherd's Purse.
Capsella Bursa-pastoris.

partly filled with water and the fragments of insects; the
latter are apparently drowned, and no doubt contribute
to the physical sustenance of the plant; but the raw-meat
coloring, the red veining, and the general form of the
flower are conducive to the attraction of carrion flies,
which are especially fitted for the cross-fertilization of
the flower. The style within the blossom is strangely like
an umbrella with five ribs, the stigmatic surface on the
inside. The folding petals and the flower's drooping position certainly protect the ripening pollen from any disturbance by the elements, but the inquisitive insect finds
easy access to it. The general coloring of the whole plant
is green with red-purple veining; the sepals are madder
purple, and greenish on the inside, the petals are dull
pink, and the umbrellalike style green. The outer surface
of the pitchers is smooth, but the inner surface is covered with fine bristles pointing downward, which mani-
festly interfere with the escape of trapped insects. The
pitchers are circled about the root in radiating lines, and
they measure 4-10 inches in length; the flower-stalk is
frequently a foot high. The plant is commonly found in
the black peat-bogs of wooded hills or in mountain tarns
where there is scant sunshine. When the plant is more
exposed to the sun its green coloring predominates. It
is common north and south, and extends as far west
as Minn.

Trumpets
Sarracenia flava   **Dull yellow, April**

A southern species with elongated, trumpet-shaped
leaves nearly erect, 12-20 inches high. The flowers a
light ochre or dull yellow, the petals narrow, long, and
drooping. 1-3 feet high. Bogs, Va. south to Fla., and
west to La.

SUNDEW FAMILY. *Droseraceæ.*

Bog plants with sticky-hairy leaves which are coated
with a fluid that attracts and retains insects—they are,
in fact, carnivorous. The small flowers are perfect, with
five petals, and few or many stamens with the anthers
turned outward. Fruit a 1- to 5-celled capsule. The tiny
red filaments of the leaves curl and clasp about a captured insect, and ultimately its juices are absorbed.

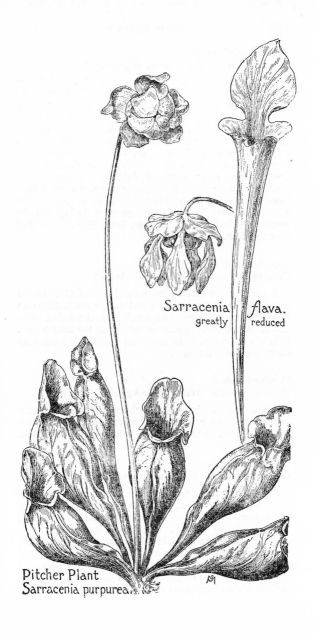

Sarracenia flava.
greatly reduced

Pitcher Plant
Sarracenia purpurea.

Round-leaved Sundew
Drosera rotundifolia   White, July-August

A *very* small plant with long-stemmed round leaves
lying close to or upon the ground, both leaf and stem
covered with long, fine red hairs. The red flower-stalk
is erect and smooth, and bears about four or six small
white flowers, which are frequently visited by the fungous
gnats and other small woodland insects. The flower-
cluster is one-sided, bends over, and the blossoms open
one at a time only in the sunshine. The glands of the
leaves exude clear drops of fluid, which appear like
small dewdrops; hence the popular name, also the Greek
δροσερός, meaning dewy. The whole plant is so saturated
with color that its sap stains paper a ruddy madder
purple. 4-9 inches high. In bogs, from Que., south, and
west to Mont.

Long-leaved Sundew
Drosera intermedia   White, July-August

A very similar species, but with elongated blunt-tipped
leaves whose stalks are long and rather erect. Differing
further from the preceding species by the naked leaf-
stalks, the red hairs appearing only upon the little leaves.
It is not so common as the other species, but occupies
about the same territory.

Slender Sundew
Drosera linearis   White, July-August

A northern species with 3-inch-long, slender or linear
leaves, also with naked, erect stalks. The white flowers
are few. Newf. to Que., west to Mich., Wisc. and Minn.

Thread-leaved Sundew
Drosera filiformis   Purple-magenta, July-September

The leaves of this larger species are merely threadlike
with no distinct stalk; they are glandular, red-hairy
throughout, the hairs terminated by a red bead or dot.
The flowers are fully ½ inch broad, and dull purple-
magenta. There are many in the cluster. 8-18 inches high.
In wet sand near the seacoast, from Mass., south. Found
in the pine barrens of N. J. Nothing is more dainty and
beautiful under the magnifying-glass than the spun-glass-
like, glandular, ruby hairs of the *Droseras*.

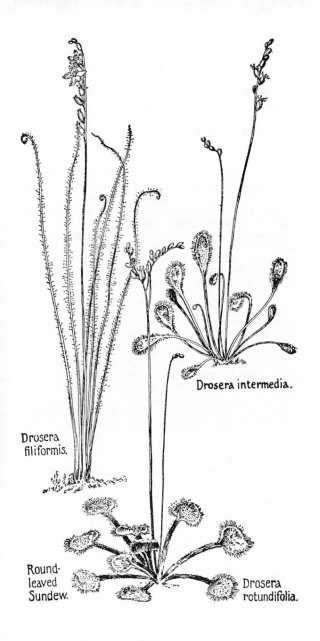

Drosera filiformis.

Drosera intermedia.

Round-
leaved
Sundew.

Drosera
rotundifolia.

ORPINE FAMILY. *Crassulaceæ.*

Rather fleshy or succulent herbs, with absolutely symmetrical small flowers; the petals, sepals, pistils, and stamens equal in number, or the last double in number. A common garden plant in this family is the houseleek.

Ditch Stonecrop
Penthorum sedoides   Yellow-green, July-September

A familiar weed of ditches and swamps with insignificant greenish-yellow, or yellow-green flowers, in slender bending clusters of 2-3 branches, at the top of the erect stalk. The latter is smooth, usually branched, and bears lance-shaped, or elliptical, pointed, light green leaves, finely toothed. The flower has five sepals but rarely any petals, ten stamens, and five pistils united below, finally forming a five-angled seed-vessel. Not fleshy-leaved. 8-20 inches high. Me., west to Minn., south to Fla. and Tex.

Wild Stonecrop
Sedum ternatum   White, April-June

A small species at home on rocky ledges and in stony woodlands from New Eng. to Ga., west to Mich. and Ark. It has little five-petaled white flowers growing on horizontally spreading branches. The leaves are small, toothless, fleshy, and rather wedge-shaped; the lower ones are generally in groups of three. The flower-cluster is three-spiked and leafy. 3-8 inches high. The name is from *sedeo,* to sit.

Live-forever or Garden Orpine
Sedum purpureum   Dull garnet-red, June-September

A common perennial, with a stout light green stem and very smooth, fleshy, dull-toothed leaves, which children are fond of splitting by lateral pressure with the fingers and forming into green "purses." It is adventive from Eurasia, and is generally an escape from gardens, establishing itself in fields and on roadsides. The small flowers in thick clusters are opaque crimson. 10-18 inches high. Common. Closely related to *Sedum telephium,* which is somewhat shorter and has paler flowers; also Eurasian and an escape from gardens.

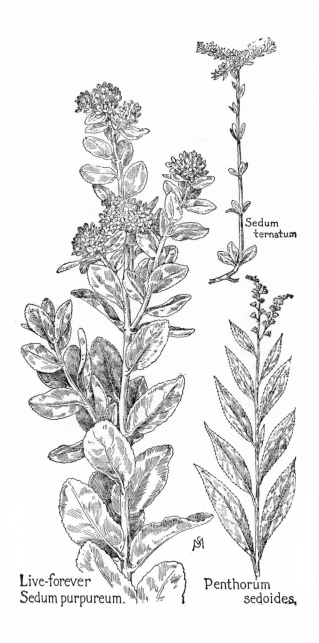

Sedum
ternatum

Live-forever
Sedum purpureum.

Penthorum
sedoides.

SAXIFRAGE FAMILY. *Saxifrageæ.*

A large family of herbs or shrubs related to the family *Rosaceæ,* but differing from it by having albumen in the seeds, and *opposite* as well as alternate leaves. The flowers are mostly perfect with usually five petals; fertilized by the aid of the smaller bees, flies, or in some instances butterflies. Among common shrubs are the hydrangea and the currant.

Early Saxifrage
Saxifraga virginiensis   White, April-May

A little plant hugging the rocks on hillsides and blooming along with the first flowers of spring; the buds are formed early, and appear like little (fine-haired) balls in the center of the rosettelike clusters of obovate leaves close to the ground. Eventually a cluster expands to a branching downy stalk bearing many little white, five-petaled, perfect flowers with ten yellow stamens. The flowers are succeeded by rather odd and pretty madder purple seed-vessels which are two-beaked; often the color is madder brown. 4-10 inches high. N. B., south to Ga., and west to Manitoba and Ark.

Swamp Saxifrage
Saxifraga pennsylvanica   Greenish-white, May

A much larger plant with less attractive, greenish-white flowers with very narrow (linear) petals. The stem is somewhat sticky-hairy and stout. The larger blunt lance-shaped leaves are scarcely toothed, and are narrowed to a rather broad stalk. 12-30 inches high. In bogs and on wet banks from Me., south to Va., and west to Minn. and Iowa. The name saxifrage is from *Saxifragus,* meaning a rock or stone breaker from its habitat in the crevices of rocks.

There are at least 12 other saxifrages within our area, but their differences and ranges should be sought in the technical manuals.

———

False Mitrewort, Foamflower, or Coolwort
Tiarella cordifolia   White, Late April-early June

An attractive little plant that decorates the moist woodland floor with its ornamental leaves all through the summer. The feathery spike of fine white flowers with

Early Saxifrage.   Saxifraga virginiensis.

five petals appears conspicuously above the leaves in late spring or early summer; the ten prominent stamens have orange anthers, and the long pistil in the center is white. The leaves remotely resemble those of the mountain maple, but they are small, rough-hairy over the upper surface, and dark green, sometimes mottled with a brownish tone. The little seed-capsule is characteristically cloven like a tiara, hence the name; the heart-shaped form of the leaf accounts for the specific *cordifolia*. 6-12 inches high. In rich woods, from Nova Scotia, south along the mountains to Ga. and Ala., and west to Mich. Common in the woods of the White Mountains.

Mitrewort or Bishop's Cap
Mitella diphylla   White, April-May

The true mitrewort is very easily distinguished from the false, by several marked differences. Halfway up the stem are two opposite leaves nearly if not quite stalkless. The flowers, instead of being borne on rather long individual stems in a thin feathery cluster, are short-stemmed and distinctly separated; the tiny white blossom has five petals beautifully fringed which remind one of a highly ornamental snow crystal. This plant is also hairy throughout. The name means *a little mitre,* alluding to the mitre-shape of the seed-pod. 8-16 inches high. Rich woods, Que., south to N. C. and Ala., and west to Minn. and Mo.

Naked Mitrewort or Bishop's Cap
Mitella nuda   Greenish-white, April-June

A much smaller and daintier species distinguished by its naked stem, which is without the two leaves and is slightly hairy. The leaves approach a somewhat round form, and the snow-crystal-like flowers are greenish-white, and few. They have ten yellow stamens. 4-7 inches high. In cool woods and mossy bogs, from Labrador south to Pa., and west to Mont.

Alumroot
Heuchera americana   Whitish-green, May-July

A stout and tall plant bearing some resemblance to *Mitella nuda* on a large scale, but the flowers are dis-

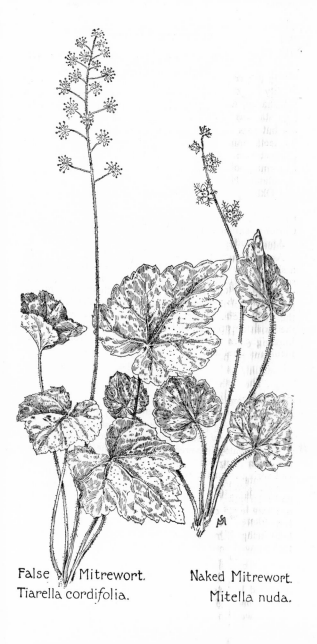

False   Mitrewort.   Naked Mitrewort.
Tiarella cordifolia.   Mitella nuda.

tinctly different; they are borne in a long loose cluster, usually 4-5 on one of the small branching stems, small, bell-shaped, with inconspicuous green petals, very prominent stamens tipped with orange anthers, of which there are but five. The leaves are heart-shaped and scalloped; the teeth blunt. The stem is more or less hairy, and is 2-3 feet high. Named for Johann Heinrich von Heucher, a German botanist of the early eighteenth century. Rocky woodlands, New Eng., west to Minn., south to Ala., La. and Okla.

Golden Saxifrage
Chrysosplenium americanum   Yellow or purple-green, April-June

An insignificant plant of cold bogs or wet places, with a slender low-growing, forking stem, with roundish fine-scalloped generally opposite-growing leaves, and fine yellowish or purplish-green flowers with orange anthers; growing close between the points where the leaves join the plant stem. In wet shady places, Que., south along the mountains to Va., and west to Mont. Stems 3-7 inches long. The name means *golden spleen*, from reputed medicinal qualities.

Grass of Parnassus
Parnassia glauca   White green-veined, June-September

An interesting perennial herb with single cream-white flowers delicately veined with green, about 1 inch broad. A single ovate olive-green leaf clasps the flowering stem; the others are long, slender-stalked and heart-shaped, and spring from the root. The flower has five petals and five straw-yellow anthers terminating the fertile stamens and alternating with the petals; a number (perhaps 15) of abortive stamens encircle the green pistil. The blossom is visited by bees and the smallest butterflies (skippers). 8-20 inches high. In bogs and wet meadows, Que., south to Va., west to S. D. and Iowa.

Heuchera
americana.

Chrysosplenium
americanum.

Grass of Parnassus.
Parnassia glauca.

ROSE FAMILY. *Rosaceæ.*

A family of over 3,000 species, highly esteemed for its luscious fruits, such as apple, pear, quince, cherry, plum and peach, and for its most beautiful flowers, such as the rose, flowering cherries, and the hawthorns. They are dependent in a great measure upon the bees for cross-fertilization. The flowers are extraordinarily rich in pollen and honey; the raspberry yields the finest flavored honey which is known. The leaves are alternate-growing, and accompanied by stipules, or small leafy formations at the base of the leaf-stalk. The flowers are regular and generally perfect, with usually five sepals and as many petals (seldom more or less), numerous stamens, and one or many pistils. Rarely the petals are absent. The family is very closely allied to *Saxifragaceæ* and *Fabaceæ.* It is mostly composed of trees and shrubs, although the herbaceous members are many, some of which it is impossible to include here, as the technical manuals list over 400 species within our area.

Meadowsweet
Spiræa latifolia Flesh-pink, June-August

A common flower on the borders of the road, in bloom throughout the early summer. A shrub with light green, nearly smooth, ovate, sharply toothed leaves, and a usually yellowish-buff stem of a wiry character, upon which are freely set the alternate leaves. The beautiful flower-spike is pyramidal but blunt and branching, and is closely crowded with flesh-pink and white flowers resembling miniature apple-blossoms, with prominent pink-red stamens. It is frequently visited by the smaller butterflies and the bees, and possesses a slight fragrance. The name is from the Greek, for a wreath. 2-4 feet high. Newf., south to S. C., and west to Mich.

Hardhack or Steeplebush
Spiræa tomentosa Deep pink, July-September

A similar species, but readily distinguished by its woolly stem (terra-cotta red) and leaves; the latter are olive-green of a dark tone above, and very whitish and woolly beneath. The slender steeplelike flower-spike is crowded with tiny, *deep* rosy pink flowers, smaller than those of the preceding species; the succession of bloom is unfortunately slow, and *downward,* so the top of the

202

Meadowsweet.
Spiræa latifolia.

Hardhack.
Spiræa tomentosa.

spike is often in a half-withered condition. 2-4 feet high.
In dry or wet ground, Nova Scotia to N. C., west to
Minn. and Ark.

————

Queen-of-the-Prairie
Filipendula rubra   Deep pink, June-July

A tall western species, also in cultivation, with handsome, fragrant, deep pink, or peach-blossom-colored flowers, and cut-lobed, deep green, smooth, large leaves of
sometimes seven divisions. It grows in moist situations
or on the prairies. The terminal leaflet is larger than the
others. The large compound flower-cluster of perfect fine-
petaled flowers is feathery in character. 2-8 feet high.
N. Y., south to N. C. and Ky., west to Wisc. and Minn.
An escape to roadsides further east.

————

Goat's Beard
Aruncus dioicus   Yellowish-white, May-July

Another tall and handsome species with a compound
flower-spike formed of many little spikes about as large
around as one's little finger. The tiny narrow-petaled
flowers are yellowish-white, and are an exception to the
general rule of the family, as they are staminate on one
plant and pistillate upon another. The stem is smooth
and the deep green leaves are compound, with sometimes
eleven small leaflets. The pistillate flower has usually
three distinct pistils. 3-6 feet high. In rich woods, Pa.,
south to Ala., and west to Ark.

————

Purple-flowering Raspberry
Rubus odoratus   Crimson-pink or magenta-pink, June-
August

A shrubby roadside species which suffers with a mis-
leading name, the rose family rarely producing a true
purple flower. This big-leaved plant exhibits a wild-
roselike flower of five broad petals whose color is at first
deep crimson-pink, and at last a faded magenta-pink.
The large maplelike leaves are 3-5 lobed and a trifle
hairy. The stem is covered with short red or brown
bristly hairs; the flower-stalks are particularly red, as
well as the calyx, or flower-envelope. The fruit is insipid
and resembles a flat, red raspberry; it is often called

Queen-of-the-Prairie.
Filipendula rubra.

Goat's Beard.
Aruncus dioicus.

Purple-flowering
    Raspberry.
Rubus odoratus.

Cloud berry.
Rubus
Chamaemorus.

Thimble-berry. 3-5 feet high. Common in stony woodlands, beside the shaded road, and in copses. Nova Scotia,
south to N. C., and west to Mich. The name *rubus* is an
ancient one for bramble, from *ruber,* red.

Cloudberry, or Mountain Raspberry
Rubus Chamæmorus   White, June-July

One of the interesting relatives of the common raspberry which finds its home among the clouds of high
mountain-tops. It is found in the peat bogs of N. B.,
and eastern Me. and N. H. The cloudberry is another
instance of a break in the family rule: the flowers are
staminate on one plant and pistillate on another. The
solitary white flower is about an inch broad. The plant-
stem is herbaceous, not shrubby, and the leaves are
rather roundish with 5-9 lobes; the stem is unbranched
and with only 2-3 leaves. The fruit is a pale wine-red,
or when nearly ripe, amber color, and possesses a delicate
flavor; the lobes are few. 3-10 inches high. Wild black-
berries and raspberries, which also belong to the genus
Rubus, are legion, and so confused that even the technical
manuals do not agree as to their identities.

Dewdrop
Dalibarda repens   White, June-September

A delicate woodland plant with a white blossom like
that of the wild strawberry, and densely woolly or fine-
hairy stems and leaves; the latter are dark green, heart-
shaped, and wavy or scallop-toothed. In form they closely
resemble those of the common blue violet. The 1-2 white
flowers about ½ inch in diameter are borne on long,
fuzzy, sometimes ruddy stems; it is said that they fertilize
in the bud before opening. 2-4 inches high. In the
northern woods, from Que., south to southern N. J.,
and west to Ohio and Minn.

White Avens
Geum canadense   White, June-August

A rather tall, fine-hairy plant with angular, branching
stem, insignificant five-petaled white flowers, and three-
divided leaves, except the simple uppermost ones; the
root-leaves of 3-5 leaflets, all toothed. The flowers succeeded by a burlike, densely bristly seed-receptable. 18-24
inches high. On the borders of woods and shaded roads.

Dewdrop.
Dalibarda repens.

Common from Nova Scotia to Ga., west to Minn. and Tex.

Rough Avens
Geum virginianum   Cream-white, May-July

A bristly hairy-stemmed plant common in low grounds and on the borders of low damp woods, with flowers and leaves similar to those of the preceding species. The stem very stout. The flower has inconspicuous cream-white petals which roll backward. Mass. to N. C., west to Ind. and Tenn.

Geum aleppicum strictum   Golden-yellow, July-August

A slightly hairy species with compound lower leaves, the leaflets wedge-shaped with round tips, the upper leaves with 3-5 leaflets irregular, oblong, and acute. Flowers golden-yellow. Fruit-receptacle downy. Moist meadows, Newf. south to N. J., west to Minn. and N. Mex.

Purple Avens
Geum rivale   Brownish-purple, July-August

An aquatic or marsh species, with lyre-shaped root-leaves, and irregular compound upper leaves; the stem-leaves few, and three-lobed. The nodding flowers brownish- or rusty-purple, with obovate petals terminating with a claw. 2 feet high. Bogs and wet meadows, Newf. south to N. J., west to Alberta.

Long-plumed Avens
Geum triflorum   Dull crimson-red, May-July

An exceedingly pretty and graceful but rare avens, with a decorative, deeply cut leaf, and a ruddy flower-stalk generally bearing three ruddy flowers with scarcely opened, acute, erect calyx-lobes. The fruit is daintily plumed with gray feathery hairs, about an inch long. 6-12 inches high. Dry or rocky soil. Western N. Y. west to Minn., B. C. and N. Mex.

Geum Peckii   Yellow, July-early September

This is a dwarf species with smooth stem and showy pure yellow flowers quite an inch broad, which is found on Mt. Washington, and other high peaks in the north. The ornamental roundish leaves are nearly smooth—except the veins. Also on the high mountains of Great Smoky National Park.

Avens.

Geum triflorum.   Geum Peckii.

Wild Virginia Strawberry
Fragaria virginiana   White, April-June

Our commonest wild strawberry, at home in the rough dry pasture lands of the north and south. Rather broad, coarsely toothed leaflets, blunt-tipped, and hairy. The flower-stalk not longer than the leaves, and with spreading hairs. The flower has many orange-yellow stamens offset by the five round white petals. The scarlet fruit is ovoid, and the tiny seeds are imbedded in pits over the surface. 3-6 inches high. Common in some of its forms throughout our range; generally in fields. The name from the Latin *fraga,* fragrant.

American Wood Strawberry
Fragaria vesca var. americana   White, May-July

A slender species with thin leaflets which are more ovate and less wedge-shaped than those of the other species, and have silk-silvery hairs on the under side. The scarlet fruit is more conical, and the seeds are borne, not in pits, but upon the shining, smooth surface. The sepals are reflexed or turned backward from the fruit. This species is remarkable for its very long, delicate runners. 3-6 inches high. In rocky woodlands and pastures. From Que. to Va., west to Ind. and Ohio., and in the Rockies.

Fragaria virginiana var. *illinœnsis* is a western form found from Ind. to Minn., and south to La. and Ala. It is larger than the typical *F. virginiana,* and the fine woolly hairs on the flower stems are mostly wide-spreading; those on *F. virginiana* are somewhat loosely set against the stem. The typical *F. vesca* is a stocky plant with strongly veined, deeply toothed light green leaflets, and the fruit is broadly conic or nearly globular. The common garden strawberry, *F. chilœnse* var. *ananassa,* often escapes from cultivation, but rarely persists.

Norway Cinquefoil
Potentilla norvegica   Yellow, June-September

A weedy plant differing from the common cinquefoil by an *extremely* hairy stem and leaf; the latter is composed also of three leaflets instead of five, and it slightly suggests the strawberry leaf. The five not very conspicuous petals are somewhat isolated in the green setting of the flower, which is very leafy in character. There are

Wild Virginia Strawberry.
Fragaria virginiana.

American
Wood Strawberry.
Fragaria vesca var americana.

15-20 stamens. 12-30 inches high. In dry or waste ground everywhere and probably introduced from Europe. The name is from *potens* for the plant's reputed medicinal powers.

Rough-fruited Cinquefoil
Potentilla recta   Yellow, June-September

A similar stout plant, with a characteristically rough, horned seed-vessel. The five rather narrow leaflets are deep green, very hairy beneath, and slightly so above. The flowers are pure yellow, and ¾ inch broad; the petals are much larger than the lobes of the calyx (flower-envelope), which is the reverse of the case with the Norway cinquefoil. Erect, 1-2 feet high. Adventive from Europe, and in the vicinity of old gardens and waste grounds. Que. to N. C., and west to Minn.

Silvery Cinquefoil
Potentilla argentea   Yellow, May-September

A small species remarkable for its silvery character. The leaflets are dark green above and silver-white beneath. The stem is also covered with the silky white wool, beneath which appears the pale terra-cotta tint of its surface. The five wedge-shaped, narrow leaflets are rolled back at the edge and quite deeply cut. The pure yellow flowers are rather small, and loosely clustered at the ends of the branches. 5-12 inches long. In dry and sterile fields, or sandy soil, Nova Scotia south to Va., and west to Mont. A native of Eurasia.

Potentilla Robbinsiana   Yellow, June-August

A dwarf Alpine species found on the summits of the White Mountains, rather soft-hairy when young, but smooth later, and with three coarsely toothed leaflets, deep green and somewhat broad. The small yellow flowers are slender-stemmed and generally solitary. 1-3 inches high. Found about the Lake of the Clouds and elsewhere on Mt. Washington.

Potentilla tridentata   White, June-August

Potentilla tridentata, also found on Mt. Washington and Mt. Wachusett, is less dwarfed, but low-growing. The three leaflets are *coarsely three-toothed* at the tip, smooth and thick. The flowers are white. 1-10 inches high. Greenland to Conn., west to Mich. and Minn.; also occasional in the mountains to Ga.

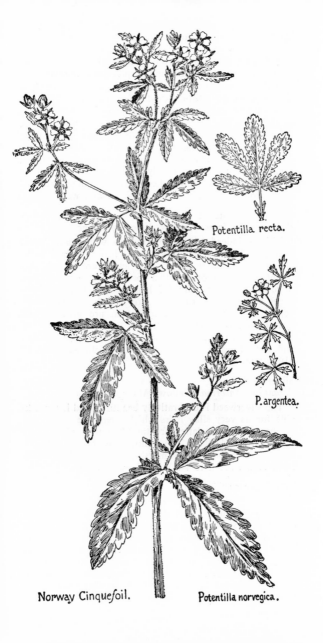

Potentilla recta.

P. argentea.

Norway Cinquefoil.　　　Potentilla norvegica.

Marsh Five-finger or Purple Cinquefoil
Potentilla palustris   Magenta-purple, June-August

This is the only purple-flowered five-finger and it is therefore readily distinguished from the others. The reddish stem is stout, mostly smooth, and a trifle woody at the base. The leaves have from 5-7 leaflets which are blunt-tipped, and sharp-toothed. The rather pretty flowers are magenta-purple within and pale or greenish without, through the influence of the somewhat longer green sepals; the blossom is nearly one inch broad, and its petals are pointed. 6-20 inches long. In swamps and cold bogs, from Greenland south to N. J., and west to Cal.

Shrubby Cinquefoil
Potentilla fruticosa   Yellow, June-September

This is indeed a shrubby species with nearly erect stems, tan-brown in color, and quite leafy; the bark is inclined to peel off in shreds. The leaves are entirely different from those of the other species; they are toothless, olive-yellow green, with 5-7 lance-shaped leaflets whose edges curve backward. They are silky-hairy. The deep yellow flowers, with rounded petals, are generally an inch broad. 1-2 feet high. It is a troublesome weed in N. Y., western Vt., Mass., and parts of the west. Swamps and wet places, Labrador, south to N. J., and west to Minn. and N. Mex.

Silverweed
Potentilla Anserina   Yellow, May-September

The silverweed is decoratively beautiful, and is remarkable for its very silky hairs which cover the under side of the leaves; the latter are tansylike with about 7-23 sharp-toothed leaflets. The yellow flowers are solitary. Stem 1-3 feet long. In salt marshes and on wet meadows, from Newf. south to N. Y., and west to Iowa.

Five-finger or Cinquefoil
Potentilla simplex   Yellow, April-August

The commonest of all the five-fingers, often wrongly called wild strawberry, with pure yellow flowers about ½ inch broad. It decorates meadow and pasture, fertile and sterile grounds, and weaves its embroidery over the stony and barren roadside. Its five deep green, shiny, long-stalked leaflets are sharply toothed, firm and smooth, altogether harder in character than the three strawberry leaflets. The whole plant is generally smooth, but some-

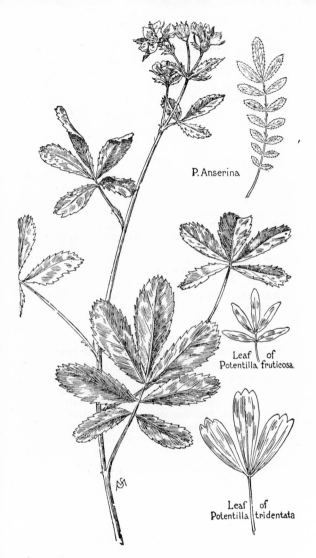

P. Anserina

Leaf of
Potentilla fruticosa.

Leaf of
Potentilla tridentata

Purple Cinquefoil.
Potentilla palustris.

times thinly hairy. Flowers solitary, fertilized mostly by
flies. Runners 6-20 inches long. Common everywhere in
the north. From Newf. to Ala., west to Minn. and Tex.
A common similar species is *Potentilla canadensis,* which
is fine-woolly over the stems, and does not creep over
the ground so characteristically as *P. simplex.*

Agrimony
Agrimonia gryposepala   Yellow, June-August

A most common weed with a glandular-hairy simple
stem, and compound leaves with a hairy stalk; spicy-
odored when crushed. The usually seven bright green,
many-ribbed ovate leaflets coarsely toothed; the inter-
posed tiny leaflets are ovate and toothed; there are generally three pairs occupying the spaces between the
larger lateral leaflets. The slender spikes of five-petaled
yellow flowers with orange anthers are not showy. The
seeds are sticky and adhere to one's clothing. 2-4 feet or
more high. Common on the borders of woods and in
thickets. Me., south to N. C., and west to Mich.; also
in N. Mex.

Indian Physic
Gillenia trifoliata   White or pale pink, May-June

Sometimes called Bowman's root, from its reputed
medicinal value, this is an erect, branched or unbranched
herb, from 18-30 inches high, with a thick rootstock and
nearly smooth stem. Leaves with 3 leaflets, their margins
doubly toothed, i.e., the teeth are themselves toothed.
Flowers in a lax, loose cluster, the petals narrow and
pointed, the dry fruits hairy, purple and red. Mostly in
the mountains from Ont. to Ga., west to Ky. and Ala.
Named for Arnold Gillen, German botanist.

Burnet
Sanguisorba canadensis   White, July-September

A showy, midsummer-blooming herb, 20-35 inches high,
always growing in wet or moist places. Leaves compound,
the 7-15 leaflets distinctly stalked and with fine marginal
teeth. At the end of the usually branched stem is a long,
finger-thick cluster of tiny white flowers crowded into a
feathery spike 1½-4 inches long, borne on a long naked

Agrimony.
Agrimonia gryposepala.

Cinquefoil.
Potentilla simplex.

stalk. Fruit dry, scarcely ⅛ inch long. Newf. to N. J., south along the mountains to N. C., west to Ohio, Ind. and Manitoba. Named from *sanguis,* blood, and *sorbere,* to absorb, in allusion to reputed styptic properties.

False Spirea
Sorbaria sorbifolia White, July

This shrublike herb or herblike shrub grows from 3-5 feet high and looks like a miniature mountain ash (*Sorbus*); hence its Latin name of *Sorbaria*—like a mountain ash. It is an Asiatic plant, commonly cultivated, and is to be looked for as an escape along roadsides or other disturbed places. It has leaves with 6-8 pairs of tapering, sharply toothed leaflets and a branched, dense cluster of small white flowers suggesting those of *Spiræa,* hence its common name of false spirea. It is closely related to the Indian physic, and has small dry fruits very different from the colored berries of the mountain ash.

PEA FAMILY. *Fabaceæ.*

An enormous family of plants comprising about 10,000 species, mostly tropical. Common garden examples are the sweet pea, locust, wisteria, lupine, and among foods the pea, bean and lentil. Sometimes called the pulse family, or *Leguminosæ.* They have butterflylike flowers, and alternate, usually compound leaves, generally without teeth. The flowers are perfect and are borne singly or in spikes; they are fertilized largely by bees and butterflies.

Wild Indigo
Baptisia tinctoria Yellow, June-August

A smooth and slender plant with deep gray-green leaves of three wedge-shaped leaflets covered with a slight bloom; they are almost stalkless. The small pealike blossoms are pure yellow, and terminate the many branches of the upright stem. The flowers are visited by the butterflies, flies, the honeybee and the leaf-cutter bee. The plant grows with a bushy luxuriance in favorable situations, and has a most remarkable habit of turning black upon withering. 18-28 inches high. In dry sandy soil everywhere.

Indian
Physic.

Sorbaria.

Burnet.

Blue False Indigo
Baptisia australis   Light violet, June-July

A beautiful, tall, and western species, with pale green smooth stem, light green wedge-shaped, short-stalked leaves with 3 leaflets, and loose flower-clusters, sometimes 10 inches long, of light, dull violet blossoms quite 1 inch long, of a soft, æsthetic hue. The peapodlike fruit is tipped with a spur. Plant 3-6 feet high. On rich alluvial soil, western Pa., south to Ga., and west to Mo., Ark. and Tex. Quite handsome in cultivation and sometimes escaping in the north.

———

Rattlebox
Crotalaria sagittalis   Yellow, June-August

The rattlebox, so named because the seeds rattle about in the boxlike, inflated, sepia-black pods, has oval pointed leaves, toothless and nearly stalkless, growing alternately along the bending stem. The yellow flowers are scarcely ½ inch long. The stems and edges of the leaves are soft-hairy. 4-12 inches high. In dry sandy soil everywhere, but not very common.

———

Blue Lupin
Lupinus perennis   Violet, May-June

This is one of our most charming wild flowers, but many western relatives are far more showy and very numerous. The pealike blossom has violet or deep purple wings and a light violet hood veined with blue-violet. Rarely the sweet-scented flowers are magenta-pink or even white. The horse-chestnutlike leaf has generally eight narrow, light green leaflets. Stem and long-stalked leaves are generally fine-hairy, and frequently show a few touches of purple-red through the green. The flower-spike is quite showy, and pinkish early in the bud. 1-2 feet high. In sandy fields, Me. to Fla., west to Minn. and La. The Texas bluebonnet is a related species.

———

Rabbit-foot or Stone Clover
Trifolium arvense   Gray-pink, August-September

A naturalized species of clover, originally from Eurasia, remarkable for its oblong fuzzy flower-heads, the corolla of which is green-white and the calyx green with

Baptisia
tinctoria.

Blue
False Indigo.
Baptisia australis.

Crotalaria
sagittalis.

Blue Lupin.
Lupinus perennis.

Rabbit-foot Clover.   Trifolium arvense.

pink tips, all in effect rather gray-pink. The light green triple leaves have narrow, long leaflets with blunt tips. The flowers are sweet-scented. 4-10 inches high. Common in poor soil, old fields, and pastures everywhere.

Red Clover
Trifolium pratense   Crimson or magenta, May-September

This is our commonest field clover and a special favorite of the bumblebee upon whom it is almost wholly dependent for fertilization. The three (rarely 4-5) rather soft, dull bluish-green leaflets are conspicuously marked by a whitish or yellow-green triangle. There are two hairy white and green stipules or leafy wings at the base of the leaf-stalk. Stem and leaves are soft-hairy. The somewhat pyramidal globular flower-head ranges through crimson or magenta to paler tints of the same colors, and even white; it yields a plentiful supply of nectar, which is scarcely reached by the short tongues of honey-bees or the butterflies. The burly bumblebee is therefore the best pollen disseminator of this particular clover. 8-24 inches high. Common in fields and on roadsides, everywhere.

White Clover
Trifolium repens   Cream-white, May-October

This is also one of our most common clovers, and a permanent resident of the grassy roadside. It is generally smooth, with roundish or heart-shaped leaflets marked less distinctly with a triangle, and frequently 4-5 leaflets are found on a single stalk. The globular flower-heads are a translucent cream-white, and the florets are sometimes more or less tinted with flesh pink. Eventually the florets are reflexed. Fertilized by bees, and rich in honey. It is the florists' substitute for the Shamrock of Ireland. 4-10 inches long. Creeping by runners. Common everywhere. A widespread variety of it, the Ladino clover, is common in pastures and often escapes. It is a larger-leaved, more robust form.

Alsike or Alsatian Clover
Trifolium hybridum   Creamy rose-pink, May-October

A species somewhat similar to our white clover, but with a branching, stout, and rather juicy stem. The leaflets are generally obovate but not reverse heart-shaped; i.e., with the lobed tip. The edges are finely toothed, and the

Red Clover.
Trifolium pratense.

surface is not marked with the triangle; a pair of flaring stipules or leafy wings are at the base of the leaf-stalk. Flower-heads similar to those of white clover but varying from pinkish-cream to crimson-pink; the withered florets brownish and turning downward, extremely sweet-scented, and rich in honey. 1-2 feet high. On roadsides and in waste places everywhere.

Yellow or Hop Clover
Trifolium agrarium **Pale golden-yellow, June-September**

A small annual species, with a smooth stem and light green, narrow and long leaflets, scarcely suggesting the clover-leaf. The stem is branched and stands nearly upright, or reclines; the leaflets are very finely but rather imperceptibly toothed. The small, dull golden-yellow florets bloom from the base of the flower-head upward, and the withered florets, turning downward and becoming brownish, resemble dried hops. 6-15 inches high. On roadsides and fields everywhere.

Low Hop Clover
Trifolium procumbens **Pale golden-yellow, June-September**

Similar in many respects to the foregoing, but lower, more spreading, and the stems and leaves fine-hairy. The leaflets are shorter and blunt-tipped, the middle one slightly stemmed and the lateral ones stemless. The stipules (leafy formations at the base of the leaf-stalks) are broader than those of the preceding species; they are pointed ovate. The tiny standard of the floret is wide-spread, and not curled up at the edges as in *T. agrarium*. 3-6 inches high. Occasional or common everywhere, especially on roadsides.

———

Yellow Melilot
Melilotus officinalis **Light golden-yellow, June-August**

This is sometimes called yellow sweet clover, but its resemblance to clover is in its character rather than its aspect. It is a foreign flower which has established itself in all waste places especially in our seaport towns. The three leaflets are long, blunt-tipped, and toothed. The light golden-yellow flowers are strung along in a delicate spike. The stem is smooth and 2-4 feet high. *Melilotus alba* is a similar, taller, white-flowered species. Both common everywhere.

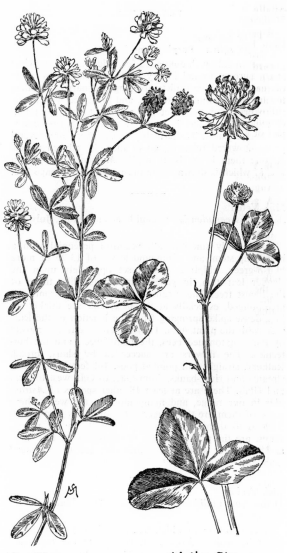

Hop Clover.
Trifolium agrarium.

Alsike Clover.
Trifolium hybridum.

Alfalfa or Lucerne
Medicago sativa　Purple, June-August

A perennial much cultivated for fodder and naturalized from Europe. Found in dry fields and sandy wastes in the east. The three leaflets are long and narrow, toothed toward the tip which is obtuse, and furnished with a tiny sharp bristle; each leaflet has a distinct stalk, and that of the middle leaflet is bent upward. The purple florets in short clusters. 12-25 inches high. There are several yellow-flowered relatives, all of them introduced weeds. Among them is the black medic, *Medicago lupulina,* a leaf of which is shown in the illustration facing page 232.

―――――

Milk Vetch
Astragalus canadensis　Greenish cream-yellow, July-
　　August

A generally smooth, tall, beautiful perennial with a branching stem, and compound leaves of 13-25 or more bluish-green, elliptical leaflets set oppositely upon the slender leaf-stem, in general appearance like those of the locust tree. The cream-yellow slender blossoms are green-tinged, especially at the base, and are thickly set in a dense spike springing from the junction of the leaf-stalk with the plant stem. They are cross-fertilized mostly by the long-tongued bees, the bumblebees, and the butterflies. The flowers are succeeded by short, broad, leathery, straight and pointed pods. 1-4 feet high. Along streams and river-banks, from Que. to Ga., west to Tex. and Utah. There are at least 18 other species of *Astragalus* in our range, and many more in the west, where some of them are the dangerously poisonous loco-weeds. Related to them, and confined generally to the prairie states, are the prairie clovers (*Petalostemon*). For these and the other species of *Astragalus,* see the technical manuals.

―――――

Tick Trefoil
Desmodium nudiflorum　Pale magenta or lilac, July-
　　August

A common weed which flourishes in dry woods. The generally leafless flower-stem rises from the root, and bears a scattered cluster of very small magenta-pink or lilac flowers, the broad upper petals of which are notched at the apex and turned backward, the lower narrow ones

Alfalfa.
Medicago sativa.

Yellow Melilot.
Melilotus officinalis.

are lilac and white; the stamens are prominent. The
flower is fertilized by honeybees and many other smaller
bees. The stout, shorter leaf-stalk is terminated by the
leaf-clusters, of three ovate, toothless leaflets. The hairy
two-jointed pods or seed-vessels stick to one's clothing
or are distributed by some similar means of transportation. 18-25 inches high. In woodlands from Me., south
to Fla., and west to Minn.

Desmodium glutinosum   Pale magenta, June-September

This species has similar flowers, but they are considerably larger and borne on a slender stalk which rises from
the plant-stem at the point where the leaf-stalks spring
outward. The broad, pointed leaflets are much larger and
a trifle hairy. The strange seed-pod like that of the foregoing species is 2-3 jointed. The name is from δεσμός,
a chain, alluding to the connecting joints of the pod.
1-4 feet high. Nova Scotia to Ga., west to Tex.

Desmodium rotundifolium   Purple-magenta, July-September

The stem of this silky-hairy tick trefoil bends or lies
near the ground. The leaflets are quite round, comparatively speaking, soft-hairy, and *not* pointed. The flowers
are light purple-magenta, and the pod 3-5 jointed, constricted nearly equally at both edges. 2-5 feet long. About
the same distribution.

Desmodium Dillenii   Pale magenta, June-September

This species has oblong lance-shaped leaflets, or quite
ovate ones, nearly if not quite smooth above, an erect and
nearly smooth stem, and branching flower-stalks bearing
very small pale magenta flowers. Pods 2-4 jointed, the
sections nearly triangular. 2-3 feet high. Me. to Fla.,
west to Wisc. and Tex.

Desmodium paniculatum   Pale magenta, July-September

A still narrower-leaved species, the deep green leaflets
scarcely 2 inches long, and linear lance-shaped, resembling willow leaves. The flower-spikes are rather horizontally branched; pale magenta flowers very small.
Pods 4-6 jointed. The slender stem 2-3 feet high. Common throughout the eastern states and west to Kan. and
Tex.

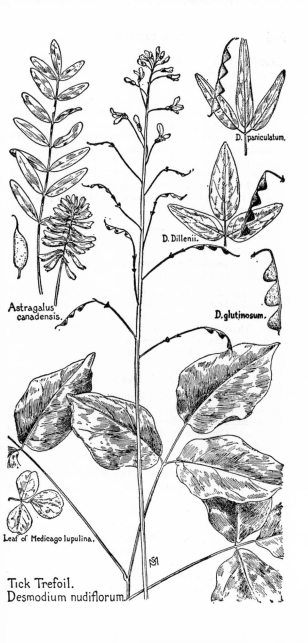

D. paniculatum.

D. Dillenii.

Astragalus
canadensis.

D. glutinosum.

Leaf of Medicago lupulina.

Tick Trefoil.
Desmodium nudiflorum.

Canadian Tick Trefoil
Desmodium canadense　Dull magenta-pink, July-September

The most showy species of the genus, with crowded flower-clusters terminating a tall, stout, and hairy stem. The leaves are nearly without stalks, or with short ones, and the three leaflets (longer-stalked) are oblong lance-shaped. The flowers (larger than those of the other species) are nearly ½ inch long, and vary in color from magenta to magenta-pink. Pods 3-5 jointed and quite hairy. 2-6 feet high. Common on the borders of copses and on river-banks, from Que., south to S. C., and west to Alberta and Ark.

Trailing Bush Clover
Lespedeza procumbens　Purple-magenta or magenta-pink, August-September

An interesting little plant with a trailing habit, its perpendicular branches rising from a stout horizontal stem. The little leaves are cloverlike. The whole plant woolly-hairy. The tiny pealike blossoms magenta-pink or a light purple-magenta. 12-25 inches long. Common in dry soil, N. H. to Fla., west to Tex. and Okla.

Lespedeza violacea　Purple, August-September

An upright and tall species with small elliptical leaflets distinctly stalked. Stem sparingly hairy and much branched. The small flowers purple or violet-purple. 1-3 feet high. Common in dry soil, and on the borders of copses everywhere.

Lespedeza virginica　Purple, August-September

An erect species with smooth, dark green, cloverlike leaves, crowding a rather straight, generally smooth stem which is terminated by the small, crowded, purple flower-cluster; smaller clusters also spring from the junction of stem with leaf-stalk. The *Lespedezas*, especially this one, are apt to exhibit two kinds of flowers; those with showy petals, which are sterile, and those petalless and minute, which are abundantly fertile. Closely related to *L. procumbens*, but with narrow leaflets. 1-3 feet high. Mass. to Ga., west to Wisc. and Tex.

Canadian Tick Trefoil. **Desmodium canadense.**

Lespedeza hirta Yellow-white, spotted, August-
September

This species has yellow-white flowers purple-spotted,
which grow in small, dense, bristly, oblong spikes. The
stem is silky-hairy, and the round ovate leaflets are
slightly separated by the conspicuous stalk of the middle
one. 2-4 feet high. Common in dry places, Me. to Fla.,
west to Mich. and Tex.

Lespedeza capitata White-streaked, July-September

The flowers of this species are clustered in small round
heads terminating a stiff, straight stalk, which is silky
hairy. The leaves have three oblong leaflets, and are
nearly stalkless. The flowers are similar to the foregoing
species, or they are white, magenta-streaked. 2-4 feet
high. In dry woods, Me. to Fla., west to Minn. and Tex.

Common Vetch
Vicia sativa Purple, May-August

A climbing annual adventive from Europe where it is
cultivated for fodder; one of the genus is also extensively
cultivated in Italy, notably about Naples, and in the
vicinity of Pompeii. The flowers, which are purple or
even magenta-pink, grow in pairs or singly at the junction of stem with leaf-stalk. The 8-10 leaflets are obtuse
oblong, notched at the tip, and the stalk terminates in
two twining tendrils. The pod resembles that of the pea,
but it is long and slender. Stem 1-3 feet long. Common
everywhere as an escape from cultivation.

Cow Vetch
Vicia Cracca Light violet, June-August

A perennial, and graceful plant, climbing by tendrils
and characterized by a fine, downy hairiness. The compound leaf has twenty or more lance-shaped leaflets terminated abruptly by a bristlelike point. The small bean-
blossomlike flower is light violet, the upper petal is lined
with a deeper violet; the cluster is sometimes quite four
inches long, and is one-sided; it grows from between
the leaf-stalk and the plant-stem. The color of the foliage
is rather gray olive-green. Fruit like a small pea-pod.
Stem 2-3 feet long. Dry soil, on the borders of thickets,
and cultivated fields, Labrador to Del., west to Wisc.

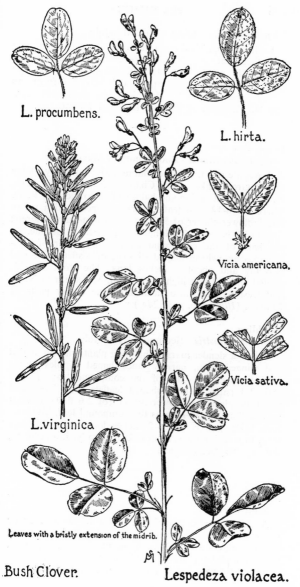

L. procumbens.

L. hirta.

Vicia americana.

Vicia sativa.

L. virginica

Leaves with a bristly extension of the midrib.

Bush Clover.

Lespedeza violacea.

Vicia americana   Light violet, May-July

Easily distinguished from the foregoing by its generally smooth character and its obtuse elliptical leaflets which are less in number (8-14) and distinctly veined. The light violet flowers are larger, and only 3-9 form the rather loose cluster. 2-3 feet long. In moist soil, Ont. and N. Y., south to Va. and Ky., and west to Cal.

Beach Pea
Lathyrus maritimus   Ruddy purple, May-August

A seaside plant, but one common also on sandy shores of the Great Lakes, Lake Champlain and Oneida Lake, N. Y., its construction and habit similar to those of *Vicia*. There are 6-12 oval leaflets, bristle-tipped, and a ruddy purple flower-cluster of 5-12 bean-blossom-shaped florets; the cluster is somewhat long-hemispherical in outline. At the base of the compound leaves are a pair of conspicuous arrowhead-shaped stipules, or leaflets. The pod is veiny and about 2 inches long. The stout stem is angled and 1-2 feet high. Sandy soil, Me. south to N. J., and west to Ore.; also throughout the cooler parts of Eurasia. (*Illus. opp. page 244.*)

Vetchling
Lathyrus palustris   Red-purple, June-July

This is a slender marsh-inhabiting plant with an angled and winged stem, narrow lance-shaped stipules (leafy formations at the base of the compound leaves), and with 2-4 pairs of lance-shaped leaflets. The loose and ruddy purple sparse flower-cluster (of 2-6 flowers about ½ inch long) is as long as the compound leaf. The narrow, veiny pod is about 2 inches long. Stem 1-3 feet long. In wet situations, from Labrador to N. J. and N. Y., west to the Pacific Coast.

Ground Nut
Apios americana   Maroon and pale brown-lilac, August-September

A climbing vine reaching a height of about four or five feet. The root is tuberous and edible. The compound leaf is composed of 3-7 toothless, ovate pointed leaflets, smooth and light green. The æsthetic flower-cluster is maroon and pale brown-lilac in color with a texture of

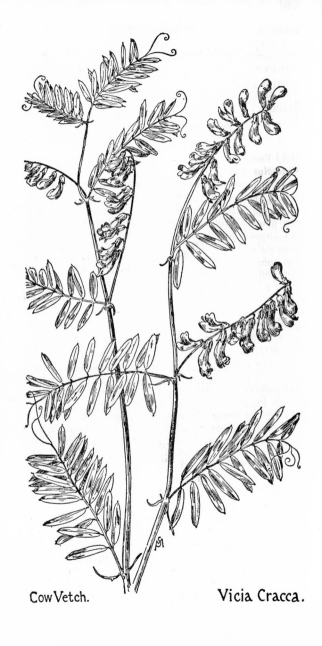

Cow Vetch.   Vicia Cracca.

velvet; the bean-blossomlike florets are cloyingly sweet, and suggest English violets with a slight and strange horse-chestnut odor. They are fertilized mostly by the various bees, including the honeybee. The name is from ἄπιον, a pear, alluding to the pear shape of the tubers. The plant is exceedingly beautiful and worthy of cultivation. On low, damp ground, from Que., south to Fla., and west to S. D. and Tex.

Wild Bean
Phaseolus polystachios   Red-purple, July-September

Another perennial climber, distinguished by its leaf of three leaflets pointed at the tip and rounded at the base. The plant is very fine-hairy and considerably branched. The flower-cluster is thin and about 4-8 inches long; the red-purple blossoms are scarcely over ⅓ inch long. The pods are stalked, drooping, and a trifle curved. Stem 5-12 feet long. In thickets, Me. south to Fla., west to Ill., Mo. and Tex. The common garden string bean, *P. vulgaris,* is a close relative.

Wild Bean
Strophostyles helvola   Greenish-white or purple, July-September

A similar, but annual species, with a low-twining stem about 6-8 feet long, the leaflets sometimes bluntly lobed and sometimes entire. The 3-10 greenish-white or red-purple flowers about ½ an inch long, in a loose cluster. The slender linear pod is fine-hairy and about 3 inches long or less. Stem branching at the base. Sandy riverbanks, and meadow borders, Que. to Fla., west along the Great Lakes to Minn., and southwest to Tex. (*Illus. opp. page 244.*)

Wild or Hog Peanut
Amphicarpa bracteata   Magenta-lilac, August-September

A dainty vine with delicate light green leaves formed of three smooth, angularly ovate-pointed leaflets, and bearing two kinds of fruit. The perfect lilac or magenta-lilac narrow blossoms are in small drooping clusters, these are succeeded by many small pods about an inch long holding generally three mottled beans. The

Ground Nut.   Apios americana.

other fruitful blossom is at the base or root of the plant
in rudimentary form with but few free stamens; it is
succeeded by a pear-shaped pod containing one large
seed—hence the name wild peanut. The name of the
plant means *both* and *fruit,* in reference to the two kinds
of fruit. The pod of the upper blossom is curved and
broad at the tip, it matures about the middle of September. The slender stem twines about the roadside shrubbery, and is from 2-7 feet long. Common everywhere in
moist ground from Que. to Fla., west to Mont. and Tex.

SENNA FAMILY. *Caesalpiniaceæ.*

A small family closely related to the pea family and
differing chiefly in having slightly irregular, but not
pealike or butterflylike, flowers in those below. Among
cultivated sorts are the redbud and the honey locust.

Wild Senna
Cassia marilandica   Golden-yellow, brown-tipped, July
   August

A showy and decorative plant with compound leaves
of 12-18 broad lance-shaped leaflets of a rather yellow-
green tone. They are smooth and somewhat sensitive to
the touch. The flower-clusters are loosely constructed.
The light golden-yellow flowers of five slightly unequal
petals are accented in color by the prominent chocolate-
brown of the anthers; the stamens are very unequal in
length. 3-8 feet high. In swamps and alluvial soil from
Pa., south to Fla., and west to Iowa and Tex. A related
form or perhaps a distinct species is *C. hebecarpa,* which
does not differ materially.

Partridge Pea
Cassia fasciculata   Yellow, July-September

An erect annual species with large showy yellow flowers, 1¼ inches across, in groups of 2-4 at the bases of
the sensitive leaves; often the five petals are purple-
spotted at the base. The 20-30 leaflets, less than an inch
long, are blunt lance-shaped and pointed with a tiny
bristle. The slender pod about 2 inches long is slightly
hairy. 1-2 feet high. In dry or sandy fields, or in wet
places. Mass. to Minn. and south to Fla.

Wild Bean.
Phaseolus polystachios.

Hog Peanut.
Amphicarpa bracteata.

Wild Sensitive Plant
Cassia nictitans   Yellow, July-September

A similar species, but tall, and with very small and inconspicuous yellow flowers. The 12-40 tiny leaflets scarcely ⅔ inch long. The flowers in groups of 2-3 at the bases of the leaves. 6-12 feet high. Me., south to Ga., and west to Ill., Kan. and Tex. Not in N. H., and if in Me. exceedingly rare, for only one record exists.

Sickle-pod
Cassia Tora   Yellow, July-September

An annual with 4-6 leaflets, mostly 6, thin, obovate, and with a bristlelike point. The yellow flowers ½ - 1 inch broad. The linear, slender pod crescent-shaped. Along rivers, Va. south, and in Miss. valley to Mo. and Ind.

This is a species which is common in Mexico and throughout tropical Am. It is also generally distributed over the semi-tropical regions of the Old World.

The Cassias are more or less natives of the tropics and are in constant use—both their fruit and leaves—for medicinal purposes. The leaves of *Cassia angustifolia* and *Cassia Senna* yield the drug senna, widely used as a purgative.

The very handsome, ornamental tree, *Cassia Fistula* of the Old World, has very long cylindrical pods which contain a sweet pulp valuable for use as a mild laxative.

Coffee Senna
Cassia occidentalis   Yellow, July-August

A smooth annual species with many branches, and 8-12 ovate or ovate lance-shaped leaflets, very acute at the tip and rounded at the base. Flowers rather small; pod linear and about 4-5 inches long. 4-6 feet high. Waste places and along the shore from Va. to Tex., and in Miss. valley to Mo. and Ind. Naturalized from tropical Am.

Cassia occidentalis is a common species of the Americas as far south as Uruguay, Argentina and Chile. In our more northern country it is probably adventive and does not progress beyond warm and sunny river valleys. In the region of the tropics its seeds are used as a substitute for coffee although they do not contain caffein.

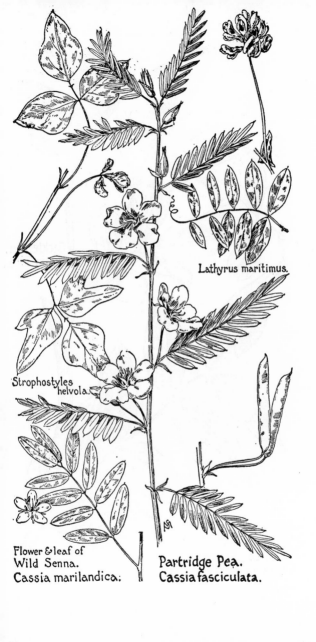

Lathyrus maritimus.

Strophostyles helvola.

Flower & leaf of
Wild Senna.
Cassia marilandica.

Partridge Pea.
Cassia fasciculata.

Sickle-pod.
Cassia Tora.

Coffee Senna.
Cassia occidentalis..

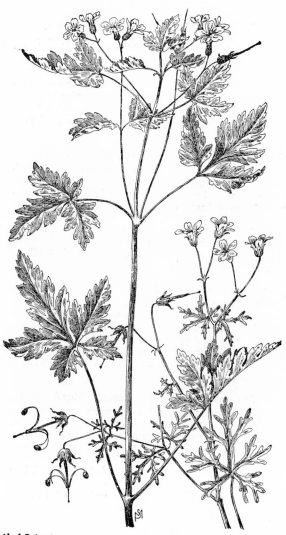

Herb Robert.
Geranium Robertianum.

Geranium Bicknelli.

GERANIUM FAMILY. *Geraniaceæ.*

A small family of plants with symmetrical and perfect flowers of mostly five parts, viz.: five petals, five sepals (usually distinct), and five stamens or twice that number. Fruit a capsule. Cross-fertilized by bees, butterflies, and the beelike flies. The related garden geranium belongs to the South African genus *Pelargonium,* which differs from our wild flowers of the genus *Geranium.*

Herb Robert
Geranium Robertianum   Magenta, May-September

A rather decorative but weak-stemmed species adventive from Europe, distinguished for its generally *ruddy* stems and strong odor when bruised. The ornamental leaves have 3-5 distinct leaflets and are deep green sometimes modified with the ruddy tinge of the plant. The flowers are deep or pale magenta, and are succeeded by long-beaked seed-vessels. 10-18 inches high. On the borders of rocky woods, from Newf., south to Va., and west to Minn.

Geranium Bicknellii   Pink-purple, June-September

A somewhat similar species, but distinguished by its 5-parted leaf, which does not have distinct leaflets; and remarkable seed-vessel the persistent style of which splits upward *from the base* and bears the seed at the tip. The flowers are pink-purple, and are generally borne in pairs. 8-16 inches high. Newf. to southern N. Y. and Pa., west to Ind. and Iowa.

Geranium carolinianum   Pale magenta, May-August

Another similar species but one more commonly distributed through the south. The leaves are deeply cut and narrowly lobed, and the pale magenta flowers are borne in compact clusters. The beak to the seed-vessel is nearly an inch long, and is short-pointed in contradistinction to that of the foregoing species, which is long-pointed. The curved sections of the beak are also shorter. The stem is fuzzy and 8-15 inches high. In poor soil from Me., south to Mex., and west. This geranium as well as the others is more or less dependent upon the small bees for cross-fertilization. The flower has ten perfect stamens, however, and the inner circle of their anthers is so near the stigma that self-pollinization may easily occur.

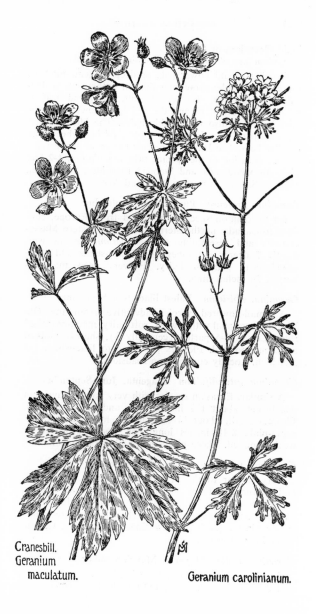

Cranesbill.
Geranium
maculatum.

Geranium carolinianum.

Wild Geranium or Cranesbill
Geranium maculatum   Magenta-pink, May-July

A delicate wild flower pale or deep magenta-pink, or quite light purple; sometimes the ten anthers are a delicate peacock-blue. The deeply cut, five-lobed leaf is rough-hairy; the stem and the unfolded flower-envelope (the bud) are also remarkably hairy. The blossoms are cross-fertilized mostly by the agency of honeybees, and smaller bees. The leaves with their brown or white spots are tne occasion of the specific title, *maculatum*. 1-2 feet high. In woodlands and wooded roadsides, from Me., south to S. C., and west to S. D. and Ark.

Geranium pratense   Purple, June-September

An uncommon species introduced from Europe, confined to Canada, northeastern Maine, and eastern Massachusetts and resembling *G. maculatum*. Leaves with mostly 7 deeply cut lobes; the flower-stems and seed-vessel beak glandular-hairy. Flowers deep magenta-purple. 24 inches high.

Geranium sibiricum   Palest lilac, June-September

A small-flowered species adventive from the Old World. An annual with a weak, soft-hairy, much-branched stem. Leaves 3-5 parted (generally 3), sharply toothed and acute-pointed. Flowers pale lilac to lilac-white. 1-4 feet high. Locally common on roadsides.

Geranium rotundifolium   Magenta, June-September

A similar, Eurasian species with very round leaves not deeply cut, about 1½ inches wide, and scallop-toothed. Flowers small, about ¼ inch broad, magenta and magenta-pink. 8-18 inches long, but mostly prostrate or weak-stemmed. Waste places and ballast but uncommon.

Geranium pusillum   Lilac, May-September

Very similar to the preceding species in habit, leaf, and flower; petals of the latter lilac or pale purple, slightly notched and about as long as the sepals. With 5 stamens only. Seeds smooth. 4-18-inch stem, reclining. Waste places, southern New Eng. south to N. C. and west. From Europe.

Geranium molle   Magenta, May-September

Another similar European species, but more soft-hairy, and the leaves cut about to the middle, the segments 3-5

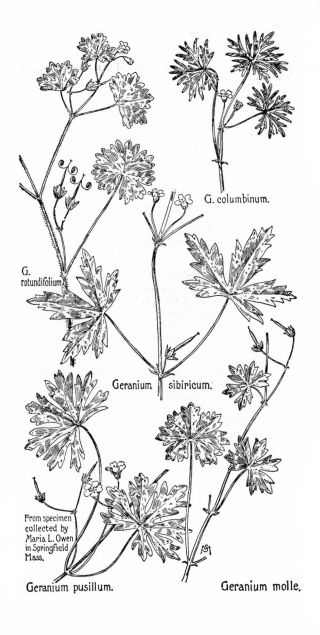

G. columbinum.

G. rotundifolium.

Geranium sibiricum.

From specimen
collected by
Maria L. Owen
in Springfield
Mass.

Geranium pusillum.

Geranium molle.

toothed. The small flowers deep or pale magenta, with 10 stamens, the sepals obtuse and not bristle-pointed. Waste places, Me. to Pa. and west.

Geranium columbinum   Magenta, May-July

Yet another similar species, minutely white-hairy, with leaves deeply cut into 5-9 narrow, nearly linear segments, the stems long and slender. The small flowers magenta, with slightly notched petals, and ovate, bristle-pointed sepals, the stems very slender. Borders of fields and roads, N. Y. to N. C., west to Ohio.

FALSE MERMAID FAMILY. *Limnanthaceæ.*

Plants with 3-6 parted very small flowers, compound (pinnate) leaves, and weak or prostrate stems.

False Mermaid
Floerkea proserpinacoides   White, April-June

A slender and weak-stemmed little plant, with small compound leaves of from 3-5 leaflets sometimes thrice cleft. The tiny white flowers with three petals are borne singly on long and slender stems proceeding from the base of the leaves. The flower is succeeded by 1-3 fleshy spherical seed receptacles which are set snugly within the remaining three sepals. 6-15 inches high. In swampy land, and on river-banks, from Nova Scotia southwest to Del. and westward. (*Illus. on page 160.*)

Floerkea proserpinacoides is distributed quite across Ontario and the northern United States to Utah, Oregon and California, and southward to Delaware, Kentucky and Missouri.

WOOD-SORREL FAMILY. *Oxalidaceæ.*

A small family of low herbs in our range, with compound leaves and perfect, regular flowers of five parts; the ten stamens united at the base. Fruit a five-celled capsule. Juice sour and watery. Cross-fertilized by the smaller bees and the beelike flies.

Wood Sorrel
Oxalis Acetosella   White pink-veined, May-July

One of the most dainty of all woodland plants, common in cool, damp situations. The leaf composed of three

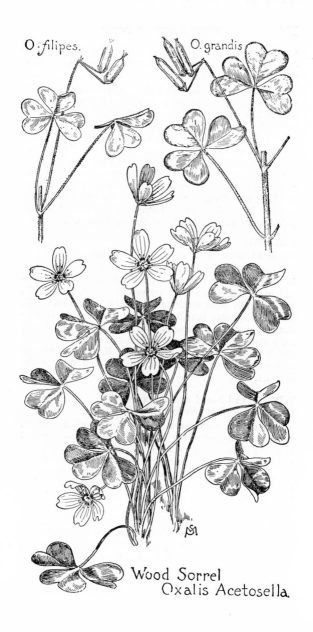

O. filipes.

O. grandis

Wood Sorrel
Oxalis Acetosella.

light green heart-shaped leaflets which droop and fold
together after nightfall. The frail flowers nearly an inch
broad, with five notched petals, are borne singly on delicate long stems, and are either pinkish-white, striped
with crimson lines, the color deepening toward the center
of the blossom, or white with crimson-pink lines. Fertilized by the smaller bees and flies. Cleistogamous flowers (a kind fertilized in the bud without opening) are
also borne on small curved stems at the base of the plant.
A stemless perennial about 3-4 inches high, growing from
a creeping scaly-toothed root. Common in thin, damp
woods from Que. to the mountains of N. C., and west
to Mich. and Wisc. A native also of the Old World, and
a most interesting flower frequently introduced in the
paintings of Fra Angelico and Sandro Botticelli.

Violet Wood Sorrel
Oxalis violacea   Pale magenta, May-June

Another most dainty woodland species also common
in the north. The leaves are similar to those of the preceding species. The flowers are variable, sometimes white,
but generally light magenta—they are *never* violet. The
long flower-stalks bear 3-6 or more blossoms, in contradistinction to *O. Acetosella* which bears but one flower
on a stalk. It is frequented by the same class of insects
which visit the last. 4-8 inches high. Rocky ground and
thin woods, from Mass. south to Fla. and west to the
Rockies.

Yellow Wood Sorrel or Lady's Sorrel
Oxalis corniculata   Yellow, May-September

One of the commonest yellow sorrels of the north,
not a woodland plant but familiar by every roadside and
in every field and garden. The light green stem erect,
rather smooth, or sparingly hairy (viewed under the
glass); the three heart-shaped leaflets (smaller than those
of the last species), long-stalked and somewhat drooping;
without small leafy formations at the junction of leaf-
stem and plant-stem. The rather deep lemon-yellow
flowers scarcely ½ inch broad, with five long ovate petals
and ten yellow stamens alternately long and short; the
heart of the blossom is green. There are 2-6 flowers on
a somewhat horizontally spreading, branched stem, which
are succeeded by hairy seed-pods ½ inch long set at
scarcely a wide angle with their stalks. Visited by the
smaller bees, flies, and also occasionally by the tiny

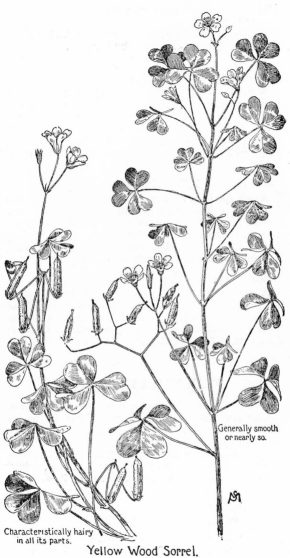

Characteristically hairy
in all its parts.

Generally smooth
or nearly so.

Yellow Wood Sorrel.

Oxalis stricta.

Oxalis corniculata,

butterflies. 3-12 inches high, with a weak stem but strong root. It is by some known as *Oxalis repens.*

Yellow Wood Sorrel or Lady's Sorrel
Oxalis stricta   May-September

A far less common species, an annual or perennial, sustaining itself by far-reaching running roots. Generally more upright than the last. With leafy formations at the bases of the leaf-stalks. Pods elongated, and erect, often set at a sharp angle with their stalks. In other respects very similar to the foregoing species. Nearly throughout N. Am.

Oxalis grandis   Yellow, May-August

A tall species with a nearly smooth erect stem and branches, or these covered with soft fine hairs. The leaflets large, often 1½ inches broad, sometimes edged with dull magenta. The yellow flowers often ¾ inch broad. 12-20 inches high. Sandy woodlands and river margins, Pa. to Ill., and south to Ga. and Tenn.

Oxalis filipes

A very slender plant, doubtfully distinct from *O. stricta,* the stem sparingly hairy, and the stems of the yellow flowers threadlike, the clusters mostly two-flowered. 9-18 inches high. In sandy woodlands, Conn. to Fla., west to Tenn. and Mo.

FLAX FAMILY. *Linaceæ.*

A small family mostly composed of not very tall herbs, slender and frail flowered, but remarkable for having furnished the world with linen from time immemorial as well as linseed oil. The perfect, symmetrical flowers (of the genus *Linum*) have five petals, sepals, styles, and stamens; the petals before expansion are rolled-up. The fruit is usually in a capsule. Mostly fertilized by the smaller bees and beelike flies.

Wild Yellow Flax
Linum virginianum   Yellow, June-August

A smooth perennial, with small yellow flowers terminating slender branches; the five tiny yellow petals scarcely give the flower a width of ⅓ inch. The small leaves are lance-shaped, thin, and one-ribbed. The sepals

L.virginianum

Common Flax.   Linum usitatissimum.

are ovate and pointed. 1-2 feet high. Dry woodlands, and
shady places, throughout the north, and south to Ga.
and Tex.

Linum sulcatum   **Yellow, June-August**

A somewhat similar species, but an annual with a
usually simple stem and alternate leaves; the stem corrugated, at least above, the sharp, lance-shaped leaves
three-ribbed, and the yellow flowers a full half-inch
broad. 1-2 feet high. In dry soil from E. Mass., west to
the Great Lakes, through the mountains south to Ga.,
and southwest to Tex. Rare along the seacoast.

Common Flax
Linum usitatissimum   **Light blue-violet, June-September**

A rather delicate-appearing and pretty annual adventive from Europe or escaped from cultivation; it has
been under cultivation since prehistoric times for its
linen fiber and its seed oil, although different varieties
are grown for linen and for linseed oil. The stem erect,
branching, and ridged, the alternate leaves lance-shaped,
sharp, and three-ribbed. The delicate blue-violet flowers,
¾ inch broad, with five slightly overlapping petals, are
fertilized mostly by the honeybee. 9-20 inches high. Along
roadsides, by railways, in cultivated fields, and in waste
places.

MILKWORT FAMILY. *Polygaceæ.*

Mostly herbs with generally alternate leaves, and perfect but irregular flowers with five sepals, the two lateral
ones petal-like, large, and colored; the others small. The
three petals are connected with each other in a tubelike
form; the lower one is often crested at the tip. The
generally eight stamens are more or less united into one
or two sets and in part coherent with the lower petal, but
free above. Stigma curved and broad; the anthers generally cup-shaped and opening by a slit or hole at the
apex. Cross-fertilization effected by the agency of bees
and the beelike flies.

Fringed Milkwort or Flowering Wintergreen
Polygala paucifolia   **Magenta or white, May-July**

An exceedingly dainty, low perennial rising from prostrate stems and roots sometimes a foot long. The few

Seneca Snakeroot.   Polygala Senega.

broad, ovate, bright green leaves are crowded at the summit of the stems, the lower ones reduced to the size of a mere scale. The leaves live through the winter and turn a bronze-red. The flowers, nearly ⅞ inch long, are generally magenta or crimson-magenta, and rarely white. The three petals are united in a tube, the lowest one terminating in a pouch containing the pistil and anthers, and furnished at the end with a fringe or beard. This last serves as a landing platform for bees, which will naturally depress the pouch by their weight; the rigid pistil and stamens, however, refusing to bend with the pouch, are forced out through a slit at the top of the latter and come in direct contact with the under parts of the insect visitor. Thus cross-fertilization is in a large measure secured by the pollen-daubed bee brushing against the exposed stigma of the next flower visited. The little plant often bears permanently closed subterranean flowers on tiny branchlets. Erect stem 3-6 inches high. Common in damp, rich woods, from Que. south to Ga., and west to Wisc. (*Color Plate 12.*)

Milkwort
Polygala polygama   Dull crimson, June-July

The tiny æsthetic, dull crimson flowers of this species are borne in delicate long clusters at the tips of the leafy stems. The leaves are light dull green, lance-shaped, and crowded on the slender stem, toothless and rather blunt, with a bristlelike tip. Rarely the flowers are nearly white; the eight stamens are more or less conspicuous. The plant also bears permanently closed flowers on subterranean horizontal branches. 5-15 inches high. Dry sandy soil, common everywhere, but only locally abundant.

Seneca Snakeroot
Polygala senega   White or greenish-white, May-June

A much less showy species with white or greenish-white flowers and fewer lance-shaped leaves, the lowest ones very small and scalelike. The small terminal flower-cluster dense. It bears no permanently closed blossoms. Stem 6-12 inches high, simple or slightly branched. In rocky woodlands, from western N. B. south to Ga. among the mountains, and west to Alberta and Ark.

Polygala sanguinea   Magenta, June-September

A branching and leafy species with globular or oblong, compact flower-clusters of deep or pale magenta blos-

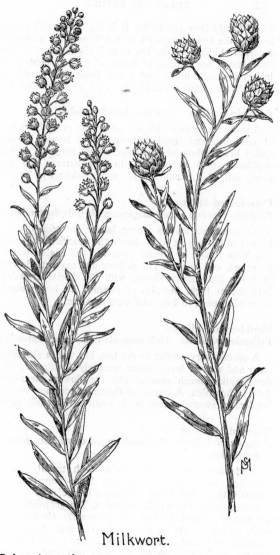

Milkwort.

Polygala polygama.   Polygala sanguinea.

soms; rarely they are white. It is the calyx which contributes the ruddy magenta to the flower; the yellowish
petals are hidden within. The stem is slightly angled. The
little leaves are similar to those of *P. polygama*. 6-12
inches high. In moist and sandy fields and roadsides,
Nova Scotia, south to S. C., and west to Minn. and La.

Polygala mariana   Magenta, July-September

A southern species with a slender stem much branched
at maturity, and small, narrow, linear leaves. Flower
spikes nearly globular, the flowers light magenta. Bracts
deciduous. 6-15 inches high. In pine barrens and dry
sandy soil, N. J. south to Fla., and southwest to Tex.

Cross-leaved Milkwort
Polygala cruciata   Dull magenta-pink, July-September

An attractive species whose leaves are generally arranged in clusters of four—hence the specific title, *cruciata*. Stem square or almost winged at the angles, widely
branched, and smooth. The delicate dull magenta flowers
in heads like clover bloom, with the florets crowded.
3-13 inches high. Margins of swamps, or low ground,
from Me. south to Fla., and west to Minn.

Short-leaved Milkwort
Polygala brevifolia   Dull magenta-pink, June-September

A species very similar to the last, but with a slenderer
stem and shorter leaves more sparingly distributed. The
flower-spikes much smaller and the flowers stemmed.
3-10 inches high. A coastwise *Polygala*, common on the
borders of swamps, from N. J. south to Fla. and Miss.

Whorled Milkwort
Polygala verticillata   Magenta-tinged or whitish, June-
    September

A slender and smooth species with usually many
branches, and with long slender lance-shaped leaves
tipped with a slight bristle, arranged in circles of 4-5, or
scattered singly among the branches. The greenish-white
or magenta-tinged flowers are compactly clustered in
conic spikes, nearly an inch long. The little florets are
distinctly stemmed. All the *Polygalas* are assisted in the
process of fertilization by the bees and some of the
smaller butterflies. 6-12 inches high. Common everywhere

Cross-leaved Milkwort.   Polygala cruciata.

in fields or on roadsides. The var. *ambigua* is nearly the same in structure, but is taller, slenderer, and only the lower leaves are in circles; the others are alternate. It is considered by some as a separate species. The flower-spikes are very long and loose, some of the lower flowers being isolated; the blossoms are a trifle larger, and mostly a pale magenta. In dry soil, Me. to Ga., and southwest to Ala. and Okla.

SPURGE FAMILY. *Euphorbiaceæ.*

Plants with usually a milky and often poisonous juice, bearing staminate and pistillate flowers on one plant or exclusively either kind on one plant, so there may be perfect or unisexual flowers; hence they are largely dependent upon insects for fertilization. The flowers are irregularly or imperfectly constructed, i.e., in some instances without petals, and in others polypetalous or even monopetalous. Fruit generally a three-lobed capsule. Represented in our area largely by the genus *Euphorbia*, but largely a tropical family. Ten other genera are also found here, and for these and other species of *Euphorbia*, the technical manuals should be consulted.

Seaside Spurge
Euphorbia polygonifolia   Whitish-green, July-September
A prostrate, spreading weed common in the sand of the seashore; stem branched and smooth. Flowers inconspicuous and usually solitary at the bases of the small linear oblong leaves. Seed-capsule round-ovoid, and ash-gray-colored. Branches 3-7 inches long. Along the Atlantic Coast from Que. to Ga. and on the shores of the Great Lakes.

Milk Purslane or Spotted Spurge
Euphorbia maculata   Whitish or ruddy, June-September
A prostrate weed common throughout North America, in open places and on roadsides. Stems usually dark red, hairy and spreading radiately like common pussley; leaves toothed, red-blotched, and dark green in color, oblong and obtuse, about 1 inch long. The whitish or ruddy inconspicuous flowers growing at the bases of the leaves. Branches 3-12 inches long. Common. The plant is green early in the summer, the leaves a dull, lifeless color with-

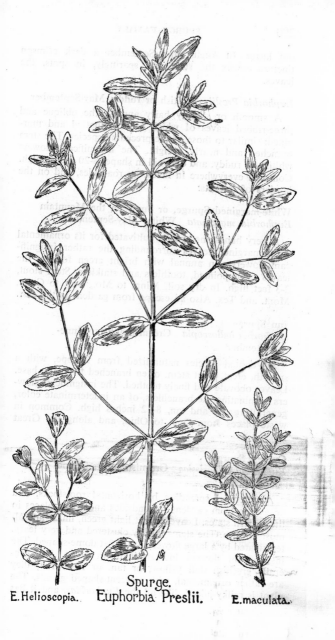

Spurge.

E. Helioscopia.   Euphorbia Preslii.   E. maculata.

out luster. In August and September a dark crimson tincture covers the stem and sparingly, in spots, the leaves.

Euphorbia Preslii   Whitish or ruddy, May-September

A smooth or slightly hairy annual, the oblique and three-ribbed leaves of which are red-spotted and margined; similar to those of the preceding species. The stem branched and nearly upright. The insignificant flowers whitish or ruddy, and obovoid in shape. 8-20 inches high. Common everywhere in fields, by roadsides, and on the borders of thickets.

White-margined Spurge, or Snow on the Mountain
Euphorbia marginata   White, May-September

A very handsome species cultivated for its ornamental white-margined leaves surrounding the rather insignificant flowers. An annual with bright green foliage, the leaves ovate-pointed, toothless and stalkless. Stem stout, 2-3 feet high. In dry soil, Minn. to Mo., west to Colo., Mont. and Tex. Also an escape from gardens in the east.

Sun Spurge
Euphorbia helioscopia   Greenish and tan, June-September

An annual species naturalized from Europe, with a smooth, erect, stout stem, often branched from the base. Leaves obovate and finely toothed. The insignificant flowers terminating the branchlets, of an indeterminate color, generally green and tan. 8-12 inches high. Common in waste places from Que. to Ohio, and along the Great Lakes.

Cypress Spurge
Euphorbia Cyparissias   Greenish and tan, June-September

A perennial spreading by horizontal rootstocks, and an escape from gardens to roadsides and waste places in the eastern states. Leaves bright light green, linear and almost filiform. The stems thickly clustered and very leafy, terminated by a large flower-cluster flat dome-shaped. The insignificant flowers indeterminate in color, but generally greenish dull yellow, or tan, or russet-red; they are rather ornamental, with crescent-shaped glands. The plant is milky-juiced, like all the *Euphorbias,* and it has

Cypress Spurge.
Euphorbia Cyparissias.

Snow on the Mountain.
Euphorbia marginata

become naturalized from Europe. It is poisonous if eaten in any quantity. Fertilized by bees and butterflies. 5-12 inches high. Common everywhere in the east.

Euphorbia agraria   Greenish-yellow, July-September

An Old World species with a tall, stocky, smooth stem, and long lance-shaped leaves, the floral ones heart-shaped and with a bristlelike tip. The seed pods finely wrinkled. Along roadsides and in fields of the Susquehanna Valley, N. Y. and Pa. Similar to *E. Cyparissias* in general appearance with the exception of the broader leaves. 8-18 inches high.

CROWBERRY FAMILY. *Empetraceæ.*

Low, heathlike plants, with very small leaves and flowers, one an Arctic-alpine plant, the other scattered in sandy, often pine-barren soils along the Atlantic seaboard. Flowers regular, often the sexes on different plants.

Crowberry
Empetrum nigrum   Greenish-purple, July-August

A low, prostrate plant, really a miniature shrub with spreading, sticky branches, making dense patches, but not over 6-8 inches high. Leaves scarcely ½ inch long, densely crowded, narrow, the margins rolled back. Flowers minute, without petals, but the greenish-purple sepals petal-like. They are stalkless and scattered among the tiny leaves, and followed by a shiny black (or pink or reddish) berrylike fruit about the size of a pea. In bogs, from Arctic regions south along the coast to Me. and thence only above timber line in the mountains of New Eng. and N. Y., west to northern Mich. and Minn. An interesting outlying station for it is at Montauk Point, L. I., probably started by birds.

———

Broom Crowberry
Corema Conradii   Brown-purple, May

A miniature shrub with minute, densely crowded heath-like leaves, much-branched and usually not over 7-10 inches high, but forming dense patches often a yard wide. Leaves crowded, scarcely ¼ inch long. Flowers minute

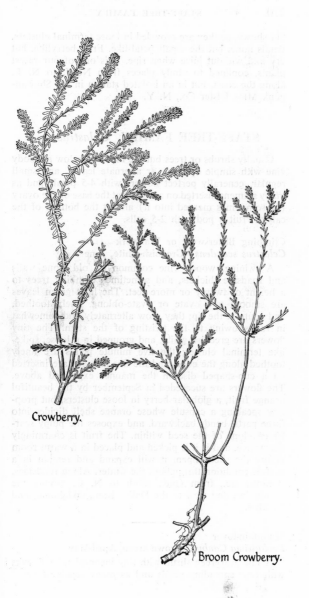

Crowberry.

Broom Crowberry.

but showy, as they are crowded in loose terminal clusters. Petals none, but the sepals petal-like. Fruit berrylike, but dry and without juice when ripe. It is one of our rarest plants, confined to sandy places from Newf. to N. J., along the coast, but in an isolated station in the Shawangunk Mts., Ulster Co., N. Y.

STAFF-TREE FAMILY. *Celastraceæ.*

Usually shrubs or trees but the first one below a woody vine with simple opposite or alternate leaves, and small regular, generally perfect flowers with 4-5 petals and as many stamens inserted on a disc set at the base of the ovary (or sometimes merged into it) and at the bottom of the calyx. Fruit a pod with 2-5 cells.

Climbing Bittersweet or Waxwork
Celastrus scandens Greenish-white, June

A twining, woody vine common on old stone walls and roadside thickets, and sometimes climbing trees to a height of twenty or more feet. The light green leaves are smooth and ovate or ovate-oblong, finely toothed, and acute at the tip; they grow alternately and somewhat in ranks owing to the twisting of the stem. The tiny flowers are greenish-white, and grouped in a loose, spike-like terminal cluster; the five minute petals are finely toothed along the edge, and the five stamens are inserted on a cup-shaped disc in the manner explained above. The flowers are succeeded in September by the beautiful orange fruit, a globular berry in loose clusters, but properly speaking a capsule whose orange shell divides into three parts, bends backward, and exposes the pulpy scarlet envelope of the seed within. The fruit is charmingly decorative, and if it is picked and placed in a warm room before the shells open, it will expand and remain in a perfect condition throughout the winter. Along roadsides, streams, etc., from Que., south to N. C. among the mountains, and west to the Daks., Kan., Oklahoma, and N. Mex.

Mountain-lover
Pachystima Canbyi Brown-green, April-May

A low evergreen shrub with tiny inconspicuous flowers with four spreading petals and as many sepals of equal

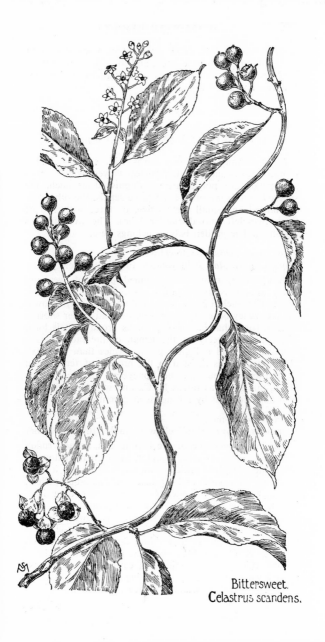

Bittersweet.
Celastrus scandens.

length, brown-green. The small blunt leaves opposite, linear-oblong, slightly toothed, and the edges rolled back. 4-12 feet high. Rocky slopes of mountains in Va. and W. Va., Ky. and Ohio.

JEWEL-WEED FAMILY. *Balsaminaceæ.*

Juicy-stemmed glistening herbs with smooth simple-toothed leaves and irregular perfect flowers whose sepals and petals are not clearly distinguished as such, the spurred sack being one of the three sepals; the other two are lateral and small. Petals five, or three with two of them two-cleft into dissimilar lobes. The five stamens are short. The garden balsam belongs here.

Pale Touch-me-not or Jewel-weed
Impatiens pallida   Pale yellow, July-September

A common, translucent-stemmed plant of wet and shady situations in the north, especially on mountainsides. The sack of the pale yellow, sparingly brown-spotted honey-bearing flower is obtuse and rather short—in fact, somewhat bell-shaped, or as broad as it is long. The spur is scarcely ⅓ the length of the sack. It is a more robust and a lighter green species than the next. Undoubtedly it is assisted in the process of fertilization by the bumblebee and the honeybee. Throughout the north, and south as far as N. C., and west to Saskatchewan and Mo., but by no means as common as *I. biflora.*

Spotted Touch-me-not
Impatiens biflora   Gold-yellow variable, July-September

The commoner one of the two species, usually ruddy stemmed; very variable in color, with smaller flowers, sometimes deeply freckled with red-brown over a deep gold-colored ground, and at other times pale buff-yellow, scarcely spotted. The sack is deep, longer than it is broad, and terminated by an incurved spur nearly one half or fully one third of its length. The flower develops its stamens first, and afterward its pistil, so cross-fertilization is almost an assured thing. 2-5 feet high. Newf. south to N. C. and Ala., and west to Ark. and Okla.

The fruit of both species is a capsule, elastically explosive when mature, and projecting its seeds. if touched, for a considerable distance—hence touch-me-not.

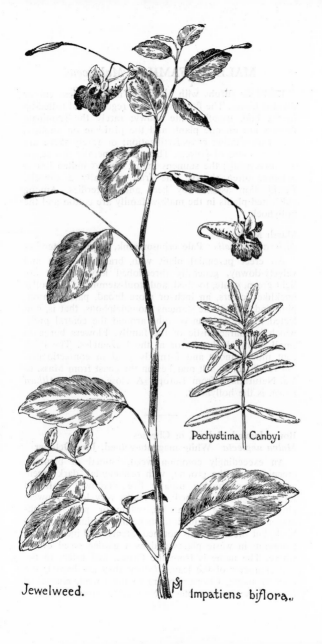

Jewelweed.   Impatiens biflora.

Pachystima Canbyi

MALLOW FAMILY. *Malvaceæ.*

Herbs or shrubs with alternate, more or less cut or divided leaves. The flowers perfect, regular, and rolled-up in the bud, usually quite showy; rarely the staminate flowers are on one plant, and the pistillate on another, thus necessitating cross-fertilization; or rarely there are all three kinds of flowers. There are generally five sepals and five petals; the stamens many, always united into a column, often showy. The fruit generally a capsule. Fertilization assisted by bees and butterflies. Among cultivated plants in the mallow family are cotton and the hollyhock.

Marsh Mallow
Althæa officinalis **Pale crimson-pink, August-September**

An erect perennial plant with branching stem and velvety-downy, generally three-lobed leaves. They are light green, ovate, toothed, and stout-stemmed. The hollyhocklike flowers, an inch or more broad, pale crimson-pink and veined; the stamens monadelphous, that is, collected in one column or tube around the central pistil, which is characteristic of the family. Flowers borne in small terminal clusters or at the leaf-angles. The thick root mucilaginous and formerly used in confectionery. 2-4 feet high. In salt marshes on the coast from Mass. to Va. Naturalized from Europe. A close relative, *Althæa rosea,* is the hollyhock.

Round-leaved Mallow, or Cheeses
Malva neglecta **White magenta-veined, June-October**

An exceedingly common weed, annual or biennial, creeping over the ground, with ornamental, dark green, round leaves having usually five shallowly scalloped lobes, irregularly toothed; the stalks very long. Flowers clustered in the leaf-angles, white or pale pinkish-magenta, magenta-veined; in shape like a miniature hollyhock, but the five petals notched. Stems 4-10 inches long. Common in waste places and as a garden weed everywhere. The name is from the Greek, and refers to the soft character of the leaves (albeit they are hard!); the popular name, Cheeses, refers to the round, cheeselike form of the seed-receptacle. Naturalized from Europe.

274

Cheeses.   Malva neglecta.

High Mallow
Malva sylvestris   Light magenta or pinkish, June-
   September

A common biennial with an erect branching stem, slightly fine-hairy or sometimes smooth. The leaves lighter green, rather long-stalked, toothed, and angularly five-lobed or occasionally seven-lobed. The flowers with the same family resemblance to the hollyhock, magenta-pink, or light magenta, the petals with about four deeper veins; the clusters (few-flowered) at the leaf-angles. 18-30 inches high. A delicate-flowered plant common on road-sides and in waste places everywhere. Adventive from Europe.

Musk Mallow
Malva moschata   White or magenta-pink, June-
   September

A very similar but perennial species, with the leaf division deeply slashed or cut. The medium green leaves with very narrow divisions and short stalks. The white or very pale magenta-pink flowers nearly two inches broad, flat, and borne in terminal clusters; they are also veined. The leaves have a delicate odor of musk when crushed. 1-2 feet high. Common from Que. to Va., west to B. C. and Mo.; from Europe.

———

Purple Poppy-mallow
Callirrhoe involucrata   Magenta, May-August

A distinctly western flower, occasionally escaped from cultivation in the east, a perennial bearing large, showy, purple-crimson or magenta flowers slightly resembling the *Malvas*. The leaves slashed like those of the preceding species, but not so deeply; the lobes more obtuse. The stem hairy, and the flowers borne singly with long stalks. 1-2 feet high. In dry ground, from N. D. south to Tex. and Utah.

———

Rose-mallow
Hibiscus palustris   Pale pink or white, August-
   September

A tall perennial with stout shrublike stems and large showy flowers. The leaves olive-green, bright above and densely white woolly beneath; ovate pointed and indistinctly toothed, with long stalks; the lower leaves three-

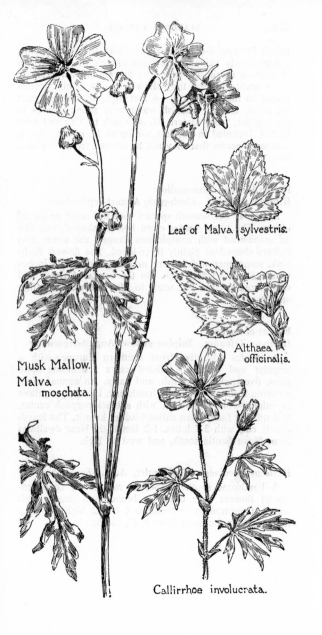

Leaf of Malva sylvestris.

Althaea officinalis.

Musk Mallow.
Malva moschata.

Callirrhoe involucrata.

lobed. Flowers 4-6 inches across, with five broad petals conspicuously veined, pale crimson-pink or white, with or without a crimson base. The flowers are borne singly or in scant clusters; they show a strong family resemblance to the hollyhock. 4-6 feet high. In marshes near the coast, and in brackish water near saline springs in the interior, from eastern Mass., south to Va., and west to Ind. Included in our last edition as *H. moscheutos,* a southern species that may not be distinct from *H. palustris.*

Halberd-leaved Rose-mallow
Hibiscus militaris   Flesh-pink, August-September

A similar but smooth species with the same period of bloom. The upper leaves often halberd-shaped, i.e., like an arrowhead with conspicuous flanges, the lower also halberd-shaped or plainly three-lobed. The flowers flesh-pink, sometimes with a dark magenta center; 2-3 inches broad. Stem 2-5 feet high. On the banks of rivers and small streams from Pa., south to Fla., and west to Minn. and Tex.

Flower-of-an-hour
Hibiscus Trionum   Sulphur-yellow, August-September

A species adventive from southern Europe, with a singular and beautiful inflated calyx resembling spun glass, five-angled, roundish, and hairy. An annual often escaping from gardens, with handsome, large, pure yellow or sulphur-colored flowers, with a black-purplish center, that quickly fade; often called bladder ketmie. The leaves deeply cut, with 3-7 lobes. 1-2 feet high. Near dwellings from Nova Scotia south, and west to Neb.

Hibiscus coccineus   Red-scarlet, August-September

A handsome southern species, with large, deep red-scarlet flowers over 6 inches broad, and deeply cleft leaves. Common in cultivation. 4-7 feet high. In deep marshes near the coast from S. C. south.

H. militaris.

H. Trionum.

Rose-mallow.
Hibiscus palustris.

ST. JOHN'S-WORT FAMILY. *Hypericaceæ*.

A small family of shrubs and herbs, with opposite, toothless leaves generally stalkless, and dotted with blackish spots. The flowers perfect, with five (or four) parts, and often with numerous stamens. Fruit a capsule.

St. Peter's-wort
Ascyrum stans   Yellow, July-August

A plant familiar in the pine barrens of New Jersey, with oval, stalkless, thickish leaves and four-petaled lemon-yellow flowers, closely resembling the next species. The stem conspicuously two-edged. 1-2 feet high. In sandy soil, N. J. and Pa., south to Tex.; also in Ky. and Mo.

St. Andrew's Cross
Ascyrum hypericoides   Yellow, July-September

A low, branching, smooth plant with small deep green leaves, oblong or narrowly obovate, stalkless and thin, growing oppositely. The lemon-yellow flowers with four petals arranged in pairs in the form of a + in a final cluster, or at the leaf-angles; petals numerous; flower ¾ inch broad. 5-10 inches high. Sandy soil, Nantucket, Mass., south to Fla., and west to Kan. and Tex.

Great St. John's-wort
Hypericum pyramidatum   Deep yellow, July-August

An erect and showy perennial with tall branching stem, the branches four-angled. Leaves ovate-oblong, pointed, stemless and slightly clasping the plant-stem. The flowers large and showy, 1-2 inches broad, deep lemon-yellow, with five narrow petals; stamens numerous. 2-6 feet high. River-banks and meadows, Que. to Pa., west to Ind. and Kan.

Shrubby St. John's-wort
Hypericum prolificum   Golden-yellow, July-August

A shrubby species with stout, branching stem, the branchlets two-edged and leafy. Leaves deep green, lighter beneath, linear-oblong, and very short-stemmed; several smaller leaflets at the junction of leaf with the stem. Flower-clusters thick, loose, and flat. The flowers golden-yellow, with numerous deep golden-yellow stamens. 3-5

Hypericum
denticulatum.

St. Andrew's Cross.
Ascyrum hypericoides.

feet high. In sandy soil, N. Y. south to Ga., and west
to Minn. and La.

Hypericum adpressum   Golden-yellow, July-August

A simple-stemmed species blooming in the same season
and with similar golden-yellow flowers. The deep green
leaves (rather closely set upon the plant-stem) oblong
or lance-shaped. The flowers in small terminal clusters,
with deep golden-yellow stamens. 1-2 feet high. In low
ground, Mass. to N. J. and Pa., south to Ga. and La.,
and west to Ind. and Ill.

Hypericum ellipticum   Light gold-yellow, July-August

A common St. John's-wort blooming in the same
season, with a simple, slightly four-angled stem. Leaves
dull light green, thin, elliptical (often perfectly so) or
oval, obtuse, and stemless, sometimes narrowed at the
base. Flowers pale gold-yellow, about ½ inch broad;
stamens numerous and golden-yellow. The pointed pods
succeeding the flowers are pale terra-cotta color. 8-20
inches high. In wet places and along streams from Que.
south to Conn., northern N. J., Pa. and W. Va., west to
Minn.

Hypericum denticulatum   Bright ochre-yellow, July-September

A slender-stemmed species generally branched above,
the stem somewhat four-angled. Leaves oblong lance-
shaped, acute, and stemless. Flowers numerous, deep
bright ochre-yellow, coppery in tone; stamens numerous,
blossom same size as the preceding. 1-2½ feet high. In
low grounds, pine barrens of central N. J., Del., south,
and west to Ill.

Common St. John's-wort
Hypericum perforatum   Deep golden-yellow, July-September

This is, generally speaking, the commonest species.
A perennial naturalized from Europe. Stem simple or
much-branched. Leaves dusky green, stalkless, small,
elliptical, or oblong-linear, more or less brown-dotted.
Flowers shiny, deep golden-yellow, with numerous stamens; the clusters terminal, on several branchlets. 1-2
feet high. Common everywhere.

St. John's-wort.

Hypericum ellipticum.　　　Hypericum perforatum.

Spotted St. John's-wort
Hypericum punctatum   Golden-yellow, July-September

A species with the same season of bloom, remarkable for its spottiness; its stem slender and round, often tinged with dull red. The leaves ovate-pointed, or oblong, thickly dotted with sepia brown, stalkless or nearly so, and often flushed with a ruddy color. The golden-yellow flowers marked with thin blackish lines, more conspicuous upon the back of the petal than on its face. 1-3 feet high. In moist places and damp thickets from Que., south to Fla., and west to Minn. and Okla.

Hypericum mutilum   Pale golden-orange, July-September

An annual, and an extremely *small-flowered* species, diffusely branched, the branchlets four-angled, and slender. The leaves light dull green, oblong or ovate, blunt-pointed, and stemless. Flowers scarcely ⅛ inch broad, pale golden-orange, or light orange-yellow, with only 5-12 stamens. 6-24 inches high. In meadows and low grounds everywhere.

Hypericum canadense   Deep golden-yellow, July-August

A very similar species, but with *linear* leaves and *tiny* deep golden yellow flowers about ⅛ inch broad, withering early in the day. The leaves light dull green and obscurely three-veined, the two side veins scarcely visible. The branches wiry, angular, and erect. The budlike, tiny pods succeeding the flowers are conspicuously ruddy, and exceed in length the five-lobed green calyx. In moist sandy soil, Que. south to S. C., and west to Minn.

Orange-grass or Pine-weed
Hypericum gentianoides   Deep golden-yellow, June-September

Also an annual, with an entirely different aspect from that of the two preceding species, although it is tiny-flowered. The stem erect, diffusely branched, and *apparently leafless;* the branches like slender wires, and the leaves minute and scalelike, leaning closely to the branchlets. Flowers deep golden-yellow, nearly stalkless, and open only in the sunlight. 5-10 inches high. In sandy soil from Me. south to Fla., and west to Minn., Mo., and Tex.

Drawn life size.

Hypericum canadense.

Marsh St. John's-wort.
Triadenum virginicum.

Marsh St. John's-wort
Triadenum virginicum   Pinkish flesh-color, July-
September

A perennial with an erect stem and stalkless, close-set, light green, ovate leaves, sepia-dotted, and with a slight bloom beneath. The stem, together with the leaves, late in the season (September) is more or less pinkish or crimson-stained, and the seed-vessels are magenta. The flowers are pinkish flesh-color, with orange glands separating the three groups of golden-yellow stamens. Flowers in small terminal clusters. 1-2 feet high. In marshes, from Nova Scotia south to Fla., and west to Mich.

ROCKROSE FAMILY. *Cistaceæ.*

Small shrubs or herbs with regular flowers, the five green sepals of unequal size, the two outer smaller ones resembling bracts, or small leaflets. Petals 3-5. But one style or none at all. Fruit a capsule (on slender stalks), splitting down the side. Visited by butterflies and honey-bees in particular.

Frostweed
Helianthemum canadense   Yellow, June-August

A perennial, remarkable for the fact that ice-crystals form about the cracked bark of the root in late autumn. Lance-oblong dull green leaves hoary with fine hairs on the under side. With two kinds of flowers, the early ones solitary, one inch broad, with showy yellow petals which are more or less crumpled in the bud and fade early and fall away; these early blossoms have innumerable stamens. The later ones have few, and are small and clustered at the bases of the leaves. Pods of the larger flower ¼ inch long; of the smaller one, not larger than a pin head. Low. In some of its forms, mostly in sandy soil from Me. south to N. C. and west to Minn. The name from the Greek words *sun* and *flower;* the flowers open only once in sunshine.

———

False Heather
Hudsonia tomentosa   Yellow, May-June

A shrubby little plant with tiny awl-shaped, scalelike leaves, oval or longer, downy, and set close to the plant-

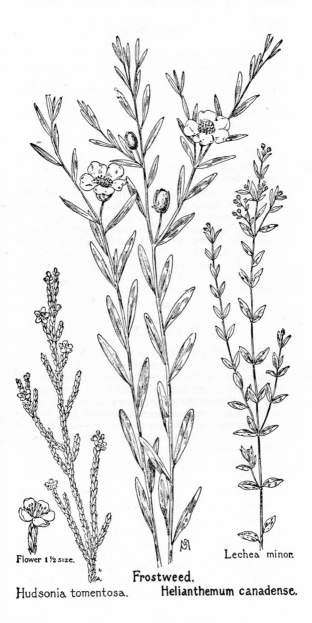

Flower 1½ size.

Frostweed.

Lechea minor.

Hudsonia tomentosa.

Helianthemum canadense.

stem. The small yellow flowers crowded along the upper branches; they open only in sunshine. The stem 5-10 inches high, hoary with down. Sandy shores, Que. to N. C., west to sandy areas in southern Canada, Ill., Ind. and N. D. The related golden heather, *H. ericoides,* has more spreading leaves and is found among the dunes from Newf. to Va.

————

Pinweed
Lechea minor　Greenish or magenta-tinted, June-September

An insignificant, fine-hairy, perennial herb, with tiny linear leaves, larger on the upper parts of the plant and very small near the base. The three tiny, greenish (or magenta-tinted) narrow petals remain within the green sepals after fading. The pod nearly globose, and appearing like a pin head. The upright smooth (when old) stem 10-18 inches high. Common in dry, sterile ground. There are seven other pinweeds in our area, but their differences are too technical to include here.

VIOLET FAMILY. *Violaceæ.*

A family of generally low herbs with perfect, but rather irregular, flowers of five petals, the lowest of which is spurred. There are five perfect stamens whose anthers turn inward and lie touching each other around the pistil. Besides the upper, showy flowers, all except the first species produce near the ground level another set of inconspicuous flowers that never open. Over 50 species of violets are found in our area; those below are the most common. *Viola* is the old Latin name for the sweet violet of Europe, *V. odorata.* Most of ours are inodorous.

Bird-foot Violet
Viola pedata　Light violet, etc., April-June

A beautiful violet, generally smooth and tufted; the leaves, dull pale green, are cut into 3-5 segments, three of which are again cut and toothed, so that the average leaf possesses nine distinct points, or more. The pale blue-violet or lilac flowers, larger than those of any other species, are often an inch long. But the most familiar tint of the common Bird-foot Violet is blue-violet, more

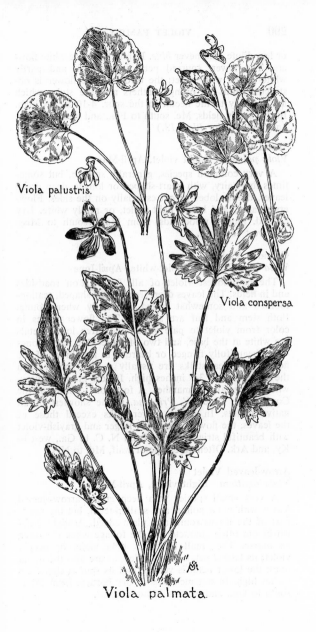

Viola palustris.

Viola conspersa

Viola palmata.

or less dilute, and never *blue*. Rarely there are white flowers. The lower, spurred petal is grooved, and partly white-veined with violet; the throat of the flower is obstructed with the orange anthers and the style, which bar the way to the nectar in the spur. 4-10 inches high. In dry sandy fields, Me. south to Fla., and west to Minn. and Tex. (*Color Plate 13.*)

Wood Violet
Viola palmata   Light violet, April-May

A very common species, generally smooth, but sometimes fine-hairy, with heart-shaped or longer, deep green leaves, deeply lobed or cut especially on the sides. Flowers smaller, and bright light violet, or rarely white. Dry ground, mostly woodlands, from Mass. south to Miss. and west to Minn.

Common Violet
Viola papilionacea   Violet-white, April-June

The commonest violet of all, familiar on roadsides and in fields. The leaves deep green, heart-shaped, scallop-toothed and somewhat coiled, especially when young. Both stem and leaf are smooth. The flower varies in color from violet to pale violet; the three lower petals are white at the base, and two of these—the lateral ones—are beautifully fringed or bearded at the throat of the flower. The leaf-stalks are usually a little longer than the flower-stalks. 3-7 inches high. In low grounds everywhere, especially in marshes. A form of it known as the Confederate violet, *V. Priceana,* is the showiest of all native violets. In it the flower-stalks exceed those of the leaves, the flowers are much larger and grayish-violet with beautiful stripes. Native from N. C. to Ga., west to Ky. and Ark. Often an escape or waif, Md. to N. C.

Arrow-leaved Violet
Viola sagittata   Light violet, April-May

A very small species with deep green, arrow-shaped leaves with blunt points, and scallop-teeth, but the upper part of the leaves sometimes plain-edged. A slight grayish bloom often characterizes the foliage when it is seen *en masse*. The small flower is light violet or deeper violet; its lateral petals are bearded, as are also the upper ones; the lower petal is veined, and its spur is short. 2-8 inches high. In wet meadows or dry borders from Mass. south to Ga., and west to Minn. and La.

Arrow-leaved Violet.
Viola sagittata.

Blue Violet.
Viola papilionacea.

Viola Selkirkii   Pale violet, May-June

Selkirk's Violet is a rather uncommon, small, woodland species generally found among the hills. The stalks are erect and smooth, the leaves dark green and heart-shaped, deeply lobed at the base. The flowers are pale violet and beardless, with deep spurs. Moist soil, from N. B. to Pa., and westward to Minn. Also in Europe and Asia.

Marsh Violet
Viola palustris   Light lilac, May-July

A small smooth species whose flower-stalks generally exceed those of the leaves, which are broad, heart-shaped and indistinctly scalloped. Sometimes the leaves are kidney-shaped. The small flowers are light violet or lilac, with purple veins; the petals are nearly, if not quite, without beards. 3-6 inches high. In marshes and wet soil, Labrador to mountains of New Eng., west to the Rockies; also in Eurasia.

Sweet White Violet
Viola blanda   White, April-May

A small species with olive-green, round heart-shaped leaves slightly scalloped, and *sweet-scented* white flowers, very small, with purple-veined petals, bearded, and *not* broadly expanded. 3-5 inches high. In swamps, wet meadows, moist woodlands, and often in dry situations, from Que. south to Ga., and local westward. (*Color Plate 14.*) A close relative, *Viola renifolia,* is slightly soft-hairy, the leaves are round kidney-formed, and the flower-petals are usually beardless. From Newf. to western N. Y. and Minn.

Lance-leaved Violet
Viola lanceolata   White, April-June

A smooth, remarkably narrow-leaved species, the leaves lance-shaped or even linear lance-shaped, indistinctly scalloped, and generally blunt. The flowers white, veined with dull purple, and the petals beardless; they are slightly fragrant. Cross-fertilized by the aid of the small bees. 2-5 inches high. Common in moist ground and on river-banks, from Nova Scotia south to Fla., and west to Minn. and Tex.

Sweet White Violet.   Lance-leaved Violet.
Viola blanda.   Viola lanceolata.

Round-leaved Violet
Viola rotundifolia   Pale golden-yellow, April-May

A very early and rather inconspicuous violet, most frequently found on woodland floors and rocky hillsides. The stalks are smooth, or very slightly fine-hairy, and 2-4 inches high; generally the flower-stalks exceed those of the leaves. The smooth deep green leaves are round or long heart-shaped, indistinctly scalloped, and small in the flowering season; but by midsummer they lie flat upon the ground and attain a diameter of 2-4 inches. The small flowers are pale golden-yellow, the lateral petals are bearded and veined with madder purple; the lower petal is also strongly veined and has a short spur. In cool and somewhat damp evergreen woods, Que., south in the mountains to S. C. and Ga., and west to western Ont.

Downy Yellow Violet
Viola pubescens   Pale golden-yellow, April-May

This is a rather tall and forking species lacking the lowly habit of the common violet. The light green stem is fine-hairy above, though usually smooth below. The leaves are deep green, broad heart-shaped, slightly scallop-toothed, and somewhat soft-hairy to the touch. The small flowers are pale golden-yellow, veined with madder purple; the lower petal, conspicuously veined, is short (set horizontally), with a two-scalloped tip and a short spur. The flowers grow singly on thin stalks from the fork of two leaf-stalks. The anthers and the style obstruct the throat of the flower, and the side petals, heavily bearded, compel the entering insect to brush against the stigma and finally against the anthers in the effort to obtain nectar. 6-17 inches high. In woodlands from Me. south to Ga., and west to S. D. and Iowa. A related, but perhaps not distinct species, is *V. pennsylvanica*. It is not so tall, the stems are slender, only slightly fine-hairy, and the leaves are generally acute at the apex and distinctly scallop-toothed. 4-12 inches high. In moist thickets or woodlands from Conn. south to Ga., west to Minn. and Tex.

Canada Violet
Viola canadensis   Pale purple, white, May-July

A smooth sweet-scented species with a tall, leafy stem resembling that of the foregoing. The heart-shaped, deep green leaves, broader or longer, with a slightly toothed

Downy Yellow Violet.
Viola pubescens.

Viola canadensis

Viola rotundifolia.

edge, on long stalks, growing alternately. The flowers springing from the forking leaf-stalks are lighter or deeper purple on the outside of the petals and nearly white on the inside, with the throat yellow-tinted; the three lower petals are purple-veined, the side petals bearded, and the middle petal is acutely tipped. Rarely the flowers are altogether white. 5-15 inches high, occasionally more. In hilly woods from Newf. south to S. C. and Ala., among the mountains and west to Saskatchewan and N. Mex.

Viola canadensis passes through various grades of purple to a decided magenta-pink. There are also similar pink phases of *Viola pedata,* but the color never seems to be constant.

Pale Violet
Viola striata   White or pale lavender, April-May

A handsome, somewhat western species with smooth, straight stems, and deep dull green, heart-shaped leaves, finely scallop-toothed, and more or less curled at the base when young, the tips acute. The moderately large flowers white, cream-colored, or very pale lavender, the lateral petals bearded, the lower one thickly striped with purple veins, and broad. The flower-stalk exceedingly long. The stigma of the flower projects far beyond the anthers, so self-fertilization is impracticable. 6-16 inches high. In moist woods and fields, N. Y. to Minn., and south along the Alleghenies to Ga. and Ala.

Dog Violet
Viola conspersa   Light purple, April-June

A low creeping violet; the light green stems with many toothed stipules (leafy formations at the angles of the stems), and small round heart-shaped yellow-green leaves, obscurely scalloped, and not pointed at the tip. The pale purple or violet flowers are small, with the side petals slightly bearded, and the lower petal purple-veined and long-spurred. Rarely the flowers are white. The seeds are straw-color. 2-6 inches high. Common in wet woodlands and along shady roadsides, from eastern Que., west to Minn., and south to Ala. and Mo. A related species, *Viola adunca,* is characteristically fine-hairy, the leaves are ovate and small, and the stipules are deeply toothed; the flower spur is generally blunt and straight, though occasionally it is abruptly bent inward. Seeds brown. In sandy soil, Que. to Minn., and northwest.

Pale Violet.   Viola striata.

CACTUS FAMILY. *Cactaceæ.*

A very large family of desert plants, confined to the New World and much developed in Ariz., N. Mex. and adjacent Mexico, a few of them reaching to our area. They are characteristically leafless, fleshy, and usually very spiny plants, reaching giant stature in the saguaro, *Carnegiea gigantea,* of Ariz. Ours are much smaller, with leaflike swollen joints, and conspicuous, showy radiate flowers. Sepals, petals and stamens very numerous. Fruit, in ours, a fleshy berry, often edible. One of the species yields the Indian narcotic, peyote.

Prickly Pear
Opuntia compressa **Yellow, July-August**

A nearly prostrate perennial succulent, often forming mats in sandy places. Leaflike joints thick and fleshy, oblongish, 2½-5 inches long, peppered with cushionlike clusters of minute barbs, which, if touched, are almost impossible to extract from one's skin. The plant, unlike its desert relatives, is usually spineless, or there may be one or two stout yellowish spines. Flowers bright yellow, 2-3 inches wide. Fruit pear-shaped, juicy, 1-2 inches long, reddish-purple and edible if all the minute barbs are removed, otherwise choking! In dry places, Mass. to Ga., often on sand dunes, west on dry prairies to Minn., Mo. and Tex. Several related species are known from the Middle West.

LOOSESTRIFE FAMILY. *Lythraceæ.*

Woody herbs in our range, with four-sided branches and generally toothless, opposite leaves and perfect flowers, though these are occasionally in two or even three forms, i.e., with long filaments (the stem part of the stamen minus the anther) and a short style, or vice versa. Petals 4-7. Stamens 4-14, sometimes the petals are absent. Cross-fertilization effected in a number of instances through the agency of bees and butterflies.

Hyssop Loosestrife
Lythrum Hyssopifolia **Pale purple-magenta, July-**
September

A smooth branching annual, with pale green stem and leaves, the latter alternate and lance-shaped, with stalk-

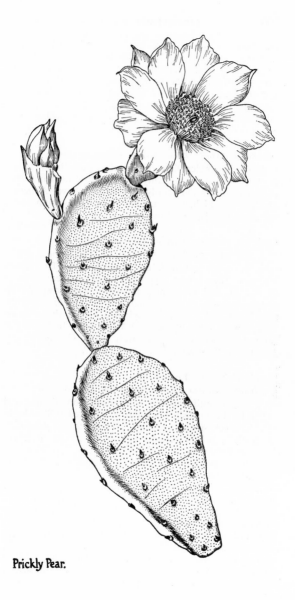

Prickly Pear.

less base, at which there are frequently little narrow leaflets growing upon a separate stalk of their own, which, lengthening, forms lateral, leafy branches above. The pale purplish-magenta flowers usually have six petals and the same number of stamens, or less; they grow singly in the angles of the leaves. 6-15 inches high. In salt marshes, from Me. to N. J., also in Ohio. Also widely distributed on the Pacific Coast and in Eurasia.

Lythrum lineare Pale purple, July-September

A similar, paler flowered species with linear leaves growing oppositely; the tiny flowers grow in two forms, explained under the family description above. A perennial 2-3 feet high. Salt marshes from N. J. south along the coast to Fla. and Tex.

Lythrum alatum Purple, July-September

A tall slim species with much darker leafage and a smooth, much-branched, and angled stem. The leaves alternate (the lowest opposite), lance-shaped, pointed at the tip, and broader at the base. The flowers deep purple-magenta, ¼ inch or more broad, and dimorphous, that is, in two forms, as explained above; the stamens very long in some blossoms. 1-3 feet high. In low moist ground, from Ont. to Ga., west to B. C.; mostly occasional in the northeast.

Purple or Spiked Loosestrife
Lythrum Salicaria Purple-magenta, June-August

A most beautiful species naturalized from Europe and called by the English, Long Purples, Spiked Willow-herb, etc. An erect, smooth, or slightly hairy slender perennial, generally much-branched. The medium green leaves lance-shaped with a heart-shaped base, growing oppositely or in circles of three, and stalkless. The long-petaled, purple-magenta (light or deep) flowers, growing in circles, with 8-12 stamens, longer and shorter; the flowers, in fact, trimorphous, that is, developing *three* relative lengths of stamens and style. Unquestionably dependent upon insects for cross-fertilization; the honey-bee, the bumblebee, and many of the butterflies are common visitors. 20-35 inches high. In wet meadows, and on the borders of swamps, from Que. south to Md., and apparently increasing its range; also found in Mich., and in eastern N. Y. It responds readily to cultivation.

Cuphea petiolata.

Lythrum Salicaria. Loosestrife. Lythrum alatum.

Swamp Loosestrife
Decodon verticillatus   Magenta, July-September

A somewhat shrubby plant, nearly smooth, with re-clining or recurved stems of 4-6 sides, and lance-shaped leaves nearly stalkless, opposite-growing, or mostly in threes; the uppermost with clusters of small, bell-shaped magenta flowers growing from their bases. Flowers with five wedge-lance-shaped petals half an inch long. Stamens 10, five short and five long. 2-8 feet long. Swampy places. Nova Scotia to Fla., west to Minn. and La.

Blue Waxweed
Cuphea petiolata   Magenta-pink, June-September

A cold and clammy, hairy, branching, homely annual, with ovate-lance-shaped dull green leaves, and small magenta-pink flowers with ovate petals on short claws. Stem branching, 1-2 feet high. Dry sandy fields, from N. H. south to Ga., and west to Kan. and La.

MEADOW-BEAUTY FAMILY.
Melastomaceæ.

Herbs, or in the tropics gorgeous shrubs and trees, comprising over 4,000 species; but only a handful of herbs reaches our area. They have opposite leaves of 3-7 veins, and perfect, regular flowers having four petals, and as many calyx-lobes; there are either four or eight promi-nent stamens; in our species the anthers open by a pore in the apex. The stigma being far in advance of the anthers, the flower is cross-fertilized, and mostly through the agency of butterflies and bees. The seeds are in a four-celled capsule.

Meadow-beauty or Deer-grass
Rhexia virginica   Magenta, July-August

A stout-stemmed perennial, sometimes branched (the stem rather square), with smooth, light green, three-ribbed leaves, sharp-toothed, ovate pointed or narrower, and stalkless. The flowers with four broad magenta or purple-magenta petals; the golden anthers large. There are eight stamens slightly varying in length; the pistil reaching beyond them secures the cross-fertilization of the flower. 10-18 inches high. In sandy marshes, from Nova Scotia to Ga., and local west to Wisc. and Okla.

Swamp Loosestrife.   Decodon verticillatus

Rhexia aristosa   Magenta-purple, July-August

A similar species, with square stem and narrow, small, linear leaves. The large rounded petals of the magenta flowers are furnished with a tiny awnlike point. In sandy swamps, and the pine barrens of New Jersey, south to Ga.; local.

Rhexia mariana   Magenta-purple, July-August

A slender, round-stemmed species, rather hairy and with short-stemmed linear-oblong, toothed leaves, three-ribbed and acute. The flowers are light magenta and similar to those of *Rhexia virginica*. In sandy swamps, and in the pine barrens of New Jersey, south and southwest to Tex. The name was used by Pliny for some unknown plant, perhaps an *Echium,* but not for this.

Rhexia ciliosa   Purple, July-September

A smooth species with a square stem and ovate almost stemless leaves with bristly fringed edges. Flowers like those of *R. virginica* but purple, the anthers oblong and straight, not spurred. 1-2 feet high. Va. to S. C.

EVENING PRIMROSE FAMILY. *Onagraceæ.*

Herbs, or sometimes shrubby. The perfect flowers commonly with four petals and four sepals (rarely 2-6), and with as many or twice as many stamens; the stigma with 2-4 lobes. Fertilized by moths, butterflies, and bees.

Seedbox
Ludwigia alternifolia   Yellow, June-September

A nearly smooth herb with many branches, and lance-shaped, toothless, opposite-growing leaves which taper to a point at either end. The solitary light yellow, four-petaled flowers, about ⅞ inch broad, with sepals nearly as long as the petals. The seed-capsule is four-sided and wing-margined, rounded at the base; the seeds eventually become loose and rattle about when the plant is shaken. 2-3 feet high. Common in swamps, from Mass., to northern N. Y., south to Fla., and west to Iowa and Kan.

Ludwigia polycarpa   Green, July-September

A less showy species with very narrow lance-shaped leaves, and tiny, inconspicuous, stemless flowers whose rudimentary petals are pale green. The flowers grow at

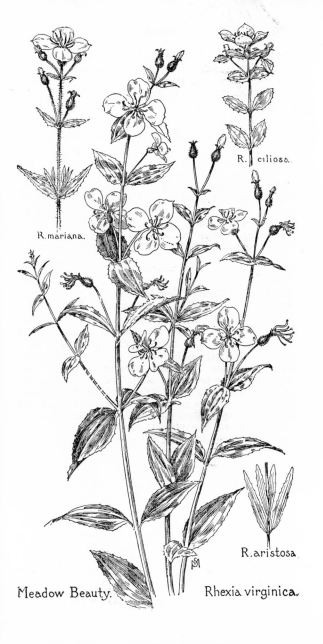

R. mariana.

R. ciliosa.

R. aristosa.

Meadow Beauty.

Rhexia virginica.

the junction of leaf-stalk with plant-stem. The four-sided, top-shaped seed-capsule is furnished at the base with linear or awl-shaped leaflets. 1-3 feet high. In swamps from Mass., southwest to Tenn. and west to Minn. and E. Kan.

Water Purslane
Ludwigia palustris   Pale reddish, June-September

A common, uninteresting aquatic species found in swamps and ditches. The tiny inconspicuous flowers without petals, or, when the plant grows out of water, with very small ruddy ones. The lance-shaped, opposite-growing, slender-stalked leaves (with the flowers growing at their bases) an inch long or less. The elongated capsule indistinctly four-sided. Stems 4-12 inches long, creeping or floating. Shallow marshes, and muddy ditches everywhere. Named for C. G. Ludwig, a German botanist.

Fireweed, or Great Willow Herb
Epilobium angustifolium   Light magenta, July-August

A tall perennial herb with ruddy stem and dark olive-green, lance-shaped, white-ribbed leaves without teeth or nearly so, resembling those of the willow. The light magenta or rarely white flowers in a terminal showy spike with four broad and conspicuous petals, eight stamens, and a prominent pistil. The slender, velvety, purple-tinged pods, gracefully curved, open lengthwise and liberate a mass of silky down in late August and September, which gives the plant a wild and disheveled appearance. 4-7 feet high. Common on newly cleared woodland, especially where the ground has been burned over throughout N. Am.

Hairy Willow Herb
Epilobium hirsutum   Magenta, July-August

A foreign perennial species which has become naturalized about towns near the coast. The deep yellow-green leaves oblong lance-shaped, finely toothed and stemless. The four-petaled magenta flowers, ⅞ inch broad, in a short terminal cluster, or between leaf-stem and plant-stem. There are eight stamens. Seed-pod long and slender, the seed wafted by means of a long tuft of silky hairs at the tip. 3-4 feet high, densely soft-hairy, stout and branching.

L. palustris   L. polycarpa.

Seedbox.

Ludwigia alternifolia.

Fireweed.
Epilobium angustifolium.

Hairy Willow Herb.
Epilobium hirsutum.

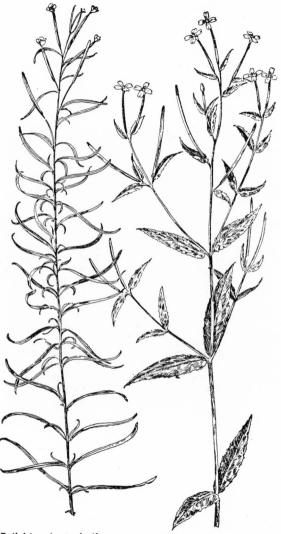

Epilobium leptophyllum.   Epilobium coloratum.

Epilobium palustre Lilac, July-August

A small uncommon species. The stem angled or marked with hairy lines, sparsely finely hairy throughout. The broad linear, obtuse leaves erect or ascending, and stalkless, with curled-back margins. The seed-capsules extremely long and with scarcely apparent slender stems. 6-12 inches high. Flowers the same as in the next species. Throughout the cooler part of our range.

Epilobium leptophyllum Lilac, July-August

A very slender swamp species, with small linear or narrow lance-shaped light green leaves with a short but distinct stalk, and tiny lilac or pale magenta flowers, scarcely ¼ inch broad. The whole plant minutely hairy together with the capsule. More branched than the next species. 1-2 feet high. In bogs from Que., southwest to Ky., and west to Colo. and Utah.

Epilobium strictum Lilac, July-August

A similar species with densely soft white-hairy stem, leaves, and seed-pod. The leaves broader and less acute than those of the last species, with short stems or none at all. The veins distinct. Flowers like those of the previous species. 1-3 feet high. In bogs from Que. south to Va., and west to Ill.

Epilobium coloratum Lilac, July-August

A very common species in the north, with a minutely hairy branching stem, often ruddy, and lanceolate leaves, distinctly but not conspicuously toothed, short-stalked, and yellow-green in color, often ruddy-tinged. The tiny flowers pale lilac, and sometimes nodding; in fact, all these small-flowered *Epilobiums* after being plucked show nodding blossoms. Seed-pod green, exceedingly long and slender, the seeds dark brown, the hairy plume, at first pale, finally cinnamon-brown. 1-3 feet high. In wet situations everywhere.

Epilobium adenocaulon Lilac, July-August

Differs from the foregoing species in having erect flowers (though they may nod at first), broader, blunter, and less toothed leaves with shorter stalks, and lighter colored seeds with a slight prolongation at the top. 1-3 feet high. In wet situations throughout the north; not south of Pa. The silky plumes of the seeds of these few last small-flowered species described may become grayish-

Willow-herb   Epilobium adenocaulon

white as in *E. adenocaulon;* but at first they are *abso-lutely white*. At best the *Epilobiums* are a difficult *genus* to separate distinctly, and are not a little puzzling to the botanist.

———

Common Evening Primrose
Œnothera biennis Pure yellow, July-August

A very familiar biennial, and nocturnal species, with light green leaves more or less lance-shaped, sometimes broad, slightly resembling those of the fireweed, slightly toothed or toothless. Large showy pure yellow flowers, lemon-scented, with eight prominent and spreading stamens; the golden pollen loosely connected by cobwebby threads. They usually open just before sundown, and fade in the strong sunlight of the following day; the sudden opening of the flower in the twilight hour is interesting and remarkable. The soft-hairy plant-stem, leafy throughout, is 1-6 feet high. Roadsides and fields everywhere east of the Rocky Mountains. The commonly cultivated *Œ. grandiflora,* from the southwest, is very large; the corolla is 3-4 inches in diameter.

Oakes's Evening Primrose
Œnothera parviflora Pure yellow, July-August

An annual, slenderer than the foregoing species, and not hairy but covered with a slight close woolliness. The calyx-tips not conspicuously close together. Dry situations, Newf. to N. J., west to Mont. A related plant, sometimes called *Œ. cruciata* has narrower petals.

Œnothera laciniata Pure yellow, May-July

A lower slightly fine-hairy species with oblong or lance-shaped leaves wavy-toothed or often deep-cleft like those of the dandelion; the small light yellow flowers borne at the bases of the leaves turn pinkish in fading. About 1 foot high. In sandy soil, from Mass. south, and west to S. D., Okla. and N. Mex.

Sundrops
Œnothera perennis Pure yellow, May-July

A small slightly hairy plant with diurnal, rather small pure yellow flowers, borne in a loose spike or at the bases of the leaves, the latter light dull green, toothless and obtuse, lance-shaped but broader nearer the tip. 10-20 inches high. In dry sunny fields, from Que. to N. C., and west to Minn. and Kan.

Evening Primrose.   Œnothera biennis.

Œnothera tetragona   **Yellow, May-September**

A slender species with very large pure yellow flowers 1½-2¾ inches broad, and long ovate leaves, wavy-toothed. The smooth seed-capsule oblong and with four broad wings. 20-34 inches high. In dry mountain woods, Nova Scotia to Ala., west to Mich. and La.

Sundrops
Œnothera fruticosa   **Pure yellow, May-July**

A similar diurnal species with flowers ½-1 inch broad, borne in a loose spike or at the bases of the leaves; the latter are oblong or lance-shaped and very slightly toothed. The stigma extends far beyond the anthers, so self-fertilization is impossible except with the agency of insects. The seed-pods strongly ribbed and winged. Very variable. 1-3 feet high. Common in fields and on roadsides everywhere. A variety of it is more slender, has very narrow, linear-lance-shaped leaves, and the less ribbed seed-pods taper into the slender stalk. It is sometimes designated as *Œ. fruticosa,* var. *linearis.*

———

Enchanter's Nightshade
Circæa quadrisulcata   **White, July-August**

An inconspicuous perennial of damp and shady woodlands, with opposite thin, frail deep green leaves, ovate pointed, remotely toothed, and long-stalked. The tiny white flowers have two petals so deeply cleft that they appear as four; they are borne at the tip of a long slender stem, which is set about with the little green burlike, white-haired, nearly round seed-pods. Plant-stem very smooth and swollen at the joints. Common in cool and moist woodlands everywhere. Named for the enchantress Circe.

Circæa alpina   **White, July-August**

A smaller species, the stem of which is watery and translucent, ruddy and smooth. The thin and delicate heart-shaped leaves are shiny, coarsely blunt-toothed, and distinctly different from those of the preceding species. Tiny leaflets, or bracts, are set immediately beneath the flowers. The burlike buds are club-shaped. 3-8 inches high. Common only in the north among the mountains. Low, 8-16 inches high.

Sundrops.
Œnothera *fruiticosa*.

Œnothera
perennis.

Circæa canadensis   White, July-August

The leaves ovate and long-stalked, coarsely toothed. Flowers small, white, 8-10 in a cluster, followed by small, bristly fruits. Que. to Mass., west to Mich. and Minn.

GINSENG FAMILY. *Araliaceæ.*

Generally herbs in our range, with compound, mostly alternate leaves and tiny five-petaled flowers in crowded clusters; stamens five, alternate with the petals; the flowers perfect or more or less polygamous; staminate and pistillate flowers occurring on the same plant. Fruit a cluster of berries, which with the root, bark, etc., are slightly aromatic. Visited by numerous woodland insects as well as the bees and occasionally by butterflies.

Spikenard
Aralia racemosa   Green-white, July-August

A tall, branching, smooth woodland herb, with a round, blackish stem, and large compound leaves of generally 15-21 ovate leaflets, heart-shaped at the base, finely double-toothed, and deep green with brownish stems. The greenish-white flowers are arranged in small round clusters which in the aggregate form a large, terminal, branched cluster. Visited by bees and the beelike flies. Fruit a round dull brown-crimson berry (in compact clusters), sometimes, when over-ripe, dull brown-purple. The large roots are esteemed for their spicy and aromatic flavor. 3-5 feet high. Rich woodlands from Que., south through the mountains to N. C., and west to Minn., S. D. and Mo.

Bristly Sarsaparilla or Wild Elder
Aralia hispida   Dull white, June-early July

A characteristically fine-hairy plant with similar leaves generally hairy on the veins beneath and irregularly double-toothed; they are perhaps longer and more pointed than those of *Aralia racemosa,* and rounded at the base. The tiny dull white flowers are arranged in somewhat hemispherical clusters, several of which crown the summit of the stem. The fruit is somewhat oblate-spheroidal in shape and huckleberry black when ripe. 12-34 inches high. In rocky woods, from Newf. south to N. C., in the mountains; west to Minn. A tall shrubby relative of these *Aralias* is the Hercules' Club, which is very spiny,

Enchanter's
Nightshade.
Circæa quadrisulcata.

Circæa alpina.

has immense compound leaves and equally large flower clusters. Known as *Aralia spinosa* it grows from Del. to Fla., and west to Ind. and Mo.

Wild Sarsaparilla
Aralia nudicaulis   Green-white, May-June

A so-called stemless *Aralia,* whose true plant-stem scarcely rises above ground, the leaf-stem and flower-stem apparently separating near the root. There is a single long-stalked leaf rising 7-12 inches above the ground, with three branching divisions of leaflets; there are about five ovate, finely toothed, light green leaflets on each division. The flower-stalk is leafless and bears 3-7 rather flat hemispherical clusters of greenish-white flowers whose tiny petals are strongly reflexed; the five greenish stamens are conspicuous. The fruit is a round purple-black berry in clusters. Common in moist woodlands, from Newf. south along the mountains to Ga., and west to Ind. and Mo. The aromatic roots are used as a substitute for the true Sarsaparilla (*Smilax officinalis*).

Ginseng
Panax quinquefolium   Pale green-yellow, July-August

The roots of Ginseng, which in the estimation of the Chinese are possessed of some potent medicinal virtue, are so much in demand for export that through the assiduity of collectors the plant has become rare. The large deep green leaf has five thin, obovate, acute-pointed leaflets, sharply and irregularly toothed; in arrangement it slightly resembles the horse-chestnut leaf. The plant-stem is smooth and green, and the compound leaves are borne three in a circle. The yellowish-green flowers (the staminate lily-of-the-valley-scented) are crowded into a single hemispherical cluster; they are polygamous. The fruit is a deep ruby-red berry, in a scant cluster. The name is a corruption of the Chinese Jin-chen, meaning manlike (from the two-legged appearance of the root). The plant is small—8-15 inches high. In rich cold woods, Que. to Ga., west to Minn.; very rare.

Dwarf Ginseng
Panax trifolium   Dull white, May-June

A tiny species with a *spherical* root, generally three compound leaves composed of about three toothed, ovate leaflets, and dull white flowers, staminate and pistillate

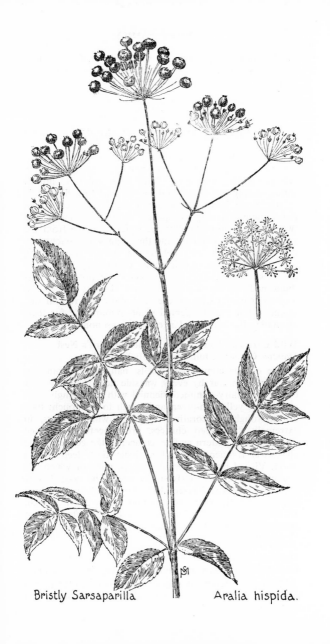

Bristly Sarsaparilla   Aralia hispida.

on the same plant, borne in a single cluster. Fruit yellow. 4-8 inches high. Que. south to Ga. in the mountains, and west to Minn. and Iowa.

PARSLEY FAMILY. *Umbelliferæ.*

An enormous family of chiefly herbs, notable examples among garden plants being parsley, carrot, parsnip, celery, caraway and anise. They have generally hollow stems, deeply cut compound leaves, and tiny flowers in mostly broad flat-topped clusters (umbels), perfect (often polygamous), having five petals, as many stamens, and two styles. In some flowers the styles protrude from the yet undeveloped blossom, and the stigmas are touched by the visiting insect long before the anthers are mature, thus securing cross-fertilization. Commonly visited by countless insects. The many species are not easily distinguished, as the flowers are very similar; in general, minute characteristics of the seed show the radical differences best. Strong-scented plants remarkable for their aromatic oil; some are dangerously poisonous if eaten.

Wild Carrot or Queen Anne's Lace or Bird's Nest
Daucus Carota   Dull white, July-September

One of our commonest weeds, naturalized from Europe, and familiar by every wayside near a dwelling. A coarse and hairy-stemmed biennial with exceedingly fine-cut leaves, yellowish-green and rough to the touch; they are thoroughly decorative. The dull white flowers, in extremely flat-topped clusters, are gracefully disposed in a radiating pattern as fine as lace; in the center of the cluster is frequently found a single tiny deep purple floret. Visited by innumerable insects, most of which are attracted by the peculiarly strong odor. The aged flower-cluster curls up and resembles a bird's nest, from which circumstance the plant derives that name. 2-3 feet high. In waste places and fields everywhere; it is often a most troublesome weed. From it was derived the garden carrot.

Hemlock Parsley
Conioselinum chinense   Dull white, August-September

A smooth, perennial species somewhat similar in appearance to wild carrot, but with a slender-branched

Conioselinum
chinense.

Wild Carrot.   Daucus Carota.

flower-cluster composed of far less showy dull white
flowers. The leaves similar, the lower long-stemmed, the
upper quite stemless. The fruit or seed is smooth, flat,
and prominently five-ribbed, the two side ribs exceedingly
broad. 2-4 feet high. In cool swamps among the hills,
from Labrador, southwest through the mountains to
N. C., west to Minn. and Iowa.

Cowbane
Oxypolis rigidior   Dull white, August-September
    A tall and slender species, poisonous to taste, and with
large tuberiferous roots. The leaves are deep green, and
altogether different in form from those of the preceding
species; they are long-stemmed and composed of 3-9
lance-shaped or broader, remotely toothed leaflets, more
or less variable in shape. The tiny dull white flowers are
in slender clusters. The seed is flat-sided, broad, and the
ribs are not sharp or prominent; the side ribs are broad.
Another denizen of the swamps; from N. Y. south to
Fla., west to Minn. and Mo. Name from the Greek for
white and sharp, in allusion to pointed bracts and white
flowers.

Cow Parsnip
Heracleum lanatum   Dull white, June-July
    A common very tall perennial with a stout, hollow,
ridged stem, sometimes stained lightly with dull brown-
red. The leaves are dark green, compound—in three
divisions, toothed and deeply lobed, rather soft-hairy
beneath, and with a leafy formation at the junction of the
leaf-stem and plant-stem. The insignificant dull white
flowers, in large flat clusters, have five petals, each of
which is deeply notched and of unequal proportions. The
seed is very broad, flat, and generally oval. 4-8 feet high.
Wet ground, shady borders of moist thickets, from
Labrador south to Ga., and west to Ariz. Named for
Hercules.

Wild Parsnip
Pastinaca sativa   Light gold-yellow, June-September
    A common biennial familiar on waysides and the bor-
ders of fields, with a tough, strongly grooved, smooth
stem, and with dull deep green, compound leaves composed of many, toothed, thin, ovate divisions. The dull

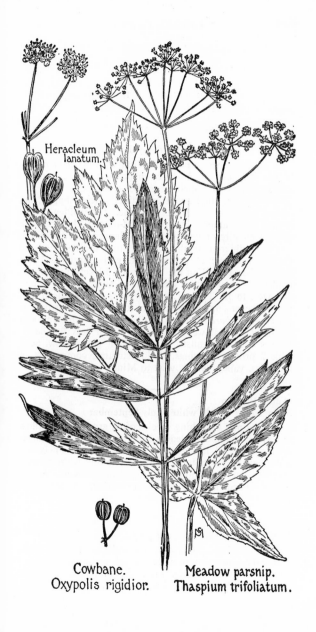

Heracleum
lanatum.

Cowbane.
Oxypolis rigidior.

Meadow parsnip.
Thaspium trifoliatum.

(in effect greenish) light gold-yellow flowers are gathered in small clusters set on slender stems, and form a broad, flat-topped cluster. The stem, 2-5 feet high, is extremely strong and difficult if not impossible to break. Seeds flat and thin. Common. Naturalized from Europe, and the ancestor of the garden parsnip.

Meadow Parsnip
Thaspium trifoliatum   Golden-yellow, June-August

A western species not very distant from *Zizia aurea*. It has medium green lance-shaped or ovate, toothed leaflets, three of which *generally* compose a leaf; the root-leaves are single, mostly distinctly heart-shaped, the others simply rounded at the base. The golden-yellow flowers are gathered in sparse flat-topped clusters. The seed is equally angled with deep flanges or ribs and is distinctly different in this respect from the flat seeds of *Pastinaca sativa;* they mature in early autumn. 15-36 inches high. Found on the borders of thickets, and woodland roads, from Ohio, west to Mo., southwest to Tenn., and west to Ill. The var. *atropurpureum* bears deep dull purple flowers, and is found from R. I. to Fla., mostly near the coast. *T. barbinode* is a similar species with stem- and leaf-joints and flowering stems more or less fine-hairy. Leaves with 3-6 leaflets. Flowers light gold-yellow. Seed with 7 prominent wings. Beside streams, commonest in the Miss. valley; N. Y., west to Minn., and south.

Water Parsnip
Sium suave   Dull white, July-September

A stout and branching species often growing in shallow water. The compound leaves deep green, with 7-15 linear or lance-shaped leaflets sharply toothed; the finely cut lower leaves generally submerged. The dull white flowers are in a flat dome-shaped cluster. The seeds are prominently ribbed, and the leaves are variable in form. 2-6 feet high. Throughout the country.

Berula erecta   White, June-July

A similar but smaller aquatic species 6-34 inches high, with 7-19 leaflets, more or less lobed, and a dome-shaped cluster of white flowers. From N. Y. to Ill. and Neb. Also in the Rockies, the Far West, and in Eurasia.

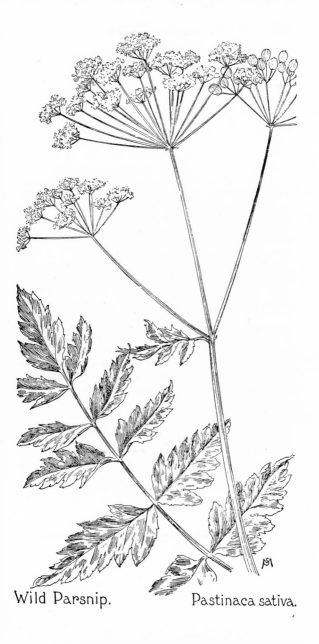

Wild Parsnip.   Pastinaca sativa.

Golden Alexanders
Zizia aurea Light gold-yellow, May-June

A very common smooth perennial, found on shaded roadsides or meadow borders. The medium light green leaves are doubly compound; generally three divisions (or leaflets, properly speaking) of 3-7 leaflets, all narrow, pointed, and sharply toothed, but varying to broader types. The stem is often branched. The tiny dull light gold-yellow flowers have prominent stamens, and are collected in many small clusters, each widely separated from the other but all forming a thin radiating cluster. Visited commonly by many flies, small butterflies, and but few bees. Seeds slightly ribbed. 16-34 inches high. Everywhere.

Caraway
Carum carvi Dull white, June-July

A common weed in the north, naturalized from Europe. Biennial or perennial; the lower basal leaves long-stemmed, the upper stemless; all fine cut, and ornamental; deep olive gray-green; the flowers grouped like those of the wild carrot, but far less showy, dull white or gray-white, in scattered thin groups like *Zizia*. The seed is oblong, slightly curved, plainly ribbed, exceedingly aromatic, and is much used as a spice in cakes, and also in confectionery. The flowers are frequently visited by various flies, bees, and butterflies. 1-2 feet high. Local from Newf. west to Minn., S. D., and Colo.

Water Hemlock or Spotted Cowbane
Cicuta maculata Dull white, June-August

An erect, slender, usually much-branched and smooth perennial herb, very poisonous to the taste. The stem marked with dull magenta lines. The leaves deep green, smooth, often tinged ruddy, with coarse sharp teeth, and conspicuously veined, the lower ones nearly a foot long. The 9-21 leaflets lance-shaped or broader. The inconspicuous dull white flowers in a thin, flat, somewhat straggling cluster; they are polygamous. The seed ovate, flat on one side, or nearly so, and inconspicuously ribbed on the other. 3-6 feet high. Visited by numberless bees, wasps, and butterflies. Wet meadows and borders of swamps, from Que. south to Fla., and west to Wyo.

Fruit twice size.

Berula erecta.

Sium suave.

Golden Alexanders.

Zizia aurea.

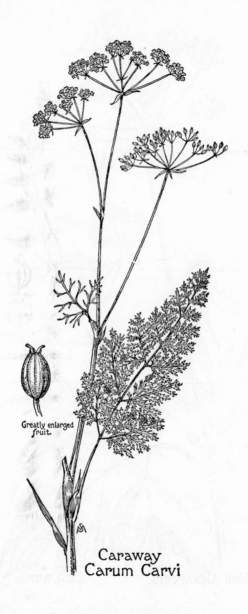

Greatly enlarged
fruit.

Caraway
Carum Carvi

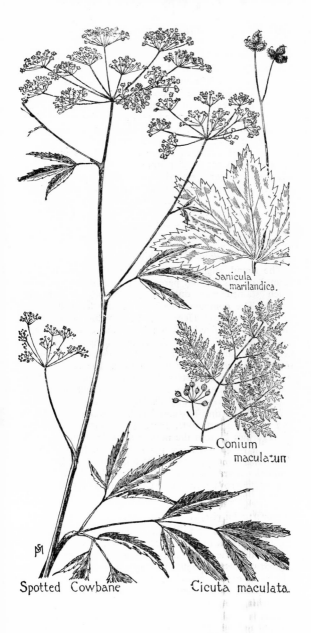

Sanicula
marilandica.

Conium
maculatum

Spotted Cowbane   Cicuta maculata.

Poison Hemlock
Conium maculatum   Dull white, June-July

A similar much-branched herb, from which is obtained a virulent poison used in medicine. It bears the name of the Hemlock employed by the ancient Greeks in putting to death their condemned political prisoners, philosophers, and criminals. Socrates died by this means. The dark green leaves are deeply dissected and toothed; the leaf-stems are sheathed at the base, and the dull white flower-clusters are slender-branched. The ovate seeds are flat and irregularly ribbed. The stem is also spotted or marked with ruddy color like that of *Cicuta*. 2-5 feet high. In waste places, Que. to Fla., west to Cal. Naturalized from Europe.

Sweet Cicely
Osmorhiza Claytoni   Dull white, May-June

The round, slightly silky hairy stem (especially when young) of this familiar perennial herb is dull green often much stained with dull madder purple—a brownish-purple. The compound leaf is cut and toothed similar to that of Poison Hemlock; when young it is distinguished by its fine-hairiness; later that characteristic is less evident; it is mostly three-divided, appears fernlike, deep green, and thin. The lower leaves are large, sometimes considerably over a foot long. The stems of the dull white flower-clusters are slender and few, consequently there is no appearance of an aggregate flat-topped cluster such as generally distinguishes the family *Umbelliferæ*. The tiny blossom has five cloven white petals and a very short style, scarcely $\frac{1}{24}$ inch long, which distinguishes it from the next species. 16-34 inches high. In moist rich woodlands, from Que., south through the mountains to Ga., west to Minn. and Mo. The large aromatic roots are anise-flavored and edible, but the similar general appearance of the Poison Hemlock often leads to dangerous if not fatal results.

Osmorhiza longistylis

This is so similar to the preceding that the differences are not obvious to the casual observer. The chief difference is that the style under the magnifying glass shows a greatly superior length; it is fully $\frac{1}{12}$ inch long or more. The roots of *O. longistylis* are more spicy than those of *O. Claytoni*. Que., south to Ga., and west to Colo.

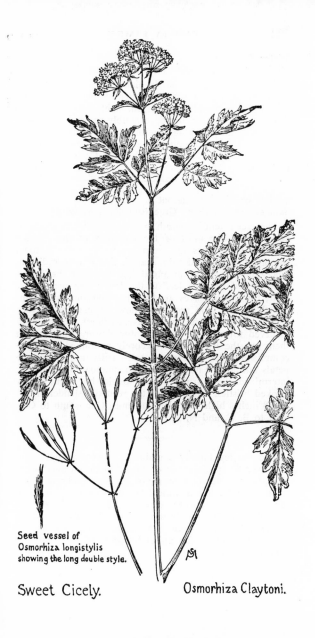

Seed vessel of
Osmorhiza longistylis
showing the long double style.

Sweet Cicely.

Osmorhiza Claytoni.

Water Pennywort
Hydrocotyle americana　Dull white, June-August

A small, creeping marsh plant, with a weak, pale green, smooth stem which frequently takes root at the joints, and a round-heart-shaped, light green leaf, thin, smooth, and shining, the edge doubly scalloped, and the stalk about an inch long. The tiny white flowers, 1-5 in a cluster, are inconspicuous and grow at the angles of the leaves. In wet places, Que. south to N. C., west to Wisc. and Ind.

Sanicle or Black Snakeroot
Sanicula marilandica　Greenish-yellow, May-July

The green stem is smooth, light green, slightly grooved, and hollow like most of the members of the Parsley Family. The leaves are deep green of a bluish tone, smooth, toothed, and palm-shaped, that is with radiating lance-shaped leaflets, arranged like those of the horse-chestnut; of the five leaflets the lower two are deeply cleft; the upper leaves are in three divisions and stem-less. The tiny pale greenish-yellow flowers are in very small clusters; the five petals of each floret are curiously incurved toward the center of the flower, and beneath them are the five stamens securely restrained from accomplishing the process of self-fertilization; later the petals unfold; the flowers are both staminate and perfect, intermixed. The fruit, a tiny ovoid bur with many hooked bristles, often retains the recurved slender styles. 18-38 inches high. In rich woodlands, Que. south to Ga., west to B. C. and N. Mex.

The Parsley Family contains 52 genera in our area, and over 80 species. It is obvious that the meager selection above is merely a sample of the most common plants of that family. The treatment has been restricted because the differences between genera, and even species, are difficult to discern—only the very small fruits have diagnostic value. The student must therefore look to the technical manuals for an elaboration of this puzzling family of plants.

Water Pennywort.   Hydrocotyle americana.

DOGWOOD FAMILY. *Cornaceæ.*

Shrubs or trees, with opposite or alternate toothless leaves, and generally perfect flowers. The genus *Cornus,* within our range, which is represented here by two species, has perfect flowers. Cross-fertilization is effected mostly by bees and the beelike flies. The sour gum or pepperidge belongs here.

Dwarf Cornel or Bunchberry
Cornus canadensis Greenish-white, May-July

An exceedingly dainty little plant and remarkable for its brilliant scarlet berries which grow in small, close clusters. The leaves are light yellow-green, broadly ovate pointed, toothless, and deeply marked by about 5-7 nearly parallel, curving ribs; they are set in circles. The flowers are greenish and tiny, closely grouped in the center of four large slightly green-white bracts, having the semblance of petals, and imparting to the whole the appearance of a single blossom about an inch broad. The flowers are succeeded in late August by a compact bunch of exceedingly beautiful but insipid scarlet berries, of the purest and most vivid hue. The commonest visitors are the bees together with many woodland flies. 3-8 inches high. In cool, damp, mossy woods; frequently found on summits over 4,000 feet high, among the Adirondacks and the White Mountains. From Greenland south in the mountains to W. Va., and west to Minn., Colo. and Cal.

Flowering Dogwood
Cornus florida Greenish-white, April-June

A medium-sized tree or large shrub whose familiar flowers, appearing just before or with the ovate deeper green leaves, have four similar broad white or rarely pinkish bracts, ribbed, and notched on the blunt tips. Fruit ovoid and scarlet, in small groups. 7-40 feet high. Me. south to Ky. and Fla., and west to Mich. and Tex. Name from *cornu,* a horn, in allusion to the hardness of the wood.

* * *

Here begins a fundamental division of the plant kingdom, based on the fact that most of the plants from here to the end of the book have their petals *united* into some sort of a bell-shaped, funnel-shaped, or salver-shaped

Flowering Dogwood.
Cornus florida.

Bunchberry.
Cornus canadensis.

corolla. There are a few exceptions, noted where they occur, but overwhelmingly these plants do not have *separate* petals. For the significance of this, and its use in the sequence of plants in the book, see "How to Use This Book."

WINTERGREEN FAMILY. *Pyrolaceæ*

Often classed as a sub-family under the Heath Family. Generally evergreen perennials with perfect, nearly regular flowers, the corolla very deeply five-parted, or five-petaled; twice as many stamens as the divisions of the corolla; the style short, and the stigma five-lobed. Fruit a capsule. Sometimes known as Pyrola Family.

Pipsissewa: Prince's Pine
Chimaphila umbellata Flesh or cream, June-July

A familiar and beautiful evergreen plant of the deep woods. The dark green leaves are thick and shining, sharply toothed along the upper half of the edge and indistinctly toothed on the lower half; they are wedge-shaped at the base, short-stalked, and arranged in circles about the buff-brown plant-stem. The flowers are dainty pale pinkish or waxy cream color; the corolla has five blunt lobes which turn backward as the flower matures, and at the base, next to the dome-shaped green ovary, is a circle of pale magenta; the ten short stamens have five double madder purple anthers; the style is remarkably short—scarcely noticeable, and the gummy stigma is nearly flat and five-scalloped. The flowers are delicately scented. Seed-pod a globular brown capsule. 6-12 inches high. In dry woods, from Que. south to Va., west to Cal.

Spotted Wintergreen
Chimaphila maculata Pale pink or white, June-August

A very similar species remarkable for its green and white marked leaves. The leaves taper gradually to a point; they are remotely toothed, dark green, and strongly marked with white-green in the region of the ribs. They are about 2 inches long. 3-9 inches high. In woods, Mass. to Ga., extending westward only as far as Mich. The name, from χειμα, winter, and φιλέω, to love.

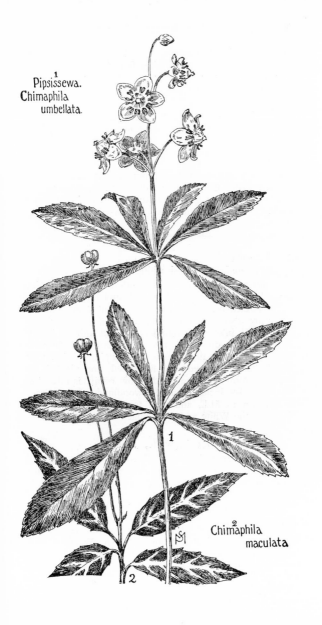

1
Pipsissewa.
Chimaphila
umbellata.

1

Chimaphila
maculata

2

One-flowered Wintergreen
Moneses uniflora Ivory-white, June-August

A very small plant, bearing a single blossom, some-what like that of the common Shinleaf. The leaves are thin, deep green, shining, round or nearly so, with rather fine indistinct teeth, and flat-stalked. The five petals of the cream-colored or ivory-white flower are a bit pointed; the ten white stamens have two-pointed dull yellow anthers, and the long green pistil bends downward; not far below the flower on the stem is a tiny bract or minute leaflet. 2-5 inches high. In pine woods, usually near brooks. From Greenland south to N. Y., and west to Mich. and Ore. Also in the Rocky Mountains, south to Colo. Flowers with the petals crinkly-edged.

Small Pyrola
Pyrola secunda Greenish-white, June-July

A northern woodland plant with ovate pointed deep green leaves, rather round-toothed, and long-stalked; the leaves circled near the base of the plant-stem. The leaf-stalks are also somewhat flat and troughed. The flower-stalk is tall, bracted or remotely set with minute leaflets, and bears a one-sided row of small greenish-white flowers which finally assume a drooping position; the corolla is bell-shaped and five-lobed; the pistil is extremely prominent. The slender flower-stalk is often bent sideways. 3-9 inches high. In woodlands, from Greenland south to Md., and west to Minn. Found on the slopes of the White and Adirondack mountains.

Pyrola virens Greenish-white, June-July

This is a small-leaved species with dainty drooping flowers, and a stem of very moderate height without bracts or minute leaflets, or at least possessing but one. The leaves are dull olive-green, obscurely scalloped-edged, rather round, and thicker than those of the common *Pyrola* (Shinleaf). The nodding, greenish-white flowers have obtuse, elliptical, convergent petals. They are slightly fragrant. 4-9 inches high. Woods, Newf. south to Md., west to Alaska; also in Eurasia.

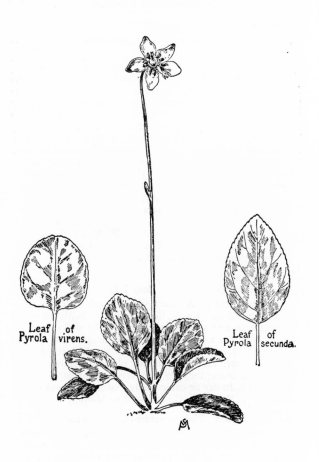

Leaf of Pyrola virens.

Leaf of Pyrola secunda.

One-flowered Wintergreen. Moneses uniflora.

Shinleaf
Pyrola elliptica   Greenish-white, June-July

Perhaps the commonest of all the Pyrolas, rather taller than *P. virens,* with evergreen, dark olive-green, elliptical, thin, and obscurely shallow-toothed leaves, the stalks somewhat flat or troughed; they exceed their stalks in length. The greenish-white waxy flowers nod; they are very fragrant; the five petals are thin and obovate, and form a protective cup about the pale ochre-yellow anthers; the pistil is extremely long, bends downward and then curves upward, exposing the tiny five-lobed stigma to the visiting insect which is most likely to alight upon the invitingly exposed pistil. The flowers form a loose cluster, each on a ruddy pedicel (stemlet), and are borne on an upright stalk generally ruddy at the base, and having a tiny leaflet or bract halfway up. Commonly visited by the beelike flies and the bees. 5-10 inches high. Rich woods, from Newf. south to W. Va., and west to B. C. (*Color Plate 15.*) The name is from *Pyrus* or *Pirum,* a pear, in allusion to the shape of the leaf.

Round-leaved Pyrola
Pyrola rotundifolia   White, June-July

A similar but much taller species, with nearly round or very broad oval leaves, thick, very indistinctly toothed or toothless, and a deep shining green; the stalks usually longer than the leaves, and narrowly margined; they are evergreen. The white waxy flowers are like those described above, but the roundish obovate petals spread open much more; they are also very sweet-scented. 8-18 inches high. In dry or damp sandy woodlands, from Que. south to N. Y. and N. C., and west to Minn.

Pyrola asarifolia   Pink or magenta, July-August

This similar species has pale crimson or magenta flow-ers, and very round heart-shaped leaves, rather wide, shining, and thick. The southern limit, northern N. Y. and New Eng., northwestward to Alaska.

Indian Pipe
Monotropa uniflora   White or pinkish, July-August

A familiar clammy, white, parasitic plant, deriving its nourishment from roots of other plants and the fungi responsible for the decayed vegetation, generally causing the rotting of trees. The stem is thick, translucent white,

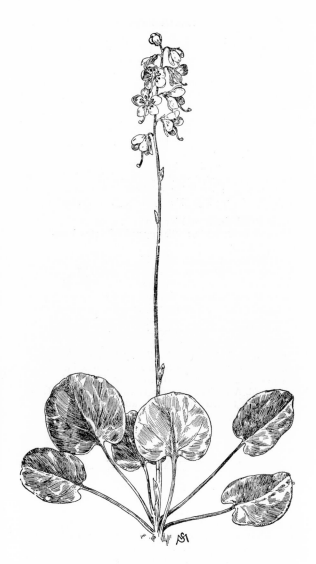

Pyrola asarifolia.

and without leaves, except for the scaly bracts which take their place. The white or delicately pink-salmon-tinted flower has 5, or sometimes 4, oblong petals, and the 10-12 stamens are pale tan color. The flower is in a nodding position, and is usually solitary, although rarely two may be found on one stem; the latter is often pink-tinged and springs with several others from a mat of entangled fibrous rootlets. The enlarged ovary finally assumes an erect position, becoming a pale tawny-salmon color; it is usually 10-grooved and 5-celled, and forms a large, fleshy, ovoid seed-vessel. The plant is at home in the dim-lit fastnesses of the forest, and it quickly withers and blackens after being gathered and exposed to sunlight. 3-9 inches high. Nearly throughout the country.

False Beech-drops or Pine-sap
Monotropa Hypopitys   Tawny-reddish, etc., June-
September

A somewhat similar parasitic plant found most frequently over the roots of oaks and pines. The stems are in clusters, and are slightly downy; they are whitish, pale tan color, or reddish, with many bracts. The small bracts are thin, papery, yellowish-red, and they turn black when withering. The small vase-shaped flowers are light crimson-red more or less touched with yellow; the tips of the petals are quite yellowish. The cluster of 3-10, or rarely more, drooping flowers is slightly fragrant. The fleshy vase-shaped seed-vessels become erect. 4-12 inches high. In dry woods from Newf. south to Fla., and west to Ore. and Ariz. The generic name is from the Greek, and means turned one-sided, in allusion to the one-sided flower arrangement.

HEATH FAMILY. *Ericaceæ.*

Mostly shrubs and a few perennial herbs with simple leaves and generally regular, perfect flowers, the corolla of 4-5 lobes, or sometimes of separate petals, and as many or twice as many stamens. Fruit a capsule or berry. Cross-fertilized by various bees, by the beelike flies, butterflies, and moths. To this family belong the blueberries, huckleberries, cranberries and the heather, as well as the gorgeous azaleas and rhododendrons of our gardens.

Indian Pipe.
Monotropa uniflora.

False Beech-drops.
Monotropa Hypopitys.

Creeping Snowberry
Gaultheria hispidula   White, May-June

The daintiest member of the Heath Family, with (often terra-cotta-colored) roughish stems creeping closely over rocky and mossy ground. The stiff dark olive evergreen leaves are tiny, broad, ovate pointed, and sparsely covered with brownish hairs beneath; the margin of the leaves rolled backward. The tiny white flowers are bell-shaped with four rounded lobes. They grow at the angles of the leaves and assume a nodding position. The berry is shining china white, ovate, and about ¼ inch long. Both leaf and berry possess a wintergreen flavor. Branches 3-11 inches long. In cool damp woods and peat bogs, frequent on hill-tops, from Newf., south to N. C., and west to Minn.

Wintergreen or Checkerberry
Gaultheria procumbens   White, July-August

The familiar wintergreen of the Middle States, common in wildernesses and all evergreen woodlands. The broad, ovate, evergreen leaf is stiff, thick, and shiny dark green, with few small teeth or toothless, and very nearly stalkless. The younger leaves are yellow-green; all are clustered at the top of the buff-brown or ruddy stem. The white, waxy flowers are vase-shaped and nodding; they grow from the angles of the leaves. The dry but exceedingly aromatic berry is pure red (a deep cherry color), often ⅓ inch in diameter, and is formed of the calyx which becomes fleshy and surrounds the seed-capsule. 2-5 inches high. From Newf. south to Ga., and west to Manitoba. The same aromatic essential oil exists in sweet birch as in this wintergreen, both now largely supplanted by synthetic substitutes.

———

Trailing Arbutus
Epigæa repens   White and pink, April-May

The mayflower of New Eng., common on the borders of rocky woods and hillsides, and blooming beside the remnants of snow-drifts in early spring. It is common in the vicinity of evergreen woodlands. The light brown stems are shrubby and tough, creeping close to the cold earth under decayed leaves and grasses; they are rough-hairy. The old dull light olive-green leaves are more or less rusty-spotted; the sides spread angularly from the

1
Trailing Arbutus.
Epigæa repens.

2
Checkerberry
Gaultheria procumbens

central depressed rib. The new leaves develop in June. The surface is rough and netted with fine veins; beneath, it is rough-hairy and much lighter in color. The most fragrant, white or delicately pink-tinted flowers are five-lobed, tubular, and possess a frosty sheen; they are in general trimorphous, that is, the stamens and styles are of three relative and reciprocal lengths; but commonly the flowers are dimorphous—confined to staminate and pistillate forms. The staminate blossoms contribute a touch of light yellow to the delicate surrounding of pure pink and white. The commonest visitors are the early queen bumblebees. The flower is nectar-bearing. Branches 6-12 inches long. Newf. south to Fla., and west to Saskatchewan. (*Color Plate 16.*)

Bearberry
Arctostaphylos Uva-ursi   White or pink-white, May-June

Also a trailing, hillside plant of a shrubby nature, with more or less ruddy, hairy-rough branches. The toothless leaves are thick, dark evergreen, round-blunt at the tip, narrowed at the base, and finely veined. The white or rarely pinkish white flowers are bell-shaped or vase-shaped, and are borne in terminal clusters. The style extends far beyond the anthers, and is touched first by the tongue of the visiting insect. The berry is an opaque red; it is dry and insipid. In dry rocky soil, from Me. south to N. J., west to Minn., S. D., and Colo. The name is from the Greek for a bear and a berry; the specific title is mere Latin repetition—*Uva,* a bunch or cluster of fruit, and *Ursus,* a bear. Both the mayflower and bearberry are difficult to grow, and the mayflower should not be picked for that purpose, or for any other. It is against the law in some states to gather it.

Although this book is devoted to wild flowers, which would normally exclude shrubs and trees, the next eight pages are devoted to them. To omit the finest plants of the Heath Family, merely because they are shrubs (or even trees in the Great Smoky National Park), did not appeal to the late Schuyler Mathews any more than it does to us.

Creeping Snowberry.
Gaultheria hispidula.

Bearberry.
Arctostaphylos Uva-ursi.

Mountain Laurel
Kalmia latifolia White, pinkish, May-June

A stout shrub or a small tree in its southern range, often forming impenetrable thickets. The stem and branches are irregular and angular in growth; the leaves are evergreen, shiny dark green, elliptical, firm, and toothless. The young leaves are a yellower green. The beautiful flowers are borne in large, dome-shaped clusters; they are exceedingly conventional and ornamental in form, bowl-shaped with five lobes, waxy white, pinkish-tinged in maturity, and pure pink in the corrugated, cone-shaped bud. There are ten depressions or pockets in the sides of the corolla in which the tips of the anthers are securely held, their filaments forming a series of arching spokes from the center of the flower which is stained with a tiny crimson star; the style is prominent and pale green. The insect visitor, commonly a moth, often a bee, struggling and pushing its way to the heart of the flower, releases the stamens and these spring backward, showering pollen over the fuzzy body of the intruder. The pollen of *Kalmia* is more or less connected by webby threads, and its adhesive character is peculiarly adapted to the purpose of cross-fertilization; the next blossom visited by the insect probably has a receptive stigma about which the pollen strings become quickly entangled. The flower-stalks are hairy-sticky, thus preventing pilferers, such as ants, who would be useless as fertilizing agents, from entering the blossoms. The seed-capsule is somewhat globular but five-lobed, and at first assumes a dull red hue. 3-6 feet high, and in its southern range often attaining a height of 20-35 feet. In woodlands, preferring sandy soil or rocky slopes, from N. B. south and west to Fla. and Ind. Named for Peter Kalm, a Swedish botanist who visited this country in the middle of the eighteenth century and sent many plants to Linnæus.

Sheep-laurel or Lambkill
Kalmia angustifolia Crimson-pink, June-July

A shrub of lesser proportions, and small, narrow, drooping leaves, elliptical or lance-shaped, evergreen, and dull olive-green often rusty-spotted, lighter green beneath. The flower is crimson-pink, small, but otherwise like that of Mountain Laurel, except that the filaments and all other parts are more or less pink-tinged. The stem is

Mountain Laurel   Kalmia latifolia

terminated by the newer leaves which stand nearly upright; beneath these is the encircling flower-cluster; below,
the leaves droop. The foliage is poisonous if eaten, as
are many other plants of the Heath Family. 8-36 inches
high. Common in swamps. Newf. south to Ga., west to
Mich.

Pale Laurel
Kalmia polifolia　Crimson-pink or lilac, June-July

A similar and even smaller species, blooming about
the same time, distinguished by its two-edged branches
which seem to grow in sections set at right angles with
one another. The narrow, evergreen leaves grow oppositely or are set in groups of three; the edges are
rolled back rather strongly; they are conspicuously white-
green beneath. The crimson-pink or often light lilac
flowers, ½ inch broad, terminate the stem. 6-20 inches
high, confined to cold peat bogs and hillside swamps,
from Labrador south to Pa., and west to Minn.

White Swamp Honeysuckle
Rhododendron viscosum　White, June-July

The wild Rhododendrons and Azaleas are also shrubs
which bear characteristically showy flowers. This species
has a much branched stem, and obovate or blunt lance-
shaped, not evergreen yellow-green or pale leaves, with
a few scattered hairs above. The twigs are hairy, and the
stem almost bare of leaves. The flowers (expanding later
than the leaves) are pure white or pink-tinged, with the
outside surface covered with ruddy, sticky hairs; they are
very fragrant; the stamens are prominent, the anthers
yellow; the pinkish pistil is longer than the stamens.
Visited most frequently by bees, butterflies, and moths,
and protected from creeping insects by the sticky-hairy
outer surface of the corolla-tube. 3-7 feet high. In
swamps from Me., south to Fla., west to Ohio and Ark.;
generally near the coast. Often called *Azalea viscosa*.
The name (Greek) means rose-tree.

Pinxter Flower or Wild Honeysuckle
Rhododendron nudiflorum　Pale or deep pink, April-
May

A more leafy shrub with branching stem, characterized
by its extremely golden yellow-green foliage which is not

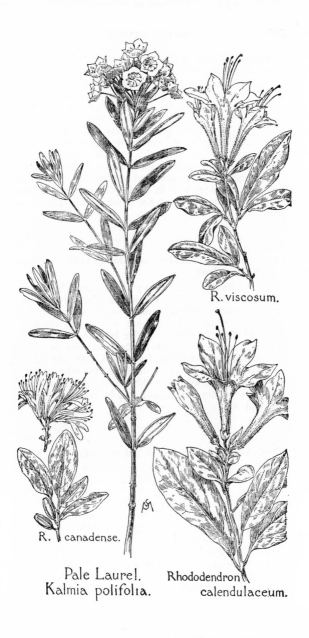

R. viscosum.

R. canadense.

Pale Laurel.
Kalmia polifolia.

Rhododendron
calendulaceum.

evergreen. The ovate leaf tapers and is pointed at both ends, the edge and surface are very slightly hairy. The delicate and beautiful flowers are pale or deep crimson-pink with the base of the tube a trifle stronger; the broader corolla lobes do not curve back conspicuously; the stamens and pistil, all exceedingly prominent, are light crimson. The flowers are delicately fragrant, grow in small terminal clusters expanding before or with the leaves, and when fading the corollas slide down the pistils, depend from them a while, and finally drop. The most frequent visitors are the honeybees and moths. 2-6 feet high. In swamps or in shady places, from Vt. south to S. C., west to Ohio and Ky. Often called *Azalea nudiflora*.

Flame Azalea
Rhododendron calendulaceum   Orange-yellow and reddish, May- June

A most beautiful and showy species, entirely southern but commonly cultivated. The leaves, which are not evergreen, are hairy and generally obovate, sometimes with only a few scattered hairs above. The flower, expanding with or before the leaves, has five broad lobes scarcely if at all backward curved; it is nearly flame color or orange-yellow more or less suffused with pink, has very little or no fragrance, and the outer surface of the tube is slightly fine-hairy and sticky. The ruddy stamens prominent. 4-12 feet high. In dry woodlands, Pa., in the mountains, to Ga. and Ala.

Rhodora
Rhododendron canadense   Light magenta, May

A familiar flower of New Eng. and one famous in the verses of the poet Emerson. The leaves are slightly hairy, light green, oval or oblong, and rather obtuse; the color deeper above and paler beneath. The flowers are narrow-lobed, light magenta, and formed somewhat like the honeysuckle, with the upper lip slightly three-lobed, and the lower in two nearly separate sections; they grow in thin clusters terminally, and precede the unfolding of the leaves or else expand with them. 1-3 feet high. Wet hillsides and cool bogs, Newf. to N. J., and eastern Pa. in the mountains. Often called *Rhodora canadensis*.

Pinxter Flower.   Rhododendron nudiflorum.

Great Laurel
Rhododendron maximum   Pink, June-July

A tall shrub, or often a tree in the mountains, with showy clusters of pink-white flowers spotted with gold-orange, and greenish at the base, the five lobes of the corolla, broad, blunt, and substantially even in shape. The leaves shiny dark green, 4-9 inches long, evergreen, leathery, drooping in the winter season, and spreading in summer. They are oblong, toothless, slightly rolled under at the edge, and dark beneath. The flower-stems are sticky-hairy, thus preventing the pilfering of creeping insects; the flowers are mostly visited by bees, but the honey they produce is said to be poisonous. 5-35 feet high. Damp woods, rare from Nova Scotia to Ohio, plentiful from Pa. to Ga.; abundant throughout the Allegheny region, where, on the mountainsides, it forms impenetrable thickets.

Red Laurel
Rhododendron catawbiense   Light purple, May-June

A species similar in many respects to the foregoing, but generally not more than 5 feet high. The leaves are broadly oblong or oval, the tips with an abrupt very small point, pale green beneath. The large flowers are light purple or lilac. This species has been hybridized with other less hardy ones, especially those of the Himalayas, and from these proceed many of the Rhododendrons familiar in ornamental grounds. 3-6, or rarely 18 feet high. In the higher Alleghenies from Va. to Ala.

Lapland Rosebay
Rhododendron lapponicum   Light purple, July-August

A dwarf species confined to the summits of high mountains in the north. The olive-green, evergreen leaves are small, oval or elliptical, and grouped in clusters on the otherwise bare stem. They are covered, together with the branches, with minute rusty scales. The flowers have a five-lobed corolla which is bell-shaped and light purple, dotted. There are 5-10 stamens. A prostrate branching plant that hugs the rocky slopes of the mountains. 2-12 inches high. Summits of the White Mts., N. H., and the Adirondacks, N. Y.; throughout Arctic Am.

The heather, *Calluna vulgaris,* of northern Europe, is established in sandy soils from Newf. to N. J. It has tiny, crowded leaves, and small pinkish flowers in narrow, spiky clusters. Usually about 18 inches high, often less.

Great Laurel.   Rhododendron maximum.

DIAPENSIA FAMILY. *Diapensiaceæ.*

Low, evergreen, perennial herbs, or tufted shrubs of a mosslike character, very closely related to the *Ericaceæ*— the attachment of the stamens to the corolla being the principal difference—with five-parted tiny flowers whose style is tipped with a three-lobed stigma. Fruit a capsule.

Pyxie or Flowering Moss
Pyxidanthera barbulata White or pink, April-May

An interesting and pretty mosslike little plant common on the pine barrens of N. J. The linear or lance-shaped leaves, scarcely ⅓ inch long, are medium green, sharp at the tip, and hairy at the base when young; they are crowded toward the ends of the branches. The white or pale pink flowers are small, with five blunt lobes, between which are curiously fixed the five conspicuous stamens; they are numerous, and apparently stemless. Branches prostrate and creeping. 6-10 inches long. In sandy soil, dry pine barrens of N. J.; also southeast Va. and eastern N. C. The name is from two Greek words, box and anther, referring to the anthers which open as if by a lid.

A related plant, *Diapensia lapponica,* with heathlike foliage, and solitary, white, waxlike flowers, grows only on alpine summits in New Eng. and N. Y., thence to the Arctic. It grows in low leafy tussocks, blooms in June or July, and is one of the most beautiful wild flowers of alpine fell-fields.

PRIMROSE FAMILY. *Primulaceæ.*

Herbs with leaves variously arranged, and with perfect, regular flowers. The corolla (usually five-cleft) is tubular, funnel-formed, or salver-formed. Stamens as many as there are lobes to the corolla and fixed opposite to them, but the corolla lacking in the genus named *Glaux.* Seeds in a one-celled and several-valved capsule.

Featherfoil
Hottonia inflata White, June-August

A peculiar aquatic plant of a somewhat spongy nature, common in shallow stagnant water. Its strange appearance is due to the cluster of inflated primary flower-stalks which are about ½ inch thick, constricted at the joints,

Hottonia inflata.

Pyxie Moss.
Pyxidanthera barbulata.

Enlarged blossom showing the alternate connection of stamens with the lobes of the corolla.

and almost leafless. The leaves are cut into threadlike divisions, and are beneath the water, densely distributed on the floating and rooting stems. The insignificant whitish flower, ¼ inch long, has a corolla much shorter than the calyx. The seed-capsule is globular. Stems sometimes 18 inches long. Shallow ponds and ditches, from Me. south to Fla.; also in southern Ind. Named for Peter Hotton, botanist.

American Cowslip or Shooting Star
Dodecatheon Meadia   Light magenta, April-May

A handsome wild flower, frequently cultivated, but confined in its natural state mostly to the country west of Pennsylvania. The blunt lance-shaped deep green leaves proceed from the root; they are generally toothless or nearly so, and their stalks are long and margined. The tall primary flower-stalk is topped by a small cluster of delicate pendulous light magenta, pink-magenta, or white flowers, the five long corolla-divisions of which are strongly turned backward. The exposed stamens are close-clustered—grouped in a conelike figure; the anthers are long, thin, and golden-yellow; the base of each is thickened and marked with magenta-purple. The flower is cross-fertilized by bees. Moist hillsides, cliffs, open woods, or prairies, from D. C. and western Pa. to Wisc., south to Ga. and Tex. Name from the Greek, meaning twelve gods.

Dwarf Canadian Primrose
Primula mistassinica   Pale magenta-pink, June-July

A delicate little plant found only in the northern part of our range, bearing a family resemblance to the yellow English Primrose. The light green leaves are blunt lance-shaped, tapering to a distinct stem, thin, green on both sides, rarely with a slightly mealy appearance beneath, and shallow-toothed. The pale magenta-pink or lighter pink corolla is five-lobed, bluntly scallop-tipped, and stained with yellow in the center (sometimes the yellow is absent). The few flowers are clustered at the top of the long slender stalk. This is apt to be mistaken for *Primula farinosa,* a cultivated European species, which is taller and has leaves white-mealy beneath (at least when young), and flowers with a more cuniform lobe, borne in thicker clusters. Confined to moist situations; Nova Scotia, central N. Y., west to northern Ill. and Mich.

Shooting Star.
Dodecatheon Meadia.

Primula
mistassinica.

Star Flower.
Trientalis borealis.

Star Flower
Trientalis borealis　White, May-June

A delicate and interesting little woodland plant with a long horizontally creeping root which sends upward an almost bare or few-scaled thin stem terminating in a circle of sharp-pointed, lance-shaped, light green leaves, thin, shiny, and tapering to both ends. There are 5-9 leaves in the circle, from the center of which proceed two threadlike stalks, each bearing a fragile, white, star-shaped flower with 6-7 pointed divisions. The stamens are long and delicate, with tiny golden anthers, which mature later than the stigma. Cross-fertilization effected mostly through the agency of beelike flies. 3-7 inches high, or rarely more. In moist thin woods, from Newf. west to Minn., and south along the coast to N. J. and Va. Common in the thin woodlands of the White Mts.

Fringed Loosestrife
Steironema ciliatum　Yellow, June-July

A rather handsome perennial commonly found in low moist situations, particularly on river flats. The smooth light green leaves are ovate or ovate lance-shaped and sharply pointed; on the upper edge of the leaf-stalk is a fringe of erect hairs—hence the specific term, *ciliatum.* The leaves are in pairs which are set at right angles with each other. The pretty, light golden-yellow flowers, not far from a pure yellow tone, are five-lobed, the divisions oval and terminated by an abrupt sharp point (called mucronate); these tips are somewhat twisted or puckered; about the center of the corolla is a terra-cotta-colored ring; within this are five straw-colored stamens alternating with five abortive ones; in the center is the pale green pistil. The smooth, erect stem 18-22 inches high or more. Common in low ground and on the borders of thickets from Que. west to B. C., south to Fla., Ala., and Ariz.

Steironema lanceolatum　Yellow, June-July

A narrow-leaved species smaller and slenderer in every respect. The leaves are lance-shaped and linear, nearly stalkless and smooth; the lower ones are much shorter and broader, and the stems are distinct and long. The flowers are similar to those of *S. ciliatum,* but smaller—a little over ½ inch broad. 8-20 inches high. Moist ground from Pa. west to Wisc., and south to Fla.; rare

Steironema ciliatum.

except in Va., Ky. and Ohio. The *Steironemas* are cross-fertilized by bees. The name is from two Greek words, sterile and thread, in allusion to the abortive stamens.

Four-leaved Loosestrife
Lysimachia quadrifolia   Yellow, June-July

A delicate and pretty species common on all lowlands, especially sandy river-banks. The light green leaves are pointed lance-shaped or broader, and are arranged in a circle of generally four, but sometimes three and six. From the bases of these leaves project slender long stalks, each bearing a single star-shaped light golden-yellow flower, prettily dotted around the center with terra-cotta red, which sometimes extends in faint streaks all over the corolla lobes. The stamens and pistil project in a cone-shaped cluster; the stigma is advanced so far beyond the anthers that self-fertilization rarely if ever occurs. The *Lysimachias* are visited by bees, by bumblebees and by honeybees, evidently for the purpose of collecting pollen. Stem smooth or very minutely hairy (under a glass), straight and round. 12-30 inches high, simple or rarely branched. Sandy soil or often moist ground, Me. west to Wisc., south to Ga.

Lysimachia terrestris   Yellow, June-August

Along with preceding species bloom the slender spire-like clusters of the simple-stemmed *Lysimachia terrestris* whose flowers are not appreciably different, though the flowers are borne in a terminal cluster, rather than solitary at the leaf-joints. The slender flower-spike is distinctly characteristic of *L. terrestris;* it forms an aggregation of misty yellow color (when a large colony of the plants is seen) which is never present with the other species. Often little elongated bulblets appear at the bases of the leaves. Leaves lance-shaped and sharp-pointed at either end; in both species apt to be sepia-dotted. Stem 8-20 inches high. Moist and sandy soil. Que. west to Manitoba, south to N. C.

Hybrid Loosestrife
Lysimachia producta   Light golden-yellow, June-August

A hybrid of *L. quadrifolia* and *L. terrestris,* widely distributed in the north. The smooth stem is simple or very slightly branched, the lance-shaped light green leaves,

Loosestrife.
Lysimachia terrestris.   Lysimachia quadrifolia

pale green beneath, grow oppositely or in circles of 3-5, and the terminal flower-spike, loosely flowered, is sometimes 18 inches long. The corolla-divisions are dotted and striped with dark red, ovate-oblong and rounded at the tips. In low damp ground on the borders of thickets, from Me. west to Mich., and south to N. C.

Moneywort or Creeping Charlie
Lysimachia nummularia   Light golden-yellow, July-September

An extremely beautiful trailing vine with a creeping, not climbing, habit, which has become naturalized from Europe, sometimes under the inappropriate name of myrtle. It takes kindly to cultivation. The leaves are dark green, shining, small, almost round, and short-stemmed. One rather large light golden-yellow flower, with five ovate divisions to the corolla, grows from the junction of the leaf-stalk and plant-stem; it is not spotted with terra-cotta like the other members of this genus. Stems 6-20 inches long. In moist ground near dwellings, mostly an escape from gardens everywhere, and in many places a troublesome weed.

Sea Milkwort
Glaux maritima   Purple-white, June

A low, fleshy seaside plant with oblong, toothless, and stalkless light green leaves, from the bases of which grow the solitary dull purple-white or pinkish flowers *without a true corolla,* but with a five-scalloped calyx. The seaside from Va. north to Que., and in salty places west to Cal.

Pimpernel
Anagallis arvensis   Red, purple, etc., June-August

A low-spreading annual; the common Poor Man's Weatherglass of England, which has become naturalized in this country. The small solitary flowers are a variety of colors, scarlet, purple, white, etc. The corolla has five broad divisions but hardly any tube. The leaves are ovate, stalkless, and toothless, and grow oppositely in pairs, or in circles. Stem 6 inches long. Waste sandy places everywhere. The flowers open only in sunshine, and close in late afternoon or when rain threatens.

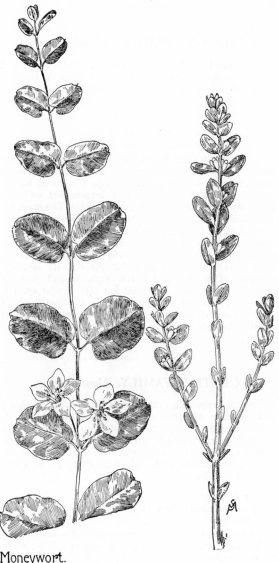

Moneywort.
Lysimachia nummularia.

Glaux maritima.

LEADWORT FAMILY. *Plumbaginaceæ.*

Perennial herbs with small, perfect, regular flowers of five parts—i.e., five-lobed corolla, five stamens, and five styles; the flower-tube funnel-formed and plaited; the ovary one-celled and bearing a solitary seed. Seaside plants.

Sea Lavender or Marsh Rosemary
Limonium carolinianum Lavender, July-September

A salt marsh plant with a slender much-branched stem growing from a thick woody root very astringent in character, the branches rather erect. The basal leaves, are blunt lance-shaped or obovate, long-stalked, toothless or nearly so, and tipped with a bristly point. The branches bear many solitary, or 2-3 (in a group) tiny lavender flowers with a curious tooth between each of the five tiny lobes; the lobes of the calyx are also very acute. The character of the plant is branchy and naked-stemmed, with flowers so insignificant that the delicate lavender color is often missed. 1-2 feet high. In salt marshes from N. Y. to Mex. A related but very similar species, differing in having a hairy calyx, is *L. Nashii,* which grows also northward to Labrador. The common Garden Thrift, *Armeria maritima,* also belongs to the leadwort family.

GENTIAN FAMILY. *Gentianaceæ*

Smooth herbs with generally opposite leaves, toothless and stalkless; *Menyanthes* and *Nymphoides,* two little-known aquatic genera, are exceptions to this rule. Flowers regular and perfect, often very showy, the corolla with 4-12 lobes; alternating with these are a corresponding number of stamens. Fertilized mostly by the bees and the beelike flies.

Lesser Centaury
Centaurium umbellatum Light magenta, June-September

An erect and smooth annual naturalized from Europe, with several short branches above, and elliptical or oblong light green leaves, somewhat acute; the uppermost rather linear. The small tubular light magenta flowers

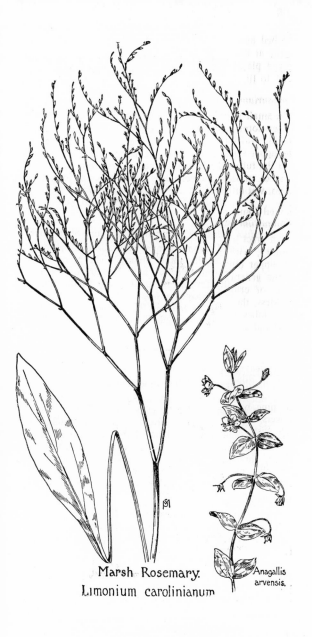

Marsh Rosemary.
Limonium carolinianum

Anagallis
arvensis.

5-lobed and very nearly stalkless. They are numerously borne at the summits of the branches. 6-12 inches high. Waste places and the shores of the Great Lakes, from Que. to Ill.

Centaurium pulchellum　Magenta-pink, June-September

A small species from Europe similar in many respects to the foregoing, but the stem very much branched, the leaves oval or long-ovate, the larger lower ones blunt, the upper small and acute. The flowers are magenta-pink, and the tube of the corolla is nearly twice as long as the 5 lobes of the calyx. 3-8 inches high. Waste places or fields, wet or shady, from southern N. Y. to Va.

Spiked Centaury
Centaurium spicatum　Magenta-pink, June-September

An erect and smooth annual naturalized from the old country, with small, blunt, oblong, light green leaves; the upper ones rather acute, and all more or less close to the generally forking stem. The very small magenta-pink, or crimson-magenta flowers tubular and 5-lobed, stalkless, the tube of the corolla a little longer than the calyx-lobes. 6-16 inches high. Shores of Nantucket, Mass., Del. and coastal Va.

Lance-leaved Sabatia
Sabatia difformis　White, June-September

A not very uncommon wild flower in the swamps of the pine barrens of N. J., with white, starlike, 5-lobed flowers nearly an inch broad, which in fading turn yellowish, and ovate or lance-shaped light green leaves with 3-5 ribs. The plant-stem slender, somewhat four-sided, branched above, or sometimes simple. The branches are borne relatively opposite. The flowers are numerous. 1-3 feet high. Pine barrens of N. J., to Fla.

Rose Pink
Sabatia angularis　White or pink, July-August

The stem of this species is decidedly and sharply four-sided; it is also rather thick and much branched. The light green leaves are 5-ribbed, ovate, acute at the tip, and somewhat clasping at the base. The delicately fragrant flowers are an inch or more broad, pale crimson-pink or sometimes white, and marked in the center with a yellow-green star (a characteristic of many of the

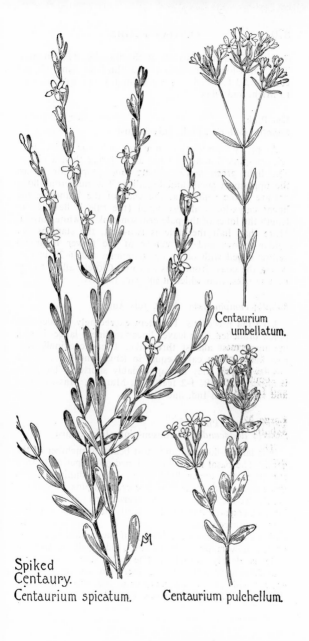

Centaurium
umbellatum.

Spiked
Centaury.
Centaurium spicatum.

Centaurium pulchellum.

Sabatias. The style is cleft at the tip—i.e., two stigmas. The calyx-lobes are about one third as long as the corolla. 2-3 feet high. Fertile ground, Conn. to Fla., west to Mich. and Okla.

Sea Pink
Sabatia stellaris   Pink, July-August

A pretty species common on salt meadows, with crimson-pink flowers as large as or larger than a nickel. The light green leaves oblong lance-shaped or linear, the uppermost small and bractlike. The numerous flowers are borne solitary at the ends of the branches; the linear calyx-lobes almost equal (the rule is flexible) in length the lobes of the pale crimson-pink or white corolla. More than half the style is two-cleft, the stamens are golden-yellow, and the center of the flower is green-yellow edged with ochre or sometimes red. 6-20 inches. Along the coast from Mass. to Fla. Closely allied to the next species, into which it appears to pass.

Sabatia campanulata   Pink, July-August

Like the preceding. The stem exceedingly slender and much branched. The leaves linear or linear lance-shaped, the uppermost almost threadlike. The exceedingly narrow lobes of the calyx equal in length the lobes of the corolla (rarely they are appreciably shorter). The style is about half-cleft. 1-2 feet high. Marshes, Mass. to Fla. and La.; also in Ind. and Ky.

Large Marsh Pink
Sabatia dodecandra   Crimson-pink, July-August

The largest-flowered and most beautiful member of the genus. The basal leaves blunt-tipped and tapering toward the base, the upper light green leaves diminishing to lance-shape and linear. The few crimson-pink flowers are nearly two inches broad, with generally ten obovate corolla lobes (an equal number of linear calyx lobes), each marked with a three-pointed ochre-edged, green-yellow base which contributes to the beauty of the central star-figure of the flower; the stamens are golden-yellow, and the style is deeply two-cleft. The wiry stems, simple or branching very little, are 1-2 feet high. Rarely the flowers are white. On sandy margins or brackish ponds from Conn. and L. I. to La. (*Color Plate 17.*)

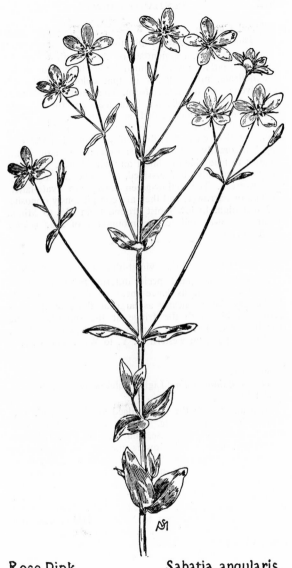

Rose Pink.   Sabatia angularis.

Fringed Gentian
Gentiana crinita   Blue, September-October

The most famous member of the beautiful Gentian group, remarkable not so much for its blue color as for the delicate, misty quality of that color, and the expressiveness of the flower-form. The plant is a biennial with a leafy, perpendicular, branched stem, the branches erect, somewhat four-angled, and each bearing a single terminal flower. The flower is deep vase-shaped with four rounded, light violet-blue lobes deeply fringed and spreading horizontally only in the sunshine; the color is the nearest to true blue of almost any wild flower. The large four-pointed calyx is four-sided, and generally a bronzy, yellow-green. The yellow-green leaves are ovate-lance-shaped or narrower, and they are conspicuously opposite. 1-3 feet high. In low moist ground from Me. to Minn., south to Iowa, and to the mountains of Ga. (*Color Plate 18.*)

Gentiana procera   Light violet-blue, July-September

A similar but annual species differing from the fringed gentian chiefly in its lance-linear or linear leaves. Its violet-blue flowers nearly as large as those of the preceding species with the fringe at the summit of the corolla short, or reduced to mere teeth. 4-18 inches high. Moist ground from western N. Y. to Wisc. and Iowa.

Ague-weed
Gentiana quinquefolia   Light violet-blue, August-October

Also an annual; the stem ridged and four-sided. The leaves, in general, ovate, sharply pointed at the tip, slightly clasping at the base, and with 3-7 ribs. The very light violet-blue or lilac flowers clustered at the apex of the branches in groups of 2-7 but generally 5. The flowers smaller, scarcely an inch long, tubular, and terminating in five triangular small bristle-pointed lobes. A common species in the west, attractive but not so beautiful as the fringed gentian. 8-22 inches high. Moist hillsides from Me. south, and west to Mich. and Mo., generally in the mountains; it is found at an altitude of over 6,000 feet on the peaks of N. C.

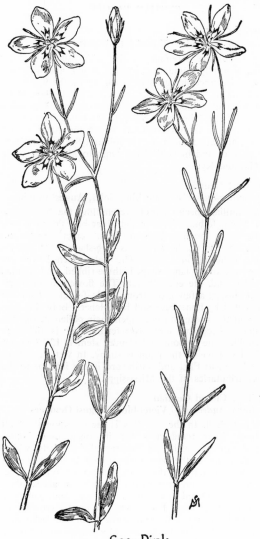

Sea Pink.
Sabatia stellaris.   Sabatia campanulata.

Downy Gentian
Gentiana puberula   Blue-violet, August-October

A handsome perennial species with usually a single stem, generally minutely hairy and rough, and with narrow, rigid, lance-shaped light green leaves, the uppermost nearly linear. The blue-violet flowers are bell-shaped with five triangular lobes, rather open-spreading. The calyx has five linear lobes quite rough to the touch. The flowers are borne in terminal clusters or at the bases of the leaves, and are seldom if ever solitary. 8-17 inches high. On prairies and in fields from Ohio to Manitoba, south to Ga. and Ky.

Soapwort Gentian
Gentiana Saponaria   Pale blue-violet, August-October

A familiar species closely resembling the bottle gentian. The pale blue-violet, or light lilac-blue flower is only partly open, the five lobes are blunt, erect, slightly cut at the tip, and the flower-cup is club-shaped, the anthers within cohering in a ring. The light green leaves are commonly ovate lance-shaped, three-ribbed, and pointed at either end, the edges rough. The flowers form a terminal cluster; a few grow from the leaf-angles. They are frequented by honeybees and bumblebees. Both this gentian and the preceding one ripen their pollen before the stigma is receptive and cross-fertilization is therefore inevitable. The smooth and slender stem is 12-27 inches high. The juice of the plant is soapy. In wet woodlands from N. Y. to Fla., and northward in the interior to the upper tributaries of the Mississippi.

Bottle or Closed Gentian
Gentiana Andrewsii   Violet-blue, August-October

A perennial. In the east this is the commonest of all gentians; it is remarkable for its tight-closed bottle-shaped corolla, which is contracted by plaits white-striped, white at the base and an intense violet-blue at the apex; sometimes the blue approaches ultramarine. The medium (sometimes rusty) green leaves are smooth, ovate lance-shaped, pointed at the tip, and generally narrowed at the base. The flowers are mostly crowded in a terminal cluster, but some grow from the leaf-bases; all are set close to the leaves, which are conspicuously arranged in pairs. Bumblebees not infrequently force an entrance into the corolla, and self-fertilization is sometimes questionable. The smooth, round stem 1-2 feet high.

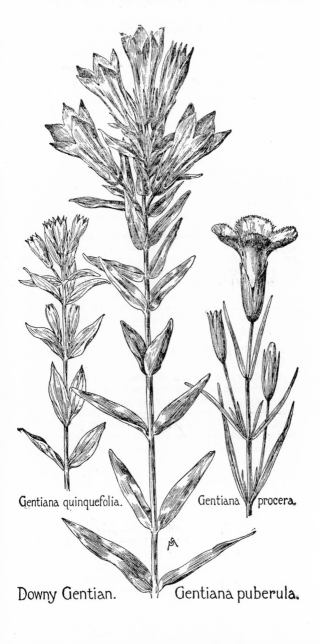

Gentiana quinquefolia.

Gentiana procera.

Downy Gentian. Gentiana puberula.

Rich woodland borders, Que. to Manitoba, south to N. C. and Mo.

Gentiana linearis   **Light blue-violet, August-September**

A much less common gentian frequenting mountain bogs. It is a smooth, slender-stemmed perennial, with light green linear or lance-linear leaves with three ribs, acute at either end. The pale blue-violet flower-cup is contracted to a funnel-form with rather scalloped lobes; the light green, simple, round stem is 10-24 inches high. Wet situations from Que. to New Eng. and N. Y., south in the mountains to W. Va.

Sampson's Snakeroot
Gentiana villosa   **Greenish-white, September-November**

A greenish-white-flowered species with a corolla narrowly open, displaying stripes of magenta-lilac on a greenish-veined background, the lobes somewhat triangular and with a tooth. The flowers are mostly in terminal clusters. The medium green leaves obovate, the uppermost acute at the tip, the lower ones blunt and short, all narrow at the base. Slender stem 8-16 inches high. Shaded woodland borders from southern N. J. to Fla., west to Ind. and La.

Gentiana Porphyrio   **Light ultramarine-blue, August-October**

A smaller and exceedingly delicate and pretty species mostly confined to the pine barrens of the southern states, with a simple or sometimes branching stem, and with solitary, bright light ultramarine-blue flowers (often speckled within) at the apex of the stem or its branches; they are much larger than bluebells. The five lobes of the corolla are deeply cut, ovate, and open-spreading. The small linear leaves are less than 2 inches long. 6-15 inches high. In moist situations from southern N. J. to S. C.; rare.

––––––

Yellow Bartonia
Bartonia virginica   **Greenish-yellow, July-September**

An attenuated, slender, stiff-stemmed little plant, simple or with a few erect branches, destitute of leaves but with small awl-shaped opposite-growing scales closely hugging the stem, which is a trifle angled, all a yellow-green. The yellow, minute, bell-shaped flowers of a

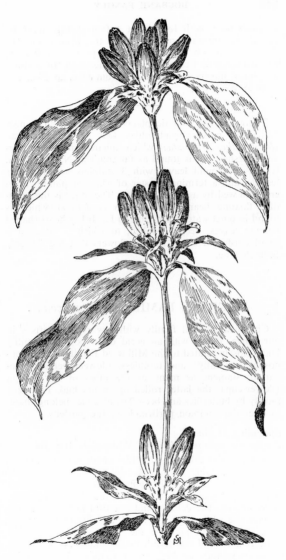

Bottle Gentian.   Gentiana Andrewsii.

greenish tone, with four blunt (often slightly toothed) lobes, are arranged oppositely on the plant-stem. The flowers are mostly terminal but inconspicuous on account of their uncertain coloring. 4-14 inches high. In pastures and bogs, mostly in damp soil, from Que. to Fla., and west to Wisc.

———

There are two aquatic plants of the Gentian Family that look most ungentianlike. One is the buckbean (*Menyanthes trifoliata*) which inhabits northern bogs and marshes, but is found as far south as N. J. and Va. It has compound leaves with 3 stalkless and toothless leaflets, and a terminal cluster of white or pinkish flowers, followed by a small, dry pod. The other is the beautiful floating heart (*Nymphoides cordatum*) which is found in quiet water from Que. to La. It has heart-shaped floating leaves, deeply 5-lobed, to which is attached a small cluster of white floating flowers that are scarcely ¼ inch long.

DOGBANE FAMILY. *Apocynaceæ.*

Chiefly a tropical family with few representatives in our range. Plants with an acrid often poisonous milky juice, closely related to the Milkweed Family. Leaves opposite (generally) and toothless. Flowers perfect, five-parted; stamens as many as the lobes of the corolla (flower-cup), the latter rolled up in the bud. Fertilized mostly by butterflies and bees. The oleander belongs here, as does the common periwinkle of the gardens.

Spreading Dogbane
Apocynum androsæmifolium   White-pink, June-July

A somewhat tall and shrublike plant, with a smooth, slender, branching stem, generally reddish on the side exposed to sunlight. The opposite growing, lusterless light blue-green, ovate leaves are toothless and ruddy, short-stalked. The delicate and beautiful little bell-shaped flowers are white-pink, five-lobed, and lily of the valley-like, striped with pink on the inside of the cup. The clusters are small and terminate the branches; their most frequent visitors are bees and butterflies. An insect inseparable from the dogbane is the so-called dogbane

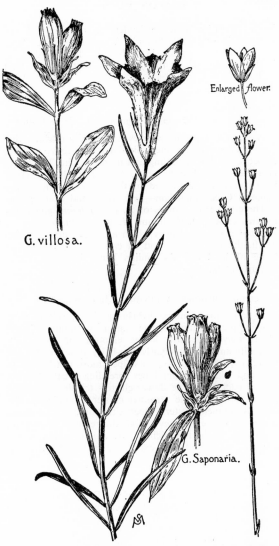

G. villosa.

Enlarged flower.

G. Saponaria.

Gentiana Porphyrio.   Bartonia virginica.

beetle, jewel-like and resplendent in metallic red and green of incomparable luster; it is scarcely ½ inch long. 1-4 feet high. Common in half-shaded field borders, or in thickets throughout the north, and south to Ga.; west to B. C. and Ariz.

Indian Hemp
Apocynum cannabinum   Greenish-white, June-August

A far less attractive species with greenish-white, tiny flowers erectly five-pointed. Similar to the above in other respects, but less spreading and more upright. The leaves narrower and abruptly acute. 1-3 feet high. On sandy river-banks, in fields, and in thickets everywhere. The name is Greek in origin—ἀπό, from, and κύων, a dog.

There are many forms of *A. cannabinum,* and many hybrids exist between it and *A. androsæmifolium.* The var. *pubescens* has leaves which are white fine-hairy beneath, the flower stem and its calyx also fine-hairy. In some of its forms the Indian hemp is found nearly throughout N. Am.

Apocynum medium   White-pink, June-August

A name for assumed hybrid species, resulting from crossing the two above species, and perhaps others. These plants may have firm leaves elliptical or long-ovate, generally smooth or slightly fine-hairy beneath, and the white or pink-tinged flowers shaped more nearly like an urn, and with the blunt lobes spreading a trifle but not curved backward. The flower clusters terminal or at the tips of branches, the terminal cluster blooming earlier than the branch clusters. Open situations, dry or moist, and rocky shores wherever both the reputed parents are known to be in the vicinity. *A. medium* is a highly doubtful entity and may exist only in the minds of its protagonists.

———

The very close relationship of the Dogbane and Milk-weed families is evidenced by their milky juice and the anatomical character of their flowers, though these last have no apparent similarity. A long time ago after much discussion and dispute among the earlier botanists the Dogbanes and Milkweeds were finally separated into two family groups.

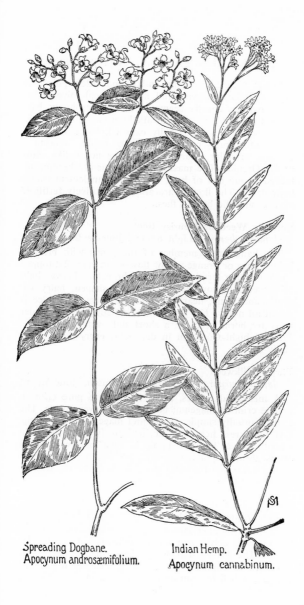

Spreading Dogbane.
Apocynum androsæmifolium.

Indian Hemp.
Apocynum cannabinum.

MILKWEED FAMILY. *Asclepiadaceæ.*

Plants with a generally milky and often poisonous juice with large leaves, and flowers deeply five-parted, the sepal-like corolla segments turned absolutely back at the time of bloom; the so-called corona within with its five concave parts thus fully exposed; the anthers and stigma remarkably connected and the pollen cohering in waxlike, granular, pear-shaped masses not unlike those of the Orchids. The masses quite frequently become attached to the feet of bees, and the entanglement causes their death. The flowers are almost exclusively fertilized by bees and the beelike flies.

Butterfly Weed or Pleurisy Root
Asclepias tuberosa　Light orange, June-September

The handsomest member of the genus with brilliant light orange or orange-yellow flowers, in erect flat-topped clusters at the termination of the branches. Leaves light olive-green, narrow oblong, or lance-shaped, hairy beneath, and veiny, nearly or quite stemless. The juice is not at all milky. The stem somewhat rough. The slender pods are borne erect on a short stalk with an S curve. 1-2 feet high. Common in dry fields everywhere, especially south.

Purple Milkweed
Asclepias purpurascens　Magenta-crimson, June-August

A misnamed species, as its flowers are pure crimson or else crimson-magenta; but they are never purple. The stem is usually simple, green, and magenta-tinged at the leaf junctures. Leaves ovate, and finely hairy beneath; smooth above. The flowers are ¼ inch long, with broad horns abruptly pointed inward. 2-3 feet high. Common in dry fields and thickets, Mass. south to N. C., west to Minn. and Okla.

Swamp Milkweed
Asclepias incarnata　Dull light crimson, July-September

A similar, rather smooth species, the stem with two downy lines above and on the branches of the flower-stalks. The leaves narrow, or lance-shaped; all short-stalked. The small flowers in small terminal flat-topped clusters, dull light crimson or dull crimson-pink. 2-4 feet

A.verticillata.

Butterfly Weed   Asclepias tuberosa

high. Common in swamps throughout our range. The var. *pulchra* is more or less hairy, has broader, shorter-stalked leaves, and dull crimson or pink or even pink-white flowers. Common north, south to Ga., east of the Alleghenies.

Common Milkweed
Asclepias syriaca   Pale brown-lilac, July-August

The commonest of all the *Asclepias*, and remarkable for its cloyingly sweet, somewhat pendulous flower-cluster, which is most æsthetic in color; it varies from pale brownish-lilac to pale lavender-brown, and from dull crimson-pink and pink-lilac to yellowish (the horns particularly) and brownish-lavender. The broad oblong leaves and stem of the plant are very finely hairy, the color is light yellow-green, and the ribs are yellowish. The rough-surfaced seed-pod is filled with the silkiest of white down, attached to flat yellow-brown seeds overlapping each other like the scales of a fish. The flower-clusters are borne at the junction of leaf-stalk and plant-stem. The flowers are mostly fertilized by bees, who not infrequently lose their lives by their feet becoming inextricably entangled with the pollen masses, or caught in the fissures of the corona. 3-5 feet high. Common everywhere.

Asclepias amplexicaulis   Lilac-green, July-August

Pale magenta-purple-stained green flowers in a solitary terminal cluster. The oblong, wavy leaves with a clasping base somewhat heart-shaped. Rather uncommon northward, but frequent in the south, especially in Fla. and the Gulf states.

Poke Milkweed
Asclepias exaltata   Cream-white, June-August

A rather tall milkweed with large ivory or cream-white flowers, whose reflexed corolla-segments are green or magenta-tinged on the outer surface; the flowers loosely clustered and drooping. The rather large leaves are thin and pointed at either end; the stem is slender and 3-6 feet high. One of our most dainty and beautiful wild flowers. Common on the borders of thickets and woods, N. H. to N. C., west to Mich. and Ky.

Common Milkweed.   Asclepias syriaca.

Four-leaved Milkweed
Asclepias quadrifolia   Magenta-pink, May-July

An early-flowering species with delicate magenta-pink flowers, the reflexed lobes of which are palest pink. The stem is slender and generally leafless below, bearing about two circles of four leaves about the middle and two pairs of opposite smaller leaves at the upper part of the stem. The plant is delicate and small, with few flower-clusters. 1-2 feet high. Woods and copses throughout the north, and south to N. C.; west to Minn. and Ark.

Asclepias verticillata   Green-white, July-September

An extremely small narrow-leaved plant with a slender stem leafy at the summit. The leaves smooth and very narrowly linear, generally grouped in circles of 4-7. Flowers greenish-white. 1-2 feet high. Common on dry hills, New Eng. to Fla., west to Saskatchewan and Tex.

MORNING-GLORY FAMILY. *Convolvulaceæ.*

Herbs, in our range, with twining or trailing stems, alternate leaves, and regular, perfect flowers with generally a bell-shaped or funnel-formed corolla, and five stamens. Self-fertilized as well as cross-fertilized. The name from the Latin *convolvo,* to roll together. Those below are often weedy pests, but the native *Ipomœa pandurata,* the wild potato-vine or manroot, has an enormous starchy root once a favorite food of the Indians. It is now rare.

Upright Bindweed
Convolvulus spithamæus   White, June-August

A small, erect or slightly twining plant scarcely a foot long, with blunt, oval, light green leaves, heart-shaped at the base, short-stemmed, about 1-2 inches long. Funnel-formed white flowers about 2 inches long, borne singly. Calyx inclosed in two large leafy bracts. In sandy or rocky fields, Que. to Va., and west to Minn. and Mo.

Hedge Bindweed
Convolvulus sepium   White, pink-tinged, June-August

A smooth-stemmed vine with arrow-shaped, triangular, grayish-green leaves, slender-stalked and acute-pointed. Handsome bell-shaped or funnel-shaped flowers ranging

Poke Milkweed.
Asclepias exaltata.

Four-leaved Milkweed,
Asclepias quadrifolia.

from pure white to pink-tinged, borne singly on long stalks; the five stamens cream-yellow, the pistil white. The five-parted calyx is inclosed in two pale green bracts. The flower generally closes before noon; it is sometimes over 2 inches broad and 3 long. Vine 3-10 feet long. Along moist roadsides and borders of fields climbing over shrubbery nearly everywhere. Also in Europe.

Japanese Bindweed
Convolvulus japonicus   Pink, June-August

A more or less trailing species, with simple or slightly branched stem, and ovate or oblong leaves, arrow-shaped or slightly heart-shaped at the base, 1-2 inches long. Flowers pink double-flowered, borne singly on long stalks, and about 2 inches long. 1-3 feet long. Common in lawns and pastures; a native of Japan.

Small Bindweed
Convolvulus arvensis   White or pink-tinged, June-September

A smooth-stemmed, very slender species with oblong and arrow-shaped gray-green leaves, the lateral lobes of which are acute. Small flowers not over 1 inch long, white or pink-tinged, and generally borne in clusters of two. The calyx *without* leafy bracts at the base. 1-2 feet long. In fields and waste places throughout N. Am.; a native of Europe.

———

Common Dodder
Cuscuta Gronovii   Dull white, July-October

A miserable parasite often troublesome in gardens, but found in low, damp, shady situations. It climbs high upon other plants by twining closely about their stalks and exhausting their juices through a thousand tiny suckers. Its threadlike, twisting stem varies in color from dull yellow to dull orange, it is crowded with bunches of tiny dull white bell-shaped flowers having five lobes. The calyx is greenish-white. All the dodders start at first from the ground, but finally securing a convenient plant upon which to climb, the root in the earth dies and they become parasitic. Common everywhere. There are 14 other species in our area, distinguished only by technical characters.

Hedge Bindweed.
Convolvulus sepium.

Common Dodder.
Cuscuta Gronovii

PHLOX FAMILY. *Polemoniaceæ.*

Herbs with alternate or opposite leaves and perfect, regular flowers with a five-lobed corolla which is rolled up in the bud, the lobes of the mature flower forming a long-tubed, salverform corolla. Stamens five. Cross-fertilized most generally by butterflies and bumblebees. The name *Phlox* is from the Greek φλόξ, meaning flame.

Downy Phlox
Phlox pilosa Purple, etc., May-June

A more southern and western species with soft-downy stem and leaves, the latter deep green, linear or lance-shaped, without teeth and stemless. Flowers from pale crimson-pink to purple and white. The calyx hairy or sticky-glandular, the corolla-tube usually fine-hairy. 1-2 feet high. In dry ground from Conn. south to Fla., west to Wisc. and Tex.

Wild Blue Phlox
Phlox divaricata Pale lilac or violet, April-June

Another rather western species with a somewhat sticky fine-hairy stem, with spreading leafy shoots from the base. Leaves wider than those of the preceding species, especially those on the sterile shoots; they are deep green, ovate lance-shaped, and acute-pointed. The pale violet or lilac flowers have generally notched lobes, they are slightly fragrant, and are gathered in loose clusters. Often the lobes are without notches. 9-18 inches high. In moist thin woodlands, Que. and N. Y., south to S. C., increasingly frequent westward to Mich. and Ill.

Ground or Moss Pink
Phlox subulata Crimson-pink, etc., April-September

A very low species with tufted stems, spreading over the ground until it forms compact masses resembling moss. The small, thickish yellow-green leaves sharptipped, linear, and close set; the plant mostly evergreen. Flowers few in a cluster terminating the short stems, varying in color from white through crimson-pink to light magenta; the petals notched. The stems fine-hairy or becoming smooth. 2-5 inches high. In sandy or rocky ground, Ont. south to N. C., west to Mich. and Ky.

Phlox paniculata—which is a tall garden species, in colors varying from pink and lilac to white, with stout,

Phlox pilosa.

Moss Pink
Phlox subulata.

smooth stem, and dark green acute lance-shaped or oblong leaves—has escaped from cultivation and is established permanently in many localities. 2-6 feet high. Its wild range is from N. Y. to Ga. and west to Ind. and Kan.

———

Greek Valerian
Polemonium reptans   Light violet, April-May

A smooth perennial with slender and weak stems finally reclining, and compound alternately growing leaves formed of 5-15 ovate lance-shaped leaflets; the uppermost leaves generally simple; all toothless. Flowers about ½ inch long, light blue-violet or rarely white, in loose clusters and nodding—bluebell-like. 8-12 inches high. In thin woods, N. Y. south to Ala., west to Minn. and Ark.

Jacob's Ladder
Polemonium Van-Bruntiæ   Violet, May-July

A much rarer species, found only by the mountain streams and in the swamps of the north. It has a stout horizontal root from which spread numerous rootlets, with erect stems smooth and leafy to the top. Leaves compound like those of the preceding species, the lower ones consisting of 15-19 nearly stalkless, ovate pointed leaflets. Flowers numerous in a somewhat long cluster, bright violet, and nearly 1 inch broad, with protruding stamens, the five lobes of the corolla rounded. 1-2½ feet high. From Vt. and northern N. Y., south to W. Va. Common only in the far north.

———

Two plants, somewhat suggesting the Greek valerian, and belonging to the related family *Hydrophyllaceæ,* are the water-leaf, *Hydrophyllum virginianum,* and its close relative *H. canadense.* The water-leaf is a rough-hairy perennial with deeply-cut, five-lobed leaves, and dense terminal clusters of white or pinkish flowers with prominently protruding stamens. It is found in rich, moist woods from Que. to Va., west to N. D. and Ark. Its close relative, *Hydrophyllum canadense,* has rounded, more shallowly lobed leaves which half hide the flower cluster, while in *H. virginianum,* the flower cluster stands well above the foliage. In moist woods, Vt. to Ga., west to Ill. and Mich., south to Mo.

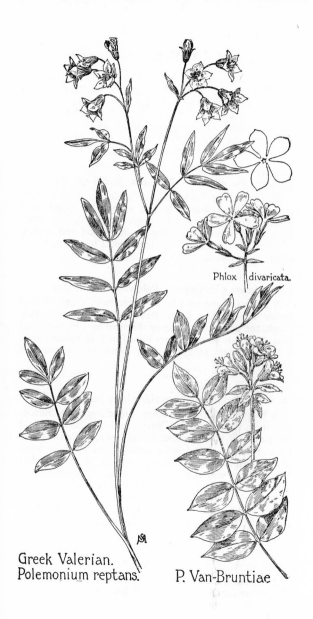

Phlox divaricata.

Greek Valerian.
Polemonium reptans.

P. Van-Bruntiae

BORAGE FAMILY. *Boraginaceæ.*

In our range annual or perennial herbs with rough-hairy stems and generally alternate, toothless, rough leaves. The blue-violet flower perfect and regular with a five-lobed corolla (*Echium* excepted), and five stamens. Flowers mostly in one-sided spikes, which at first are somewhat rolled up, straightening as the blossoms expand. The heliotrope and forget-me-not belong here.

Hound's Tongue
Cynoglossum officinale Magenta, June-September

An ill-smelling, Eurasian, weedy biennial with branching stem, lance-shaped leaves, except the basal ones which are oblong and long slender-stemmed. The small magenta or rarely white flowers, five-lobed and loosely arranged on a fine-hairy curving stem. 2 feet high. Fields nearly everywhere.

Wild Comfrey
Cynoglossum virginianum Pale violet, April-May

A perennial species with a simple hairy stem, without leaves above. The basal leaves oblong lance-shaped, rough, the upper ones clasping the stem by a heart-shaped base. The pale violet flowers on a few long naked stems. 1-2½ feet high. In thin woods, Conn. to Fla., west to Mo. and Okla.

___

Virginia Stickseed
Hackelia virginiana Lavender-white, June-September

A biennial with a fine-hairy, branching stem, slender and spreading. The basal leaves vanishing, as a rule, at the period of bloom, rather broad ovate; the stem-leaves light green, ovate and lance-shaped, growing quite small toward the top of the plant, acute at either end. The flower-spikes very slender and bearing tiny white flowers of a lavender tinge. The tiny burlike fruit covered with barbed prickles. 2-4 feet high. Common on the borders of dry woods, Que. south to Ala. and La., west to Minn. and Okla. Formerly known as *Lappula.*

___

Virginia Cowslip
Mertensia virginica Violet-blue, March-May

A beautiful species frequently cultivated, having light violet-blue flowers nearly 1 inch long. The stem smooth

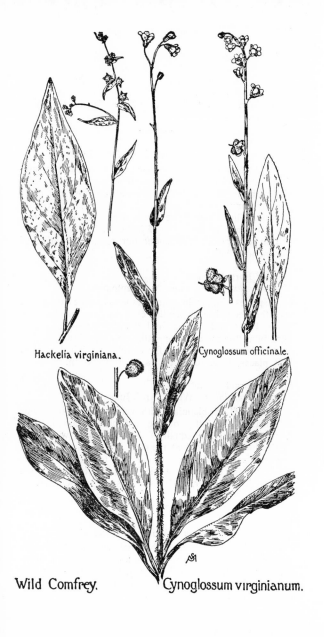

Hackelia virginiana.

Cynoglossum officinale.

Wild Comfrey.

Cynoglossum virginianum.

and erect, sometimes branched. The deep green leaves
toothless, ovate pointed or obovate, strongly veined, and
stalkless; the trumpetlike flowers with five lobes are rarely
white. 1-2 feet high. On river meadows and along river-
banks from N. Y. and N. J., south to Ala., west to Wisc.
and Kan.

———

Forget-me-not
Myosotis scorpioides   Light blue, May-July

The true forget-me-not of gardens, escaped from cultivation, and found in wet ground or marshes. A perennial with slender, sprawling, fine-hairy stems, and gray-
green oblong lance-shaped leaves, stemless or nearly so.
The small light blue flowers with a golden eye, in small
clusters somewhat curved. 6-15 inches high. Beside brooks
and in wet places throughout our range. A native of
Europe and Asia.

Smaller Forget-me-not
Myosotis laxa   Pale blue, May-September

A species similar in many respects to the foregoing,
with the fine-hairiness bending close to stem and leaf, the
leaves blunt and oblong, and the very small and pale
light blue flowers on long stalks, loosely clustered. The
calyx lobes as long as the flower-tube. 6-19 inches high.
Wet places, Que. south to Va., west to Minn.

Spring Forget-me-not
Myosotis virginica   White, April-June

An annual or biennial, with very bristly-hairy stems
and leaves, the latter oblong and obtuse. Small white
flowers; the calyx unequally five-cleft, bristly, with some
of the bristles hooked at the tips. 3-15 inches high. On
dry banks from Me. to Ga. and west to Mich. The var.
macrosperma, by some considered a separate species, is a
western form, larger, and has a looser flower-cluster.

———

Corn Gromwell
Lithospermum arvense   White, May-August

A rough-hairy annual or biennial, with erect, branching stems and foliage resembling that of *Myosotis,* but a
brighter green. The small white flowers scattered on the
spikes and stemless or nearly so. 6-18 inches high. Sandy
roadsides and fields everywhere.

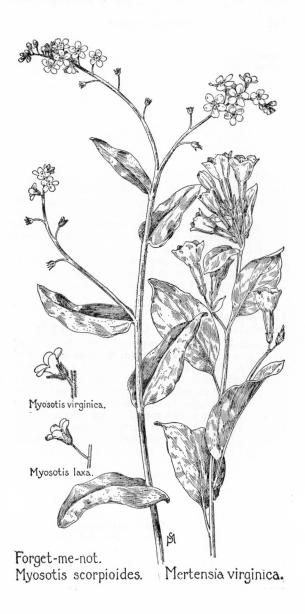

Myosotis virginica.

Myosotis laxa.

Forget-me-not.
Myosotis scorpioides.   Mertensia virginica.

Gromwell
Lithospermum officinale   Cream-white, May-August

A similar taller species with a much-branched stem, gray-green, few-veined, rough and stemless leaves rather broad lance-shaped. The cream-white flowers with corollas funnel-formed and a little longer than the five-pointed hairy calyx. 1-3 feet high. Que. to N. J., west to Minn. Both of these last species are naturalized from Europe. *Lithospermum* is formed of the Greek words *stone* and *seed,* referring to the hard seed.

Indian Paint
Lithospermum canescens   Orange-yellow, March-June

An indigenous species, the so-called Puccoon of the Indians. A perennial, soft-hairy and rather hoary, with obtuse linear-oblong leaves, stemless and hairy. The orange-yellow flowers with a broad corolla, salver-formed and five-lobed, about ½ inch long. 6-18 inches high. Cross-fertilized by bees and butterflies. In dry soil, Ont. south to N. J. and Ala., and west to Manitoba and Ariz. Rare in New Eng. The roots yield a red dye.

False Gromwell
Onosmodium virginianum   Cream-white, May-July

A densely harsh-hairy perennial herb, the hairs of which lean toward stem and leaf, the stem slender and branching. The light green leaves oblong lance-shaped. Flowers cylindrical, cream-white, with five long sharp lobes; the style threadlike and extending far beyond the mouth of the corolla; the calyx with five sharp segments; the flower-cluster at first curved, finally erect and long. Flowers ⅓ inch long. The stigma matures before the anthers; it is mostly cross-fertilized by the butterflies. 1-2 feet high. Me. south, and west to Kan. (*Illus. on page 408.*)

Small Bugloss
Lycopsis arvensis   Light violet, June-September

A rough-bristly annual species, naturalized from Europe, with a branching stem and lance-shaped leaves. The light blue-violet flowers in crowded clusters, the calyx nearly as long as the curved corolla. 1-2 feet high. In fields and on roadsides near dwellings, throughout the U. S. The name is from λύκος, a wolf, and ὄψις, a face; but the flower's face scarcely looks that way!

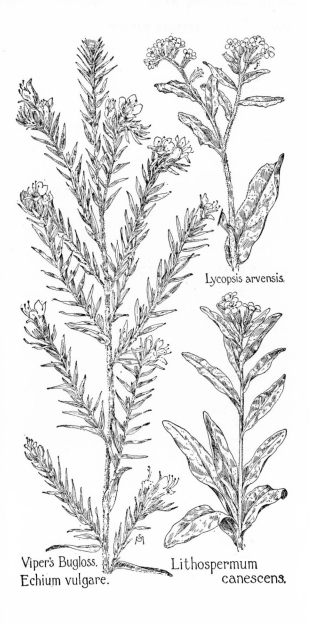

Lycopsis arvensis.

Viper's Bugloss.
Echium vulgare.

Lithospermum
canescens.

Viper's Bugloss
Echium vulgare　　Blue-violet, June-July

Sometimes called blueweed, and in fact a flower sufficiently approaching a blue tone to justify the name; but
the blossoms actually range between lilac, purple, and
violet of a bluish cast. It is a biennial with an exceedingly
bristly-hairy stem, and hairy, silvery light green leaves,
linear lance-shaped, toothless and stalkless. The flowers
are rather showy, tubular or vase-shaped, with five
rounded unequal divisions; the four stamens, which, with
the pistil, are pink, extend far beyond the limit of the
corolla. The flower-spike one-sided, at first closely coiled,
but finally long and but slightly curved; the flower is
light ultramarine-violet. 1-2½ feet high. Roadsides and
pastures throughout the U. S. Naturalized from Europe.

VERVAIN FAMILY.　*Verbenaceæ.*

Generally herbs (at least in our range) with opposite
leaves and perfect, more or less irregular flowers in terminal clusters. In the tropics most of them are shrubs
and trees, including the teak. The corolla with united
petals, uniform in shape, or two-lipped, the tube generally
cylindrical and spreading into 4-5 lobes. Four stamens,
two long and two short, or very rarely only two. Probably self-fertilized, though cross-fertilization may occur.

European Vervain
Verbena officinalis　　Purplish or white, June-September

A troublesome annual weed with a four-sided, slender,
nearly smooth, branching stem, and minutely hairy
leaves, deeply cleft and sharp-toothed; the upper ones
lance-shaped and toothless, the lower ovate and sharply
divided; all deep green. The small pale purple or white
flowers in branching spikes about 5 inches long, inconspicuous and uninteresting. 1-3 feet high. In waste places
everywhere. Naturalized from Europe.

White Vervain
Verbena urticifolia　　White, July-September

A similar perennial species with white flowers; usually
with erect slightly rough-hairy stem four-sided and
grooved, and coarsely toothed, deep green leaves, all or
nearly all with distinct stems, acute, and slightly hairy.

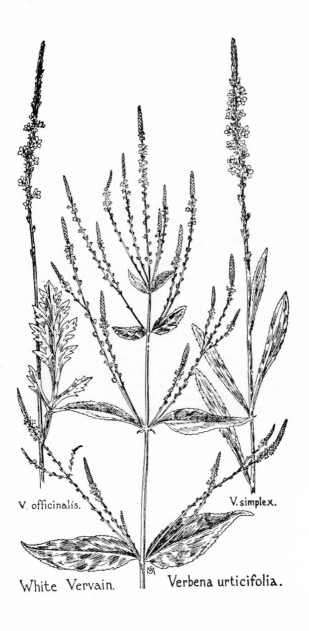

V. officinalis.

V. simplex.

White Vervain.

Verbena urticifolia.

The flower-spikes at length very long, the white flowers very small. 3-5 feet high. In fields and waste places, from Me. south, and west to Minn., S. D., and Tex. It has many forms or varieties, but these are disputed by the experts.

Narrow-leaved Vervain
Verbena simplex   Pale violet, June-August

A small, rough-hairy species with a slender, often simple stem. Leaves linear and lance-shaped, the lower ones broad at the tip and wedge-shaped at the base, all more or less toothed and veiny. Flower-spikes few or single, densely clustered with pale violet flowers about ¼ inch wide. 8-22 inches high. Dry borders of fields, Ont. south to Fla., and west to Minn. and Okla.

Blue Vervain
Verbena hastata   Blue or violet-blue, July-September

One of the handsomest yet commonest members of the genus. The stem erect, stout, four-sided and grooved, roughish, and dull green. The short-stalked leaves dark green, lance-shaped or oblong lance-shaped, acutely incised with double teeth, and with a rough surface; the lower leaves are more or less three-lobed. The flower-spikes are numerous and branch upward like the arms of a candelabra; the flowers bloom from the foot of the cluster upward, a few at a time, leaving behind a long line of purple-tinged calyx; the tiny blossoms are deep violet-blue or blue. *Verbena hastata* is a special favorite of the bumblebee, and it is also closely attended by the honeybee. In fields everywhere. The garden verbena, *Verbena hortensis,* is a rare escape.

LOPSEED FAMILY. *Phrymaceæ*

This family has only one species.

Lopseed
Phryma leptostachya   Crimson-magenta, July-August

A tall plant. The stalk is four-sided, hollow, and strong-fibered, branching divergently above. The deep green leaves are thin, coarsely toothed, and arranged in pairs, each pair set at right angles with the next; the upper leaves nearly stemless and ovate pointed; the lower oval. The slender flower-spike bears little two-lipped flowers

Blue Vervain.   Verbena hastata.

(the lower lip is three-parted) set in pairs at right angles with each other. This plant is considered as being related to the plantains by some authorities. In woods, Que. south to Fla., west to Minn. and Okla.

MINT FAMILY. *Labiatæ.*

An enormous family of aromatic herbs (shrubs and trees in the tropics) the foliage of which is covered with tiny glands containing a strong-scented volatile oil of wide use in condiments and perfumes. The flowers are usually small, tubular, with an entire or two-lobed upper lip and a three-lobed lower lip. The stem is generally *square,* and the leaves grow opposite each other. The tiny flowers are gathered in more or less conspicuous spikes, or are clustered at the base of the leaves; they are honey-bearing, and are almost exclusively cross-fertilized by honeybees, bumblebees, and the smaller bees. The name from *Labiæ,* the lips. Among garden plants are lavender, rosemary, sweet marjoram, coleus and the scarlet salvia.

Blue Curls or Bastard Pennyroyal
Trichostema dichotomum   Pale violet or magenta, July-September

This is an annual species whose light violet, magenta-pink, or rarely white flowers are generally in pairs at the terminating branchlets of the somewhat woolly-sticky stiff stem. The leaves are narrowly oblong or lance-shaped, and a trifle sticky, with an aromatic pennyroyal-like odor. The flowers are too scattered to form a panicle or cluster, and they are remarkable for the *extraordinary length* of the violet stamens which extend in a curving line far beyond the five-lobed corolla, or flower-cup—hence the name Blue Curls. The Latin name also refers to the hairlike stamens. After the corolla fades and falls, the little nutlets within the calyx are in plain view. 6-20 inches high. In dry sandy fields, from Me. south to Fla., west to Mich. and Mo. A narrow-leaved form, which grows with the type, is distinguished by some as the var. *lineare.*

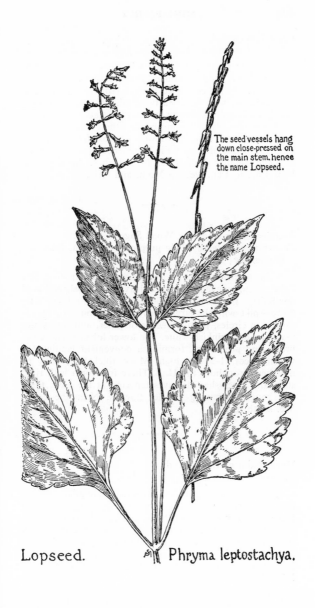

The seed vessels hang
down close-pressed on
the main stem, hence
the name Lopseed.

Lopseed.　　　Phryma leptostachya.

False Pennyroyal
Isanthus brachiatus   Pale violet, July-September

A slender branching annual with lance-shaped, tooth-less or slightly toothed, conspicuously three-ribbed leaves, and extremely regular-lobed flowers (for one of the family *Labiatæ*), with five nearly equal, obovate, spreading divisions. The pistil greatly exceeds the stamens in length, the latter scarcely extending beyond the corolla; it is evident, therefore, that the flower is cross-fertilized. The most frequent visitors are the bumblebees, the honeybees, and the smaller butterflies. 8-16 inches. In dry soil, New Eng. to Fla., west to Minn. and Ariz.

———

American Germander or Wood Sage
Teucrium canadense   Pale purple or magenta, July-September

A downy perennial with a stiff perpendicular stem, and light green, unevenly toothed leaves, lance-shaped and fine-hairy, particularly underneath. The rather long flower-spike with the large nearly ¾-inch-long flowers arranged in circles, purple, deeper or paler, and sometimes magenta, or a pinkish-white. The lower lobe of the flower broad and prominent, forming a convenient landing for visiting bees. 1-2 feet high. Moist thicket borders, or marshes throughout the U. S. There is a form with rigid stem and lance-shaped leaves tapering at the base, thick and roughish, having smaller flowers. Near the coast, Me. south to Fla.

———

Horse Balm or Rich Weed
Collinsonia canadensis   Pale yellow, July-September

A stout-stemmed, yellow-flowered perennial species, tall and branching, with large ovate sharply toothed leaves and a nearly smooth stem. The pale yellow flowers with 2 long divergent stamens and a prominent pistil, strongly lemon-scented. Flower-cluster very loose. Named for Peter Collinson, an English botanist. 2-4 feet high. In damp rich woodlands, from Que. to Fla., west to Mich. and Ark.

Blue Curls.   Trichostema dichotomum

Onosmodium virginianum.

Isanthus brachiatus.   Teucrium canadense.
Perilla frutescens.

Note the long lower lip of the
corolla and its slightly
fringed edge.

Rich Weed.   Collinsonia canadensis.

Perilla frutescens White, July-September

A coarse and aromatic perennial species introduced into the gardens of this country from China and India, and escaped to roadsides near dwellings. The large, ovate, coarsely toothed leaves deep purple-tinged beneath, and with a bronze tone above, the green completely suffused with the other color. Strongly scented. Flowers tiny, in terminal clusters, and dull white or pale magenta. 1-3 feet high. In waste places, New Eng. to Fla., west to Ill. and Iowa.

Bugle
Ajuga reptans Blue, May-June

A sprawling, weedy Eurasian perennial, often cultivated and escaping from gardens anywhere in our range. It is scarcely 8 inches high, partly creeping and apt to form mats. The leaves are opposite, essentially stalkless. Flowers in a dense, leafy cluster, the blue corolla nearly an inch long, faintly hairy. While this type is rather rare in cultivation, there are many showy horticultural forms with white, purple, pink and blotched flowers, and one with metallic crisped leaves. Any of these may be found as escapes.

Wild Marjoram
Origanum vulgare Pinkish-purple, July-September

A Eurasian perennial herb with a creeping rootstock, the stems erect, branched, and from 16-30 inches high. Leaves opposite, ovalish, stalked, without marginal teeth. Flower-clusters at the ends of small branches, rounded or nearly flat-topped, the corolla scarcely ½ inch long. This is the plant known as pot marjoram by the herb fanciers and has been grown for centuries. It is commonly cultivated here for its aromatic foliage and has escaped to fields and roadsides from Mass. to N. C.; not common.

The genus *Mentha* is a tribe of odorous perennial herbs with little tubular flowers mostly in close clusters; the plant-stems square. Almost all the species are naturalized from Europe, and there are many hybrids. Name from the Latin name of the mint. The mints are commonly fertilized by flies.

Wild Marjoram.

Bugle.

Horse Mint
Mentha longifolia   **Pale purple, July-August**

Flowers in rather crowded, slender, leafless spikes, sometimes disconnected. Leaves ovate-oblong and ovate lance-shaped, almost stalkless, sharp-pointed and sharply toothed, often smooth above, but the whole plant generally finely white-haired. Plant-stem square. 18 inches high. Roadsides and field-borders, New Eng. to Mo. *Mentha alopecuroides* has larger leaves, stemless, broadly oval and obtuse, often approaching heart-shape, coarsely toothed and more veiny. Mass. to Pa.

Spearmint
Mentha spicata   **Pale purple, July-August**

Flowers variable in depth of color; clusters crowded like those of the preceding species, but especially narrow and pointed. Plant-stem green, but ultimately reddish, square, and *nearly* smooth. Leaves oblong or ovate lance-shaped, unevenly toothed. 12-20 inches high or more. Wet places and roadsides or in cultivated ground everywhere. This is the mint for juleps and mint sauce.

Peppermint
Mentha piperita   **Pale purple, July-August**

Flowers in narrow, loose, disconnected, leafless, terminal spikes, and often on a rather long stem proceeding from between the plant-stem and leaf-stalk. Leaves long-ovate, deep green, smooth, and regularly toothed, slightly rough beneath. They taste of menthol, which spearmint does not. Plant-stem purplish, 18-36 inches high. Along brooks and in cultivated ground everywhere.

Water Mint
Mentha aquatica   **Pale purple, August-September**

The flowers in a roundish or nearly oblong terminal cluster; frequently there are one or more clusters between the plant-stem and the upper leaf-stalks. Leaves ovate or round-ovate. The plant is characterized by downy hairs (rarely it is smoothish) which generally point downward. Wet places throughout our area, but not common. 18-28 inches high or more. In the var. *crispa* the plant is smooth, but the leaves somewhat crisped.

Mentha longifolia.

Mentha spicata.

Peppermint.

Mentha piperita.

Wild Mint
Mentha arvensis **Light purple, July-August**

The tiny bell-shaped flowers clustered in circles about the plant-stem at the junction with leaf-stalks. Leaves ovate, blunt-toothed, and distinctly stalked, but these hidden by the dense, stalkless flower-clusters. 6-20 inches long. It is our only *native* mint. The plant is more or less hairy throughout, and has the odor of Pennyroyal. In wet places through the northern United States across the continent and south to Va. It has many different forms, which are poorly differentiated and puzzling to the amateur. Our illustration is of the typical form.

Bugleweed
Lycopus virginicus **White, July-September**

A mintlike weed but inodorous, with small white flowers remotely suggesting a bugle shape. Stem slender, four-angled, and generally smooth. The light green leaves ovate lance-shaped and very coarsely toothed. The tiny flowers clustered at the bases of the leaves have but two perfect stamens; the other two, if present, are quite abortive. Fertilized mostly by the beelike flies, and the small bees. 6-24 inches high. Common.

Cut-leaved Water Horehound
Lycopus americanus **White, June-September**

A similar species, with some leaves so deeply toothed that they appear incised, and others incised to an appearance of lobes. The stiff stem generally smooth, simple or branched. The flower-cup tiny and but little larger than its green calyx. 1-2 feet high. Common.

Balm
Melissa officinalis **Blue or white, June-August**

Cultivated for two thousand years this lemon-scented perennial has such a delightful odor that an old Arab saying that "Balm makes the heart merry and joyful" is still true. It grows 1-2 feet high and becomes rather bushy. Leaves more or less oval, crinkly on the margins, and short-stalked, always opposite. Flowers rather sparse, only a few in each cluster at the leaf-joints. Corolla pale blue to white. Originally a native of Asia, it came through Europe to N. Am. and has escaped from gardens from Me. to S. C., west to Mo. and Ark.

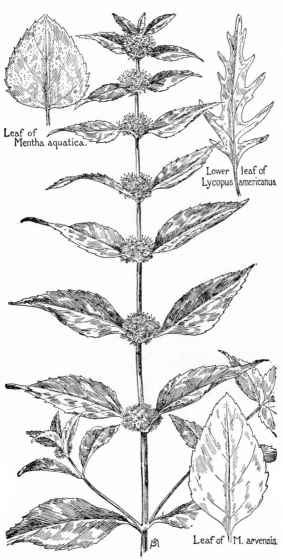

Leaf of
Mentha aquatica.

Lower leaf of
Lycopus americanus.

Leaf of M. arvensis.

Wild Mint.   Mentha arvensis

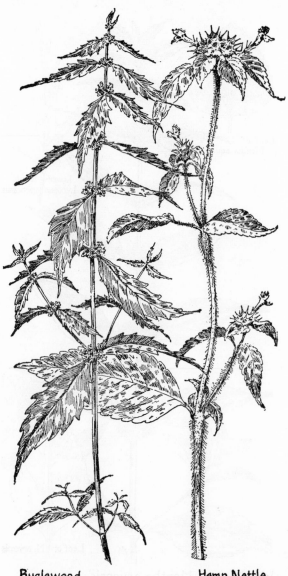

Bugleweed.
Lycopus virginicus.

Hemp Nettle.
Galeopsis Tetrahit.

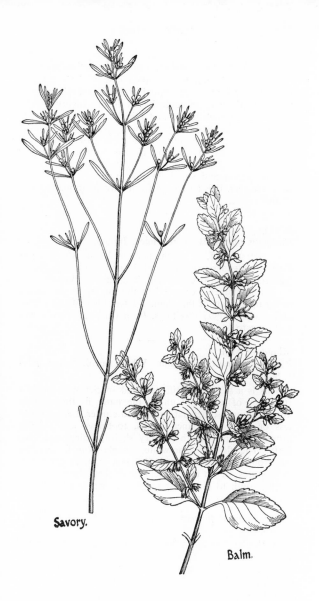

Savory.

Balm.

Savory
Satureja hortensis   Pinkish-purple, July-September

While this is commonly called savory, it is actually the summer savory, an annual from the Mediterranean region cultivated for centuries. It is *the* savory of the cooks and of such flavor that Nicholas Culpepper, writing in 1652, advised everyone to "keep it dry by you all the year, if you love yourself and your ease, and it is a hundred pounds to a penny if you do not." It grows 12-30 inches high, has opposite, bright green, rather narrow leaves and small flowers in more or less one-sided clusters. It is an escape from gardens in many parts of our range.

———

Hyssop
Hyssopus officinalis   Pale violet, June-September

A coarse, stiff, aromatic perennial naturalized from Eurasia. Slender-stemmed and lance-leaved; the leaves stiff and pointed at either end. The tubular flowers with projecting stamens, crowded at the angles of the leaves at the upper part of the plant. 1-3 feet high. Waste places and roadsides near dwellings, from Que. south to N. C., and west to Mont.

———

Mountain Mint
Pycnanthemum virginianum   White, purple-dotted, July-September

This is a stout and stiff-stemmed species with a slight fragrance of mint; but unlike the latter its tiny flowers are borne in a somewhat flat-topped cluster. Leaves stalkless or nearly so, lance-shaped, toothless, and slightly aromatic; stem smooth or very slightly hairy, and very leafy. The flowers lilac-white, purple-spotted, standing out from the globular heads. 1-3 feet high. In dry fields, or pastures, or on the borders of thickets, from Vt. and Mass., south to Ga., west to N. D. The name meaning *crowded flower-clusters*.

Pycnanthemum flexuosum   White, purple-dotted, July-August

A similar species, with smooth linear leaves, sharp-pointed and light green. The stem and leaves stiff. The tiny flowers white, speckled or dotted with purple. 1-2 feet high. Dry fields, N. H. south to Fla., west to Wisc. and Tex.

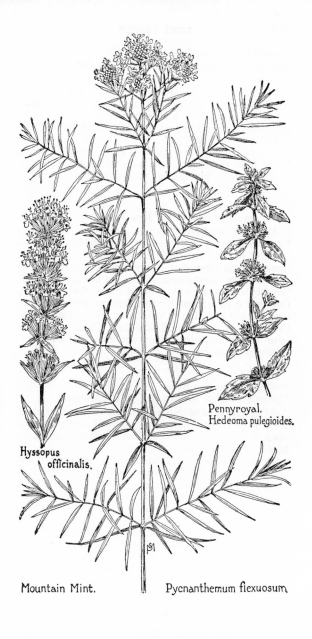

Hyssopus
officinalis.

Pennyroyal.
Hedeoma pulegioides.

Mountain Mint. Pycnanthemum flexuosum.

American Pennyroyal
Hedeoma pulegioides   Pale light violet, July-September

A small annual, exceedingly odorous. The stem erect, finely hairy, with upward-reaching branches; the small light olive-green leaves with few teeth, ovate lance-shaped, blunt-pointed, and narrowed at the base. The tiny pale violet or lavender, tubular flowers with a three-lobed underlip. Fertilized mostly by bumblebees, honeybees, and the smaller bees. 6-15 inches high. Common in dry fields everywhere. The essential oil of Pennyroyal is efficacious in driving away mosquitoes.

Lyre-leaved Sage
Salvia lyrata   Light violet, June-July

A slightly rough-hairy, slender plant, with conspicuous light violet flowers nearly an inch long, which are cross-fertilized mostly by the bumblebees. The lower leaves are somewhat lyre-shaped, the upper pair (sometimes two pairs) midway up the stem, similar but less cut, or lobed; the tubular flowers with a broad three-lobed lip which furnishes a convenient landing-platform for insect visitors; 1-2 feet high. In dry woodlands, and beside thickets, Conn. to Fla., west to Ill. and Tex. There are several other species of *Salvia* within our area, but they must be sought in the technical manuals.

Oswego Tea or Bee Balm
Monarda didyma   Scarlet-red, July-September

A brilliant and showy wild flower whose scarlet-red color is strongly relieved by its usual background of shady woodland. Commonly found beside streams on the border of the woods.

The *Monardas* are peculiarly adapted to the visits of butterflies, although they are also commonly visited by bees, the bumblebee in particular. The two anther-bearing stamens are prominent, as well as the two-parted stigma, and neither can be passed without friction by butterfly or bee, both of which have the long tongue necessary to reach the nectar. The somber dark green leaves are broad lance-shaped, sharply toothed, and stalked; the small leaves just beneath the flower are often tinged ruddy. The stem, rather hairy-rough and square, is about 2 feet high, or more. Moist ground, New Eng. south to N. C. and west to Mich. (*Color Plate 19.*)

Oswego Tea.   Monarda didyma.

Wild Bergamot
Monarda fistulosa **Magenta-purple, June-September**

A similar species with a downy, slender stem, and deep green leaves, the upper ones somewhat stained with the pure pale lilac or whitish tint which characterizes the flower-bracts. The flowers with a less expanded throat, paler or deeper magenta-purple. 2-3 feet high. Dry grounds, Que. to Ga., west to Manitoba and Tex.

Downy Blephilia
Blephilia ciliata **Light purple, June-August**

A woodland species rather similar in many respects to *Monarda*. The small tubular flowers about ½ inch long, with a three-lobed underlip, light purple or violet, and fine-hairy. The lance-shaped leaves almost toothless (except the lower ones), white-downy beneath, and quite stalkless. The stem downy and mostly simple. 1-2 feet high. In dry woods, Mass. south to Ga. and west to Wisc. and Ark. The name is Greek for *eyelash,* in allusion to the hairy bracts.

Catnip
Nepeta Cataria **Lilac-white, July-October**

An exceedingly common weed to which many of the animals of the tribe *Felis* are greatly attached. The stem is densely downy as well as the deeply round-toothed leaves, and both are sage-green in color. The pale lilac or lilac-white and spotted flowers are also downy, and gathered in small terminal clusters, which are rarely 4 inches long. Leaves strongly aromatic. 2-3 feet high. Common everywhere. Naturalized from Europe.

Ground Ivy or Gill-over-the-Ground
Glechoma hederacea **Light purple, April-May**

A small creeping plant, adventive from Europe, common in all moist shady places. It takes the place of our Trailing Arbutus, in the moist fields of England in April, but often a pestiferous weed here. The pale purple flowers, spotted darker near the throat, and often with the calyx magenta-tinged, have two lips, the upper one two-cleft, and the lower, three-cleft; the deep green leaves,

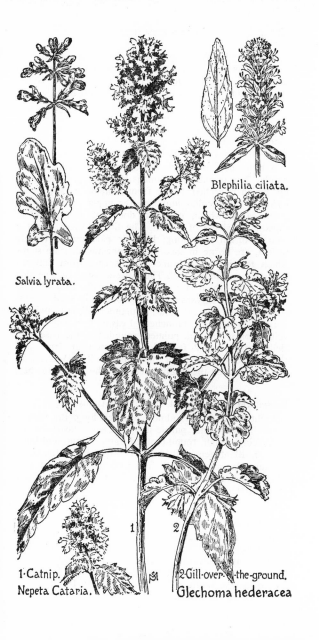

Salvia lyrata.

Blephilia ciliata.

1·Catnip.
Nepeta Cataria.

2·Gill-over-the-ground.
Glechoma hederacea

scalloped and rather heart-shaped, are often stained with magenta, as well as the stem; the latter takes root at the joints, and reaches out sometimes fully 3 feet. Newf. south to Ga., and west to Minn., Neb. and Kan.

———

Mad-dog Skullcap
Scutellaria lateriflora   **Pale purple, July-August**

A bitter perennial herb, not aromatic, with two-lipped tubular flowers, the four stamens located under the upper lip, which is arched. Name from *scutella,* a dish, in allusion to the peculiar hump on the upper section of the green calyx, which, however, does not even remotely suggest the shape of a dish. The little flowers, about a quarter of an inch long, light or pale purple (rarely white), are borne in succession along the delicate stems which terminate the branches or spring from between leaf-stalk and plant-stem. The flowers borne on one side of the stem which later is decorated with the odd little hoodlike green calyxes containing four white seeds. Plant-stem smooth, square, and sometimes slightly twisted, upright and much branched. Leaves narrowly ovate, veiny, coarse-toothed, pointed, rounded at the base, and slender-stalked. 1-2 feet high. Common in damp and shady places, throughout the country. The *Scutellarias* are fertilized by the smaller bees and the leaf-cutter bee.

Scutellaria ovata   **Light violet, July-August**

Light violet flowers almost an inch long, the whitish lower lip sometimes purple-stained. Leaves heart-shaped, very veiny, rough, round-toothed, rather blunt, and long-stalked. Plant-stem soft-hairy. 1-3 feet high. Banks of streams, Pa. south to Ala. and west to Minn. and Tex. The plant is very variable and at least three varieties are recognized.

Scutellaria serrata   **Light violet, May-June**

Flower an inch long, narrow, and its upper lip only a trifle shorter than the lower one. Leaves ovate or long-ovate, toothed, tapering at both ends, and smooth. Green and nearly smooth, slender plant-stem, 1-2 feet high. In woods, Pa. south to N. C., and west to Ill. The most showy of all the genus.

Mad-dog Skullcap.   Scutellaria lateriflora.

Scutellaria incana   **Light violet, July-August**

The flowers, stems, and under sides of the leaves generally covered with soft white hairs; flower nearly an inch long. Leaves ovate or narrow-ovate, stalked, and some slightly heart-shaped at the base. 2-4 feet high. Riverbanks from N. Y. to Ill., south to Va., west to Ark.

Scutellaria elliptica   **Light violet, May-July**

Flowers ½ inch long or a trifle more. Leaves distant, oval or long-ovate, veiny, round-toothed, the longer-stalked lower ones sometimes slightly heart-shaped, the upper on short, margined stalks. Plant-stem with spreading hairs. Dry or sandy ground, or woods. 12-30 inches high. Southern N. Y. and Pa. south and west to Mo. and Ga. The var. *hirsuta* is a larger, more hairy form with coarse leaves. Pa. to Fla., west to Mich., Miss. and Tex. Formerly and often still called *S. pilosa.*

Scutellaria integrifolia   **Light violet, June-August**

Flower bright light violet, and an inch long, in a striking terminal cluster. Leaves oblong lance-shaped, or narrower, mostly toothless, obtuse, short-stalked and downy together with the plant-stem. 6-20 inches high. Dry ground, borders of fields, woods. The seaboard states from Mass. to Fla.; also in Ohio, Ky. and Tenn. A handsome species.

Scutellaria parvula   **Violet, May-July**

A low species with flowers ¼ inch long, borne on very short stems at the junction of leaf-stalk with plant-stem. Leaves opposite-growing, toothless, round to lance-ovate or slightly heart-shaped, about ½ an inch long. Stem spreading, 3-10 inches high. Sandy banks and moist places, and a very variable species. The var. *ambigua* is minutely fine-hairy or smooth. Que. to Va. and Ala., west to N. D. and Tex.

Scutellaria galericulata   **Blue-violet, July-August**

Flowers ¾ inch long, growing in the same position as those of the foregoing species. Leaves ovate lance-shaped, the lower sometimes with a slight heart-shaped base, toothed, and acute. Stem smooth and slender. 1-2 feet high. Common in wet shady places and along streams, Que. to Del., west to the Pacific Coast; also in Eurasia.

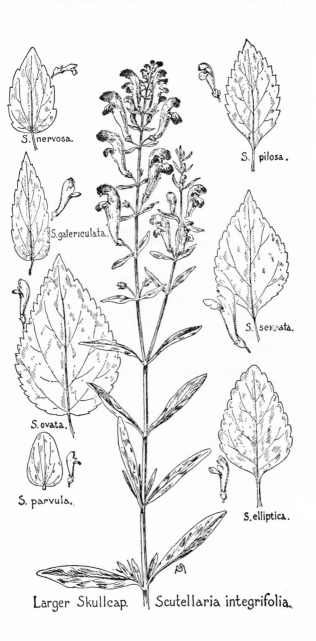

S. nervosa.

S. pilosa.

S. galericulata.

S. serrata.

S. ovata.

S. parvula.

S. elliptica.

Larger Skullcap. Scutellaria integrifolia.

Scutellaria nervosa   Pale blue-violet, June-August

Flowers a trifle more than ¼ inch long. Leaves about an inch long, roundish or ovate, slightly toothed, and the lower ones slightly heart-shaped. The floral leaves toothless. Stem smooth and slender, 1-2 feet high. Moist woods and thickets, N. J. south to Tenn., and west to Iowa.

———

Self-heal or Heal-all
Prunella vulgaris   Purple, light or deeper, June-September

A very common Eurasian, weedy, low perennial with generally a single stem, and tubular, two-lipped, hooded flowers proceeding from a spike or head of closely set, sometimes rusty-colored green, floral bractlike leaves. Flower tiny, purple, but sometimes flesh-color or white, the lower lip slightly fringed. Generally fertilized by the bumblebee, the common yellow butterfly is also a constant attendant. Leaves ovate-oblong, narrowing toward the tip, slightly or imperceptibly toothed, with generally two small bractlike leaves at the base of the stalks. Plant-stem slightly hairy. 6-13 inches high. Very common along roadsides nearly everywhere; a very variable species, one form with deeply cut leaves distinguished as *P. laciniata,* which is known only from Pa. and D. C.

———

False Dragonhead
Physostegia virginiana   Pink-lilac or lighter, July-August

A smooth perennial with upright, slender stem, stalk-less lance-shaped leaves mostly toothed, and large, 1-inch-long, showy flowers crowded in terminal, leafless spikes. Flower pale pinkish-lilac, often variegated with white, and funnel-shaped, the upper lip a little hooded, the lower three-parted; the throat inflated. Plant-stem smooth, 1-4 feet high. Wet grounds, from Que. to Del., west to Minn. and Tex. Very variable. One form, known as *P. denticulata,* slender and generally low, with scallop-toothed, or imperceptibly toothed leaves, and very slender flower-spikes is found from Va. to Fla. and Tex.; also Ark. (*Illus. opp. page 434.*)

Self-heal.   Prunella vulgaris.

Wild Thyme
Thymus serpyllum Purple, June-September

A European, rather weedy, plant closely related to cultivated thyme, but usually cultivated only for ornament, from which it escapes in many parts of our range. Stems rather woody, weak and sprawling, not over 12-16 inches long. Leaves opposite, short-stalked, ovalish, scarcely ¾ inch long. Flowers in a terminal, spiky, rather showy, crowded cluster which may be 2-4 inches long (rarely 8 inches), the purple corollas about ½ inch long. It generally escapes into woods and fields.

Dittany
Cunila origanoides Purple to white, August-October

A native, woodland, rather woody perennial herb, its stiffish branches forked. Leaves opposite, scarcely stalked, with a broad base and tapering tip; highly and pleasantly aromatic, not over 1½ inches long. Flowers in terminal close clusters, or these scattered among the upper leaves, the corolla nearly ½ inch long, generally purple, more rarely white. It is usually not over 12-18 inches high, and inhabits dry, sandy or rocky sites from southern N. Y. to Fla., west to Ind., Mo., Ark. and Okla. It is often called stone mint.

Horehound
Marrubium vulgare White, August-September

A white-woolly, bitter, and aromatic perennial, branched at the base, with small tubular dull white flowers circled about the plant-stem at the leaf junctions. Leaves round-ovate, stalked below, but essentially stalkless above, and scallop-toothed. 1-2 feet high. Cultivated, and escaped into waste places. Naturalized from Eurasia. The name from the Hebrew *marrob,* a bitter juice. (*Illus. opp. page 434.*)

Motherwort
Leonurus Cardiaca Pale lilac, June-August

Perpendicular-growing decorative herbs without any particular odor, with deeply cut leaves, and tiny flowers encircling the plant-stem at the point of junction with the leaves. The name from λέων, a lion, and ὀυρά, tail— lion's tail, alluding to the form of the flower-spike, but a poor simile. The upper lip of the tiny, tubular but

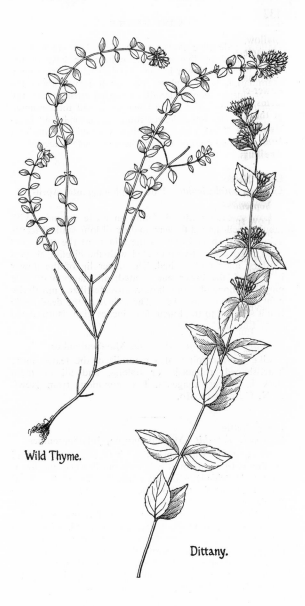

Wild Thyme.

Dittany.

shallow, pale lilac flower is bearded. The green calyx characterized by five thornlike points; the base of the calyx, when the flower is gone, marked with a cross upon examination with a glass. The small leaves about the flower-clusters conventionally arranged around the tall stems, wedge-shaped toward the stem, and three-pointed at the tip. The lower leaves rounded, slashed, and long-stalked. 2-4 feet high. A familiar perennial naturalized from Asia and common everywhere in waste places about dwellings.

———

Dead Nettle
Lamium amplexicaule   Pale purple-magenta, April-September

Low spreading annual, found on waste grounds. With tubular, bell-shaped flowers, and small long-stalked leaves below, heart-shaped ones in the middle of the stem, and others above directly connected with the circling flower-clusters; all round-toothed. The upper lip of the flower is bearded, the lower one spotted; all magenta or pale purple. A honey-bearing flower, cross-fertilized mostly by honeybees and bumblebees. The foliage of the dead nettle is not stinging to the touch. 6-18 inches high. Naturalized from Eurasia.

Lamium purpureum   Magenta, May-September

Like the foregoing, also naturalized, the leaves more heart-shaped, roundish, or oblong, and all of them stalked. Flowers magenta. Less common, from Newf. to N. C., west to Mo.

———

Hemp Nettle
Galeopsis Tetrahit   Magenta-purple, July-September

An annual, with spreading branches, and several circling clusters of small pale magenta flowers (the lower lip purple-striped) gathered at the stalks of the floral leaves. Name from the Greek, *weasellike,* from the fancied resemblance of the flower to the head of a weasel. The tiny flowers white-hairy, the flower-cup bristly. Leaves ovate, toothed, hairy, and pointed. Plant-stem square, very hairy, with hairs pointing downward, and conspicuously swollen below the joints. Cross-fertilized by the bumblebees and smaller bees. 10-18 inches high. Common in waste places and gardens everywhere. Naturalized from Eurasia. (*Illus. on page 416.*)

Motherwort. Leonurus Cardiaca.

Hedge Nettle
Stachys palustris   **Magenta-purple, or paler, July-
September**

Hairy perennial herbs, with tubular bell-shaped flowers, clustered in circles, 6-10 in each circle, and forming
a terminal spike. The upper part of the light magenta-
purple flower and its green cup (calyx) hairy. Leaves
stalkless, or the lower ones short-stalked, ovate lance-
shaped or longer, scallop-toothed, downy-hairy, rather
obtuse, and rounded at the base. Plant-stem square, 1-3
feet high. Wet grounds, common in some of its forms
nearly everywhere.

Stachys hispida   **Magenta-purple, July-September**

Like the foregoing, but with mostly smooth flowers,
leaves sometimes smooth, and nearly all distinctly stalked;
the plant-stem taller, commonly smooth on the sides,
but stiff-hairy at the angles. The flower-spike slender.
Stem 2-4 feet high. On wet grounds, Mass. to Ky., west
to Manitoba and Ark. There are 14 other species of
Stachys in our area, but their identification is difficult.

NIGHTSHADE FAMILY. *Solanaceæ.*

Mostly herbs with alternate leaves and regular, perfect
flowers; the five-lobed corolla with generally five stamens
and a very small stigma. Plants strongly scented, often
narcotic and extremely poisonous, but sometimes harm-
less and edible; fruit usually a many-seeded round berry
with the calyx generally adhering to its base. The potato,
tomato, tobacco and petunia are the widest-known members of the family. There are over 3,000 species, most of
them from Tropical Am., many of them shrubs and trees.

Nightshade or Bittersweet
Solanum Dulcamara   **Violet, purple, June-September**

A weak but woody, vinelike plant with variable dark
green leaves from ovate to triangular in outline, some
lobed and others formed of three leaflets, the two lateral
ones quite small, all without teeth. The small flowers in
diminutive loose clusters, with deeply five-cleft corolla,
violet or purple, or sometimes lilac-white, the yellow
conic center colored by the five stamens. The fruit (at
first green) an oval, translucent ruby-red berry, hanging

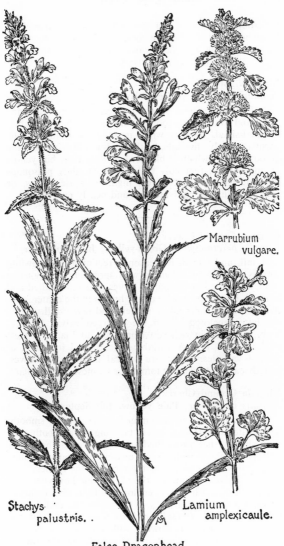

Marrubium
vulgare.

Stachys
palustris.

Lamium
amplexicaule.

False Dragonhead.
Physostegia virginiana.

or drooping in small clusters. The flower is visited by honeybees and the beelike flies. 2-8 feet high. In moist thickets and by waysides nearly everywhere. Naturalized from Eurasia. (*Illus. opp. page 438.*)

Black Nightshade
Solanum nigrum   White, July-September

A Eurasian species with an erect, smooth, branching stem, and ovate, wavy-toothed, thin-stalked leaves slightly unequal-sided. Flowers white in small side clusters, the corolla deeply five-lobed; the calyx adhering to the globose berry, which is black when fully ripe, but yellow in one variety; reputedly edible, but certainly poisonous in some varieties. 1-2½ feet high. In waste places, or near dwellings in cultivated ground nearly everywhere.

Clammy Ground Cherry
Physalis heterophylla   Green-yellow, July-September

A tall, and late in its season a reclining or sprawling species resembling *Solanum,* with spreading, sticky-hairy stem, and broad heart-shaped leaves coarsely toothed and pointed. Flower greenish-yellow, brown in the center, with five triangular short lobes; anthers and berry dull yellow, the latter enclosed within the enlarged calyx. 1-3 feet high. Common in rich soil from Que. to Fla., and west to Colo. and Tex. A variable species, and including at least 3 varieties. There are several cultivated relatives, usually called strawberry tomato or Chinese lantern-plant.

Virginia Ground Cherry
Physalis virginiana   Pale yellow, July-September

A branching and erect-stemmed species, mostly smooth. The ovate lance-shaped leaves tapering toward both ends very slightly shallow-toothed and light green. The flower dull pale yellow with five brown-purple spots; anthers deep yellow. The stigma matures before the anthers, and extends beyond them. Fertilized by the honeybee and bees. The reddish berry enclosed within the enlarged calyx. 1-3 feet high. Rich soil, Conn. to La., and west to Minn. and Ark. *Physalis pubescens,* a relative of the strawberry tomato, is downy, with angular leaves. The flower light green-yellow, brown-spotted at the throat, with violet anthers. Fruit green-yellow. Escaped from cultivation eastward.

Black Nightshade. Solanum nigrum.

Thorn Apple or Jamestown or Jimson Weed
Datura Stramonium   White, July-September

A rank-smelling annual, poisonous weed with a smooth, green or purple stout stem, and thin ovate, acute, angularly coarse-toothed leaves, slim-stalked. The white or pale violet trumpet-shaped flowers about 4 inches long, with a light green calyx less than half the length of the corolla, which has five sharp-pointed lobes. The green fruit-capsule, ovoid, about 2 inches long, and covered with stout prickles, the longest of which are at the tip of the capsule. 1-5 feet high. In waste places and vacant city lots nearly everywhere. Naturalized from Asia. The leaves are the source of dangerously poisonous alkaloids. Some students regard the purple-stemmed form as a separate species, *D. Tatula,* but they are not fundamentally different. *Datura Metel,* a native of Tropical Am., has white trumpetlike flowers 6-7 inches long and ovate leaves toothless or nearly so. Capsule evenly prickled. A garden escape in waste places. All are poisonous if eaten.

FIGWORT FAMILY. *Scrophulariaceæ.*

Commonly herbs with opposite or alternate leaves and perfect, irregular flowers with two sets of stamens (2-5), longer and shorter ones; corolla two-lipped or nearly regular. Fruit a two-celled and generally many-seeded capsule. A large family of bitter-juiced plants; some are narcotic-poisonous, others like the foxglove yield valuable drugs (digitalis). The beautiful Chinese tree, *Paulownia,* belongs here.

Great Mullein
Verbascum Thapsus   Yellow, June-September

A very common, picturesque, velvety-leaved weed of rocky pastures and roadsides, naturalized from Europe. The basal leaves at first in the form of a rosette, large, ovate, thick-velvety, and white-green. The stem stout and erect, with a few smaller, acute-pointed leaves; the terminal flower-spike cylindrical, woolly, and dotted with scattered light yellow flowers; corolla five-lobed, and anthers golden-yellow. Rarely the flowers are white. 2-5 feet high. In barren fields and waste places everywhere.

Solanum Dulcamara. Physalis virginiana.

Thorn Apple.
Datura Stramonium.

Fruit capsule.

Moth Mullein
Verbascum Blattaria   Yellow, white, June-September

A smaller species with smooth stem and thin, light green, glossy leaves, mostly oblong with deeply cut, notched, and toothed margins; the upper leaves lance-shaped and clasping at the base. The flowers, similar in shape to those of the preceding species, are light yellow or white, tinged on the back with lavender, and set on slender stalks; the five stamens are fringed with ruddy hairs, and the anthers are deep orange. The slender flower-spike is 1-2 feet long, and a trifle woolly. 2-5 feet high. In waysides, waste places, and pastures everywhere. Eurasian.

Blue Toad-flax
Linaria canadensis   Lavender, June-September

An extremely slender and smooth annual or biennial species with few small, thickish, linear, light green leaves, toothless, stalkless, smooth, and shining. The small pale violet or lavender flowers about ⅓ inch long, two-lipped, and spurred; the lower lip large and three-lobed, with a white, convex, two-ridged palate; the upper lip with two acute divisions; the spur curving and threadlike. 5-30 inches high. Common in dry, sandy soil, from Me. south, and local west to the Pacific Coast. The name from *Linum*, flax.

Toad-flax or Butter-and-Eggs
Linaria vulgaris   Yellow and orange, July-October

A very common but beautiful perennial weed natural-ized from Europe, with erect smooth stem, and gray-green linear, stalkless and toothless leaves growing alternately but near together. The flowers are about an inch long including the slender spur, and two-lipped, the upper lip two-lobed, light yellow, the lower lip three-lobed and pouch-shaped, tapering to the tip of the slender spur and furnished above with a protruding gold-orange palate which nearly closes the throat of the corolla; the four stamens are tipped with ochre-yellow anthers; the style is greenish. The flowers are assisted in the process of fertilization by bumblebees and butterflies. 1-3 feet high. In fields, pastures, and city lots everywhere.

Great
Mullein.
Verbascum Thapsus.

Moth Mullein.
Verbascum Blattaria.

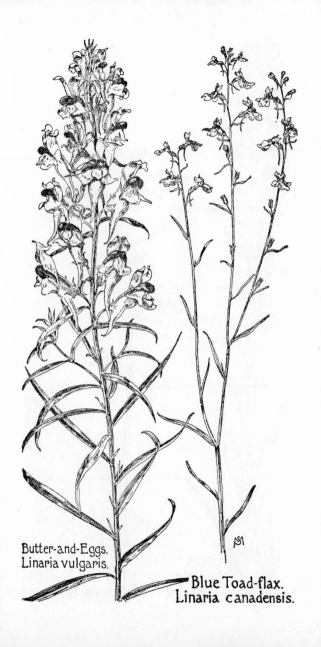

Butter-and-Eggs.
Linaria vulgaris.

Blue Toad-flax.
Linaria canadensis.

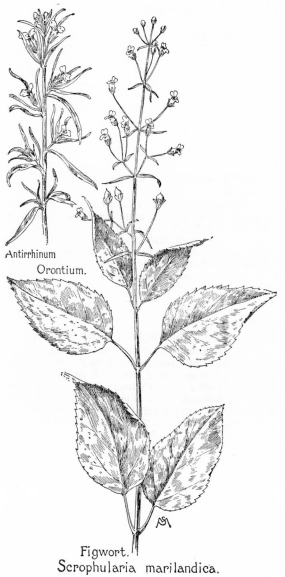

Antirrhinum
Orontium.

Figwort.
Scrophularia marilandica.

Small Snapdragon
Antirrhinum Orontium   Light purple, June-August

A smooth annual with erect stem and light green linear leaves. The flowers light purple or white, showy, solitary, and with a sac-shaped, two-lipped corolla; the upper lip two-lobed, the lower three-lobed. About 1 foot high. In fields and waste places near dwellings. Adventive from Eurasia. The garden Snapdragon, *A. majus,* is a very rare escape from cultivation.

Figwort
Scrophularia marilandica   Green-magenta, July-September

A smooth perennial with a slender four-sided, grooved stem and slender-stalked, ovate lance-shaped, toothed, light green leaves. Flowers small, sac-shaped, and clustered on long, nearly leafless branchlets; the two-lipped corolla green without, and shiny brown-magenta within. 3-7 feet high. In thin woods and thickets, from Que. to S. C. and Ala., west to Minn.

Turtle-head
Chelone glabra   White, pink-tinged, July-September

A smooth-stemmed plant superficially resembling the Bottle Gentian, with smooth, bright deep green, toothed, short-stalked, lance-shaped leaves 3-6 inches long. The flower not unlike a turtle's head, about an inch long, white, and delicately tinged at the tips with magenta-pink or crimson-pink; the corolla two-lipped, the upper lip arched over the lower one. The stamens dark and woolly. 1-3 feet high. On wet banks, in swamps, and beside brooks, from Newf. to Ga., west to Minn. and Iowa.

Pentstemon or Beard-tongue
Pentstemon hirsutus   Magenta-white, May-July

A perennial with slender and straight stem woolly almost to the base. Leaves light green, slightly woolly, oblong to lance-shaped, slightly toothed, the upper ones toothless, the lower ovate and stalked. The flowers whitish, tinged with dull magenta, the corolla trumpet-shaped, two-lipped, two lobes on the upper, three on the lower

Turtle-head.   Chelone glabra.

lip, and the throat nearly closed by a palate on the lower lip covered with long hairs. There are four stamens and a sterile stamen, which is hairy or bearded a little more than half its length. Cross-fertilized mostly by butterflies. 1-3 feet high. Que. to Va., west to Mich.

Pentstemon lævigatus Pale violet, May-June

A very similar species, smooth *except* the somewhat sticky-hairy top of the stem bearing the flowers; the latter ¾ inch long, pale violet, the corolla as in the foregoing species, but the throat wider open and scarcely or not at all hairy; the sterile filament hairy on the upper side only. The stem ruddy, and the light green leaves more or less so at the edge. 2-3 feet high. In thickets or moist fields, from Pa. to Fla. and Miss. *Pentstemon Digitalis,* with stem-leaves ovate lance-shaped, the lower longer and wider, is closely related. Its flowers are white, larger, and the corolla abruptly inflated. 2-5 feet high. Me. and N. Y., south to Va. and Tex., and west to Minn. *Pentstemon* is mostly confined to the west, outside our range. Some are so beautiful that they are commonly cultivated. Among these western garden species are *P. acuminatus, P. barbatus,* and *P. cobæa.* Any of them may become occasional escapes.

Monkey-flower
Mimulus ringens Purple, June-September

A smooth perennial with an upright square stem often considerably branched, and light green, smooth, lusterless leaves with irregular obscure teeth, lance-shaped or oblong, opposite-growing and clasping the stem. The flowers are a rich clear purple; the corolla two-lipped, the upper lip erect and two-lobed, the lower with three wide-spreading lobes; there are two yellow spots near the narrow throat. The pistil and four stamens are white; the five-pointed, green calyx is stained with dull purple. The few flowers are long-stalked and spring from the angles of the upper leaves. 1-3 feet high. In swamps and beside brooks, generally in meadows, Que. to Va. and Tenn., and west to Saskatchewan. (*Color Plate 20.*) Rarely the flowers are white. The name from the Greek for *ape,* or *buffoon,* in allusion to the fancied grin on the face of the corolla.

Lindernia dubia.

Pentstemon hirsutus.

False Pimpernel
Lindernia dubia　　Pale dull lilac, July-September

A branching and spreading little annual with rounded ovate or oblong, smooth leaves, scarcely toothed, the upper ones stalkless and clasping the plant-stem slightly. The pale dull lilac flowers ¼ inch long; the upper lip of the corolla two-lobed, the lower three-lobed and flaring not unlike *Mimulus*. 4-9 inches high. Common in low, wet ground everywhere.

Culver's Root
Veronicastrum virginicum　　White, July-September

A very tall, smooth, perennial species, commonest in the west, with simple, straight stem, and lance-shaped or oblong leaves growing in circles about the plant-stem, sharply toothed and smooth. Flowers small, white or pale lavender, with rather a long tube to the corolla, and with prominent stamens, in dense terminal spikes 3-6 inches long. 2-7 feet high. In meadows and moist woods, Vt. to Ga., west to Ont. and Manitoba.

American Brooklime
Veronica americana　　Lavender-blue, May-September

A perennial species with a hollow, smooth stem, which creeps over the ground and finally becomes erect and branching. The leaves long-oval or oblong lance-shaped, light green, slightly toothed, with short, flat stalks. The tiny flower is lavender-blue violet-striped, with a white center; the corolla four-lobed, the lower lobe narrower than the others, the two divergent stamens light purple. The frail, quickly fading flowers are set on slender stalks, in loose terminal spikes. 6-15 inches high. On banks of streams and in damp places everywhere.

Marsh Speedwell
Veronica scutellata　　Lavender-blue, May-September

A similar species. The flowers on rather zigzag stalks, and with linear, acute, shallow-toothed leaves, slightly clasping the stem. Fruit capsule flat, notched, and broader than it is long. 6-20 inches high. In swamps and bogs, Newf. to Va., west to Minn. Local in Cal.; also in Europe.

V. officinalis.

V. alpina.

V. serpyllifolia.

Veronicastrum
virginicum.

American Brooklime.   Veronica americana.

Common Speedwell
Veronica officinalis Light lavender, June-August

A woolly species with prostrate but finally erect stem. Leaves light green, oval or obovate, toothed, and narrow at the base. The flowers light lavender, striped with light violet; corolla four-lobed. The flowers are set closely on slender spikes, rising from the leaf-angles. 3-10 inches high. Common in dry fields and wooded uplands, Que. south to S. C., west to Mich. Also in Europe.

Veronica alpina var. *unalaschcensis* Dark blue, July-August

A small mountain species with the slender stem generally simple, the leaves indistinctly toothed or toothless, elliptical or ovate. Lavender-blue, or dark blue flowers in short clusters. 2-12 inches high. On the high mountains of New Eng., also in the Rockies. The seed-capsules of *Veronica* are in effect notched.

Thyme-leaved Speedwell
Veronica serpyllifolia White, pale lavender, April-May

A small species, generally found in the grass, with a slender, creeping, branching stem and small oval leaves, toothless, short-stalked, and opposite-growing. Flowers like those of American Brooklime but white or pale lavender with deeper stripes; they are less frail than those of the other *Veronicas*. 2-10 inches high. In fields and thickets throughout our range; also in Eurasia, and perhaps introduced here. Named for St. Veronica.

Fern-leaved False Foxglove
Aureolaria pedicularia Pure yellow, August-September

A handsome annual or biennial species with a rather sticky fine-hairy, leafy, branching stem, round in section. The light green leaves are fernlike, and deeply cut into many toothed lobes; they are nearly stalkless. The showy, pure light lemon-yellow flowers are bell-shaped with five broad, spreading, rounded lobes. The blossoms measure a full inch or more in diameter. The outer surface and the throat of the corolla, the stamens, and the toothed lobes of the calyx are fine-hairy. Both flower and fruit are very beautiful, and the plant would be worthy of cultivation if its character permitted; but the *Aureolarias* are parasitic on the roots of oaks. 1-3 feet high. Visited

Downy False Foxglove.   Aureolaria flava.

frequently by the bumblebee and the light brown butterfly. On the borders of dry woodlands and thickets, from Me. to Pa. and Ga., west to Minn. and Mo.

Downy False Foxglove
Aureolaria flava   Pure yellow, July-August

A handsome species with a simple stem and yellow-green leaves, ovate lance-shaped, broadest at the base, slightly coarse dull-toothed or toothless, the edge wavy. Both stem and leaves are velvety-downy with soft hairs, the leaves with their stalks magenta-tinged. The showy, pure yellow or light lemon-yellow flowers about 1½ inch long, trumpet-shaped like foxglove, with five lobes, the broad throat downy on the inside. Stamens four, two short and two long; hairy. The flowers set in a close terminal cluster, rather one-sided. Cross-fertilized mostly by butterflies and bumblebees. 2-4 feet high. Thin woodlands, Me. south to Fla., west to Wisc. The two yellow-flowered species above are considered by some as belonging to *Gerardia,* but their yellow flower and parasitic habit seem to separate them from true *Gerardias.*

Purple Gerardia
Gerardia purpurea   Magenta-purple, August-September

One of the daintiest of the *Gerardias;* an annual with a generally smooth stem, slim, straight, and rigid, the branches widely spreading. The leaves are yellowish-green, small, and linear, with acute tips. The downy, lighter or deeper magenta-purple flowers are cup-shaped, with five wide, flaring lobes; there are four stamens bearing rather large deep golden-yellow anthers. The flower is commonly visited by various bees, the yellow butterfly, and the brown butterfly. Secd-capsule spherical. 12-26 inches high. In moist soil, generally near the coast, or in the vicinity of the Great Lakes, from Nova Scotia to Fla., west to Minn. The var. *paupercula,* not quite as tall, has a smooth, simple or branched stem, and the smaller flower is about ½ inch long; seed-capsule is elongate-spheroidal. 6-17 inches high. Me. to Pa., west to Wisc.

Sea-side Gerardia
Gerardia maritima   Magenta, August-September

A similar and even lower species confined to the salt marshes of the coast. The linear leaves are rather fleshy, and obtuse at the tips; the upper ones are unusually

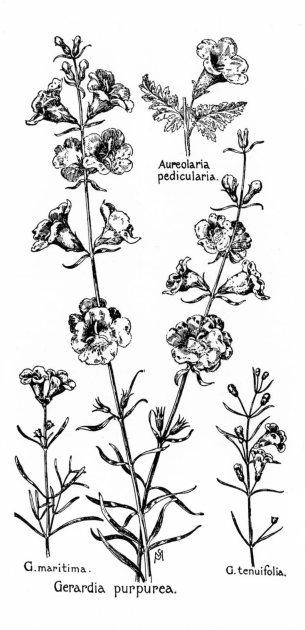

Aureolaria
pedicularia.

G. maritima.

Gerardia purpurea.

G. tenuifolia.

short. The light magenta flowers, about the same size as those of the preceding species, are not downy, but smooth. 4-14 inches high. From Nova Scotia to Fla. and Tex.

Slender Gerardia
Gerardia tenuifolia   Magenta, August-September

A very slender species with linear, acute-pointed leaves. The light magenta flowers have two of the five lobes not so fully expanded as the others; the calyx-lobes are short and acute. 10-20 inches high. In dry fields and along roadsides. Common in some of its forms everywhere. Named for John Gerarde, a celebrated herbalist.

Painted Cup
Castilleja coccinea   Scarlet, green-yellow, June-July

An odd species, annual or biennial, with the flower's corolla almost hidden in the long, cylindrical, two-lobed calyx, which is generally tipped with brilliant scarlet. The plant-stem is ruddy, soft-hairy, slender, and simple. The leaves are light green, parallel-veined, and slightly hairy or smooth, the lower ones oblong or broader, clustered, and undivided, the uppermost generally three-lobed— sometimes five-lobed; all are stalkless, and each looks as if it had been stained on the tip with deep vermilion or scarlet, more or less vivid according to the individual plant. William Hamilton Gibson calls the color of the Painted Cup "the brightest dab of red the wild palette can show." The color of the inconspicuous flower is greenish-yellow, the corolla is tubular and two-cleft. The blossoms, completely eclipsed by the red floral leaves, form with these a dense terminal cluster. Rarely the red of the leaves is displaced by yellow. Like the *Aureolarias*, this plant is also parasitic in nature. 12-20 inches high. Common in low, wet meadows, from Mass. to S. C. and Ky., west to Manitoba and Tex. Named for Domingo Castillejo, a Spanish botanist.

Castilleja septentrionalis   Whitish yellow-green, June-September

A pale green-leaved species living on the bleak and rocky summits of mountains in the north, or on the north shore of Lake Superior. A slender perennial, generally smooth except at the uppermost parts, and the stem is

Painted Cup.
Castilleja coccinea.

Castilleja
septentrionalis.

usually simple. The light green leaves are (mainly) tooth-less, stalkless, and 3-5 ribs run nearly parallel with each other, meeting at the somewhat acute tips; the upper leaves are lance-shaped, the lower linear. The floral leaves or bracts are rather obovate with a few broad teeth; the color is pale or whitish yellow-green, or else green-white tinged with dull magenta. The yellowish flowers are about as long as the bracts, and are inconspicuous. All are crowded at the summit of the stem. 6-20 inches high. In damp rocky places, Labrador to summits of New Eng. (Mt. Washington), Minn., S. D. in the Black Hills, and the Rockies, Colo.

———

Eyebright
Euphrasia americana   White, yellowish, etc., July-August

A tiny annual with ovate or lance-shaped leaves slightly resembling *Castilleja* in aspect, confined to the coast of Me. and southern Canada. The pale olive-green leaves are indistinctly dull-toothed and small on the lower part of the plant, and the upper, floral leaves are somewhat jagged and bristly toothed. The inconspicuous flowers are whitish and deep purple-veined. The corolla is two-lipped and a trifle notched, the lower lip three-lobed and spreading, the upper two-lobed (with reflexed sides), beneath it are the four stamens. 4-10 inches high. Newf., eastern Que., and coast of Me. *Euphrasia Oakesii* is a very dwarf form scarcely attaining a height of 2½ inches, with tiny yellowish flowers, and more rounded leaves with rounded teeth, growing in the alpine regions of the White Mts. (under the crest of Mt. Monroe); also on Mt. Katahdin, Me.

———

Yellow Rattle
Rhinanthus Crista-galli   Yellow, July-August

A slightly similar, taller annual confined to the same situations, with lance-shaped or oblong, dull green leaves coarsely toothed, and growing oppositely, the floral ones deeply cut and with bristle-tipped teeth. The flowers straw-color, and crowded on a one-sided leafy spike. The corolla two-lipped, the upper lip without lobes but slightly toothed on either side partway down, the lower three-lobed. Four stamens. Fruit-capsule round but flattened; the seeds when ripe rattle in the inflated pod. 6-20 inches

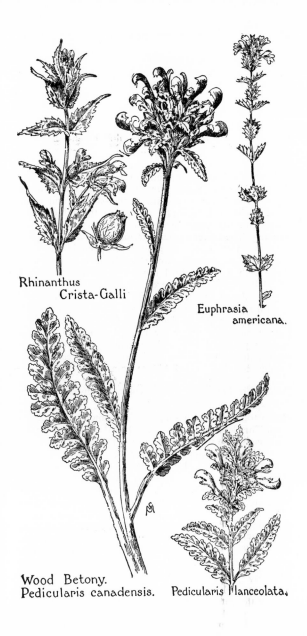

Rhinanthus
Crista-Galli

Euphrasia
americana.

Wood Betony.
Pedicularis canadensis.

Pedicularis lanceolata.

high. Rocky soil, Labrador to the coast of New Eng., the alpine regions of the White Mts. and in N. Y.; possibly introduced from Europe elsewhere.

————

Beefsteak Plant or Lousewort
Pedicularis canadensis　Magenta, dull green-yellow, May-July

Also known as Wood Betony. A very slightly hairy species with simple stem, and soft-hairy leaves, dull dark green and finely lobed, growing on grassy slopes or in copses. The lower leaves are feather-shaped and often stained with dull magenta, as is also the rather stout plant-stem; the upper leaves are sparse and grow alternately. The flower-cluster is terminal and dome-shaped, the flower two-lipped, the prominent upper lip dull dark whitish-opaque magenta, and strongly curved in a hook-shape with a two-toothed tip; the lower is three-lobed and dull green-yellow. The coarse and hairy, light green calyx is tinged at the edge with dull crimson-magenta. Bractlike leaves are set close in the flower-cluster, which lengthens to an oblong shape as the flowers develop. The four stamens are under the hooded upper lip and admirably protected from rain or other pollen-destroying agents; the flower is fertilized mostly by bees and the bumblebees. 5-12 inches high. Common everywhere.

Pedicularis lanceolata　Straw-color, August-September

A species with less crowded flowers, few of which bloom together, and a simple, nearly smooth light green stem. The deep green leaves are broad lance-shaped and finely cut in the semblance of a fern; they grow oppositely or nearly so. The upper and lower lips of the corolla are pale straw-color, and press against each other nearly closing the throat of the flower. The bees are common visitors. 12-34 inches high. In swampy places, Mass. south to N. C., west to S. D.

————

Cow-wheat
Melampyrum lineare　Greenish-white, July-September

A delicate, low annual commonly found in the half-shaded borders of woods especially in the northeastern states, with slender, wiry, gray-green, branching stem, and yellow-green, lance-shaped leaves, the lower ones

Cow-wheat: Melampyrum lineare.

toothless and the upper with generally 2-4 bristlelike teeth or lobes near the base, all set in pairs and growing oppositely. The frail greenish-white flowers are cylindrical, opening into two lips, the lower lip three-lobed, and tinged straw-yellow. The flowers grow singly from between the leaves, and are less than ½ inch long; their common visitors are the yellow butterfly, the spotted brown one, and the white cabbage butterfly. 4-10 inches high. Throughout our range. The name from the Greek, meaning *black wheat*.

BROOM-RAPE FAMILY. *Orobanchaceæ.*

Fleshy parasitic herbs having yellowish scales instead of leaves; the flowers usually perfect, irregular, 2-lipped, solitary or crowded in a dense, conelike cluster. Stamens four. The tiny seeds borne in a capsule.

Beech-drops or Cancer Root
Epifagus virginiana   Dull magenta, buff-brown, August-October

A parasitic plant which draws its sustenance from the roots of the beech tree. The stem is tough, straight, almost upright-branched, stained with brown madder, and set with a few small, dry scales. The curved tubular, dull magenta and buff-brown upper flowers are purple-striped; although generally sterile they are complete in every part, the style slightly protruding beyond, and the stamens just within the throat. The tiny lower flowers are cleistogamous—closed to outward agencies and self-fertilized. A few of the upper flowers are cross-fertilized by bees. 6-20 inches high. Beech woods, Que. south to Fla., and west to Wisc. and Mo. The name means *on the beech.*

Squawroot
Conopholis americana   Pale dull yellow, May-July

A pale parasitic plant, the stem hidden by the overlapping, light tan-colored, lance-shaped or ovate pointed scales; the plant resembling an erect cone. The flowers perfect, set in a many-scaled dense spike, the upper lip hooded, the lower small and three-lobed, the stamens protruding; the lips are pale ochre-yellow fading toward the corolla. 3-8 inches high. In rich woods over tree roots, Nova Scotia to Fla., west to Mich. and Ala.

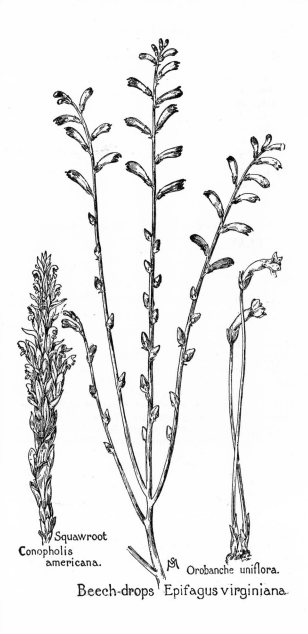

Squawroot
Conopholis
    americana.

Orobanche uniflora.

Beech-drops Epifagus virginiana

Naked Broom-rape or One-flowered Cancer Root
Orobanche uniflora Purplish, April-June

A beautiful little parasitic plant bearing a few brownish ovate bracts near the root, and sending up 1-4 erect, slender, one-flowered stalks; the curved tubular, five-lobed flower is purplish or light violet, or rarely cream-white, ¾ inch long, externally fine-hairy, and delicately fragrant. Cross-fertilized mostly by the smaller bees, and the bumblebees. 3-6 inches high. In moist woods, Newf. to Fla., west to B. C. and Tex.

PLANTAIN FAMILY. *Plantaginaceæ.*

Homely herbs—weeds—generally with coarse, strong, ribbed leaves springing from the root, and insignificant flowers in long narrow spikes, perfect, or polygamous—that is, staminate and pistillate on the same plant or different plants—and even cleistogamous—that is, fertilizing in the bud.

Common Plantain
Plantago major Dull white, May-September

The familiar weed of unkempt dooryards and grass-plots, with ovate, dark green, slightly hairy or smooth leaves, the long stems trough-shaped, the ribs conspicuous, and the edge generally toothless, or rarely coarse-toothed. The flowering spikes are cylindrical, blunt-tipped, and closely set with the dull, greenish-white, four-lobed, perfect florets which mature the threadlike style *before* the corolla is *fully open,* the former projecting. The four stamens mature much later and thus insure cross-fertilization. Seed-capsule ovoid and opening near the middle, the seeds reticulated. Flowering stalks 6-18 inches high. Common everywhere; also in Eurasia.

Plantago Rugelii Dull white, June-September

Similar to the preceding; the leaves thinner, the flowering spikes less dense and attenuated above, and the seed-capsules cylindrical-oblong; the latter open below the middle and quite within the four lobes of the calyx. The seeds are *not* reticulated. Common everywhere.

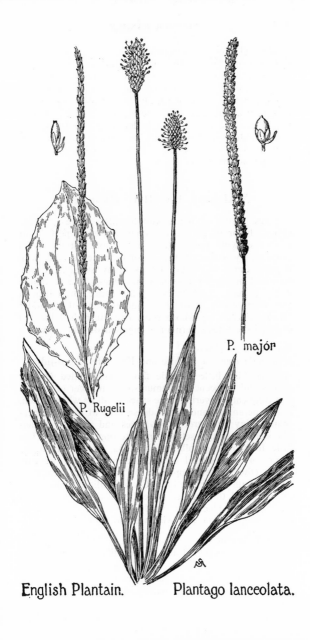

P. majór

P. Rugelii

English Plantain. Plantago lanceolata.

English Plantain or Ribgrass
Plantago lanceolata   Dull white, April-October

A similar more or less fine-hairy European species, naturalized and very common. The leaves are long lance-shaped, nearly erect, generally three-ribbed, acute and toothless; at the base of the leaves the hairiness is dark rust-color. The flower-spike is dense and short, bearing similar dull white flowers. But the conspicuously grooved stalk is 8-22 inches high. Old fields and waste places throughout our range.

MADDER FAMILY. *Rubiaceæ.*

Trees, shrubs or herbs with toothless leaves growing oppositely or in circles; the regular flowers perfect, or staminate with rudimentary pistils, or pistillate with rudimentary stamens; the corolla funnel-formed with 4 (sometimes 5) lobes and as many stamens. Cross-fertilized mostly by bees and butterflies. A large family in the tropics, to which belong the coffee, the cinchona tree from which is obtained quinine, and the madder (*Rubia tinctorum*) whose roots once furnished the red dye and the artist's permanent pigment of that name.

Houstonia or Bluets
Houstonia cærulea   White and lilac, etc., April-July

A familiar little wayside flower also called Quaker Ladies and Innocence; communistic in manner of growth and frequently covering large spaces with its white bloom. It is a perennial, and forms dense tufts of oblong lance-shaped, tiny light green root-leaves and slender, thread-like stems sparingly set with minute opposite bracts. The little four-lobed corolla is about ½ inch in diameter, white, or white-tinged on the lobes with lilac, or pale violet (the nearest approach to blue); the center is stained with golden-yellow. Cross-fertilized mainly by the bees and the smaller butterflies. 3-6 inches high. In moist grassy places or sandy waysides, from Nova Scotia south to Ga. and Ala., west to Wisc.

Large Houstonia
Houstonia purpurea   Lilac or deep lilac, May-July

A taller southern species. The stem smooth or slightly hairy, the light green leaves pointed, broad, ovate (the upper ones smaller and narrower), with 3-5 ribs, the

Houstonia   Bluets.
purpurea.   Houstonia caerulea.

largest nearly 2 inches long. The deep lilac or pale lilac, long-tubed flowers in small clusters; the thin lobes of the calyx longer than the globular seed-pod. 6-16 inches high. In thin or open woodlands, from N. J. south (especially in the mountains) to Ga. and Ala., and west to Okla. A related species, *H. canadensis,* has thicker leaves ½ inch long, with the edges conspicuously hairy-fringed, and flowers in small clusters. 5-7 inches high. On the rocky shores of the Great Lakes, and south in woodlands to Pa., W. Va., Ky., and Ark. There are various intergrading species passing to *H. longifolia,* which has thinner, linear and acute leaves, often a full inch long; the root-leaves are not hairy-fringed. 5-18 inches high. From Me. south to S. C., and west to Saskatchewan and Ark.

Partridgeberry or Twinberry
Mitchella repens   Cream-white, pinkish, May-June

A little trailing vine with dark green evergreen leaves green-white-veined and wide, slightly heart-shaped at the base. The commonly four-lobed twin flowers (sometimes conjoined with 8-10 lobes) are cream white and fine-hairy inside, but faint crimson-pink and smooth outside, they terminate the short branches, and are two-formed, i.e., staminate (with abortive pistil) and pistillate (with abortive stamens). Cross-fertilized by the same insects which visit the Mayflower and *Houstonia.* 6-12 inches long. In woods from Nova Scotia to Fla., west to Minn., and Tex. Named for Dr. John Mitchell. Berry red.

Yellow Bedstraw
Galium verum   Yellow, May-August

A slender, rather erect, perennial herb naturalized from Europe, with a smooth, squarish stem a trifle woody at the base. The narrow, linear, rough, light green leaves, in circles of 6-8, are about an inch long. The tiny, yellow, four-lobed flowers are in small terminal clusters, or at the leaf-angles. 8-30 inches long. In dry waste places and borders of fields nearly throughout our range.

Cleavers or Goosegrass
Galium Aparine   White, May-August

An annual species with the usual weak reclining stem characteristic of the *Galiums,* which hang upon shrub-

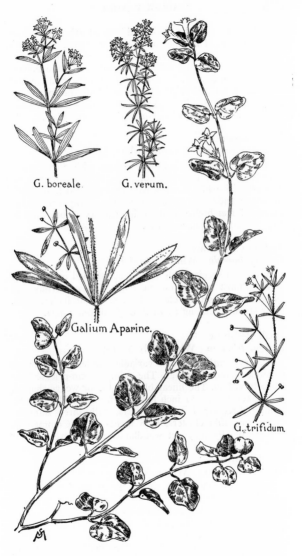

G. boreale.   G. verum.

Galium Aparine.

G. trifidum.

Partridgeberry.   Mitchella repens.

bery by means of the backward-hooked prickles of both leaf and stem. The blunt lance-shaped, light green leaves with roughened edge and rib are nearly 2 inches long, and set in a circle of 6-8. About two tiny white flowers are borne on a stalk. Fruit burlike, in pairs, and covered with short, hooked bristles which facilitate transportation. 2-5 feet long. Shady thickets and roadsides throughout our range. The following *Galiums* are perennials.

Wild Liquorice
Galium circæzans   Greenish-white, May-July

A smooth or slightly downy species with broad, ovate leaves in fours, three-ribbed, and about an inch long. The greenish-white flowers, with four pointed lobes hairy on the outside, are borne on stalks usually forked but once. 1-2 feet high. Common in rich dry woods, Me. to Fla., west to Minn. and Tex.

Northern Bedstraw
Galium boreale   White, June-July

A smooth species with acute lance-shaped or narrower leaves almost smooth on the edge. The numerous tiny white flowers set in close clusters. 15-30 inches high. Near streams, among rocks throughout our range.

Small Bedstraw
Galium trifidum   White, July-August

A very *small,* delicate, variable species, often much entangled among bushes. The minute stem-prickles are scarcely visible. The linear blunt-tipped or wedge-shaped, deep green leaves, ½ inch long, set in fours. The minute, usually three-lobed, white flowers, with three stamens, are in tiny thin clusters. 6-18 inches high. Common in sphagnum bogs and wet woodlands everywhere.

Rough Bedstraw
Galium asprellum   White, May-August

A very common, weak, and reclining species, with the usual square stem set with backward-hooked prickles. The light green leaves slightly blunt lance-shaped, and prickly-rough on edge and rib, are set in circles of 4-6. The profuse tiny white flowers are in thin, airy, terminal clusters; they are peculiarly, perhaps unpleasantly, odorous. 2-6 feet long. In damp soil, Newf. to N. C., west to Neb.

Rough Bedstraw.
Galium asprellum.

Wild Liquorice.
Galium circæzans.

Sweet-scented Bedstraw
Galium triflorum　Greenish-white, June-August

A similar species with the flowers usually borne in clusters of three, and with the same bristly-rough stem; the leaves broad lance-shaped, bright shining green, bristle-pointed, slightly rough-edged, and set usually in sixes. The foliage fragrant after drying. 1-3 feet long. Rich woodlands throughout our range.

HONEYSUCKLE FAMILY. *Caprifoliaceæ.*

A family of predominately woody plants including trees, shrubs, and a few herbs. It is retained here because it includes some charming wild flowers and the honeysuckles, but strictly speaking there are few wild flowers in the family. They have opposite leaves, and perfect regular (occasionally irregular) flowers, with generally a funnel-shaped corolla, five-lobed, or sometimes two-lipped. Cross-fertilized by the larger long-tongued bees, moths, butterflies, and the hummingbird.

Elder
Sambucus canadensis　Cream-white, June-July

A common smooth-stemmed shrub with a compound deep green, smooth leaf of 5-11, usually 7, fine-toothed, acute-pointed, ovate leaflets. The tiny cream-white flowers in broad flat clusters (with five prominent white stamens), are fertilized mostly by honeybees. The purple-black berries, in broad clusters, ripen in August. 4-10 feet high. Borders of fields and copses, in low ground, throughout our range. The fruit is much used to make elderberry wine.

Red-berried Elder
Sambucus pubens　Dull white, April-May

A similar shrub with twigs and leaves slightly fine-hairy, and warty gray bark. There are 5-7 finely toothed ovate lance-shaped leaflets which are a trifle downy beneath. The fine dull white flowers with yellowish stamens are borne in a sugar-loaf-shaped cluster. The extremely beautiful small, scarlet-red, or rarely white berries, in a compact cluster, ripen in June. 2-12 feet high. In rocky woodland borders, Nova Scotia south to N. C. (among the hills), and westward to Ind. and Ill.

Red-berried Elder.   Sambucus pubens.

Hobble-bush or Wayfaring Tree
Viburnum alnifolium   White, May-June

A shrub with coarse, light green, veiny, sharp-toothed, heart-shaped leaves, rusty-woolly on the ribs beneath, together with the young branchlets. The flat flower-cluster is composed of two kinds of flowers: the marginal dull white broad-petaled and the central, smaller, perfect flowers. Fruit a coral-red berry, set in a scant cluster. Stem 3-10 feet high, reclining; the branches often take root and trip up the "wayfarer." The commonest visitors are the bees. In low or moist woods, Nova Scotia south in the mountains to N. C., west to Mich. There are over a dozen other viburnums in our range.

Feverwort or Horse Gentian
Triosteum perfoliatum   Madder purple, May-July

A coarse perennial, sometimes called Tinker's-weed and often Wild Coffee, common in rich woodlands. The stout, simple stem is rather sticky-fine-hairy, and the opposite-growing, light green or medium green, oval leaves are acute at the tip, and narrowed at the base and through which the stem passes; the edge is toothless and somewhat undulating. The flowers are an inconspicuous purplish-brown or madder purple; they grow at the junction of the leaves with the plant-stem; the corolla is five-lobed, tubular, and scarcely longer than the long-lobed calyx, which remains attached to the mature fruit; this is ½ inch long or less, orange-scarlet, densely fine-hairy, and contains three hard nutlets. 2-4 feet high. In rich soil, from Que. south to Ala. and Ky., and west to Minn., Iowa, and Kan.

Twin-flower
Linnæa borealis var. *americana*   Crimson-pink, June-
August

A delicate and beautiful prostrate vine common in the northern woodlands, with a terra-cotta-colored, somewhat rough-woody stem, and a rounded, about 8-scallop-toothed, short-stalked, light evergreen leaf with a rough surface. The fragrant little bell-shaped flowers, in pairs, terminate a 3- to 4-inch-long stalk, and nod; they are delicate crimson-pink, graded to white on the margins of the five lobes. The tiny calyx divisions are threadlike. 6-20 inches long. In mossy, mountainous woods, Greenland to N. Y. and N. J., west to Alaska. (*Color Plate 21.*)

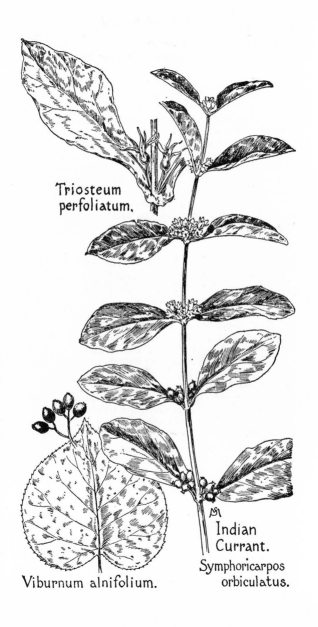

Triosteum
perfoliatum.

Viburnum alnifolium.

Indian
Currant.
Symphoricarpos
orbiculatus.

Coral-berry or Indian Currant
Symphoricarpos orbiculatus   Pink and white, July

A shrub with erect, generally madder brown branches very slightly woolly-hairy on the younger growths. The dull gray-green leaves are ovate, toothless (rarely some of the larger leaves are coarsely toothed), and have distinctly short stalks. The five-lobed flowers are tiny bell-shaped, and grow in small clusters at the angles of the leaves, or terminally; the corolla pink graded to white, and somewhat filled by the fine hairiness of style and stamens. The small berries in small terminal clusters are first coral-red and finally dull crimson-magenta. The smaller bees and honeybees are common visitors. 2-5 feet high. Rocky slopes. Mass., banks of the Delaware River in N. J. and Pa., south to Ga. and Tex., west to the Dakotas.

Snowberry
Symphoricarpos albus   Pink and white, June-August

A familiar shrub of old-fashioned gardens and door-yards still commonly cultivated, with smooth, erect, gray-brown branches, and oval, dull gray-green leaves lighter beneath, toothless, and a trifle wavy-margined. The young shoots are ochre-brown. The tiny, five-lobed, bell-shaped flowers are pink graded to white, and are borne in terminal and leaf-angle clusters. The corolla is conspicuously fine-hairy within; and the stamens and style almost protrude. The honeybee is a constant visitor, and the flowers continue to bloom even after the large snow-white waxy berries appear; the latter are a conspicuous feature of the bush in early September. 3-4 feet high. On roadsides, escaped from cultivation, and on rocky banks, from Que. south to Pa. and W. Va., and west to Minn.

————

Fly-honeysuckle
Lonicera canadensis   Naples-yellow, May-June

A thin straggling bush with smooth, brownish stems. The thin leaves bright light green on both sides, ovate lance-shaped, sometimes very broad at the base, toothless, short-stalked, and hairy-edged. The Naples-yellow or honey-yellow, five-lobed flower, about ¾ inch long, is funnel-formed and borne in pairs at the leaf-angles. Fruit two small ovoid red berries. 3-5 feet high. Moist woods, from Nova Scotia south to Pa., and west to Minn.

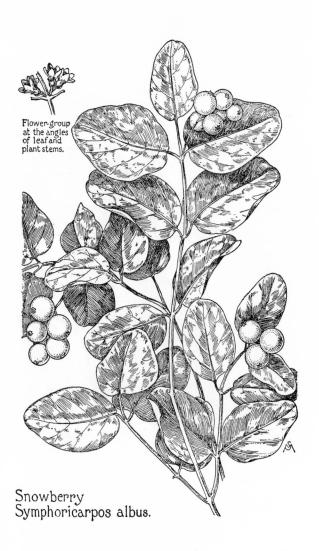

Flower-group
at the angles
of leaf and
plant stems.

Snowberry
Symphoricarpos albus.

Fly-honeysuckle. Lonicera canadensis

Mountain Fly Honeysuckle.
Lonicera villosa.

Mountain Fly-honeysuckle
Lonicera villosa Yellow, May-June

A similar species but with thickish, blunt ovate leaves fine-hairy beneath. The Naples-yellow flowers in pairs, almost united. The ovaries unite and form one two-eyed, gray-black ovate berry. 1-3 feet high. In boggy woods, Labrador to Pa., west to Minn.

Lonicera Morrowi Cream-white, May-June

A Japanese shrub in frequent cultivation, with hollow stems. Leaves dark green, oblong, rather rough, paler beneath. Corolla-lobes widespread, the calyx teeth hairy. Berries bright red. 4-6 feet high. It is an occasional escape.

Trumpet or Coral Honeysuckle
Lonicera sempervirens Scarlet and yellow, April-August

A scentless, but beautiful species, common in cultivation, twining and climbing high, and evergreen southward. The large deep green oblong leaves are whitish beneath; the top ones are united, and seemingly perforated by the stem, which terminates in a small cluster of large, tubular, deep Naples-yellow flowers, often deeply tinged red outside. Berry scarlet. The most useful visitor is the hummingbird, though many bees and butterflies assist in the transfer of pollen. 8-15 feet high. Copses, Conn. to Fla., west to Okla.; elsewhere as an escape from gardens.

Bush Honeysuckle
Diervilla Lonicera Naples-yellow, May-June

A very common shrubby species with smooth stem and leaves and exceedingly small honey-colored or Naples-yellow flowers, with 5 recurving, rather equal lobes marked slightly with dull rusty-orange. There are 5 prominent yellow stamens. The deep olive-green leaves are ovate, sharp-pointed, and fine-toothed. The flowers grow in small clusters, terminally, and at the junction of leaf- and plant-stem. The fruit is an oblong capsule with beaked tip. 3-4 feet high. In dry woodlands or in thickets, from Newf., south to Ga., and west to Ind. and Iowa. Named for Dr. Dierville, who carried the plant from Canada to France about 1707.

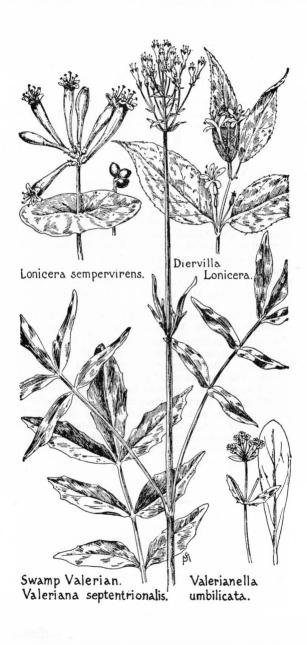

Lonicera sempervirens.

Diervilla
Lonicera.

Swamp Valerian.
Valeriana septentrionalis.

Valerianella
umbilicata.

VALERIAN FAMILY. *Valerianaceæ.*

Herbs with opposite leaves, and perfect, or sometimes staminate and pistillate, flowers: the corolla tube narrow and five-lobed; stamens 1-3. Commonly visited by bees. The genus *Valeriana* is remarkable for its ill-scented roots.

Swamp Valerian
Valeriana septentrionalis Pale magenta-pink, June-July

An erect, smooth plant, with compound leaves of from 5-11 (rarely less) deep green, lance-shaped, obtuse leaflets, indistinctly shallow-toothed or toothless; the root-leaves are long-stalked, ovate, and rarely small-lobed. The dull magenta-pink or paler pink or white flowers are tiny, and clustered in a loose terminal spike; the three stamens *very* prominent. 10-30 inches high. In wet or swampy ground, from Que. south to N. J., west to S. D., and in the Rocky Mts. to Ariz. A very variable species.

Garden Valerian, Great Wild Valerian or Vandal-root
Valeriana officinalis Magenta-crimson, white, June-July

A common cultivated species, often escaping to roadsides and margins of cultivated fields and often, inappropriately called "garden heliotrope." A native of Europe. The stem more or less fine-hairy especially at the joints, and the compound leaves with 11-21 lance-shaped, sharply toothed leaflets, the upper ones toothless. The flowers are pale magenta-crimson or white, set in compact, rather rounded clusters terminating the stout stem. The strong-scented roots are medicinal. 2-5 feet high. Que. south to Del., west to Minn. Name from *valere,* to be strong.

Valerianella umbilicata Dull white, May-July

A smooth forking-stemmed annual with succulent wedge-shaped leaves, and insignificant dull white flowers funnel-formed and five-lobed, gathered in small terminal clusters. 18-34 inches high. In moist places, from N. Y. west to Ill. and Tenn.; not common. *Valerianella olitoria,* the corn salad, a species from Europe, naturalized in the Middle States and south, has similar leaves, but pale violet flowers. 6-12 inches high.

Climbing Wild Cucumber. Echinocystis lobata.

GOURD FAMILY. *Cucurbitaceæ.*

Climbing vines generally with tendrils, and with lobed leaves growing alternately. The flowers staminate and pistillate on the same plant or different plants. Stamens mostly three. Cross-fertilized by bees and flies in general. Here belong the cucumber, all the melons, and the pumpkins.

Climbing Wild Cucumber or Wild Balsam Apple
Echinocystis lobata   Greenish-white, July-September

A beautiful, rapid-growing, and luxuriant annual climber; the light green, thin leaves, with 3-7 (mostly five) sharply angular lobes, are rough on both sides. The small, sharply six-petaled staminate flowers are borne in many loose clusters, and the pistillate flowers singly or in twos, at the angles of the leaves; the petals and the three prominent stamens with yellowish anthers are greenish-white. The spiral tendrils are three-forked. Cross-fertilized mostly by bees and wasps. The cucumberlike fruit is 2 inches long or less, green, ovoid, and thickly covered with slender, weak prickles. 15-20 feet long. Beside rivers and in waste places, throughout our range. The name (Greek) means *hedgehog* and *bladder,* in allusion to the armed fruit.

One-seeded Bur-cucumber
Sicyos angulatus   Greenish-white, July-September

Also an annual climber with branching tendrils and a five-lobed, far less deeply cut light green leaf; the stem is sticky, hairy, angular, and coarse. The small five-lobed flowers are likewise staminate and pistillate; the former are borne, five or six, in a cluster on a long stalk, the latter are almost stalkless; both are set in the angles of the leaves. The yellowish fruit, 3-10 together, is armed with fine tough bristles; a single fruit contains but one seed. 15-25 feet long. In moist places and along rivers, from Me. south to Fla. and west to Minn., Kan., and Tex. The name is Greek, for *cucumber.*

Climbing Wild Cucumber   Echinocystis lobata

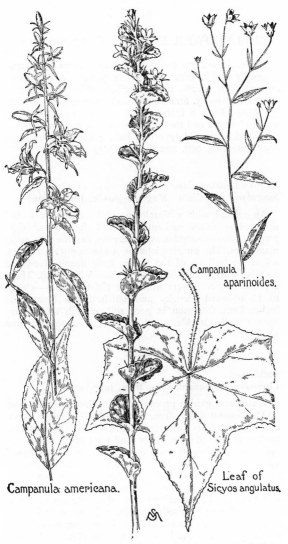

Campanula
aparinoides.

Campanula americana.

Leaf of
Sicyos angulatus.

Venus's Looking-glass.   Specularia perfoliata.

BELLFLOWER FAMILY. *Campanulaceæ.*

Herbs, in our range, with alternate leaves and acrid, generally milky, juice; the perfect flowers in a spike or solitary. The corolla usually bell-shaped and five-lobed, often very showy. Stamens five, alternating with the corolla-lobes. Fruit a many-seeded capsule. Cross-fertilized mostly by bees and the beelike flies. The garden campanulas, which are old favorites, belong here, among them the Canterbury bell, and the Coventry bells.

Venus's Looking-glass
Specularia perfoliata   Magenta-purple, June-August

An annual with a simple, wandlike stem, weak and disposed to recline, and small, curved, shell-shaped, light green, scallop-toothed leaves clasping the rough, angled plant-stem. The purple-violet or magenta-purple flowers, set at the hollows of the leaves, have deeply five-lobed corollas with five stamens and a three-lobed pistil. There are also earlier flowers which are cleistogamous—closed to all outward agencies and self-fertilized. Stem 5-22 inches long. Common in poor soil on hills and in dry open woodlands, Me. south to Fla., west to Ore. and Utah.

Bellflower
Campanula rapunculoides   Blue, July-August

A common garden perennial, naturalized from Europe, and a frequent escape from cultivation. The simple, erect, and rigid stem is light green and slightly rough-hairy, the leaves are thin, fine-hairy, and light green, the upper ones broad lance-shaped, the lower arrowhead-shaped with a heart-shaped base; all are irregularly scallop-toothed. The bell-shaped blue flowers have five acute lobes, and hang downward mostly on *one side* of the stem; the pistil is white and protruding; the stigma three-lobed and purple-tinged; the linear lobes of the green calyx are strongly turned backward. The common visitors of the flower are the honeybee and bumblebee. 1-3 feet high. In fields and on roadsides, Nova Scotia to Del. and Ohio.

Bellflower.

Campanula
rapunculoides

Harebell or Bluebell
Campanula rotundifolia   Light violet, June-September

A most dainty and delicate perennial plant, yet one so remarkably hardy that it survives the cold and storms of mountain-tops over 5,000 feet above sea-level. It is common in the Chasm of the Ausable River and on the summits of the White Mts. In spring the plant displays a tuft of round leaves (hence the name *rotundifolia*), small and sparingly toothed; these wither before the time of flowering (rarely they remain until that time), and are succeeded by a tall wiry stem, with linear, pale olive-green leaves and a succession of airy blue-violet bells depending from threadlike pedicels (flower stalks). The corolla is five-lobed, and graded in color from light violet or pale lavender to white at its base; the prominent pistil is tipped with a three-lobed stigma, which is at first green and finally white; the five anthers are a delicate lavender tint. The chief visitor is the bumblebee, who must clasp the prominent stigma before he can enter the inverted bell; in the bustling endeavor to reach the base of the blossom some of the pollen obtained from a previously visited flower is brushed off and cross-fertilization is effected. The harebell is also visited by bees and the beelike flies. 6-18 inches high. On rocky cliffs, dry or moist, in barren, sandy fields or grassy places, and in shade or sunshine, on mountain-top or meadow. Greenland south to N. J., west to Ind. and Iowa, and in the Rocky Mts. south to Ariz.; also in the mountains of Cal. Also a native of Europe and Asia, and identical with the bluebell of Scotland.

Marsh Bellflower
Campanula aparinoides   White or lavender, June-August

A species common in grassy swamps, with branching, slender, weak, reclining stems, bristly rough on the angles, like *Galium asprellum*. The light green, linear lance-shaped leaves are rough on edge and midrib; indistinctly shallow-toothed, and stalkless. The single white or pale lavender flowers scarcely ⅓ inch broad, deeply cleft into five acute lobes spreading open like a deep saucer, are arranged terminally. 6-20 inches high. In wet grassy ground everywhere, west to S. D., Saskatchewan and Colo. (*Illus. for this and* C. americana *are opp. page 482.*)

Harebell   Campanula rotundifolia.

Tall Bellflower
Campanula americana Light violet, July-September

A tall annual or biennial with a slightly fine-hairy, erect, slender, green stem, rarely branched. The ovate or ovate lance-shaped, stalkless, light green leaves are long and drooping; the lower ones are narrowed at the base to a stalk; all are acute-pointed and toothed. The dull-toned light violet or nearly white flowers grow from the angles of the leaves and form a slender terminal spike; the one-inch-wide corolla has five long, acute, spreading lobes; the style curves downward and then upward, extending far beyond the mouth of the flower. The commonest visitors are the honeybee, the bumblebee, and the "Yellow-Jacket." Flower-stalk frequently 18 inches tall. In moist shady places, Ont. south to Fla., and west to Minn. and Okla. The name is from the Italian *campana*, a bell, in allusion to the shape of the corolla.

LOBELIA FAMILY. *Lobeliaceæ.*

A family of perennial herbs or shrubs in the tropics, with milky acrid often poisonous, juice. The perfect but irregular flowers have a five-lobed sometimes 2-lipped, corolla; the five stamens united in a tube. Cross-fertilized by bees, the beelike flies, and the hummingbird. Named for De L'Obel, an early Dutch herbalist.

Cardinal Flower
Lobelia cardinalis Deep red, August-September

A most beautiful species, remarkable for its rich, deep red which largely influences the color of stem and foliage. The leaves are dark green, smooth or nearly so, oblong lance-shaped, and slightly toothed; the upper ones stalkless. The showy flower-spike is loosely set with deep cardinal red flowers, the triple-lobed lips of which are a rich velvety color. Rarely the plant produces deep pink or white flowers. Fertilized by hummingbirds, and rarely by bumblebees; but the long tongue of the hummingbird is the only practicable means of cross-fertilization. The length of the flower-tube is too great for the tongue, and the pendant lip too inconvenient for the feet of the average insect. The plant multiplies mostly by perennial offshoots. 2-4 feet high. Common everywhere in low moist ground. (*Color Plate 22.*)

Cardinal Flower.
Lobelia cardinalis.

Indian Tobacco. Lobelia. inflata

Great Lobelia
Lobelia siphilitica   **Light blue-violet, July-September**

A slightly hairy plant with a stout, leafy, and usually
simple stem; the leaves light green, 2-6 inches long,
pointed at both ends, nearly if not quite smooth, irregularly toothed, and stalkless. The light blue-violet or rarely
white flowers nearly an inch long; the calyx stiff-hairy.
1-3 feet high. Common in low moist ground, from Me.
south to Ga. and La., west to Kan., Neb., and S. D.

Downy Lobelia
Lobelia puberula   **Blue, August-October**

A similar species with similarly colored flowers in long
somewhat one-sided spikes, and with fine soft-hairy
leaves. The hairy tube of the corolla is less than ½ inch
long, and the lobes of the lip are rather broad and
smooth. 1-3 feet high. In moist sandy soil, southern N. J.
south to Fla., west to Ill. and Tex.

Spiked Lobelia
Lobelia spicata   **Pale blue-violet, July-August**

A still smaller-flowered species, bearing very long slim
spikes of pale blue-violet flowers with a usually smooth
short calyx. The stem simple and leafy, the light green
leaves nearly toothless, lance-shaped (abruptly so at the
base of the plant), or oblong, obtuse, but the upper ones
nearly linear. 1-4 feet high. In dry sandy soil from Que.
south to Ga., southwest to Ark. There are many and
quite confusing forms of the spiked lobelia to which
various names have been applied, but they add little to
elucidating a difficult complex.

Kalm's Lobelia
Lobelia Kalmii   **Light blue-violet, July-September**

A small species generally found beside brooks, or on
wet banks, with slender branching stem, and narrow,
blunt-tipped leaves sparingly toothed or toothless; the
upper ones linear. The light blue-violet flowers less than
½ inch long and scattered loosely over the spikes. The
fruit-capsule not inflated (as *Lobelia inflata*), but small,
and top-shaped or nearly globular. 6-18 inches high. On
wet meadows and wet river-banks, Newf. south to Pa.,
west to Minn.

L. siphilitica.

L. puberula.

Spiked Lobelia.
Lobelia spicata.

Water Lobelia.
Lobelia Dortmanna.

Indian Tobacco
Lobelia inflata   Light blue-violet, July-October

The commonest species; growing everywhere in dry or wet soil, within the wood or out on the meadow. An annual with a simple or branching slightly hairy stem. The thin light green leaves oval pointed, and sparingly wavy-toothed, the uppermost very small, narrow, and acute. The tiny flowers scarcely ¼ inch long, varying in color from light blue-violet to pale lilac and even white. The calyx smooth, the inflated, nearly spheroidal fruit-capsule about ⅓ inch long. Very acrid and poisonous to taste, and commonly used in medicine. Newf. south to Ga., west to Minn. and Miss.

Water Lobelia
Lobelia Dortmanna   Light violet, July-September

An aquatic species, smooth, slender, and simple-stemmed. Leaves all submerged, thick, linear hollow, and tufted at the *base of the stem.* Flowers in a loose terminal spike, light violet, ⅓ inch long. 6-18 inches high. Borders of ponds, Newf. to N. J., and northwestward to Minn.

COMPOSITE FAMILY. *Compositæ.*

Mostly perennial herbs in our area, but shrubs and even trees in the tropics. It is an enormous family remarkable for its compound flower-heads which are often radiate in character. Some have a central disc composed of tiny tubular florets surrounded by brightly colored rays, as in the common daisy. In other cases the florets are strap-shaped as in chicory and dandelion; in cone-flower and sunflower the tubular florets of the central disc are perfect and the ray-flowers neutral (without stamens and pistil); in aster and goldenrod the inner tubular florets are perfect and the outer ray-florets are pistillate; in thistle and burdock the florets are all tubular and perfect but lacking rays. It is important to distinguish plants that have only tubular flowers in a central disc, as in the first species below; and another large group which has also ray flowers in the head, as in aster. The family is the most difficult to unravel for the amateur, having over 700 species and many varieties in our area, of which those below are limited to the most common

New York Ironweed.   *Vernonia noveboracensis.*

types. The family contains many beautiful garden flowers, such as cosmos, zinnia, gaillardia, pyrethrum, dahlia and the chrysanthemum.

Tall Ironweed
Vernonia altissima   Madder purple, August-September

A tall smooth-stemmed plant found in moist situations, with lance-shaped, toothed, deep green leaves and a terminal cluster of brownish-purple or madder purple flowers remotely resembling bachelor's buttons without rays; the small flower-heads appear hairy or chaffy. 5-8 feet high. Western N. Y. south and west to Ill. and La.

New York Ironweed
Vernonia noveboracensis   Madder purple, August-September

The common species eastward, differing from the tall ironweed in its usually slightly rough stem, longer lance-shaped deep green leaves, and acute, bristle-tipped, brown-purple scales of the flower-heads. The æsthetic dull purple (rarely white) flowers resemble rayless bachelor's buttons. 3-7 feet high. In moist ground, often near the coast, from Mass. south to Miss., west to Ohio. Named for Wm. Vernon, an early English botanist.

Climbing Hempweed or Boneset
Mikania scandens   White, flesh-pink, July-September

An attractive, twining vine generally climbing over bushes on damp river-banks. The light green leaves triangular heart-shaped, and the bristly, dull white or flesh-colored flowers resembling those of boneset. 5-15 feet long. Me. to Fla. and Tex. Named for J. G. Mikan of Germany.

Joe-Pye-Weed
Eupatorium purpureum   Magenta-crimson, August-September

A familiar, tall plant with a stout stem on which the roughish, pointed ovate, toothed, light green leaves are grouped in circles at intervals. The dense terminal flower-clusters with many soft-bristly, æsthetic-toned dull magenta-crimson florets, lighter or deeper, or sometimes dull white. Frequented by the honeybee. 3-12 feet high. Common everywhere on borders of swamps or low damp

Mikania scandens.

Blazing Star.
Liatris scariosa.

Joe-Pye-Weed
Eupatorium purpureum.

ground. (*Color Plate 23.*) Named for Mithridates Eupator.

White Thoroughwort
Eupatorium album White, August-September

A similar, but small, rough-hairy species with white flowers, the scales of which are very long and white. The light green, veiny leaves are stalkless or nearly so. 1-3 feet high. In sandy soil and pine barrens, from L. I., N. Y., to Fla. and Tex.; also in Ohio.

Upland Boneset
Eupatorium sessilifolium White, August-October

A hillside species with generally smooth, opposite, ovate lance-shaped, horizontally spreading leaves tapering to a sharp point. The white flowers with long, slender but blunt scales, are in flat clusters. 2-6 feet high. In woods or on wooded banks, Vt. to Ga., and west to Minn. and Mo.

Boneset or Thoroughwort
Eupatorium perfoliatum Dull white, July-September

The common, familiar species whose leaves have been used in a bitter tonic decoction or tea. Leaves very light green, pointed, opposite, and so closely joined that two appear as one perforated by the plant-stem, which with the leaves is remarkably wool-hairy. The very dull white florets, in terminal clusters, furnish an abundance of nectar for the visiting honeybee as in all *Eupatoriums* and *Vernonias*. 2-5 feet high. Common everywhere in wet ground.

White Snakeroot
Eupatorium rugosum White, July-September

The most attractive and graceful member of this generally coarse genus. The large-toothed leaves are deep green, smooth, thin, slender-stalked, and nearly heart-shaped. Flowers white (not dull) and peculiarly downy, like the garden *Ageratum*. 1-4 feet high. Rich woods and copses, N. B. south to Ga., and west to Saskatchewan and Tex. The juice is poisonous.

Eupatorium aromaticum White, August-October

A very similar species with short-stalked leaves, dull-toothed and blunt-pointed; the flowers a trifle larger. Near the coast, from Mass. to Ga.; also in Ohio and Tenn.

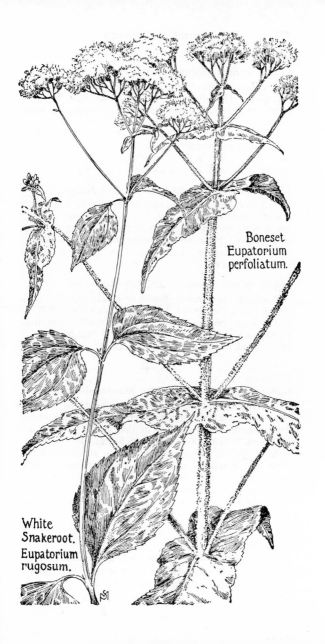

Boneset
Eupatorium
perfoliatum.

White
Snakeroot.
Eupatorium
rugosum.

Tall Blazing Star
Liatris scariosa Magenta-purple, August-September

A tall, stout, handsome species belonging to a beautiful genus. The showy flower-spike set with magenta-purple to pale violet, tubular, perfect flowers, the heads sometimes ⅞ inch broad. Leaves deep green, hoary, narrow lance-shaped, and alternate-growing. The flowers exhibit many æsthetic and variable tints. 2-6 feet high. By roadsides and in fields, southern Pa. to northern Ga., west to S. D. and Tex. (*Illus. opp. page 494.*)

Liatris squarrosa Magenta-purple, July-August

A lower species (beginning to bloom in July) with smooth or often hairy, stiff, linear leaves, and with the few flowers on the spike bright magenta-purple, the head an inch long; the scales enveloping them are leaflike with sharp, spreading tips. 6-22 inches high. Del. to Fla., west to S. D. and Tex.

Liatris spicata Purple-violet, July-September

A commoner species, smooth or nearly so, with linear leaves and a closely set flower-spike sometimes fully 14 inches long; the heads about ⅓ inch broad, range from purple to violet or rarely to white. 2-5 feet high. Moist low ground, N. Y. to Mich. and La.

Galinsoga
Galinsoga ciliata Dirty white, June-October

A pernicious Tropical Am. annual weed that has captured every part of our area since the publication of our first edition; nearly always in dooryards, gardens and roadsides. It grows 8-20 inches high, has opposite, short-stalked, ovalish, hairy-margined leaves, about 1¾ inches wide; the uppermost stalkless and almost stem-clasping. Flower-heads small, not over ¼ inch wide, in a lax, loose, rather sparse cluster, the small, inconspicuous rays dirty white. It is practically a cosmopolitan pest. Named for M. Martinez Galinsoga, Spanish botanist.

Cup-plant
Silphium perfoliatum Yellow, July-September

A tall, coarse perennial, 3-7 feet high, the stout, smooth stem commonly 4-angled. Leaves large, 4-10 inches long, opposite, coarsely toothed, rough, their bases joined to

Cup-Plant.

Galinsoga.

form a shallow "cup" through which the stem passes, hence the name, cup-plant. Flower-heads nearly 2½ inches wide, yellow, grouped in an open, not dense cluster. In woods, Ont. to Ga. west to S. D. and Okla.; often naturalized in the east in waste places. Its relative, *Silphium laciniatum,* which is taller and has slashed leaves, is the famous compass plant of the middle west, whose lower leaves tend to point north and south. It is found on prairies, Ohio to Minn., south to Ala. and Tex.

Grass-leaved Golden Aster or Silver Grass
Chrysopsis graminifolia   Golden-yellow, August-October

An asterlike but golden-yellow flower growing in dry soil generally near the coast. The shining leaves linear, soft, and grasslike, but silvery green-gray with fine-hairiness, the lower ones long. The small heads ½ inch broad, solitary at the tips of the branches, the ray-flowers pistillate, the disc-flowers perfect. The slender stem 1-3 feet high. Del. to Fla., west to Ohio and Tex.

Curved-leaved Golden Aster
Chrysopsis falcata   Golden-yellow, Late July-August

A much lower species with larger flowers, also found in the coastwise states. The stems very woolly, and the small linear leaves gray-green and crowded together. The pretty, rich golden-yellow heads are an inch broad. 4-10 inches high. From Mass. to the coastal plain of N. J.

Chrysopsis mariana   Golden-yellow, August-September

A stout, showy species, the stem and leaves of which are silky with soft hairs when young, but become smooth with age. The gray-green leaves are lance-shaped and stalkless, and the golden-yellow flower-heads are nearly an inch across, the scales below somewhat sticky and hairy. The commoner golden aster of New York and the south, found on dry sandy roadsides near the coast. 1-2 feet high. From southern N. Y. to Fla., west to Ohio and La.

The genus *Solidago,* the goldenrods, includes about 60 species in our area, of which about 25 are commonly found throughout the northern United States. These are distinguished with considerable difficulty, mostly by dif-

C. falcata.   C. graminifolia.

Golden Aster.   Chrysopsis mariana.

ferences in stem, leaf, and flower; the stem may be rough,
smooth, covered with hairs, or with bloom, or angular,
or round; the leaf may be triple-ribbed, feather-veined,
or more or less distinctly ribbed or toothed; the flower-
heads may have few or many large or small rays. The
central tubular florets are perfect, and are cross-fertilized
by many insects, chief among which are the butterflies
and the beelike flies; the flowers furnish an abundance
of honey for all. The Latin name, *Solidago,* means to
make whole, alluding to some curative quality of the
plant. There are some hybrid forms.

Stout Goldenrod
Solidago squarrosa　Golden-yellow, August-October

A not very common species, the stem hairy above and
rarely branched, with large, broad, coarsely toothed,
feather-veined leaves, and with rather showy flowers;
the 10-16 rays nearly ⅓ inch long, the tubular florets
15-24 in a single flower-head the scales of which are
strongly curved outward. The flower plume generally
straight. Plant 2-5 feet high. On rocky hillsides, and the
margins of woods, N. B. south to the mountains of
N. C. and west to Ohio and Ind. (*Illus. on page 508.*)

Blue-stemmed Goldenrod
Solidago cæsia　Late August-October

A late-blooming, graceful, slender woodland goldenrod,
with a distinct bluish or purplish, plumlike bloom on the
bending stem. The leaves dark green, feather-veined,
smooth, sharply toothed, lance-shaped, and sharp-pointed.
The heads in small oblong clusters at the junction of leaf-
stalk with plant-stem, and *not* in a distinct terminal
cluster; 3-5 rays in a single flower-head, ¹⁄₁₆ inch broad,
quite long, and very light golden-yellow. 1-3 feet high.
Common on shaded banks and margins of woods everywhere.

Broad-leaved Goldenrod
Solidago flexicaulis　August-September

A similar species, but with broad, olive-green, feather-
veined leaves pointed at both ends; the stem lighter green,
zigzag, angled in section, and rarely branched. The light
golden-yellow flowers in small clusters (like *S. cæsia*),
with but 3-4 rays. 1-3 feet high. Rich, moist, wooded
banks, Nova Scotia to Ga., west to N. D. and Ark.

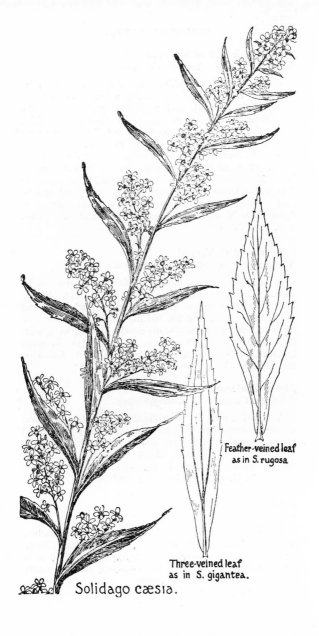

Feather-veined leaf
as in S. rugosa

Three-veined leaf
as in S. gigantea.

Solidago cæsia.

White Goldenrod or Silverrod
Solidago bicolor   August-September

A very common species; the only one with white flowers. Leaves elliptical, feather-veined, rough-hairy, very lightly toothed, and dark olive-green above, the ribs beneath hairy. Stem simple or branched, upright, and gray-hairy. Tubular florets cream-yellow, surrounded by 3-12 white rays; flower-clusters mignonettelike, small, and at the leaf-junctions or crowded in a cylindrical terminal spike. 10-30 inches high. On dry barren ground, Nova Scotia to Ga., and west to Wisc. and Mo. A yellow-flowered relative has densely woolly stem and leaves, and is considered a separate species, *S. hispida*. It is found from Newf. to Ga., west to Minn. and Ark. (*Illus. opp. page 510.*)

Large-leaved Goldenrod
Solidago macrophylla   July-September

A northern species mostly confined to damp, rocky woods. The deep green leaves are ovate, thin, sharply toothed, feather-veined, and very long-stalked. Leaf- and plant-stem usually smooth, but the latter sometimes fine-hairy at the top. Flower-heads nearly ½ inch long, with 8-10 long golden-yellow rays. 1-4 feet high. Wooded hillsides. Catskill Mountains of N. Y., north to Labrador and Hudson's Bay. (*Illus. on page 508.*)

Alpine Goldenrod
Solidago Cutleri   August-September

A dwarf alpine form confined to mountain-tops and about 8 inches high. The large flowers, thickly clustered at the summit of the stout simple stem, with about 12 rays. The florets robust, about ¼ inch high. Leaves usually obovate and finely toothed. Mountain summits of Me., N. H. (Mt. Washington), and N. Y.

Seaside Goldenrod
Solidago sempervirens   August-November

A species frequenting salt-marshes and sea-beaches. Stem stout and smooth; flower-cluster large, leafy, short, and straight, with large showy heads having 7-10 deep golden-yellow rays. Leaves lance-shaped, smooth, toothless, and with 3-5 obscure nerves. 2-8 feet high. Me. to Fla. and Tex.

Seaside Goldenrod.   Solidago sempervirens.

Bog Goldenrod
Solidago uliginosa   August-September

The stem stout and smooth; leaves smooth, lance-shaped, obscurely seven-veined, slightly toothed or toothless; those at the root very long. The heads are light golden-yellow, with 5-6 small rays, and are crowded on the wandlike or straight stem. 2-4 feet high. Newf. to northern N. J. and N. C., west to Minn.

Showy Goldenrod
Solidago speciosa   August-October

A handsome, stocky plant with a ruddy, stout, smooth, round (in section) stem, and large, smooth, firm, feather-veined, olive-green leaves, rough-edged or obscurely toothed; the upper ones oblong lance-shaped, the lower ovate. Flower-heads with about 5 large golden-yellow rays and prominent stamens; the showy flower-cluster is dense, branched, and somewhat pyramidal in outline. 3-6 feet high. Rich ground and copses. Mass. south to N. C. and Ky., and west to Minn. and Ark.

Sweet Goldenrod
Solidago odora   August-September

An anise-scented species, very odorous when crushed. Leaves bright green, smooth, indistinctly three-ribbed, shining, and dotted. The slender stem, often reclining, is usually smooth, and nearly cylindrical in section. Flower-heads small, with 3-4 golden rays nearly ⅓ inch long. The flower-cluster one-sided. 2-3 feet high. In dry sandy soil, Vt. to Fla., west to Mo. and La.

Spreading Goldenrod
Solidago patula   August-October

Very common in swamps; with stout stem (angled in section) and spreading branches. The large, rough, fine-toothed, feather-veined leaves smooth beneath. Flower-clusters small; the rather large heads with obtuse green scales and small rays. Vt. south to Ga., and west to Wisc. and Tex.

Rough-stemmed Goldenrod
Solidago rugosa   July-September

An exceedingly hairy or rough goldenrod, very common on wooded roadsides and margins of fields. Leaves dark green, feather-veined, very hairy, and deeply toothed. Stem hairy, straight, cylindrical, and thickly

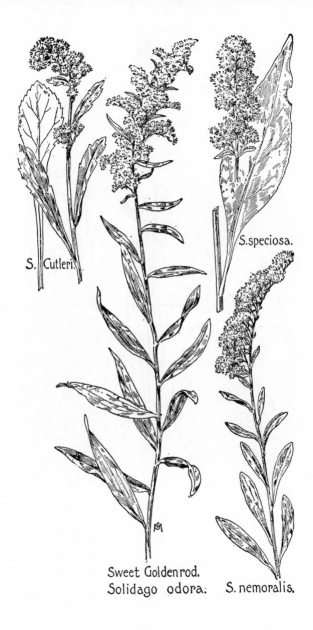

S. Cutleri.

S. speciosa.

Sweet Goldenrod.
Solidago odora.

S. nemoralis.

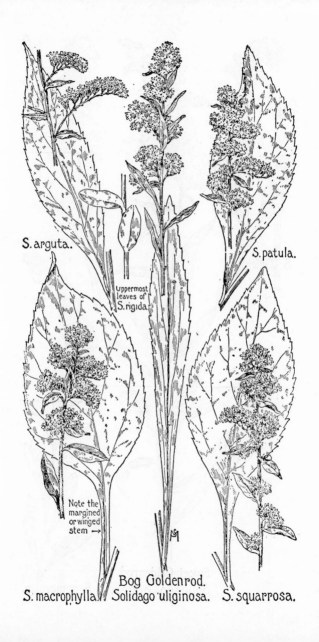

S. arguta.

S. patula.

Uppermost
leaves of
S. rigida

Note the
margined
or winged
stem →

S. macrophylla.

Bog Goldenrod.
Solidago uliginosa.

S. squarrosa.

Solidago rugosa.

set with leaves. The flower-clusters small, weak in color, and terminating several branches also thickly set with leaflets; the flower-heads light golden-yellow; 6-9 rays and 4-7 tubular florets. The plant often branched like an elm at the top, but presenting a variety of forms. 1-7 feet high. Dry ground everywhere.

Elm-leaved Goldenrod
Solidago ulmifolia July-September

A like species with but few differences, viz., stem slender, smooth or woolly at the summit, leaves thin, pointed, and tapering toward the base. Heads with about four deep yellow rays, the scales long lance-shaped. 2-4 feet high. Common in low moist copses or woods, from Nova Scotia south to Ga., west to Minn. and Tex.

Sharp-leaved Goldenrod
Solidago arguta July-September

A common and very graceful species; one of the earliest goldenrods, with very light golden-yellow heads having 5-7 large rays and small, light green, obtuse scales. The flower-cluster plumelike and reclining. The stem angled, smooth, and angular in section, sometimes ruddy brown. Leaves deep green, indistinctly feather-veined, large, thin and sharply coarse-toothed, generally elliptical lance-shaped, the upper ones nearly if not quite toothless. 2-4 feet high. Copses and rich thin woods, from Me. south to N. C.

Early Goldenrod
Solidago juncea July-September

Another very common, slender species often found in company with the foregoing and blooming a little later. Leaves smooth, yellow olive-green, and slightly three-ribbed, the upper ones toothless, the lower broad lance-shaped, with sharp and spreading teeth; a tiny leaf-wing grows at either side of each leaf-stalk. The flower-clusters are spread somewhat like an elm in larger plants; but in the smaller ones they are one-sided. The golden-yellow heads about ⅙ inch long, with 8-12 small rays. 2-4 feet high. On dry rocky banks and roadsides, Nova Scotia to N. C., west to Minn. (*Color Plate 24.*)

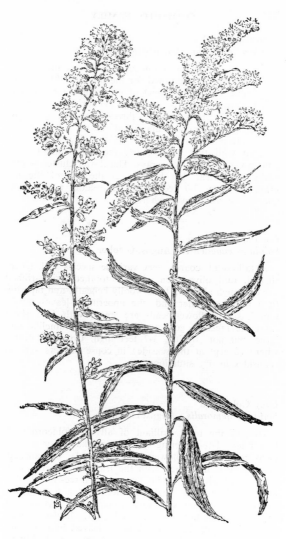

Silverrod.
Solidago bicolor.

Late Goldenrod.
Solidago gigantea.

Late Goldenrod
Solidago gigantea   August-October

A common but by no means a late-flowering golden-rod, generally distinguished for the plumlike lilac bloom (but sometimes light green) of its straight, smooth, dignified stem, which is perfectly cylindrical in section. Leaves dark green, plainly three-ribbed, smooth, and toothed only along the upper half of the edge, narrow and sharp-pointed. The stems of the flower-heads are covered with tiny white hairs; the heads small, light golden-yellow, 7-15 long rays. The flower-cluster is generally cylindrical, but bending at the top of the unbranched stem. 3-7 feet high, but seldom tall. Copses and dry roadsides everywhere.

Canada Goldenrod
Solidago canadensis   August-October

A tall, stout, coarse, very variable species with lance-shaped, dull olive-green, sharply toothed, triple-ribbed leaves, rough above, a trifle woolly beneath, and tapering to a point at either end, the uppermost leaves nearly toothless. The flower-heads are small, with 5-15 short rays; the greenish golden-yellow clusters plumelike and large, but not striking. 3-7 feet high. Common everywhere (except at the seaside) in copse borders and on roadsides in dry situations.

Gray Goldenrod
Solidago nemoralis   August-October

One of the most brilliant of all the goldenrods. A rather low, late-flowering species remarkable for its rich deep golden-yellow flowers and its simple, unbranched, green-gray stem, which with the leaves is covered with minute grayish hairs. The leaves are three-ribbed, dull olive-green, rough, thick, dull-toothed, and generally broad lance-shaped, somewhat wider at the farther end, the lower ones tapering to a stalk; little leaflets are on either side of the bases of the larger leaves. Flower-heads with 5-9 rays, the cluster generally forming a thickly set one-sided plume. 6-25 inches high. Common everywhere, beside sandy roads and in dry pastures, except at the seaside. (*Illus. cpp. page 506.*)

Canada Goldenrod.   Solidago canadensis.

Hard-leaved Goldenrod
Solidago rigida   August-October

A less common species distinguished for its spreading, *flat-topped* cluster, which is usually quite thick. The stout, leafy stem is covered with dense fine hairs; the rough, thick, narrowly oval leaves, feather-veined and extremely rigid, the upper ones broad at the base and clasping at the stem, toothless or nearly so. The large flower-heads with about 30 tubular florets and 8-14 large rays. 2-5 feet high. Dry soil, Conn. south to Ga., and west to S. D. and Tex.

Lance-leaved Goldenrod
Solidago graminifolia   August-early October

A slightly fragrant species, distinctly different from all the foregoing. The very small flowers in a *flat-topped* cluster, and the *very small,* toothless, lance-shaped, narrow willowlike, light green leaves with 3-5 ribs and very rough edges. The stem is straight, angular in section, with the ridges minutely rough, and terminates in a thin, wiry-branched flower-cluster not at all showy in color; the tiny flower-heads in small crowded groups; 12-20 minute rays. 2-4 feet high. On river-banks, borders of damp woods, or in moist situations everywhere.

Slender Goldenrod
Solidago tenuifolia   August-September

A somewhat similar, resinously fragrant species; the difference apparent in the slenderer, smoother stem and the very narrow, linear, dotted leaves, commonly one-ribbed. The tiny flower-heads, with 6-12 rays, in numerous groups of 2-3, forming a flat-topped cluster. 15-18 inches high. In dry sandy soil mostly near the coast, Nova Scotia to Fla.; reported from La.

———

The genus *Aster,* named from ἀστήρ, a star, is a varied and beautiful, late-flowering tribe which, with *Solidago,* monopolizes the roadsides and byways in autumn. The species are distinguished with considerable difficulty, as there are over 65 in our area, of which those below are merely representative types. Asa Gray once wrote of "the great if not insuperable difficulties" of *Aster.* The ray-florets are pistillate, the tubular florets (upon the disc) perfect. Our wild asters are closely related to the

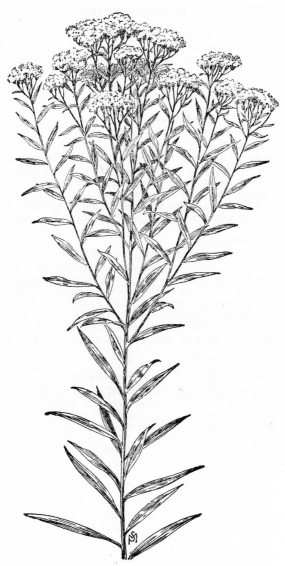

Lance-leaved Goldenrod. Solidago graminifolia.

goldenrods, but differ in never having yellow flowers. A few of them, by hybridization, mostly done in England, have produced the beautiful Michaelmas daisies of our gardens. The common, annual garden aster, however, is an Asiatic plant (*Callistephus chinensis*) having nothing to do with our native asters.

White Woodland Aster
Aster divaricatus   White, September-October

A small white aster, not showy but common in thin woods. The stem is rather smooth, a trifle zigzagged, and quite slender; the olive-green leaves are coarsely toothed, slender-stemmed, heart-shaped, sharp-pointed, and smooth. The white heads, as broad as a "nickel," have 6-9 rays; disc-flowers turn madder purple with age. 1-2 feet high. Me. to Ga., west to Ohio. (*Illus. on page 521.*)

Large-leaved Aster
Aster macrophyllus   Lilac, August-September

A stout, stiff, purplish-stemmed species with few, rough, large, 4-8 inches long, closely toothed basal leaves, the upper ones ovate, almost stalkless, and sharp-pointed. Heads about an inch broad, with 10-16 bluish lilac, or rarely lilac-white, rays; disc-flowers turning madder brown with age. 2-3 feet high. Common, damp thin woods or dry banks, N. B. to Pa., west to Minn. (*Illus. on page 531.*)

Showy Aster
Aster spectabilis   Violet, August-October

A very handsome species found chiefly near the coast, with but few showy, deep blue-violet heads about as broad as a fifty-cent piece, with 15-25 rays often ¾ inch long. The olive-green leaves, mostly toothless, are oblong lance-shaped and rough. The stiff, generally simple stem, 1-2 feet high, is slightly rough below. Sandy soil, Mass. to S. C.; also in uplands in N. C.

Rough-leaved Aster
Aster radula   Violet, August-September

A low slender species with few large, violet-blue heads and a rough stem and leaf, the latter dark green, stalkless, sharply toothed, strongly veined, and oblong lance-shaped. The upper leaves closely clasp the stem. The heads with about 22 rays nearly ½ inch long. 1-2 feet high. In wet situations and moist shady copse borders,

Aster spectabilis   Aster radula

Newf. to Va., generally near the coast. A dwarf form, var. *strictus,* has nearly toothless leaves and usually solitary flowers; White Mts., N. H.

New England Aster
Aster novæ-angliæ   Purple or magenta, August-October

A familiar and common species with numerous handsome heads about an inch broad, which vary from light violet to light purple or white, and sometimes to magenta. The stem stout, branched, and rough; the olive-green, soft-hairy leaves lance-shaped, toothless, thin, and clasping the stem by a broad base rounded at either side. The heads, rarely larger than a silver quarter, have usually 30-40 narrow rays, and terminate the branches in large clusters. 2-6 feet high or higher. Moist sites, New Eng. to Ala. and far west. It is one of the plants involved in the creation of Michaelmas daisies. (*Color Plate 25.*)

Spreading Aster
Aster patens   Light violet-purple, August-October

A common and very variable species on dry ground, with ovate-oblong, stalkless leaves, heart-shaped at the base and clasping the main stem, toothless or nearly so, but rough on the edge and on the upper surface. Stem rough-hairy, slender, and widely branched. Heads with 20-30 light violet-purple rays nearly ½ inch long, and spreading, pointed green tips beneath. 1-3 feet high. In dry open places, from Mass. to Fla., west to northern N. Y., Mo. and Kan. (*Illus. on page 521.*)

Wavy-leaved Aster
Aster undulatus   Light violet, September-October

An aster easily recognized by its remarkable *broad-stalked* leaf, which is heart-shaped where it clasps the plant-stem; some leaves are pointed heart-shaped, and the upper ones have an undulating margin. Stems stiff and very rough. Heads light blue-violet, with 9-15 rays. 1-3 feet high. In dry places and on shaded roadsides, Me. to Fla., west to Ind. and Miss. (*Illus. on page 527.*)

Heart-leaved Aster
Aster cordifolius   Lilac or lighter, September-October

A familiar, small-flowered aster with variable leaves. Stem slender, smooth, and much branched; the light green leaves rough or fine-hairy, and usually pointed heart-shaped with large sharp teeth; the upper ones short-

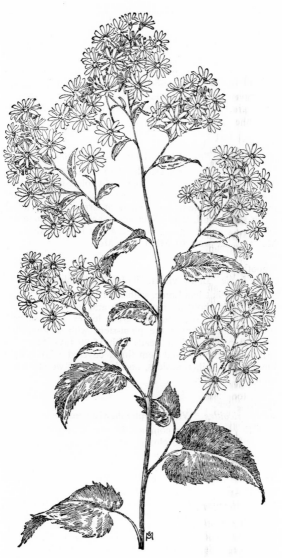

Heart-leaved Aster.   Aster cordifolius.

stalked or stalkless, ovate or lance-shaped. The lilac or blue-lavender heads, about ⅝ inch broad, with 10-20 rays, are crowded in dense clusters like those of the lilac; the disc-florets turn magenta or madder purple with age. 1-4 feet high. Common everywhere, and in a great variety of forms, for some of which a number of varietal or specific names have been proposed; not here maintained.

Arrow-leaved Aster
Aster sagittifolius   Light violet, August-October

A rather showy species. The stem stiff, erect, and with nearly upright branches. The light olive-green leaves thin, broad lance-shaped, and sparingly toothed toward the top of the stem, but somewhat arrow-shaped lower down. The small, light violet heads are showy; there are 10-14 rays about ¼ inch long. 2-4 feet high. In dry soil, Me. to Fla., west to Minn. and Mo.

Smooth Aster
Aster lævis   Light violet, September-October

Variable but handsome, with light violet or paler blue-violet heads about an inch broad, and nearly if not entirely toothless, smooth, light green leaves, lance-shaped, stalkless and clasping the plant-stem with a somewhat heart-shaped base. The heads with 15-30 rays. Stem 2-4 feet high, smooth, and sometimes covered with a light bloom. Dry soil, roadsides, and borders of woods; common everywhere.

Heath Aster
Aster ericoides   White, September-November

A tiny white aster common in dry open places. Stem generally smooth and closely set above with tiny, heath-like, linear, light green leaves, the few basal ones blunt lance-shaped and slightly toothed; all are rather rigid. The tiny white heads are like miniature daisies; there are 16-24 narrow rays sometimes lightly tinted with magenta. This aster has spread beyond its original limits through cultivation by bee-keepers; its yield of nectar is large. 1-3 feet high. Common from Me. to Pa. and far westward. It is one of the parents of some Michaelmas daisies. Here, also, belongs the plant treated in our last edition as *Aster multiflorus,* a species now merged with *Aster ericoides.*

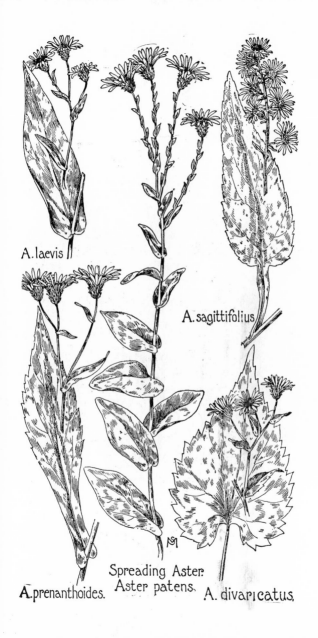

A. laevis

A. sagittifolius

A. prenanthoides.

Spreading Aster.
Aster patens.

A. divaricatus.

Aster ericoides.

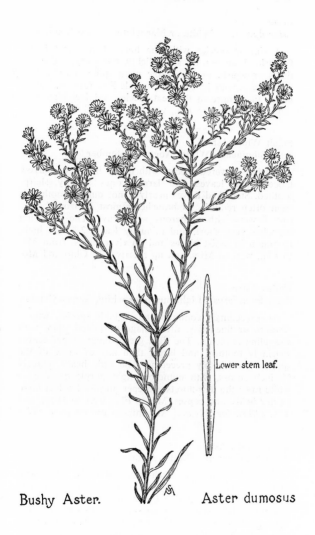

Lower stem leaf.

Bushy Aster.   Aster dumosus

Bushy Aster
Aster dumosus   White or lilac-white, August-October

A similar species with fine linear leaves and loose
flowering branches, the stem slightly fine-hairy, and some
times brownish, or the whole plant quite smooth. The
little heads, with 15-25 white or pale lilac rays, are rather
larger than those of the next species. 1-3 feet high. Dry
sandy soil, Mass. to Fla., west to Ark. and La.

Small White Aster
Aster vimineus   White, August-September

A white-flowered species with larger linear, or narrow
lance-shaped leaves, the largest ones slightly sharp-
toothed. Stem and leaves nearly if not quite smooth, the
stem often reddish, its branches almost horizontal. The
tiny flowers with numerous white rays. The flowering
branches very short, and minutely leafy. 2-4 feet high.
Common in moist places and on river-banks, from Me.
to Fla., west to Miss. and up the river to Ohio and Mo.

Calico Aster
Aster lateriflorus   Light purple or white, August-October

An exceedingly common and variable species, with a
smooth, or fine-hairy, often magenta-stained stem, with
straggling branches. The light green, lance-shaped leaves
sparingly toothed, and larger than any of those of the
species immediately preceding. The little heads scarcely
½ inch across, with numerous light purple or lilac or
white rays; the disc-florets a deeper purple. 1-5 feet high.
In dry fields, and copses, Me. to Fla., west to Minn. and
Tex. (*Illus. for this and A.* vimineus *are on page 531.*)

Tradescant's Aster
Aster Tradescanti   White, August-October

A slender-stemmed, much-branched white aster, with
numerous heads about ⅝ inch broad, and with long
lance-shaped leaves, the lower ones slightly toothed,
smooth on both sides, thin, and tapering to a sharp point.
The small heads with white or lilac-white rays clustered
about the short upward-turned branches. 2-4 feet high.
In wet fields and swamps, Nova Scotia to N. Y., west
to Mich.

New York Aster.
Aster novi-belgii.

Tradescant's Aster.
Aster Tradescanti.

Panicled White Aster
Aster simplex   White, August-October

A very tall species with white or lilac-white heads a trifle larger than a nickel, borne in somewhat flat-topped, loose or scattered clusters; the leaves dark green, very nearly if not quite smooth, long lance-shaped, and obscurely toothed; the upper ones toothless. The stout, much-branched stem is 3-8 feet high. Common in some of its many forms in low moist ground everywhere.

Long-leaved Aster
Aster longifolius   Light violet, August-October

A doubtful species with remarkably narrow, toothless (or nearly so) leaves 3-8 inches long, and pale violet or light purple heads as large as a silver quarter. It is by some regarded as a form of *A. simplex,* and by others as a variety of the New York aster. It is doubtful if the species really exists.

New York Aster
Aster novi-belgii   Lilac or blue-violet, August-October

Heads large pale violet, lilac or blue-violet, with 15-24 rays, nearly ½ inch long. The stalkless, usually toothless light green leaves are thin, long, and smooth, or the small upper ones clasping the stem, t' e lower very slightly toothed. 10-35 inches high. The variations of *A. novi-belgii* are rather numerous and one of them may be the disputed *Aster longifolius.* The New York aster is found in moist places, even in salt marshes, from Newf. to Ga., mostly near the coast.

Aster prenanthoides   Pale violet, September-October

A northern species. The upper part of the stem is hairy in lines, and occasionally brownish; the rough (but smooth beneath), ovate lance-shaped leaves are contracted to a long wide finally heart-shaped base at the plant-stem. The heads, about as large as a silver quarter, are pale violet or nearly lilac-white. 1-3 feet high. Margins of woods and banks of streams, N. Y. to Tenn., west to Minn. and Iowa. (*Illus. on page 521.*)

Purple-stemmed Aster
Aster puniceus   Light purple, August-October

A common and extremely variable species with usually madder purple stem, rough-hairy and stout. The light green leaves, lance-shaped or narrower, sparingly and

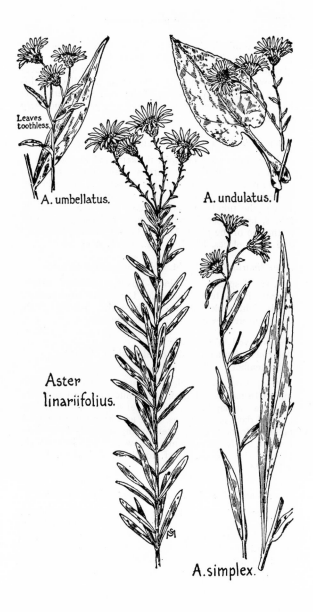

Leaves
toothless.

A. umbellatus.

A. undulatus.

Aster
linariifolius.

A. simplex.

coarsely toothed, clasp the upper branches. Heads about the size of a silver quarter or larger, light violet or light lilac-purple with 20-24 rays. 3-7 feet high. In moist places and swamps everywhere. Of the many varieties the differences are mostly in shape of the leaf, character of the hairiness, and other vegetative features; perhaps not very stable.

Aster umbellatus   White, August-September

A common aster in moist thickets, and the borders of damp woods. With few narrow white rays which are generally curved backward. The flowers are borne in flat-topped clusters. The small heads numerous but not showy, the tubular florets purpling with age. The veiny leaves, long lance-shaped and very rough-edged, extend to the top of the plant. 2-7 feet high. Common in shaded and moist places, Newf. to Ga., mostly near the coast.

Aster linariifolius   Light violet, September-October

A small species with linear leaves, one-ribbed, rough-edged, without teeth, and rigid. The rather large solitary heads light violet or rarely lilac-white. 1-2 feet high. Common everywhere in dry situations.

Sharp-leaved Wood Aster
Aster acuminatus   White or lilac-white, August-September

A low woodland species with large, scrawny heads having 10-16 narrow white or lilac-white rays, and generally magenta tubular florets. The large, sharp-pointed, coarse-toothed dark green leaves, thin, and broad lance-shaped, tapering to both ends, often arranged nearly in a circle beneath the few long-stemmed flowers. 10-16 inches high. In cool rich woods, Newf. to N. C. and Tenn. In the White Mts.

Aster tenuifolius   Lilac-purple, September-October

A species confined to the salt marshes of the coast from Mass. to Fla. and Miss. Stem very smooth and generally zigzagged. The few leaves long linear, tapering to both ends, toothless, and thick or fleshy. The rather large heads an inch broad or more, lilac-purple or paler, borne on a generally simple or slightly branched stem. 8-25 inches high.

Purple-stemmed Aster.   Aster puniceus.

Aster acuminatus.

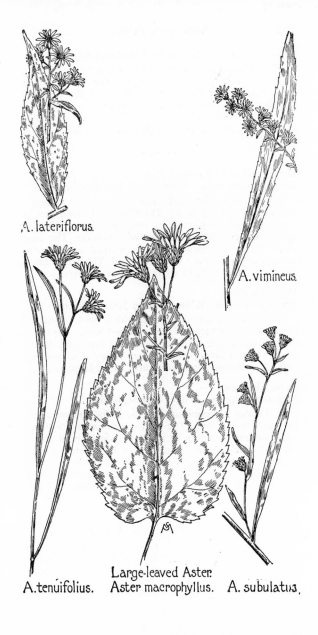

A. lateriflorus.

A. vimineus.

A. tenuifolius.

Large-leaved Aster.
Aster macrophyllus.

A. subulatus.

Aster subulatus Pale purple, August-October

Also a salt marsh aster, found from N. B. to Fla., and near salt deposits elsewhere. The leaves linear lance-shaped, toothless, and flat, those on the branches very small and awl-shaped. The numerous, very small pale purple heads with *very short rays* scarcely extending beyond the disc; disc-florets purplish. 6-24 inches high.

Horseweed or Butterweed
Erigeron canadensis White-green, June-October

A very common annual weed, and the most unattractive member of the genus. The white and green flower-heads are extremely small, ¼ inch long; the rays do not spread, but connect in the form of a cylinder. The dark green leaves are linear, remotely toothed or toothless, and the upper ones are often cut-lobed. The bristly hairy stem is 1-7 feet high. In waste places everywhere.

Daisy Fleabane
Erigeron annuus White or lilac, June-September

An annual and asterlike species with a spreading-haired stem and coarsely toothed, lance-shaped leaves, the lower ones broader. The white or pale lilac flower-heads are about ½ inch broad, with a green-yellow disc. 1-4 feet high. A common weed everywhere in waste places.

Daisy Fleabane
Erigeron strigosus White, May-September

A singular common species; the hairs not spreading but close to the stem. The light green leaves are linear and toothless or nearly so, the lower ones broad at the tip. The little daisylike heads are ½ inch broad, with a large green-yellow disc; occasionally the white rays are lilac-tinged, and sometimes they are extremely short or altogether absent. 1-2 feet high. Common in fields and on roadsides everywhere.

Robin's Plantain
Erigeron pulchellus Lilac or pale violet, May-June

A rather large-flowered plant which is frequently gregarious, tinting the roadside or field with its delicate lilac. The light olive-green stem and leaves are *very* soft-hairy, the basal leaves broad at the tip and indistinctly toothed. The showy heads, 1 inch broad, vary from lilac

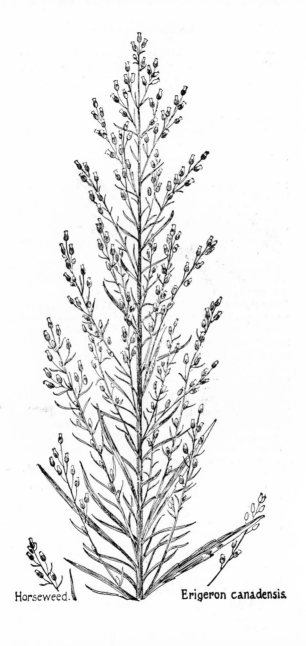

Horseweed.   Erigeron canadensis.

or magenta to a violet-purple; the somewhat green-yellow disc is broader than the fine rays are long. Fertilized by bumblebees and honeybees (the most frequent visitors) and butterflies. 10-22 inches high. Common everywhere. (*Color Plate 26.*)

Common Fleabane
Erigeron philadelphicus

A similar but taller plant with light magenta or pale pink flowers and a soft-hairy (rarely smooth) stem; 1-2 feet high. Common throughout our range, but less frequent than *E. pulchellus,* and blooming to August.

Everlasting or Pussy-toes
Antennaria plantaginifolia   White, May-June

A small plant with short white hairs; the three-ribbed basal leaves broad near the tip, the stalks nearly as long as the leaf. Upper stem leaves lance-shaped. The linear scales of the small, ¼-inch-long flower-head are green or purple at the base, and white or purplish at the tip. The styles crimson. Dry soil, Que. to Fla., west to Minn. and Tex. It has many forms for which various names have been applied, such as *A. Parlinii* of our last edition, but it is doubtful if they are valid. Another form of it is *A. fallax* of our last edition. If valid it is separated only by technical characters.

Pussy-toes
Antennaria neglecta   Dull white, April–early May

The commonest species of pussy-toes and a very woolly, small plant with slender stem and runners. The one-ribbed basal leaves wedge-shaped or blunt lance-shaped, and indistinctly stalked; the few stem-leaves linear. The head of the pistillate plant ⅜ inch long, with linear bracts greenish, brownish, or purplish below, and white at the tip. 8-12 inches high. Dry barren fields and sunny hillsides everywhere. An exceedingly variable plant with several named forms or varieties. Among them are the *A. neodioica* and *A. canadensis* of our last edition. Both are now considered as mere forms of *A. neglecta*. Both *A. neglecta* and *A. plantaginifolia* are variable and difficult species for the amateur and even for the experts. The eighth edition of Gray's Manual admits 32 "species," while Dr. Gleason very sensibly recognizes only six species of *Antennaria* in our range.

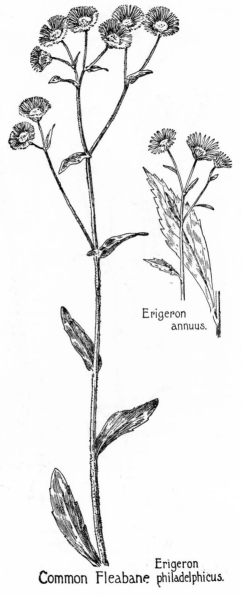

Erigeron
annuus.

Erigeron
Common Fleabane philadelphicus.

Pussy-toes.
Antennaria neglecta.

Daisy Fleabane.   Erigeron strigosus.

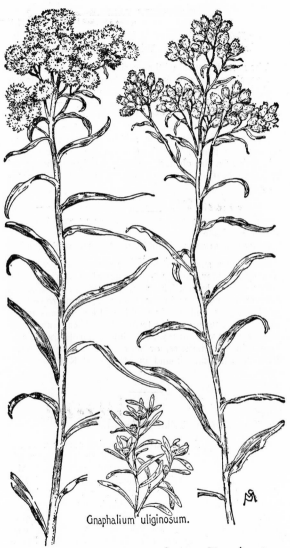

Gnaphalium uliginosum.

Pearly Everlasting.   Sweet Everlasting.
Anaphalis margaritacea.   Gnaphalium obtusifolium.

Pearly Everlasting
Anaphalis margaritacea   White, July-September

The most beautiful of the everlastings, the linear leaves are sage green above and white beneath; the heads are globular, with miniature petal-like white scales surrounding the central yellow staminate flowers, arranged not unlike the petals of a water-lily. Cross-fertilized mostly by moths and butterflies, though many other insects are common visitors. Staminate and pistillate flowers grow on separate plants. The stem is white and woolly, terminated by a flat cluster, sometimes 6 inches broad, of close-set heads. 1-3 feet high. Common throughout N. Am.

Marsh Fleabane
Pluchea purpurascens   Pinkish-purple, August-September

A resinous, sticky and aromatic annual herb, with the odor of camphor, usually 8-20 inches high, with alternate, rather ovalish leaves. These are toothed on the margin, have short stalks, or in the upper leaves narrowed toward the base and nearly stalkless. Flower-heads in an open leafy cluster, mostly terminal, the heads about ½ inch long and without rays, but pink or purple and showy. Found in salt marshes, or more rarely in fresh ones, Mass. to Fla.; rare inland in Mich. and Kan.

Coltsfoot
Tussilago Farfara   Yellow, March-June

One of the earliest of spring-blooming plants; a perennial from Europe widely naturalized in gardens, roadsides and fields. Early in the season it sends up a scaly, bracted but leafless stalk, 4-15 inches high, covered with silky white down. At the summit is a solitary flower-head, brilliantly yellow, about 1½ inches wide, apparently but not truly rayless. The minute flowers are densely crowded in the head. After the flowers wither the basal leaves appear. They are long-stalked, the blade heart-shaped but with a deep cleft at the base suggesting a colt's foot, and at first white-woolly. Not common anywhere.

Coltsfoot.

Marsh Fleabane

Sweet Everlasting
Gnaphalium obtusifolium   Cream-white, August-
September

Less showy than the pearly everlasting, but possessing
an aromatic odor resembling that of slippery elm. The
heads cream-white and ovoid, not expanding to the water-
lily shape until the seed is ripe. The stem (much branched
at the top) together with the linear leaves is white-hairy
and delicate sage-green. 12-25 inches high. Very common in dry open places and stony pastures everywhere.
The name, from the Greek, means a tuft of wool.

Clammy Everlasting
Gnaphalium Macounii   Cream-white, July-September

A similar fragrant species, but with a leafy, glandular-
sticky stem, woolly and nearly white; the leaves are a
little broader—linear lance-shaped, with a dense woolliness beneath; they partly clasp the stem. Flower-scales
a yellowish cream-white. 2-3 feet high. On dry or moist
open hillsides or banks, from Que. to Tenn. and far west.

Low or Marsh Cudweed
Gnaphalium uliginosum   Brownish-white, July-
September

An insignificant low annual with white-woolly stem
and linear, sharp-pointed leaves, rather broader at the
tip. Heads tiny, ovate, with brownish scales. The many-
branched stems are 3-7 inches high. Common on low
ground, Newf. to Va., and west to Ind.

Elecampane
Inula Helenium   Deep yellow, July-September

One of the tall picturesque weeds characteristic of the
Composite Family. Leaves olive yellow-green, white-
veined, rough above, fine-hairy beneath, toothed, the
lower ones stalked, the upper ones partly clasping the
plant-stem, which is woolly and often toned with purple-
gray. The showy but somewhat disheveled head, set
amid flattish leaflets, has many narrow, curving, deep
lemon-yellow ray florets which are pistillate, and a broad
disc of central, tubular, perfect florets, at first yellow,
and finally tan color. Heads about 2½ inches wide. Two
or three flower-heads are grouped together at the termination of the stalk. 2-6 feet high. Naturalized from
Europe, but never very common. (*Color Plate 27.*)

Tickseed.

Cone-flower.

Cone-flower
Ratibida pinnata   Pale yellow, June-August

For other cone-flowers see *Echinacea* and *Rudbeckia*. *Ratibida* is a coarse perennial, 20-40 inches high, with alternate, much cut and divided leaves, the segments mostly toothed. Flower-heads solitary or few, on perfectly naked stalks, the central cone about ½ inch high, the downward-pointing pale yellow rays from 1½-2½ inches long; at first spreading, but ultimately hanging down far below the central cone. In prairies or more rarely in dry woods, Ont. to Ga., rarely near the coast, much more common from Ohio to Minn. and Okla.

Tickseed
Coreopsis rosea   Pink, July-August

The tickseeds are common in cultivation, especially *Coreopsis tinctoria,* which is prevailingly yellow, comes from the west, but is fairly common as an escape in the east. Within our range is *Coreopsis rosea* with a weak and sprawling stem, scarcely over 12-15 inches high, the very narrow leaves opposite, occasionally divided into fine segments. Flower cone much shorter than the faintly notched or 3-toothed rays. Mostly in wet places, or even in the water, in coastal regions from Nova Scotia and New Eng. to Ga.; especially common on L. I. and N. J.

Great Ragweed
Ambrosia trifida   Green, July-September

Perhaps the tallest member of the Composite group, not excepting *Lactuca.* Stem stout, hairy or nearly smooth, and filled with a frostlike pith; leaves deeply three-lobed and sharp-pointed, the teeth irregular and acute. The insignificant small flowers form a terminal, pointed cluster (these are staminate), or spring from between the opposite-growing leaves and the stem (these are usually pistillate). 6-15 feet. Common throughout our range. This and the next are one of the chief causes of hay fever as their pollen is copious. (*Illus. on page 558.*)

Roman Wormwood or Hogweed
Ambrosia artemisiifolia   Green, July-September

A common weed with remarkably ornamental, cut leaves resembling those of *Artemisia* (Composite Family). An annual with a much-branched, fine-hairy stem

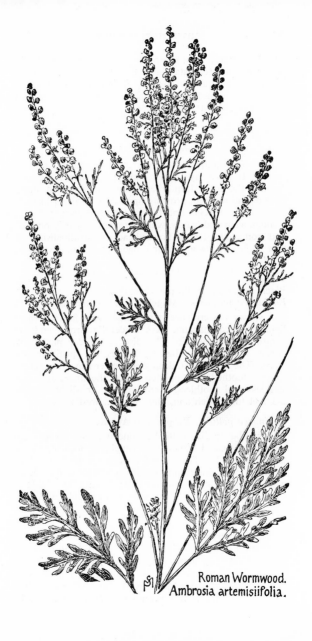

Roman Wormwood.
Ambrosia artemisiifolia.

and thin, lifeless light green, dissected leaves. The slender spikes of the green staminate flowers are numerous and somewhat decorative. The tiny fruit is furnished with 6 short acute spines. 1-5 feet high. Troublesome in dooryards and gardens everywhere.

Oxeye
Heliopsis helianthoides   Yellow, August-September

Like the sunflower, with perfect ray- and disc-flowers, the 10 straplike rays rather showy; the stem and leaves smooth, the latter deep green, broad lance-shaped, three-ribbed, and toothed, growing oppositely. 3-5 feet high. In copses, Que. to Ga., and far westward. A variety having a rough stem and leaves, which are less narrowly pointed, and somewhat larger flower-heads is distinguished as var. *scabra*. It has a similar range, but is unknown south of Md.

Black Sampson or Purple Cone-flower
Echinacea purpurea   Magenta, July-September

A showy western species with handsome flowers whose light or deep magenta rays gracefully droop and are two-toothed at the tip. The disc is madder purple, its florets are perfect; the ray-flowers are pistillate but sterile. The five-ribbed, deep green lower leaves are rough, sharply toothed, and pointed ovate; the upper ones are stalkless and toothless. Stem smooth or slightly hairy. 2-3 feet high. Rich soil, Ohio to Ga., west to Okla.

Echinacea pallida   Purple, July-August

A similar species with the same magenta flowers and long lance-shaped leaves, very rough, without teeth, and three-ribbed. The flowers are a deeper color when they at first expand. Rare on roadsides and fields in New Eng., where it has come from the west; Ill. and Ala., west to Minn., Neb., and Tex. The name from Greek for *hedgehog* or *sea-urchin*.

Tall Cone-flower
Rudbeckia laciniata   Golden-yellow, July-August

An allied plant with golden-yellow flowers whose rays droop; the central green-yellow cone, at first hemispherical, is finally elongated and brown. Nearly smooth, deep green leaves, the lowest compound, the intermediate ir-

Heliopsis
helianthoides.

Rudbeckia
triloba.

Echinacea pallida.

regularly 3-5-parted, the uppermost small and elliptical. The branching stems 3-10 feet high. In moist thickets, Que. to Fla., west to Mont. and Idaho. The double-flowered var. *hortensia* is the familiar golden glow of our gardens. Named for Olaus Rudbeck, a Swedish botanist.

Rudbeckia triloba   Golden-yellow, August

Flower-disc purple-brown, at first hemispherical, and afterward oblong-ovoid; about 8-10 golden-yellow rays, deeper at the base, and somewhat long-oval. Upper leaves rough, thin, bright green, ovate lance-shaped, lower ones three-lobed, tapering at the base, and coarsely toothed. Stem hairy, much branched, and many-flowered; the heads small, about 2 inches broad. 2-5 feet high. On dry or moist ground, N. Y. south to Fla., west to Mich. and Okla.

Black-eyed Susan or Cone-flower
Rudbeckia hirta   Deep golden-yellow, June-August

A biennial. The commonest eastern species, although its seed originally came from the west mixed with clover seed. Both stem and leaves are very rough and bristly; the former *exceedingly tough,* the latter dull olive-green, lance-shaped, toothless or nearly so, and scattered along the rigid stem; the lower leaves broader at the tip and three-ribbed. The deep gold-yellow ray-flowers are neutral without stamens or pistils; they curl backward; the disc is madder purple, and the tiny florets encircle it in successive bloom, creating a zone of yellow when the pollen is ripe. 1-2 feet high. Common in dry or sandy meadows throughout our range and a pestiferous weed in some eastern fields. (*Color Plate 28.*)

Helianthus annuus   Yellow, July-August

The common garden sunflower; an annual with generally three-ribbed and heart-shaped leaves, and golden-yellow flower-heads 1-10 inches broad. 2-12 feet high. Everywhere as an escape; native in the west.

Tall Sunflower
Helianthus giganteus   Yellow, August-September

A tall species with a rough dull magenta stem and rough, bright green, lance-shaped leaves, pointed and finely toothed, nearly stalkless, the upper ones quite so, and all growing alternately, but rarely some growing op-

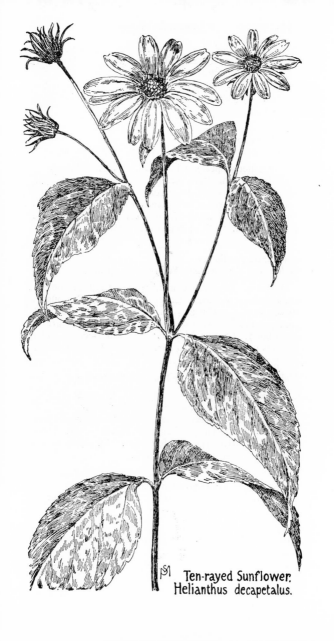

Ten-rayed Sunflower.
Helianthus decapetalus.

positely. The light yellow heads about 2 inches broad, with 10-20 rays; the disc dull yellow, with perfect florets, and the rays neutral, that is, without stamens or pistil. 3-12 feet high. Common in swamps and on the borders of wet meadows from Me. to Fla., west to Alberta and Colo.

Small Sunflower
Helianthus microcephalus   Yellow, July-September

A southerly species with many very small heads ½-1 inch broad. The stem slender and generally branched; leaves mostly opposite, broad lance-shaped, toothed, rough, and short-stalked. Heads with 5-10 yellow rays. 3-6 feet high. Common in thickets and on the borders of woods, Pa. south to Ga., west to Mo.

Woodland Sunflower
Helianthus divaricatus   Yellow, July-August

A slender, smooth-stemmed species (a trifle fine-hairy above) with opposite lance-shaped, toothed, roughish, three-ribbed, and nearly or quite stalkless leaves 3-7 inches long. The yellow heads, 2 inches broad, are few or solitary. 2-5 feet high. Common in thickets and on borders of woods, Me. to Fla., west to Manitoba and La.

Helianthus strumosus   Yellow, July-September

A species similar in aspect, color, situation, and time of bloom; but the stem very smooth below, and often with a bloom; the leaves rough above, and pale (sometimes minutely hairy) beneath. Heads about 1 inch wide, with 5-15 rays. 3-6 feet high. Me. south to Fla., but mostly west to Minn. and Tex.

Ten-rayed or Thin-leaved Sunflower
Helianthus decapetalus   Yellow, August-September

A rather showy species having 10-12 rays, with many pure yellow or deeper yellow flowers 2-3 inches broad. The slender tall stem is rough above and smooth below; the deep green leaves are broad lance-shaped, a trifle rough, thin, and short-stalked; they grow oppositely. 2-5 feet high. Borders of copses and low damp woods, Que. to N. C., west to Wisc. and Mo.

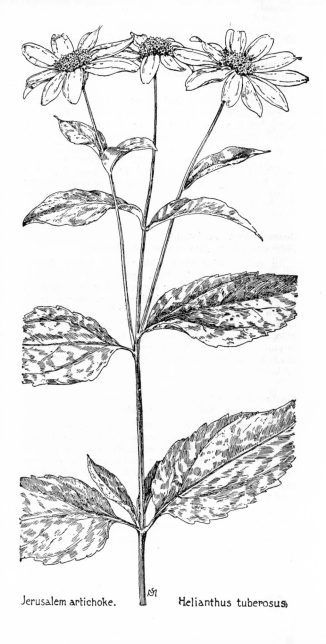

Jerusalem artichoke.   Helianthus tuberosus.

Jerusalem Artichoke
Helianthus tuberosus   Golden-yellow, September-
   October

A species once extensively grown for its edible tubers,
now running wild in fence rows and roadsides. The name
Jerusalem is a corruption of the Italian *girasole,* sunflower. Stem stout and rough-hairy; the ovate lance-
shaped, three-ribbed, rough leaves grow oppositely (a
few upper ones alternately). The golden-yellow heads,
sometimes 3 inches broad, have 12-20 rays. 5-12 feet
high. Damp soil throughout our range; perhaps not wild
in the east.

Beggar-ticks or Stick-tight
Bidens frondosa   Rusty-green, July-October

An uninteresting weed with rayless, bristly flower-
heads, indeterminate in color, approaching rusty-green,
surrounded by little leaflets; the branching stem purplish.
Leaves of 3-5 divisions, toothed and lance-shaped. Seed-
vessels two-pronged (the prongs toothed), less than ¼
inch long, and sepia-brown; attaching readily to woolly
animals or clothing. 1-8 feet high. Common everywhere
in moist soil. The name, from *bis* and *dens,* means two-
toothed. The specific name, from *frondosus,* means *full
of leaves.*

Smaller Bur Marigold
Bidens cernua   Yellow, July-October

A species with very narrow lance-shaped smooth
leaves, coarsely and sharply toothed. The similar, bristly,
half globular, rusty flowers generally nod; the rays, if
any, are short and small. The seed-vessels are narrower
and four-pronged. 6-36 inches high. In wet soil, N. B.
to N. C. and far west.

Larger Bur Marigold
Bidens lævis   Yellow, August-October

A more attractive species with light golden-yellow rays,
which, when perfect, are rather showy. The heads sometimes over 2 inches broad. Leaves narrow lance-shaped
and coarsely toothed. Seed-vessels with 2-4 prongs. 10-24
inches high. In swamps and wet places. New Eng., south,
and west to Minn. Perhaps not distinct from the last.

Bidens laevis.   Beggar-ticks.   Bidens *frondosa*.

Bidens cernua

Sneezeweed
Helenium autumnale   Yellow, August-September

A nearly smooth plant with toothed, lance-shaped, alternate leaves and decoratively handsome flower-heads, 1-2 inches broad, with the toothed, golden-yellow rays turned considerably backward; the globular disc is yellow and chaffy, the drooping rays pistillate and fertile; cross-fertilized mostly by bees. 2-6 feet high. Common in wet meadows and on river-banks everywhere.

Mayweed
Anthemis Cotula   White, June-October

A daisylike flower about an inch broad, with white, three-toothed, neutral rays (i.e., without stamens or pistils) and a yellow disc which becomes elongated with age. The small leaves, cut and slashed to absolute form-lessness, are remarkable for their disagreeable odor and acrid taste. The flower-heads of the true chamomile of the gardens, *Anthemis nobilis,* are used in making a horrible concoction called "chamomile tea" and for making a hair rinse to keep blondes blond. 8-20 inches high. Common about dwellings and on roadsides everywhere; a native of Europe.

Yarrow or Milfoil
Achillea Millefolium   Gray-white, June-October

A very familiar roadside weed adventive from Europe, with remarkable gray olive-green, feathery, dissected, stalkless leaves of a rather long-oval outline, and pleasantly aromatic, minute, grayish-white flowers in flat-topped clusters. The gray-green, stout, and tough stem is fine-hairy. The perfect disc-florets are at first yellowish, but finally gray-brown; the 4-6 pistillate rays are white, or rarely crimson-pink. Fertilized mostly by bees and the smaller butterflies. 1-2 feet high. Common everywhere, by the wayside and in fields; possibly native in the west.

Wild Chamomile
Matricaria maritima   White, July-September

A weedy European plant somewhat resembling the mayweed, but the leaves not quite so finely divided. It is an annual or sometimes biennial herb, its crushed foliage

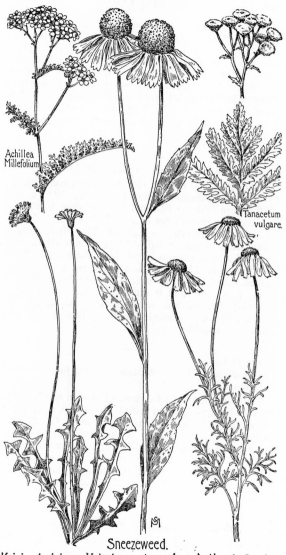

Achillea
Millefolium

Tanacetum
vulgare.

Sneezeweed.
Krigia virginica. Helenium autumnale. Anthemis Cotula.

generally inodorous, while that of the mayweed has the strong smell of chamomile. Leaves much cut, the segments almost threadlike. Flower-heads not very numerous, rather scattered, about ¾ inch wide, white. The tiny tubular flowers in the central disc are minutely 5-toothed. Also called corn mayweed and scentless chamomile. The related *Matricaria Chamomilla* is the so-called German chamomile, is an annual, and is aromatic. Both are found in waste places nearly throughout our area.

Chrysogonum
Chrysogonum virginianum   Yellow, April-June

A low perennial herb of rich woods and rocky places, never very common, but found from Pa., W. Va. and southeastern Ohio to Fla. and La. The stem is solitary, or sometimes several, not over 15 inches high and often flowering when much less than this. The whole plant is sticky from glandular hairs. Leaves long-stalked, oval to roundish, but narrowed both ends, the margins finely round-toothed. Flower-heads solitary or a few long-stalked, about 1½ inches wide. The plant has a tendency to bend its stem, and is often cultivated for its early-blooming flowers. The name is from the Greek for *golden* and *knee* in allusion to the yellow flowers and often bent, kneelike stem.

Oxeye Daisy
Chrysanthemum Leucanthemum   White, June-September

The commonest of all common Eurasian weeds of the field and wayside, often called Farmer's Curse, yet a prime favorite with children and artists! The flower's form is a *summum bonum* of simplicity and decorative beauty. The golden-yellow disc, depressed in the center, is formed of perfect flowers; the white rays are pistillate. The dark green leaves are ornamentally lobed. 15-25 inches high. The name, from the Greek, means *golden flower*.

Feverfew
Chrysanthemum Parthenium   White, June-September

A tall, branching species commonly cultivated, with small daisylike flowers in generous clusters; the stem smooth, the ornamental leaves broad and deeply lobed.

Chrysogonum.

Wild Chamomile.

Heads small, with large yellow discs of perfect florets. 1-2 feet high. Naturalized from Europe, and mostly an escape from gardens, especially in its double-flowered form.

Tansy
Tanacetum vulgare   Orange-yellow, July-September

A common weed naturalized from Europe, generally an escape from gardens belonging to old dwellings. The flatly clustered dull orange-yellow flower-heads resemble those of the daisy minus the white rays; inner florets perfect and marginal ones pistillate. The compound, deep green leaves, ornamentally toothed and cut, are strongly aromatic. 18-30 inches high. Throughout our range. (*Illus. opp. page 552.*)

Tall Wormwood
Artemisia caudata   Green-yellow, July-August

A weed with inconspicuous, tiny, green-yellow flowers in long slender clusters, the little flower-heads mostly nodding; the marginal florets pistillate, the central ones perfect. The bitter-tasting, long, linear, deeply cut leaves with threadlike divisions. 2-5 feet high. On coastal sands, N. B. to Fla., but also as a weed, in a related form, throughout our area.

Mugwort
Artemisia vulgaris   Green-yellow, July-August

A familiar, uninteresting weed naturalized from Eurasia, found in all waste places or near old houses. The smooth green leaves deeply cut, and with lobes coarsely toothed at the tips. The inconspicuous green-yellow heads *erect,* not nodding, in a simple, leafy spike. 1-4 feet high. Throughout eastern N. Am.

Wormwood or Absinth
Artemisia absinthium   Green-yellow, July-August

A somewhat similar species with ashy-gray foliage. Leaves small and often deeply subdivided, covered with fine hairs so the color is somewhat gray. The insignificant light yellow-green flower-heads are gathered in a scattering cluster. The long terminal spikes are rather disheveled and picturesque. 2-4 feet high. Escaped from gardens nearly everywhere. The young flower-heads yield a bitter oil which is an ingredient of the forbidden absinthe.

Oxeye Daisy.
Chrysanthemum Leucanthemum.

Feverfew.
Chrysanthemum Parthenium.

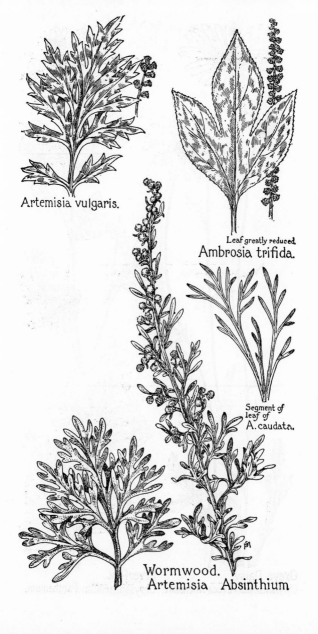

Artemisia vulgaris.

Leaf greatly reduced.
Ambrosia trifida.

Segment of
leaf of
A. caudata.

Wormwood.
Artemisia Absinthium

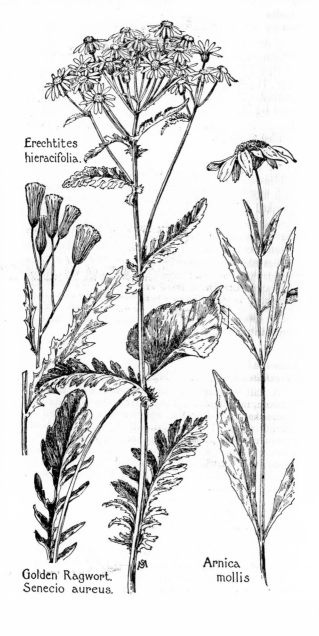

Erechtites
hieracifolia.

Golden Ragwort,
Senecio aureus.

Arnica
mollis

Arnica
Arnica mollis Pure yellow, June-September

A delicate, pure yellow, daisylike flower with 10-14 three-toothed rays, found only upon mountain summits of New Eng. and N. Y. in moist situations, but also in Que. The deep green leaves long lance-shaped, slightly toothed, and stemless—at least the upper ones. The hairy stem 1-2 feet high.

Golden Ragwort
Senecio aureus Deep gold-yellow, May-July

An early blooming perennial with handsome deep golden-yellow, daisylike flowers (8-12 rays) nearly an inch broad, in terminal clusters on the grooved, brown-streaked stem; the disc-florets perfect, the rays pistillate. The thick root-leaves in early April resemble violet leaves; they are small, heart-shaped, scallop-toothed, dark green above and magenta-red beneath; later they become elongated. The long stem-leaves more or less deeply lobed, the uppermost small and clasping the plant-stem. The plant is woolly-hairy when young. 12-32 inches high. Common in wet meadows everywhere. There are 18 other species of *Senecio* in our area, but they must be sought in the technical manuals.

Fireweed
Erechtites hieracifolia White, July-September

A tall, uninteresting, annual weed with generally smooth, rank-odored stem and leaves. The latter are thin, lance-shaped or broader, and irregularly toothed or deeply incised. The stem is full of sap, heavy, and grooved; the insignificant heads are brush-shaped, mostly green by reason of the superior flower-envelope, and tipped with the white of the tubular, fertile florets. 1-7 feet high. Common in burned-over clearings or waste places everywhere.

English Daisy
Bellis perennis White or pinkish, May-November

This is *the* daisy of the poets and artists, common all over Europe, but usually called here English daisy. It is very different from the common white daisy of our fields, which is better called oxeye daisy (see *Chrysanthemum Leucanthemum*). The English daisy is a low perennial,

Cornflower.

English Daisy.

with mostly basal leaves which are narrowed at the base to a winged stalk, and not over 1½ inches long. There is a solitary flower-head at the end of a stalk 4-6 inches high, the pert head about one inch wide, typically white, but in some horticultural forms red or pink. Widely cultivated and often escaping, especially in the north. Sometimes called bachelor's-button.

Cornflower
Centaurea cyanus　Blue, May-September

An annual, European garden favorite, now widely established as an escape, especially in the northern states and adjacent Canada. It grows 9-28 inches high and its narrow, very slender leaves are temporarily and sometimes permanently ashy-grey. Flower-heads solitary at the ends of the branches, 1-1½ inches wide, the marginal rays cut or fringed, hence its other name of ragged sailor. It is the national flower of Germany. There are eleven other species of *Centaurea* in our range, some of them native in the prairie states, especially the basket-flower (*C. americana*), which is often cultivated. Other native species are collectively known as star thistle, although they are not prickly. The cornflower is also called bachelor's button from its popularity as a boutonniere.

Burdock
Arctium Lappa　Light magenta, July-October

A familiar, rank-odored, deep-rooted weed, common in all waste places and difficult to eradicate. It has large, dull green, veiny leaves, the lower heart-shaped, the upper ovate; woolly beneath. The globular flower-head a hooked-bristled green bur with magenta or often nearly white, perfect, tubular florets with a five-cleft tip. The stem is generally much branched. 4-8 feet high. About ruins of old dwellings or in waste places. Nearly everywhere. A related species, *A. tomentosum,* is a very woolly-stemmed form, local and rare from N. H. to D. C.

Smaller Burdock
Arctium minus　Light magenta, July-October

A smaller species, with smaller, generally narrower leaves, the lower ones deeply heart-shaped, their stalks hollow and hardly furrowed; flower-heads almost stem-

Smaller Burdock.　　Arctium minus.

less on the branches, about ¾ inch broad. The inner spines erect and shorter than the lilac pink or light magenta or white florets. 2-5 feet high. Common. Both species are naturalized from Europe.

Common Thistle
Cirsium vulgare Magenta, July-October

A biennial species naturalized from Europe, generally found in pastures. The narrow, white-spiny, dark green leaves hug the plant-stem for an inch or so with prickly wings, the upper surface prickly-hairy, the lower webby-woolly with light brownish fine hairs. The green flower-envelope is armed with spreading spines; the perfect, tubular florets, densely clustered, vary from (rarely white) crimson-magenta to light magenta; the pollen is white. Flowers remarkably sweet-scented, rich in honey, and fertilized mostly by the bumblebees (often becoming intoxicated) and butterflies. Heads sometimes 3 inches broad, generally solitary at the ends of the branches. 2-4 feet high. Common throughout N. Am. (*Color Plate 29.*)

Yellow Thistle
Cirsium horridulum Corn-yellow, May-August

A species with light corn-yellow (rarely magenta), flattish flower-heads nearly 3 inches broad; it is exceedingly plentiful in the salt marshes of L. I. and N. J. The oblong lance-shaped, light green leaves smooth, clasping, and very yellow-spiny; the flower-heads set in the smaller encircling upper leaflets, with *very* narrow, rough, spineless scales. 2-4 feet high. Common in wet or dry sandy soil along the seacoast, from Me. to Tex.

Tall Thistle
Cirsium altissimum Magenta, July-October

A rather common species with magenta (rarely white) flower-heads about 1½ inches broad and weak-bristled, rough-hairy, stalkless leaves, deeply cut into linear lobes, white-woolly beneath. The outer scales of the flower-heads are slightly woolly and weak-bristled. Stem downy, 3-6 feet high. Common on roadsides and in fields, Mass. to Fla., and far west.

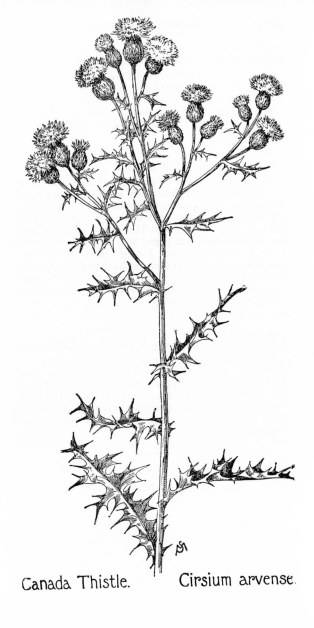

Canada Thistle.   Cirsium arvense.

Swamp Thistle
Cirsium muticum   Magenta, July-October

A species with similar leaves and flowers, but the blunt, prickleless scales of the heads glutinous, woolly, and close-pressing. The flower with a naked stem, or with a few tiny bracts at its base. 3-8 feet high. Common in swamps and moist low woodlands everywhere.

Pasture Thistle
Cirsium pumilum   Light magenta, July-September

The largest-flowered thistle of all, with solitary heads 2-3 inches broad, the florets light magenta-lilac or nearly white; they are exceedingly fragrant, rich in honey, and are frequented by the bumblebee, who imbibes to the point of abject intoxication! The slightly glutinous scales are nearly smooth and tipped with slender prickles, and at the base are tiny bracts. The light green leaves narrow and frequently cut into three-prickled lobes, the prickles shorter than those of the common thistle and very numerous. Stem only 12-30 inches high. In dry pastures and fields, Me. to Va. and W. Va.

Canada Thistle
Cirsium arvense   Lilac or pale magenta, July-September

A pernicious weed, naturalized from Europe, with small lilac, pale magenta, or rarely white heads about ⅞ inch broad. The dull gray-green, whitish-ribbed leaves are deeply slashed into many very prickly, ruffled lobes. Flowers staminate and pistillate; also fragrant. 1-3 feet high. Common in pastures, fields, and on roadsides throughout our area.

Dwarf Dandelion
Krigia virginica   Golden-yellow, May-August

A small annual species of dandelion with many long, slender flower-stalks rising from a circle of small, irregularly lobed leaves, each stalk bearing a single golden-yellow flower-head scarcely ¾ inch broad; later it becomes branched and bears a few leaves. The hairy down of the seeds is short. 2-12 inches high. Common in dry soil or on sandy banks, Me. to Fla., west to Mich. and Mo. (*Illus. opp. page 552.*)

Chicory.
Cichorium Intybus.

Fall Dandelion.
Leontodon autumnalis.

Krigia biflora Golden-yellow, May-October

A similar but tall perennial species with smooth stem covered with a slight bloom, and smooth basal leaves distinctly stalked, scarcely toothed, but with a wavy outline. A small bract clasps the flowering stem about halfway up; from this proceed 2-5 branches bearing deep golden-yellow flowers 1¼ inches broad. 1-2 feet high. Moist pastures and fields, Mass. to Ga., and far westward.

Fall Dandelion
Leontodon autumnalis Light golden-yellow, July-November

A small dandelion, naturalized from Eurasia, with a long, branching flower-stalk, which is set with tiny bracts or scales about ½ inch apart. The blunt-lobed, narrow, small basal leaves are dull green and smooth. The light golden-yellow flower-head erect in the bud about an inch broad, in twos or threes, or rarely solitary. The slender stalks of these dandelions above described are somewhat wiry, not tubular like those of the common spring dandelion. 7-18 inches high. In fields and along roadsides, Greenland to N. J., and rarely inland to Mich. Name from the Greek for *lion* and *tooth*. The var. *pratensis* is similar, but the flower-envelope and the tip of the flower-stalk immediately below it are very fine-hairy with blackish hairs. Newf. to Pa.

Chicory or Succory
Cichorium Intybus Violet-blue, July-October

A very common but beautiful weed naturalized from Europe, found on roadsides and in waste places particularly about the seaboard towns. Stem stout, tough, and stiff, with generally lance-shaped, dark gray-green, coarse-toothed leaves. The violet-blue flower-head, similar in form to the dandelion, closes in rainy or cloudy weather and opens only in sunshine. There are few florets in a single head but these are highly developed with gracefully curved, branching styles; the exposure of the double stigmatic surface thus, in a measure, insures self-fertilization in the absence of insects. The most frequent visitors are the bees—the honeybee, the leaf-cutter bee and various species of ground bees. 1-3 feet high.

Canada Hawkweed.
Hieracium canadense.

Orange Hawkweed.
Hieracium aurantiacum.

Orange Hawkweed
Hieracium aurantiacum   Tawny-orange, July-September

An odd but attractive plant, naturalized from Europe and often called devil's-paintbrush. It has a stout stem, and a flower-cup closely covered with sepia-brown hairs, the rusty character of which gave it the common name in England of Grim the Collier. The coarse, blunt, lance-shaped leaves covered with short gray hairs are nearly all at the base of the plant. The tawny-orange flowers (with light golden pistils), strap-rayed and finely fringed at the edge, are grouped in a small terminal cluster, and are quite delicately fragrant. Visited by the bees and the smaller butterflies. 7-16 inches high. In fields, woodlands, and along roads, from Newf., south to Pa., and west to Minn. Such a troublesome weed in fields and pastures that some counties have laws for its eradication.

Canada Hawkweed
Hieracium canadense   Pure yellow, July-September

A generally smooth species; the light green, lance-shaped leaves with coarse and wide-spread teeth, and the dandelionlike, very small yellow heads in a loose branching cluster terminating the leafy stem. In October the plant is decorated with tiny brown globes of down. 1-4 feet high. In dry woods and fields, Newf. to N. J. and far westward.

Hieracium paniculatum   Yellow, July-August

A similar northern plant with a drooping-branched loose flower-cluster, generally smooth stem and lance-shaped leaves, and smaller yellow flowers. The thin leaves almost stemless, and very slightly, if at all, toothed. 1-3 feet high. Nova Scotia to Ga., west to Ohio and Mich.

Rattlesnake-weed
Hieracium venosum   Light gold-yellow, May-July

An early flowering species, with deeper yellow flowers closely resembling small dandelions, and generally leaf-less (or with 1-3 tiny bracts), few-haired stems, branch-ing to a few-flowered cluster. The light green leaves are dull magenta on the ribs, edges, and under side; they are hairy, scarcely toothed, and clustered at the root. 12-30 inches high. Common in woodlands and thickets, N. H. and Vt. to Ga., rare inland to Mich.

Hawkweed.

Hieracium scabrum.   Hieracium paniculatum.

Hieracium scabrum   Yellow, July-September

The simple stem stout, and remarkable for its hairy character. The obovate or very blunt obovate, almost toothless leaves are rough-hairy and light dull green. The small terminal flower-cluster with several small heads of yellow flowers (the floral envelope a hairy green) is conspicuously irregular and angular in its branching. 1-3 feet high. Common in dry woods north, Nova Scotia to Ga., west to Minn.

Hieracium Gronovii   Yellow, July-October

A similar plant with a slenderer stem, often ruddy, rough-hairy (slightly so above), and very leafy and hairy below. The leaves like *H. scabrum*. The seed-vessels very tapering at the summit. The blossoms open only in sunshine, and very quickly wither. 1-3 feet high. Dry soil, Mass. to Fla., west to Mich., Kan. and Tex. The name from ἱέραξ, a hawk.

———

Smooth-stemmed White Lettuce
Prenanthes racemosa   Dull lilac, August-September

A tall weed with inconspicuous, narrow flowers of a dull lilac tint, grouped in a rather narrow wandlike cluster. The somewhat thickish light green leaves smooth and with a slight bloom, scarcely toothed, and blunt lance-shaped. The green floral envelope and its stalk are hairy. 2-5 feet high. In moist fields, Que. to N. J. and far westward.

Rattlesnake-root or White Lettuce
Prenanthes alba   Dull cream color, August-September

A commoner and more interesting species with drooping, dull cream-colored flowers, occasionally touched with pale lilac; the green floral envelope has about 8 magenta-tinged sections; the stamens are quite prominent and cream-colored. The smooth, deep green leaves are varied in form, the lower ones broad, three-sided, and remotely toothed, the upper ones deeply cut, and the uppermost lance-shaped with two small lateral lobes or none at all. The smooth stem is stiff, round, and generally dull, deep magenta-tinted, with a bloom. 2-4 feet high. Common in thin woods, Que. to N. J. and far westward.

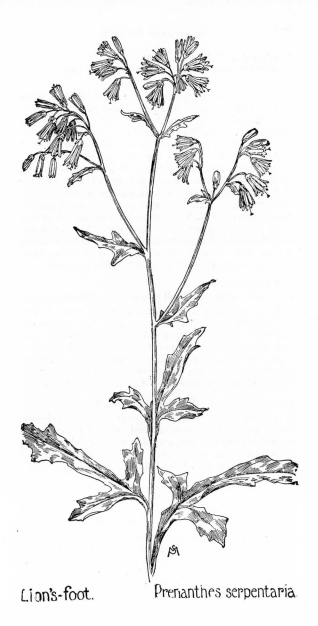

Lion's-foot.   Prenanthes serpentaria.

Lion's-foot or Gall of the Earth
Prenanthes serpentaria **Dull cream color, July-
September**

A similar smooth species, the stem of which is green
and without a bloom. The leaves also very variable, a
trifle roughish, and shaped (but more angularly) like
those of *P. alba*. The flower-cluster is inclined to be
somewhat flat-topped, and the pendulous, bell-shaped,
dull cream-colored heads are enclosed in a somewhat
bristly, hairy, green envelope, which is sometimes a trifle
magenta-tinted. The curled branches of the style are
slender and prominent, as in all the *Prenanthes*. 1-3 feet
high, usually 2 feet. In thickets, or dry sandy ground,
Mass. (rare) and N. Y., south to Fla. and Miss. A related
form on alpine summits of New Eng. (Mt. Katahdin)
and N. Y. and far northward, has deep madder brown
flowers and variously shaped leaves. 4-12 inches high.
It is considered by some as *P. trifoliolata* var. *nana*.

Tall White Lettuce
Prenanthes altissima **Dull cream color, July-September**

A tall, generally smooth species, with a green or magenta-tinged stem. The leaves (except the uppermost)
variously shaped but long-stalked. The numerous narrow, pendulous, dull cream-colored flowers with a smooth
green envelope, are borne in a narrow terminal spike, or
in small clusters at the leaf-angles. 3-7 feet high. In woodlands and thickets, Newf. to Ga., west to Mich. and La.

Prenanthes Bootii **Whitish, July-August**

A dwarf species with stout, ruddy stem, large flower-
heads, and thick, narrow, variously shaped leaves. Flowers whitish and fragrant, enclosed within a dull magenta-
tinged envelope. 4-12 inches high. Alpine summits of
N. Y. and New Eng. Found on Mt. Washington.

———

Common Dandelion
Taraxacum officinale **Golden-yellow, May-June**

The familiar grass-plot, yellow flower of the country
and city, naturalized from Europe. The heads are sometimes 2 inches broad, and are supported on a pale green,
hollow stem; the perfect flowers are orange-gold in the
center of the head, and light golden-yellow on the straps
of the margin. The seeds are neutral brown, and spiny

Red-seeded
Dandelion.
Taraxacum laevigatum.

Common
Dandelion.
Taraxacum officinale.

at the upper part. The deep green leaves are irregularly and angularly broad-toothed, the jagged edge bearing a remote resemblance to the row of teeth in a lion's jaw, hence the common name, a corruption of the French *dent-de-lion*. 3-14 inches high. The silky down forms a beautiful globe when the seeds ripen and the acute divisions of the flower-envelope are reflexed. Common everywhere.

Red-seeded Dandelion
Taraxacum lævigatum   Yellow, May-June

A similar but smaller species with flower-heads scarcely over an inch broad, pure yellow, but deeper in the center; the two-pointed straps or bracts of the floral envelope usually have a thickened point or knob near the tip. The outermost straps are magenta-tinged; the smooth leaves are very deeply cut into thin, irregular, sharp, backward-tending lobes or narrow angular divisions. The seeds are bright terra-cotta red, and spiny over the upper half of the surface. In similar sites to the common dandelion, but more rare, except in the north.

Wild Lettuce
Lactuca canadensis   Pale yellow, June-September

A tall biennial species often 6 feet high, with a smooth, stout, leafy stem branching at the top in a thin, scattered flower-spike with insignificant pale yellow ray-flowers mostly enclosed within the green floral envelope. Both stem and leaves with a slight bloom; the leaves slightly like those of the dandelion, but the upper ones often merely toothed or lobed, and the lower sometimes 12 inches long. 4-10 feet high. Common in wet soil, Que. to Fla. and far westward. The most common and variable of the plants known as wild lettuce.

Lactuca hirsuta   Pinkish-white, July-September

A less leafy and more hairy species, found in similar situations. The leaves like those of *L. canadensis,* but fine-hairy; the reddish stem hairy at the base; the scattered flower-cluster with insignificant dull lilac, or dingy pink-white flowers. 2-4 feet high. Que. to Va., and along the coast to La. and Tex.; rare or wanting inland.

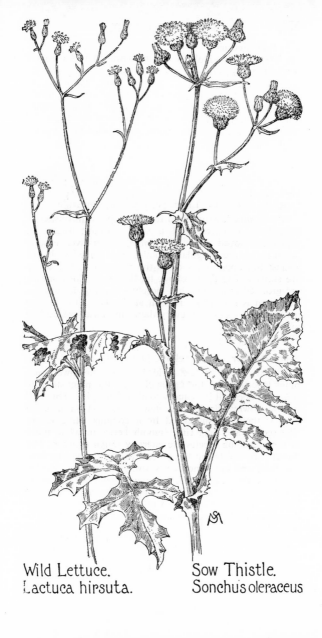

Wild Lettuce.
Lactuca hirsuta.

Sow Thistle.
Sonchus oleraceus

Tall Blue Lettuce
Lactuca biennis **Dull purple or white, July-September**

The tallest member of the genus, with a stout, straight, smooth stem, leafy up to the straggling, large flower-cluster of insignificant flowers which are never fully expanded. The green flower-heads tipped with inconspicuous dull purplish or whitish rays. The deeply lobed leaves are large and irregularly wavy-toothed. 3-15 feet high. Damp shady places, Newf. to N. C. and far westward.

Sow Thistle
Sonchus oleraceus **Light yellow, May-September**

A tall annual, naturalized from Europe, with thistlelike prickle-edged leaves, and a stout, hollow, succulent, smooth, grooved stem. The large, decorative, usually lobed leaves are irregularly toothed and armed with soft spines; the upper ones clasp the plant-stem, the lower are stalked. The light yellow, thistle-shaped flower-heads are grouped in a somewhat loosely spreading flat cluster. The stem is sometimes reddish at the base. 1-6 feet or more high. Common everywhere in waste places or manured soil.

Sonchus asper **Light yellow, May-September**

Similar, but with less divided leaves, the lower ones blunt lance-shaped, the upper clasping the plant-stem by rounded lobes, all irregularly toothed and spiny. The light yellow downy, flat-headed flowers are set in a loose cluster; they are succeeded by a copious white down. The seeds have long ribs, smooth between, while those of the preceding species are laterally rough between. The flowers are assisted in the process of fertilization by bee-like flies, and the honeybee is always a common visitor. Formerly the milk-juiced, succulent leaves were used as a pot herb. Waste places everywhere, and a native of Europe. The Greek name *Sonchus* (Sow Thistle) is a degrading title for such a decorative-leaved plant!

Arrowhead   *Sagittaria latifolia*

PLATE 1

Wakerobin   *Trillium erectum*

PLATE 2

Large Flowering Trillium   *Trillium grandiflorum*
PLATE 3

Day Lily   *Hemerocallis fulva*

PLATE 4

Nodding Pogonia   *Triphora trianthophora*

PLATE 5

Hooker's Orchis   *Habenaria Hookeri*

PLATE 6

Large Purple Fringed Orchis *Habenaria fimbriata*
PLATE 7

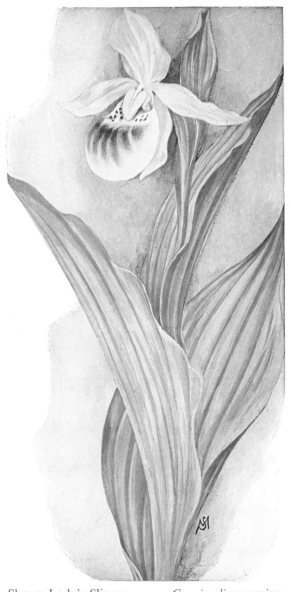

Showy Lady's Slipper   *Cypripedium reginæ*

PLATE 8

Bouncing Bet   *Saponaria officinalis*

PLATE 9

Evening Lychnis   *Lychnis alba*

PLATE 10

Marsh Marigold   *Caltha palustris*

PLATE 11

Fringed Milkwort   *Polygala paucifolia*

PLATE 12

Bird-foot Violet   *Viola pedata*

PLATE 13

Sweet White Violet   *Viola blanda*

PLATE 14

Shinleaf   *Pyrola elliptica*

PLATE 15

Trailing Arbutus   *Epigæa repens*

PLATE 16

Large Marsh Pink   *Sabatia dodecandra*

PLATE 17

Fringed Gentian   *Gentiana crinita*

PLATE 18

Oswego Tea   *Monarda didyma*

PLATE 19

Monkey-flower   *Mimulus ringens*

PLATE 20

Twin-flower   *Linnæa borealis,* var. *americana*

PLATE 21

Cardinal Flower   *Lobelia cardinalis*

PLATE 22

Joe-pye Weed   *Eupatorium purpureum*

PLATE 23

Early Goldenrod   *Solidago juncea*

PLATE 24

New England Aster   *Aster novæ-angliæ*

PLATE 25

Robin's Plantain   *Erigeron pulchellus*

PLATE 26

Elecampane   *Inula Helenium*

PLATE 27

Black-eyed Susan   *Rudbeckia hirta*

PLATE 28

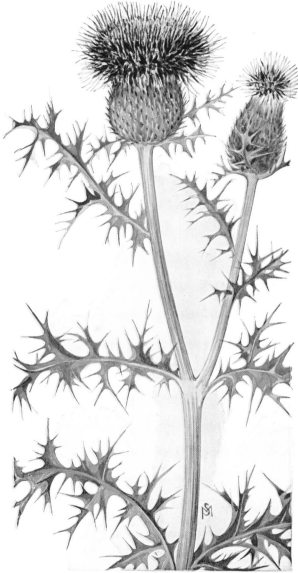

Common Thistle · *Cirsium vulgare*

PLATE 29

DE CANDOLLE'S FLOWER-COLOR SYSTEM
REVISED by F·S·M

Flowers of the tropical and sub-tropical zones are Xanthic and Cyanic, usually intense in hue.

GOLDEN YELLOW

GOLDEN ORANGE

XANTHIC

ORANGE

SCARLET

Xanthic flowers are never associated with Cyanic flowers in one group and rarely if ever pass into the albino form.

CARDINAL RED

THE THREE INDEPENDENT NORMAL PRIMARY COLORS

NORMAL BLUE   NORMAL YELLOW   NORMAL RED

Blue associates with Cyanic series, Yellow and Red with both the series.

Flowers of the north-temperate zone are almost exclusively confined to the Cyanic series.

CRiMSON

MAGENTA

CYANIC

PURPLE

VIOLET

Cyanic flowers are never associated with Xanthic flowers in one group. They are commonly pale, and invariably pass into albinos.

VIOLET BLUE.

PLATE 30

FLOWER COLORS OF THE NORTH TEMPERATE ZONE.

Xanthic except 1 & 2	Cyanic except 11	Cyanic except 17
EVENING PRIMROSE 1	HARDHACK 9	FORGET-ME-NOT 17
BUTTERCUP 2	MEADOWSWEET 10	INDIAN TOBACCO 18
BLACK-EYED SUSAN 3	PAINTED CUP 11	HAREBELL 19
COLUMBINE HORNS 4	PUR. FRINGED ORCHIS 12	SELF-HEAL DEEPER 20
COLUMBINE SEPAL 5	WILD GERANIUM 13	ASTER SPECTABILIS 21
JEWELWEED SAC 6	FIREWEED 14	CHICORY 22
JEWELWEED LIP 7	FLOWERING WINTERGREEN 15	BOTTLE GENTIAN 23
TAWNY HAWKWEED 8	VIOLETS. 16	BOTTLE GENTIAN DEEP 24

PLATE 31

INDEX

INDEX